Thousands of Heroes Have Arisen

Sikh Voices of the Great War 1914-1918

Sukwinder Singh Bassi

Helion & Company Limited

Helion & Company Limited
Unit 8 Amherst Business Centre
Budbrooke Road
Warwick
CV34 5WE
England
Tel. 01926 499 619
Email: info@helion.co.uk
Website: www.helion.co.uk
Twitter: @helionbooks

Published by Helion & Company 2019 Reprinted in paperback 2021
Designed and typeset by Mary Woolley (www.battlefield-design.co.uk)
Cover designed by Paul Hewitt, Battlefield Design (www.battlefield-design.co.uk)

ISBN 978-1-914059-07-0

British Library Cataloguing-in-Publication Data.
A catalogue record for this book is available from the British Library.

Contents

List of Illustrations

List of Maps

Glossary

Akalpurkh	Sikh word for God, literally meaning "a timeless being who never dies."
Akhand Path	Continuous nonstop recitation of all the verses in the Guru Granth Sahib from the beginning to the end.
Akhbar	Newspaper
Amrit	Holy water provided to Sikhs at religious ceremonies such as baptism.
Anand	Bliss
Anna	Former monetary unit of India, equal to one sixteenth of a rupee.
Ata	Flour
Aurangzeb	Mughal Emperor of India (1618-1707).
Avatar	A manifestation of a deity or released soul in bodily form on earth; an incarnate divine teacher.
Babiha	Small hawk.
Babu	Respectful title or form of address for a man, especially an educated one.
Badmash	Dishonest or unprincipled man.
Badshah	Persian word for King.
Bahadur	Brave; honorific title given to officers in British India.
Bahisht	Heaven
Baisakhi	A Sikh festival held annually to commemorate the founding of the Khalsa by Guru Gobind Singh in 1699.
Bajra	Pearl millet or similar grain.
Bande/Vande Mataram	"I praise thee, Mother", referencing Mother India.
Bandobast	Arrangements or organisation.
Bara	Older or senior relative or officer.
Basant	Punjabi spring time festival associated with the flying of kites.
Bellum	Persian Gulf boat holding about eight persons and propelled by paddles or poles.
Bhagat	Devotee of the Lord.
Bhang	The leaves and flower tops of cannabis, used as a narcotic.
Bharat	Alternative name of India.
Brahmin	Member of the highest Hindu (priestly) caste.
Bunga	Place of residence at Sikh places of learning.

Caste	Each of the hereditary classes of Hindu society, distinguished by relative degrees of ritual purity or pollution and of social status.
Chamar	Untouchable or Dalit community of India.
Charas	Cannabis resin.
Chet	Punjabi month equated with Mid-March to Mid-April.
Chhavi	Weapon
Chittak	Unit of weight, equal to a quarter of a seer.
Coolie	Unskilled native labourer in India, China, and some other Asian countries.
Crores	Ten million; one hundred lakhs, especially of rupees, units of measurement, or people.
Cucherry	Court
Dacoities	Acts of violent robbery.
Dal	Split pulses, in particular lentils.
Dasam Granth	Scripture of Sikhism composed by the 10th Guru, Guru Gobind Singh.
Dharma	Eternal law of the cosmos, inherent in the very nature of things. (Indian religions).
Dharna	Mode of compelling payment or compliance, by sitting at the debtor's or offender's door until the demand is complied with.
Dholki	Indian drum.
Diwali	Hindu festival of lights.
Doaba	Region of Punjab that lies between the Beas River and the Sutlej River.
Dogra	Ethnic group of northern India, predominately found in the regions of Jammu & Kashmir and Punjab.
Dooli	Stretcher/litter
Durbar	Royal court of an Indian state/ large gathering.
Fateh	"Victory"; a commonly used greeting.
Fauji Akhbar	Newspaper for Indian Soldiers fighting abroad during the Great War.
Feringhi	Derogatory term for foreigners, especially Europeans.
Gaddi	Throne or seat of high ruling position.
Ghadar/Ghadr	Revolt or Rebellion.
Ghadarites	Members or followers of the Ghadar party.
Ghari	Unit of time.
Ghi	Clarified butter, made from a cow or a buffalo.
Granth/Grunth	Holy book, associated mainly with Sikh religion.
Granthi	Professional readers of the Sikh scriptures.
Gur	Type of unrefined, solid brown sugar made from boiling sugar cane juice until dry.
Gurbani	Term used to describe compositions of the Sikh scriptures.
Gurdwara	Sikh temple or place of worship.
Gurmata	Order on a subject that affects the fundamental principles of Sikh religion and is binding upon all Sikhs.

Gurmukhi	Language of the Sikh scriptures.
Guru Granth Sahib	Holy Scripture of the Sikhs.
Guru Maharaj	Reverential term for the Sikh Gurus.
Gutka	Small volume of Sikh hymns chosen from Sikh scriptures.
Harmandir	'The Abode of God', also known as the Golden Temple.
Hindustan	Alternative name for India.
Hukka	Oriental tobacco pipe with a long, flexible tube which draws the smoke through water contained in a bowl.
Izzat	Honour
Jagir	Land granted in recognition of service, such as military service.
Janamsakhis	Literally 'birth stories'; professed to be biographies of Guru Nanak.
Japji Sahib	First sacred composition found in the Guru Granth Sahib, written by Guru Nanak.
Jat	Ethnic group of northern Indian sub-continent.
Jatha	Armed parade, especially of Sikhs.
Jawar	Sorghum, grain of the millet family.
Jhatka	Meat from an animal that has been killed instantaneously.
Jormela	Sikh religious gathering.
Kalgiwala/Kalgidhar	One who wears a plume in his turban, reverential name of Guru Gobind Singh.
Karam	Fate, destiny, predestination resulting from one's actions or deeds.
Karobar	Business, trade.
Katak	Punjabi month equated with Mid-October to Mid-November.
Khalsa	Brotherhood of "pure" Sikhs initiated by the tenth Sikh Guru, Gobind Singh.
Khatri	Caste from northern Indian sub-continent.
Khichri	Indian dish consisting chiefly of rice and split pulses.
Khir	Indian dish of sweet rice pudding.
Kos	Distance of approximately three kilometres.
Labana	Indian ethnic group.
Lakh	Hundred thousand.
Lambardar	Village officials of high status, with revenue collecting powers.
Maghar	Punjabi month equated with Mid-November to Mid-December.
Mahabharat	Epic Sanskrit poem of India, dealing chiefly with the struggle between two rival families.
Maharaja	Indian king.
Mahatma	Revered personage regarded with love and respect; a holy person or sage.
Mahommedans	Followers of the Islamic prophet Mahommed.
Maidan	Open space used for public meetings or sporting activities.
Majha	Central region of the Punjab.
Malwa	Region of Punjab south of the Sutlej River.
Maulvi	Highly qualified Islamic scholar.
Maund	Indian unit of weight.
Mazhbis	Members of untouchable caste who adopted Sikhism.

Mela	Fair or Hindu festival.
Misls	Confederacies, originally organized primarily for military purposes.
Mems	Women, usually used in the context of European women.
Mukhti	Transcendent state attained as a result of being released from the cycle of rebirth.
Mullah	Muslim learned in Islamic theology and sacred law.
Munsif	Judge
Musalman	Punjabi word for followers of Islam.
Naam	Sign, symbol and song of God, in Sikhism.
Najat	Salvation
Obol	An ancient Greek coin worth one sixth of a drachma.
Pagri	Turban
Pahlwan	Wrestler/strongman
Panth	Religious tradition, meaning Guru's path.
Panth Da Dass	Servant of the Guru's path.
Parda	Seclusion of women from the sight of men or strangers.
Parlo	Destruction/end of the world.
Patwari	Government official who keeps revenue records of land ownership.
Pauri	Section/paragraph
Phagun	Punjabi month equated with Mid-February to Mid-March.
Pice	Former monetary unit of India, equal to one quarter of an anna.
Pir	Muslim saint or holy man.
Pucca	Solid/permanent.
Rais	Person belonging to aristocracy, usually wealthy landowners.
Rajput	A member of a Hindu military caste.
Risala	Cavalry
Rishi	Hindu sage or saint.
Sabha	Indian word for gathering, council or assembly.
Sahib	Term of respect for Europeans in British India.
Santokhsar	Sacred pool in the city of Amritsar.
Satguru	True guru
Sat Sri Akal	Sikh greeting meaning 'Truth is the Ultimate God'.
Sawan	Punjabi month equated with Mid-July to Mid-August.
Seer/Ser	Varying unit of weight (about one kilogram) or liquid measure (about one litre).
Sepoy	Indian soldier serving under British rule.
Shabads	Hymns from Sikh scriptures.
Shaheed	Martyr
Shahinshah	Emperor
Shudar/Shudra	Lowest rank of the Hindu castes.
Sirdar/Sardar	A leader; an honorific term for a Sikh.
Sircar/Sirkar/Sarkar	Government
Sowar	A member of an Indian cavalry regiment.
Swarga/Surga	Heaven
Sufi	A Muslim ascetic and mystic.

Tamasha	A grand show, performance, or celebration, especially one involving dance.
Tehsil	Area serving as an administrative centre.
Tehsildar	Revenue collecting officer of a sub-administrative area of a district.
Thanadar	Thana commander: police chief.
Tola	Unit of weight in India.
Tonga	Light horse-drawn two-wheeled vehicle.
Udasis	Journeys undertaken by Guru Nanak, in the Sikh tradition.
Vakil	Lawyer/solicitor
Vaar/Varan	Chapters
Vidyala	School, place of learning.
Waheguru	Name given to God in Sikhism.
Wardi-Major	The Indian adjutant of a cavalry regiment, usually an appointment held by a Jemadar.
Wasakh/Vasakh	Punjabi month equated with Mid-April to Mid-May.
Wilayat/Valait	Term used to describe a foreign country, especially Great Britain.
Zaildar	Official with the power over an administrative area covering many villages.
Zemindar	Landowner, especially one who leases his land to tenant farmers.
Zenana	Part of a house for the seclusion of women.
Zulum	Crime/injustice

Foreword

Germany invaded Belgium on 4 August 1914; on that day Britain declared war on Germany and two days later Britain invited the Government of India to send troops to Egypt to strengthen the Suez Canal defences thus releasing regular British troops to reinforce the Western Front. Just three weeks later troops from India sailed from Karachi and Bombay, initially towards Egypt and the defence of the Suez Canal but then diverted en route to the Western Front to meet the more imminent threat.

The first troops to land in France on 26 September 1914 were the XV (Ludhiana) Sikhs, attached to the 8th (Jullundur) Brigade of 47th Sikhs, 59th Scinde Rifles (Frontier Force) and 1st Battalion The Manchester Regiment who were themselves part of the 3rd (Lahore) Division. The British *Times* newspaper reported "The arrival of the Indian Corps at Marseilles was a landmark in history. No episode in this extraordinary war was more remarkable or, for Britons, more inspiring than the presence of Indian troops on the Continent of Europe."

By the end of the War 1,381,050 men (including 283,037 British and 1,096,013 Indian troops) of the soldiers stationed in India had been sent for service overseas.

Much has been written about the critical role that the soldiers of the Indian Army played in defeating Germany and its partners but not so much is known about the feelings and reactions to European War of those individual soldiers, a high proportion of whom were Sikhs, who were part of the force sent from India.

Sukwinder Bassi has painstakingly researched and compiled a selection of the thousands of archived letters of Sikh soldiers writing home from France and Mesopotamia which are held in the archives of the British Library in London. In so doing he has provided this poignant anthology recording of what life was like in those critical days. He has grouped these selected letters into relevant and extremely readable tranches to achieve a coherent and supportive history of the thoughts and observations of those Sikhs involved in those world changing events.

Many histories have been written about the huge and vital contribution of the Indian Army to the British Empire's forces in the Great War in strategic and tactical terms, and of the specific and gallant actions of the Sikh regiments who took part, but this is the first publication of the writings home of individual Sikh soldiers actively participating in the war in France, Mesopotamia and elsewhere.

This work is an integral and important addition to the history of the Indian Army in the Great War and of the men of the Sikh regiments in particular. This gallant record is kept vibrant by the Jullundur Brigade Association, by the Sikh community in the United Kingdom through such entities as the Anglo-Sikh Heritage Trail and the Maharaja Duleep

Singh Centenary Trust, as well as by the British and Indian army regiments which actively commemorate their enduring respect and comradeship of their shared histories with the Sikh Regiment.

Major General Peter Davies CB
President
The Jullundur Brigade Association
(www.jullundurassociation.org)
London, April 2019

Poems
1914 & 2014

A National Song for Sikh Children

Nectar sweet hath Gobind given us,
Our name and fame will live forever,
Tyrants by us have been out driven,
Deny not this O India ever,
Young and old have stood unflinching,
Caring nought for bow or arrow,
Bliss for them to dwell unceasing,
In the faith their Guru brought.

Once the day we sway'd the Punjab,
Once the day our banners waved,
Delhi, Kabul, all the country
Feared and bow'd before our name.
Renown'd were we with bow and arrow
Sword and spear were by us plied,
Dreading nought in bloody battle,
Foemen countless at each Singh's hand died.

To distant climbs do we now travel,
China, Greece, Japan, Ceylon,
America too, and Afric's shores,
No part is there we haven't known.
Our veins do course with Gobind's blood,
At our aspect dire e'en lions quail,
No fear for sword or spear or arrow,
And this our rulers know full well.

Country and rulers do we love,
And who this truth will dare gainsay?
For India's sake our blood hath flow'd,
And for this work are we beloved,
Our guide is he who for his faith
Did give his sons in sacrifice.

Lala Lal Chand, *The Loyal Gazette* (Lahore), 12th April 1914.

When the Sikhs Came to War!

The Sikhs were fearless fighters on the British side
They fought with spirit and pride, ready to collide!
The Sikhs could survive being hit by a shell
They made massive contributions at Neuve Chapelle.
To the city of Marseille
They came to make the enemy pay.
Sikhs never gave up on burning sands
Even though they were fighting on foreign lands.
They wore their turbans and uniforms with pride
They never looked down, frightened or cried.
They fought with character and passion
Even though their food was a system of ration.
The Sikhs that died but were never found to cremate
Are inscribed in memorial at the Menin Gate.
They hailed from India, of the Punjab and,
Came to aid Britain in NO MAN'S LAND!
And to this day Britain pays loyal respect
To the Sikhs full of intellect.
In the town of Ypres they faced up to gas
Continued to fight as the bodies started to mass.
Killed tons of opposition during the war
Singhs fighting like lions - Roar!!
After fighting for their lives
As the century mark sparked, the story continues to thrive.
About the Sikhs fighting (*Another man's war)*
They deserved Victoria Cross's but no one saw.
The valour of the Sikhs
Who stood on high peaks, after their well-earned sleeps.
To kill the enemy
When cowardice was never a remedy.
Fortunately people saw the impact the Sikhs made
In the First World War, more explosive than a grenade!

Amar Singh Bassi, age 11
November 2014

Chronology of Selected Events

1914

May 3: *Komagata Maru* leaves Yokohama for British Columbia.
May 23: *Komagata Maru* arrives in Vancouver.
Jul: Agitation in Punjab surrounding demolition of wall of Rakabganj Gurdwara.
Aug 4: Britain declares war on Germany.
Sep 26: Lahore Division, 15th and 47th Sikhs inclusive, disembark at Marseille.
Sep 27: *Komagata Maru* returns to Calcutta.
Sep 29: Sikhs killed during Budge Budge Harbour incident.
Oct 19-Nov 22: First Battle of Ypres.
Nov 3-Nov 5: Battle of Tanga.
Nov 5: Britain declares war on the Ottoman Empire.
Nov 7: Siege of Tsingtao ends.
Nov 11-Nov 18: Battle of Basra.

1915

Feb 15-Feb 22: Singapore sepoy mutiny.
Feb 19-Jan 9, 1916: Gallipoli Campaign.
Mar 10-Mar 13: Battle of Neuve Chapelle.
Apr 22-May 25: Second Battle of Ypres – Germany first uses poison gas.
Apr 26: First Lahore Conspiracy case commences.
May 15-May 25: Battle of Festubert.
Jul 7: High numbers of deaths in the Punjab from plague.
Sep 12-Oct 7: First advance on Baghdad.
Sep 25-Sep 28: Battle of Loos – British employ poison gas for the first time.
Nov 22-25: Battle of Ctesiphon.
Dec 11-Dec 25: Senussi Campaign; actions at Wadi Seinab and Wadi Majid.
Dec 15-16 Apr, 1916: Siege of Kut-al-Amara.

1916

Apr 29: Surrender of Kut-al-Amara garrison.
Jul 1-Nov 18: Battle of the Somme.

1917

Mar 11: Capture of Baghdad.
Apr 6: USA enters the war.
Apr 9-May 16: Battle of Arras.
Jun 7-Jun 14: Battle of Messines.
Jul 31-Dec 2: Third Battle of Ypres.
Nov 20-Dec 6: Battle of Cambrai.

1918

Mar 3: Russia signs Treaty of Brest-Litovsk and leaves Great War.
Mar 21: German offensives begin.
Aug 8: Allied offensives begin.
Sep 19-Sep 25: Battle of Megiddo.
Oct 30: Turkey signs Armistice.
Nov 11: Germany signs Armistice to end the Great War.

Preface

Like Nightingales we've left the woods we know. May God keep others from the way we go!

Great shells wander twenty miles seeking out their mark, roaring madly in their rush, maxim bullets bark.

The day after Imperial Germany failed to meet the 3 August 1914 deadline for withdrawal from Belgium, Great Britain declared war on Germany. Great Britain and her empire were now at war. The centrepiece of this great empire was the 'Jewel in the Crown', India. The British had arrived in India as traders in the 17th Century and over the next 300 years slowly moved from trading to eventually ruling the sub-continent. In the middle of the 19th century the inevitable British expansion north by war and treaty, brought them to the border of the powerful Sikh Empire established by Maharaja Ranjit Singh.

The Sikhs had built themselves an empire in the Punjab, the land of five rivers (Ravi, Sutlej, Chenab, Jhelum and Beas), which they ruled from the late 18th century. This empire was built on the shrewdness of Ranjit Singh, but when he died in 1839, there was no worthy successor and the court of Lahore descended into anarchy.

Skilfully biding their time until the opportune moment, the British went to war with the Sikh Empire, the last part of the sub-continent not under British control. Two sanguinary Anglo-Sikh wars later, the British fought and manipulated their way to victory. By 1849, the British had added the prize of the Punjab to their empire.

Although eventually victorious, the British had come close to defeat for the first time in India, against an army that fought them to a standstill more than once. Post annexation the British took a keen interest in the Sikhs. How could the British subdue the Sikhs so that they would not rise again? They started to enlist discharged Sikh army soldiers into British Indian army regiments. This enlistment was a great success for it was these Sikh soldiers who came to their aid during the first major challenge to British suzerainty, the so-called Indian Mutiny of 1857. In fact, not just the Sikhs but many Punjabi regiments comprising Muslims, Hindus and Sikhs had remained loyal to the British. Sikhs now came to be readily accepted into the British Indian army to become the frontline of British imperial design across the world.

By 1914, the British had ruled all of India (now India, Pakistan and Bangladesh) for more than six decades. During this period, Punjabi soldiers including Sikhs had enlisted in large numbers, approximately half the British Indian Army being recruited from the Punjab. Sikhs contributed approximately 25 percent of the total Punjabi recruits during the Great War. More remarkable as their proportion of the Punjab population was approximately 12 percent at the time.

However, there were other parallel Sikh movements during the years of the Great War worthy of note. There was a world of religious and educational renaissance against imperial repression in the Punjab. There was also the story of emigrant Sikhs who had seen the freedom enjoyed by other peoples of the world and realised that their rights at 'home' were being denied. They had seen racism in the empire and seen laws passed in the colonies which said they were not welcome. Some emigrants decided to fight against these laws by trying to circumvent them. Others decided that an armed revolution was needed to free Indians from imperial rule.

My interest in the Great War was sparked by many factors over the last few years. Growing up as a second generation Sikh in London, my identity and background were a powerful force in my life. I now had a family of my own and I wanted my children to know their roots and the many struggles that are part of their heritage, as they would not be taught this at school. Through a chance internet search in 2014 I came across the Anglo-Sikh Heritage Trail (ASHT), run by Harbinder Singh Rana, an organisation which was dedicated to preserving and commemorating shared history between the British and Sikhs. The organisation was running a day trip to the battlefields of the Great War in northern France and Belgium. I took my son Amar, who was eleven years old at the time. The trip was an eye opener in many ways as we visited the Indian memorial at Neuve Chapelle and listened to a rendition of the last post at the Menin Gate in Ypres in Belgium. What struck us both at these places was the name Singh, rows and rows with the surname Singh, my son noticed that the name 'Amar Singh', his name, appeared often. He would go on to write a poem about his trip, which is included herein. This was also my first meeting with Harbinder and author Amarpal Singh Sidhu.

I had a strong interest and love of Sikh history, in the various battles fought by the tenth master, Guru Gobind Singh and the sacrifice of countless Sikh martyrs. I had a love of military history in general and world war two in particular as my Great Uncle had fought in the Burma campaign. With the centenary commemoration of the Great War due to begin, I was keen to research for any family connection.

'Who do you think you are?' one of my favourite TV programmes gave me the idea of establishing whether there were any links to the Great War on the paternal side of my family. Although I did not find any links, I did find out that my Great Grandfather, Bhuja Singh Bassi, had arrived in England as early as 1935 and had worked as a pedlar in East London. Further my paternal Great Uncle, still alive, mentioned that his father had stayed briefly with *Shaheed* Udham Singh and had even helped him collect funds for an unknown project. Udham Singh went on to assassinate the ex-Lieutenant Governor of the Punjab, Michael O'Dwyer, who had presided over the Jallianwalla Bagh massacre of 1919 in Amritsar.

However, I could not find a connection to the Great War. Then in a chance conversation with my mother, I asked her the question, was there anyone in her family who was a soldier? To my surprise, she believed there was. Recounting distant memories, she said "when I was very young, I remember my father saying that a family event could not be held because my grandfather was then in France." My mother related that she was 10 when her Grandfather died and that he was in his eighties. She remembered that he was tall and stern, but handsome. The timeline seemed to fit, and what reason could there have been for a British Indian subject to be in France in the early 20th century?

His name was Dalip Singh. Just hearing that name conjured up many things in my mind. His name felt important; there was an element of magic to it. Did he fight on the Western Front? Since he had survived and made it back to India, what stories did he have to tell?

Suddenly the Great War was not about Tommies and trenches for me, it was about Dalip Singh, I had my connection and I wanted to know more. This now felt personal, it was about my own community, and it was a story that had to be told. It became a labour of love.

Thousands of Indian soldiers fought and died in the Great War. However, this book will try and narrate the experiences of Sikh soldiers and Sikhs alone. This is not meant to undermine the contribution of others, but as you can imagine the Great War is a very large canvas!

For me, an archive of censored letters written by Indian soldiers kept at the British Library was a key discovery. Along with other sources of primary information such as newspaper articles, testimonies, statements and other records, I now had the information I required for a book. After all, who could better describe their wartime experiences than the Sikhs themselves?

The Indian mails censor reports kept at the British Library hold English translations of extracts of letters to and from Indian soldiers based in France during the Great War. They also include letters from Indian soldiers injured and convalescing in England. Censorship is common in military circles. Indian mail censorship was active all over the world from Hong Kong to the Middle East. Correspondence was closely scrutinised and weekly reports sent off by the Chief Censor. The task of censoring the Indian mails was huge, with approximately 50,000 letters passing through the Censorship per week on average (in March 1915).

The Indian mails censor reports in France covered the period December 1914 to March 1918. The archive is extensive and there are thousands of letters bound in 26 volumes. Luckily, the British categorised all Indian soldier letters (more about this later), and at the top of each translated letter, the receiver or writer would be described by their 'class'. So for example letters written to and from Sikhs are clearly identified and comprise the bulk of the information in this book. For the sake of completeness all the Sikh letters were transcribed from the 26 volumes. This, as you can imagine was a very long and pain staking process, which took the better part of three years! Furthermore, each Sikh letter is transcribed in its original archival format to ensure authenticity. So if a letter was written to a soldier from Jullundur, Jalandar or another variation of the spelling of the Punjabi town, the original spelling is maintained. I was only able to access records from two original censorship sources, from France and Port Said. Other such archives may also exist, but as I was unable to locate them, and thus are not included.

The censorship was based in France and initially the names of soldiers were redacted. However, this was quickly reversed. Thus for each letter included, the name, regiment and sometimes rank are recorded. Letters to Sikh soldiers would also show the name of the sender, sometimes the relationship and the location from which the letter was sent. Letters to and from Sikh soldiers came from all over the world and all over the Punjab. Over the period of the French censorship, a total of 1,070 letters sent to and from Sikh soldiers are recorded. Since these were in various languages, translators were employed who were proficient in understanding the 'native' languages. With regards to the Sikh letters, there were two main languages: 601 in Urdu and 427 in *Gurmukhi*. There are probably some things that would be lost in translation, but the Censors tended to be very knowledgeable in the Indian languages, so I believe that we can rely on the quality of their translations. There were also a small number (14) originally sent in English and 28 sent in other/mixed or unknown languages.

Nearly 700 of these Sikh letters are included in this book. The Censor of Indian mails reports did not record all the letters sent by Indian soldiers. Mostly extracts from the letters they felt best represented the feelings of the different classes. Letters would have parts of them removed if they contained sensitive information. Some letters would not be passed if they were wholly inappropriate or incited sedition. The letters would be expected to pass through many levels of scrutiny, but in practice this did not always happen. Eventually, the soldiers came to know of the censorship and used a variety of methods to circumvent the system, which meant that some letters would not pass through the censorship.

Another great archive kept at the British Library is that of the Criminal Investigation Department (CID) reports covering Punjabi newspapers, both in English and vernacular languages. These secret reports were used to ensure that the newspapers and editors remained pro-British.

Apart from the Censor of Indian mails reports, I accessed many different records held at the British Library and I would like to thank the staff of the British Library Asian and African reading room for their advice. I would like to acknowledge the assistance of the University of Cambridge library for allowing me access to a hand-written archive of censored letters sent by Indian soldiers based at Port Said in 1918. I also take this opportunity to thank the National Archives of Australia for permission to publish a letter from a Sikh widow of a Sikh soldier who fought for the Australian Imperial Force during the Great War. The Canadian National Archives, the Royal Pavilion & Museums, Brighton & Hove and the National Army Museum for permission to publish images from their collections.

I am grateful to Dr Kevin Greenbank, from the Centre of South Asian studies, Cambridge, for his help with the archives of *The Khalsa Advocate* newspaper, and having a spare memory stick on hand when I needed it most! Further, I acknowledge the advice and encouragement from military historian Amarpal Singh Sidhu (author of *The First Anglo-Sikh War* and *The Second Anglo-Sikh War*), which was always helpful.

I would like to express my appreciation to my colleague, Deanna Westwood, who advised me on my use of English and Colonel (Retd) Harisimran Singh Sandhu, whose diligence and attention to detail would be invaluable. I would also like to give a special mention to Avtar Singh Bahra for the kind access to his private collection of Great War images. My gratitude also goes to Herminder Singh Sandhu, Silverfox pictures and the Staffordshire Regimental museum for the powerful artwork created for the book. My further gratitude goes to my publisher Helion & Company and my editor Dr Michael LoCicero, for believing in the idea of this book and making a dream a reality! I am also grateful to Harminder Singh Gill, chairman of the Saragarhi Foundation, for his kind and generous support during the publication process. I would finally like to give sincere thanks to Harbinder Singh Rana, for his help in getting this book published, and for his unstinting support throughout the process.

I dedicate this book to my family, my wife Kuljit, my son Amar and my daughter Sanjana. Its aim is to reveal to the reader the thoughts and writings of the Sikh people during the period of the Great War. I hope that this would give them sufficient insight into the Sikh psyche during this time, what they did and why they did it.

I have arranged the chapters according to the themes that I identified. Each 'voice' in the chapter is arranged in chronological order, which allows the reader to see the Great War story unfold. In my opinion, the striking power of this story is that it is told by the protagonists themselves. The war becomes alive, it becomes about people, it becomes about soldiers, families, friends and loved ones. It becomes about the human experience of a Great War of the 20th century, whose effects are still being felt a 100 years later.

Sukwinder Singh Bassi
London, Summer 2018

Introduction

The Great Guru Nanak blessed the earth, from Heaven coming, taking birth.

In the Sikh wars of 1846 and 1849 they fought the British in a manner which compelled admiration for their military genius and prowess, displaying soldierly qualities of the highest order.

All the ground is covered with corpses. So many corpses are there and all have perished in forty seconds. As a man climbs a plum tree and shakes down the plums, they fall and lie in heaps.

The blood of martyrs never goes to waste. It shall bear fruit at last.

Who are the Sikhs?

Late in the 15th century, the village of Sultanpur in the Punjab, northern India was in mourning at the apparent drowning of a man in the Bein River. Three days later this man would reappear with a message for all humanity – this man would become known as Guru Nanak.

Guru Nanak's message was simple: 'There is no Hindu and there is no Muslim (*Naa Koee Hindu Naa Mussalmaan*); only human beings and any religious labels are meaningless in the eyes of God'; Sikhism was born as a new religion. In his universal message to mankind, Guru Nanak highlighted the need to earn an honest living, chant the name of God and sharing one's wealth with the needy.

Guru Nanak (1469-1539) was born into a Hindu family but was soon to question the wisdom of the rituals and traditions of his time. He was an advanced thinker at an early age and studied the religions of Hinduism and Islam which surrounded him. As a child he astounded his contemporaries and teachers with his poetry and deep philosophical thinking. Guru Nanak would go on to reject the Hindu sacred thread ceremony and debate extensively with Hindu and Muslim holy men, elevating the spiritual importance of the soul rather than pilgrimages, penance and other rituals.

Guru Nanak preached that there was only one God and that humans through meditation on God's name and singing *His* praises through divine words could experience God without the need of rituals or a priestly class. He also taught that in the eyes of God, all are equal regardless of caste, creed or gender. These were revolutionary ideas in a time where religious intolerance was unrelenting under the fledgling Mughal Empire.

Driven by his love of God and his determination to spread *His* message (See Appendix VI), Guru Nanak took his divine message far and wide over the next 30 years. He took on major journeys across continents, known as *udasis* in the Sikh tradition. These journeys would take him to the spiritual centres of the world's major religions where he would share his vision of

God. He journeyed to Tibet and Sri Lanka, centres of the Buddhist world, Mecca and Baghdad of the Islamic world and the major centres of Hinduism across India. (Recent research has also shown evidence of Guru Nanak reaching as far west as Rome and Turkey).

Guru Nanak thus became one of the most far reaching travellers of his time. Guru Nanak would finally settle in Kartarpur surrounded by his followers, before passing the 'divine light' to his greatest disciple, Guru Angad.

Pre-British Sikh History

The Sikh message was continued and propagated by his nine successors for over 200 years, ending with the passing of the tenth Guru in 1708. The fifth Guru, Arjan Dev (1563-1606) would compile the hymns of the first five Gurus in a holy text called the *Adi Granth*. The original scribe of the *Adi Granth* was Bhai Gurdas (1551-1637). Bhai Gurdas would become a renowned Sikh Scholar, writing his *Varan*, which Guru Arjan would describe as the 'key' to the *Adi Granth*. The hymns of the first five Guru's, Guru Nanak, Guru Angad, Guru Amar Das, Guru Ram Das and Guru Arjan himself were compiled in a script called *Gurmukhi (mouth of the Guru)*, under the *larivaar* style of writing, which meant the words were in a continuous form (i.e. no breaks between words). Thus the Guru's writings were preserved in their original form and essentially ratified by the fifth Guru before inclusion in the *Adi Granth*. The *Adi Granth* notably not only contained hymns of the Sikh Gurus, but also of Hindu and Muslim saints, to acknowledge the universality of 'truth'. The words of the holy text would be known as *Gurbani*. Sikhs also believed in the doctrine of *Karma*, in that previous good actions had resulted in birth as a human.

The fifth Guru would also oversee the building of the most famous Sikh place of worship, the *Harmandir*, or Golden Temple in Amritsar. Highlighting the nonpartisan nature of the faith, a Muslim *Sufi* Saint, Mian Mir, was invited to lay the foundation stone of the temple. The *Harmandir* (the abode of God) building was completed in 1577, and had four entrances, implying that all were welcome. Although destroyed by Afghan invaders several times, the temple as it stands today was rebuilt in 1764. Maharaja Ranjit Singh would later adorn it with gold leaf in the early 19th century to make it the 'Golden Temple'.

The appearance of the Sikh Guru's also coincided with the Mughal Empire in India (1526-1857). Although some Mughal Emperors were enlightened and tolerant rulers, others were not. Guru Arjan Dev was executed by the Emperor Jahangir in 1606 in Lahore, while the ninth master, Guru Tegh Bahadur was executed in 1675 in Delhi. These events were to have a far-reaching effect on Sikh history, bringing about a change in the outlook of Sikhs as a community.

After the execution of Guru Arjan, his successor Guru Hargobind opted to resist tyranny by taking up arms against Mughal persecution, fighting battles invariably against unfavourable odds and emerging victorious. Mughal-Sikh relations were then amicable until the execution of Guru Tegh Bahadur. The tenth and final Sikh Guru, Guru Gobind Singh (1666-1708) further added to the *Adi Granth* by including the hymns of his father, Guru Tegh Bahadur. The holy text would now take on a whole new meaning and would now be known as the *Guru Granth Sahib*. The remarkable text was over a 1,000 pages in length, was written in a unique script and multiple languages, entirely in poetry and set to music. The names given for God were *Waheguru* or *Akaal Purakh*, although there were numerous other names used for God within the scripture.

Guru Gobind Singh surrounded himself with many disciples and poets. Of these the most prominent was Bhai Nand Lal (1633-1713). Bhai Nand Lal was an extraordinary poet whose deep conviction and understanding of *Gurbani* manifested itself in great writings and poetry such as the *Zindginama*, *Divan-e-Goya* and *Tankhah Nama*. (See Appendix VI).

After the execution of his father, Guru Gobind Singh realised that if the Sikhs were to survive something had to change radically. In 1699, during an assembly of Sikhs on the first day of *Baisakhi* (annual spring harvest festival) at Anandpur (Punjab), he made a call to his followers for sacrifice. Five fearless men came forward; these five men would forever become known as the *Panj Pyare* (the five beloved ones). The Guru then proceeded to induct these five men into the brotherhood of warrior-saints, known henceforth as the '*Khalsa*'. He adorned them with the five symbols of identity, known as the five K's: *Kara* (steel bangle), *Kirpan* (a sword), *Kacherra* (long cotton shorts), *Kesh* (long unshorn hair) and *Kanga* (small comb), each having a different special symbolic meaning, for a baptised Sikh. Each Sikh was then baptised into the brotherhood by drinking *amrit* (holy water) and given the name 'Singh', which meant that all previous lineage was forgotten. Thus from one event a religious order was given a distinctive dress and appearance, along with a martial spirit.

However, there was no end to Mughal persecution, especially when they saw Sikhism and its new order as a threat to the spread of Islam in India. The atrocities came to a head during the rule of the Mughal Governor of Punjab, Wazir Khan. At the battle of Chamkaur (1704), against massive odds Guru Gobind Singh, lost two of his sons in battle, and was forced to seek refuge in a jungle. His two younger sons and mother were betrayed and presented to Wazir Khan. The cruel governor sentenced the two boys to be bricked alive. Guru Gobind Singh was made aware of the deaths of his sons and his mother and wrote a letter to the Emperor Aurangzeb, holding him accountable for the actions of his officials. The letter written in Persian became known as the '*Zafarnama*' (literally, "epistle of victory").

> A famous line from the *Zafarnama* states:
> "All modes of redressing the wrong having failed, raising of sword is pious and just."
> (Verse 22).

The *Zafarnama* is part of the many writings attributed to Guru Gobind Singh, compiled in the *Dasam Granth*. The *Zarfarnama* was said to have had a profound effect on the Emperor Aurangzeb, who then expressed a wish to meet with the Guru. This meeting, however, did not take place. Two Afghans, supposedly hired by Wazir Khan, tried to assassinate the Guru. Although they did not kill the Guru, he succumbed to his injuries a short while later. Before his 'divine light' passed, the Guru passed the Guruship to the holy book of the Sikhs, the *Guru Granth Sahib*. The pages would be known as *Angs* (limbs) and the *Guru Granth Sahib* would now be the living Guru for the Sikhs.

The passing of Guru Gobind Singh in 1708 would fuel the start of a long and bitter confrontation with the Mughals for over six decades. Prior to his passing away the tenth Guru had met and passed the mantle of leadership to a man who would later become known as Banda Singh Bahadur. The Guru instructed his Banda to raise the suppressed masses against the tyrannical rule of the Mughals. Banda's struggle would see the first attempt to create a *Khalsa Raj* (Sikh state). His tactics and military prowess won him many victories, including the killing of Wazir Khan to avenge the killing of the Guru's sons. However, eventually after a prolonged siege, Banda was captured and executed along with many of his followers in 1716 in Delhi.

The succeeding few decades of the 18th century were extremely arduous for the Sikhs. A combination of Mughal atrocities and invasions from Persia and Afghanistan compounded their plight. Thousands of Sikh lives were lost when the Mughal governor of Lahore, Zakaryia Khan, placed a bounty on a Sikh head. Forced to flee to jungles, Sikhs continued to wage a guerrilla war, exacting reprisals upon brutal Mughal officials and soldiers. They also evolved their own strategies and tactics to harass and inflict casualties upon invading Afghan armies under Ahmad Shah Abdali.

By the 1760's, the Sikhs were loosely organised in 12 groups called *Misls* and began to slowly fill the vacuum left by a disintegrating Mughal Empire. These *Misls* would converge during their battles against the Afghans and, in 1765, overran the Afghan controlled city of Lahore, declaring sovereignty over the Punjab.

The *Misls* had come together to effectively replace the Mughal government of the Punjab, and by the end of the 18th century, the whole region was under the control of the various *Misls*. In 1783, in a complete reversal of fortune, Sikh troops led by Jassa Singh Ahluwalia and Baghel Singh entered the Red Fort, the seat of Mughal power in Delhi. Two years later, Baghel Singh would return to oversee the building of several Sikh historic shrines, linked with major events in Sikh history. The Sisganj Gurdwara would be built on the spot where Guru Tegh Bahadur was executed, and Gurdwara Rakabganj where his body was cremated.

The 12 *Misls* needed to unify and the foresight of one Ranjit Singh, leader of the *Sukerchakia Misl* allowed this to happen. A marriage with the daughter of another *Misl* leader and the powerful influence of his mother-in-law Sada Kaur, Ranjit Singh, a one-eyed man fought to consolidate the power of the *Misls*. He achieved this and was declared the Maharaja of the Punjab in April 1801. Thus, in less than a 100 years from the passing of Guru Gobind Singh, his *Khalsa* were now rulers of the Punjab, which is even more remarkable considering the number of lives lost during the 18th century.

The shrewd Maharaja Ranjit Singh built a Sikh Empire beyond the Punjab and took victorious armies to the borders of Afghanistan and the snowy peaks of Tibet. He was able to do this with the help of generals such as Hari Singh Nalwa and Zorawar Singh. The Maharaja was acutely aware of the threat of the British, who by now were well entrenched in India.

In 1809, the Maharaja signed the Treaty of Amritsar with the British which effectively sealed the Sutlej River as the border between him and the British. The Maharaja now consolidated his empire and modernised his army with the help of European officers from Russia, Spain and France. Soldiers also joined from adjoining lands such as the Gurkhas. By the force of diplomacy and war, the Sikh Empire now stretched from the borders of Tibet in the east to Afghanistan in the west and included Kashmir to the north.

Maharaja Ranjit Singh died in June 1839 and his court fell into disarray. Deception and intrigue were rife, and the *Khalsa* army were restless in the absence of a strong leader. The British took advantage of the situation and events on the Sutlej River border spiralled towards the inevitable clash of arms between the Sikhs and the British, which is what the British wanted.

The first Anglo-Sikh War started in December 1845, just six years after the death of Ranjit Singh. Five battles ensued and victory went to the British. Misled by their generals, who were in league with the British, the Sikhs put up a stiff fight and caused heavy British casualties at the battle of Ferozeshah. Further undermined by duplicitous generals, the Sikh army was finally defeated at the battle of Soboran in February 1846. None of the Sikh army surrendered and fought desperately to the end. A treaty was signed in the aftermath of the defeat, but Sikh indignation at British interference in the running of the Punjab led to a second Anglo-Sikh War within three years. Again the Sikhs were defeated and in March 1849 the last Sikh Maharaja, the child Duleep Singh, gave up his throne on British annexation.

Sikhs and the British period

The defeat at the hands of the British would have a deep and long lasting effect on the Sikh nation. The British took no time in disbanding the Sikh Army and demilitarising the Punjab; 'placards were placed in all major cities and villages demanding the surrender of arms.'[1] Over 40,000 disbanded Sikh soldiers now had no means of employment.

The British devised a strategy to subdue and sustain the people. Firstly, they targeted the Sikh aristocracy and the royal family. The child Maharaja Duleep Singh was converted to Christianity in 1853 and left for England a year later. Many Sikh families of note were targeted, and their titles and lands removed. Many embittered Sikh soldiers left the Punjab and migrated south and elsewhere.

Another element of British policy was the control of Sikh Gurdwaras:

> The British adopted a very strict and rigid policy detrimental to the growth of Sikhism. After annexation, The Golden Temple, Amritsar, along with 6 other gurdwaras and The Gurdwara at Tarn Taran were practically controlled by the British authorities through a Manager of these Gurdwaras appointed by the British Government. The Waqf Act of 1861 gave the Control and Management of the holy places of the Hindus and Muslims to the Committees concerned but in the case of the Sikh Gurdwaras, The Act was not applied on political grounds. The properties of the Sikh places of worship were transferred and given over to the Udasi Mahants and others, throughout the Punjab.[2]

The British would then lend support and patronage to these families, *Mahants* (Managers) and other organisations, effectively binding their prospects to the British and engendering loyalty to the Raj. Post annexation, with the loss of Sikh prestige and power, many ex-Hindus who had adopted Sikhism, fell back into the fold of Hinduism. In fact, there were British officials that believed that the 'sect' of Sikhism would disappear within a few years.

Simultaneously the levels of Sikh education and employment started to dwindle. Urdu became the language of British administration in the Punjab as well as the army. Sikhism was under threat from many angles and the population numbers started to decline. The British were obsessed with classification and this was highlighted by the censuses conducted under British rule. For the British everyone had to fall under a particular category. You were either a Sikh or a Hindu, you could not be both. The definition of what it was to be a Sikh changed with each census.

1 Khushwant Singh, *A History of the Sikhs: Volume II: 1839-2004* (New Delhi: Oxford, 2004), p. 88.
2 David Petrie, *Developments in Sikh politics, 1900-1911: A Report* (Amritsar: Chief Khalsa Diwan, 1972), p. 7.

In a bid to forestall against the rise of Sikh nationalism, the British began recruiting disbanded Sikh soldiers in to their army. As early as 1846, some older Sikh soldiers were recruited into British Indian army regiments. The preference some years later was to recruit soldiers who were under the age of 20, and thus not affiliated too closely with the old Sikh army. The British also took the decision to maintain 'orthodox' Sikh traditions. Even within this recruitment policy the British maintained a 'divide and rule' element. *Jat* Sikh soldiers were the preferred Sikh 'caste' for soldiering duties, this policy would be reversed, but the different 'Sikh castes' would still be kept apart.

The British encouraged religious observance amongst Sikhs, with many regiments having their own *granthis*. British officers would pay respect to the *Guru Granth Sahib* and religious festivals would be celebrated with their soldiers. Sikh soldiers would be sworn into the army by taking an oath of allegiance on the *Guru Granth Sahib* to the British. Thus, British policy created a strange juxtaposition for Sikhs. On one hand, the brave martial *Khalsa* soldier was positively endorsed in recruitment into the army and, on the other hand, the British were wary of the Sikh nation rising again. Yet, they sought to foster their 'national' pride in the army by "studiously nationalising" them and encouraging them to "regard themselves as a totally distinct and separate nation."[3]

An event then took place which would have a far reaching effect on the Sikhs and the British, the 'Indian Mutiny' of 1857. Hindu and Muslim sepoys had turned on their European officers in Meerut and Delhi and mutinied. The mutiny spread all over northern India but did not have much effect in the Punjab. In fact, Punjabi regiments of Sikhs, Hindus and Muslims were instrumental in supressing the 'rebellion'. Post-mutiny, Sikh soldiers came to be more readily accepted into the British Indian army and many more took up the opportunity with alacrity.

The British paid acute attention to detail in their recruitment policies towards Sikhs. Lots of research was completed and recruiting handbooks were produced. Each District and *Tehsil* (area serving as an administrative centre) below it was a given a value which measured the quality of recruits (See Appendix III). For example in the Amritsar District there were three *Tehsils*: Amritsar was rated 'very good', as was Tarn Taran, but Ajnala was rated 'fair'. Ratings across the districts ranged from 'very good' to 'very bad'.[4]

Each caste (e.g. *Jat*, *Khatri*, etc.) would be further sub-divided into sub-caste. For example Sandhu, Sidhu and Gill were well known *Jat* sub-castes (or tribes). The detail even went down to the description of the style of *pagri* (turban).

Another Sikh handbook written in 1900, took the attention to detail and classification still further. Sikhs were divided firstly by geographical classification, describing their sub-geographical area as either: *Manjha*, *Malwa* or *Doaba*. Each 'caste' was then further broken down into sub-castes or clans, with details of lineage, intermarriage conventions, and the approximate number of the clan.

The handbook includes Sikh prayers, the prevailing Sikh 'sects' of the time, and Sikh customs. The four main customs described as *karams;* related to birth, baptism, marriage and death. These were then related to how much leave a solider may need to complete or take part in these customs. For example, a soldier would need 10 days for their marriage or 17 days to partake in

3 Ibid., p. 11.

4 Robert Worgan Falcon, *Handbook on Sikhs for the Use of Regimental Officers* (Allahabad: Pioneer Press, 1896), p. 69.

funeral rites. Sikh festivals and fairs were also examined, along with the 'characteristics' of Sikh life, their physical prowess and dress, to village life and the names of kitchen utensils!

The handbook included detailed instructions for recruiting. Rewards were given to good and reliable recruiters; assistance of civil authorities such as *Tehsildars* was sought and encouraged. The best season for recruiting was said to be from the 'beginning of January to the end of April as at that time the men had time on their hands as there was little to do in the fields'. A list of fairs was also appended to the handbook, described by their names, location, dates and which 'type' of Sikhs would attend. The fairs were recognised as good places to recruit soldiers. Recruitment would become a very important issue during the war as the demand for manpower increased year on year.[5]

During the late 19th and early 20th centuries, Sikhs soldiers fought colonial campaigns all over the world. Thousands of Sikhs also left the Punjab and took up posts in other Asian countries. This allowed further emigration to the west coast of America and Canada, as well as Latin America. Many ex-soldiers and farmers from the Punjab also tried to settle in Australia and New Zealand.

Back in the Punjab the two-pronged policy of encouraging Sikh enlistment in the army and keeping Sikhs 'on a leash' outside the army continued. The Indian Arms Act (XI) of 1878 was passed. Under this Act, no person could go armed or carry arms, except under special exemption or by virtue of a licence. Any instrument which could be used in 'attack or defence' would fall under the word 'Arms'. Under the Act, the *Kirpan* would be bracketed under 'sword'.

Early in the 20th century, many representations were made to the Government to redress this issue with regards to Sikhs, who were enjoined religiously to carry the *Kirpan*. Fearing that the ban on the keeping of a *Kirpan* would affect the recruitment of Sikhs to the Indian army, the Government gradually relaxed the requirements over the period 1914-18. The size and shape of the *Kirpan,* however, remained undefined, and prosecutions of Sikhs for wearing or carrying the *Kirpan* continued. In 1914, for example, Sikhs were only allowed to wear the *Kirpan* in the Punjab, a Fateh Singh was imprisoned in Burma for carrying a *Kirpan*, *The Khalsa Akhbar* newspaper (7 August 1914), called for the man to shun his release if it was 'conditional on him abandoning his *Kirpan*'. It was only in 1918 the British allowed Sikhs to wear the *Kirpan* outside the Punjab.

A powerful six volume study of 'The Sikh religion – its Gurus, Sacred Writings and Authors' by Max Arthur Macauliffe was published in 1909. In the introduction Macauliffe effuses:

> The Sikh religion differs as regards the authenticity of its dogmas from most other theological systems. Many of the great teachers the world has known have not left a line of their own composition and we only know what they taught through tradition or second-hand information. If Pythagoras wrote of his tenets, his writings have not descended to us. We know the teachings of Socrates only through the writings of Plato and Xenophon. Buddha has left no written memorial of his teaching. Kungfu-tze, known to Europeans as Confucius, left no documents in which he detailed the principles of his moral and social system. The founder of Christianity did not reduce his doctrines to writing and for them we are obliged to trust to the gospels according

5 A.H. Bingley, *Handbooks for the Indian Army: Sikhs* (Simla: Government of India, 1899), p. 52.

> to Matthew, Mark, Luke and John. Muhammad did not himself reduce to writing the chapters of the Quran. They were written or compiled by his adherents and followers. But the compositions of Sikh Gurus are preserved, and we know at first-hand what they taught.[6]

This was significant as the translations of histories of the Gurus and their writings were made in English. In his preface, Macauliffe was at pains to advocate a translation of the Sikh religion since '*old gyanis*' (professional interpreters) were dying out. Many recommendations as to the accuracy of his translation are included from learned Sikhs and Sikh organisations of the period. (This included the *gyani* of the Golden Temple and the Amritsar Singh Sabha). Macualiffe had started his work in 1893 and used the '*Suraj Parkash*' as a main source. The *Suraj Parkash* was a work which encompassed thousands of verses depicting the lives of the Gurus. Written by Bhai Santokh Singh and was completed in the year 1843. (Some Sikh scholars have since questioned the authenticity of these writings).

One of the main controversies in Macauliffe's work is the inclusion of 'predictions' made by the Gurus themselves. Quoting the *Suraj Parkash* in volume V of his work, he states that the ninth Sikh Guru, Guru Tegh Bahadur, predicted the advent of British rule in India and that the tenth Guru, Gobind Singh, reiterated this, and told how the 'Sikhs and English will join forces and how beneficial this English rule would be for the Sikhs'. Other similar 'books of prophecy' such as the '*Sau Sakhi*' (100 stories), purporting to be genuine were also circulating during the 19th century, newer 'updated' versions, regularly appearing. One version foretold of the Anglo-Sikh victory during the Mutiny, another of the return of the deposed Maharaja Duleep Singh. As the level of Sikh education and religious instruction lowered, these prophecies gained traction and were promoted in newspapers. Sometimes if a lie is repeated enough, it becomes a fact! Max Macauliffe would also give 'a lecture on the Sikh religion and its advantages to the state' in London in 1903. The British would go on to use the tenets of the Sikh religion against the Sikhs themselves to inspire them to fight for the British and to be obedient subjects.

The Press Act of 1910 controlled the flow of information in the Punjab; the Act increased controls over new printing presses and newspapers by requiring the proprietors to furnish security deposits of between Rs. 500 and Rs. 5000. The deposits could be forfeited if anti-government articles were published. Local Governments were also allowed similar powers. In 1914, the Sikh newspaper *The Khalsa Akhbar*, was added to the growing list of forfeitures when it allegedly wrote an objectionable article about the 'Gurdwara Rakabganj wall'. Thus press controls and propaganda became weapons during the Great War period in the Punjab.

New 'canal colonies' were established in what was previously arid unirrigated land; an example was the Chenab Colony, now in West Punjab in Pakistan. Sikh farmers were recruited from East Punjab and again the preference was for *Jat* Sikhs. These farmers were given free land, effectively lifting many out of the social class in which they had existed. These colonies were a great success, and a boon to the Sikhs. Little did the Sikhs of that period know that they would lose all this land that they worked so hard to develop during partition some decades later. Thus,

6 Max Arthur Macauliffe, *The Sikh Religion: Its Gurus, Sacred Writings and Authors* (New Delhi: S. Chand & Company, 1985), p. Liii.

Sikhs were in demand, in both the army and the canal colonies, and the population of Sikhs started to rise.

Simultaneously, in political, religious and communal affairs, Sikhs were being affected in several different ways. During the latter half of the 19th century, Christian missionaries made their way to the Punjab and made some high profile conversions. In addition, a Hindu movement called the Arya Samaj started to convert lower caste Sikhs to its ranks. The Arya Samaj was particularly critical of the Sikh Gurus and their philosophy. Derogatory texts such as '*Khalsa Panth ki Haqiqat*' (Truth of the *Khalsa* religion) were published to further hurt Sikh sensibilities. Some separate Sikh identities or sects started to emerge. *Nirankaris*, *Radha Soamis* and *Namdhari* (or *Kukas*) all vied for converts. The meaning of what it meant to be a Sikh started to be diluted. Of these sects, perhaps the only sect which wrought the attention of the British was the *Kukas*. Its leader, Ram Singh, was anti-British and encouraged boycotting British goods. Things came to a head with the British in 1872 when over 70 *Kukas* were brutally killed by the British by tying them to the mouths of canons and firing. These killings did not have the expected effect; many Sikhs disapproved of *Kuka* activities. Ram Singh was arrested and deported to Rangoon. The Sikhs were now seen to be a thoroughly 'loyal' community.

To arrest this apparent decline in Sikhism, and to ward off threats from Christian and Hindu missionaries, prominent Sikhs founded the Singh Sabha movement to improve and educate the Sikh people through a programme of socio-religious reform. The main aims of the movement were to "propagate the true Sikh religion and restore it to its pristine glory, to publish and circulate historical and religious books, to spread current knowledge in Punjabi and print newspapers and magazines in Punjabi"[7], and to ensure that they obtained patronage from the Government to confirm that they were closely associated with the Sikh educational programme. Punjabi and by default *Gurmukhi* was a strong focus of activities as the Singh Sabhas knew that, in effect, if you killed Punjabi, you would kill Sikhism.

The first Singh Sabha was founded in Amritsar in 1873. Membership was allowed for any Sikh who believed in the teachings of the Gurus, but the majority of its members tended to be from the upper classes. The Singh Sabha would hold big conferences close to important Sikh festivals to allow their message of reform to reach a wider audience. The Amritsar Singh Sabha was a relatively conservative organisation and promoted harmony with the Government and was seen to be 'loyal'. As a reaction to the creation of the Amritsar Singh Sabha, Singh Sabha's were formed all over the Punjab, with the largest being the Lahore Singh Sabha. In contrast to the Amritsar Singh Sabha, its membership was taken from across all the social classes. The Lahore Singh Sabha was created in 1879 and was again concerned with ensuring that the Sikhs had an educational programme and was seen as more aggressive in its approach than the Amritsar version. Some Singh Sabha's evolved different characteristics; for example the Singh Sabha of Bahsaur was much stricter on religious discipline and outlook than other Singh Sabhas. However, these differing Singh Sabhas resulted in rivalries, and public disagreements became commonplace. More organisational reforms followed, but the different organisations did not work well in partnership and a solution was needed.

7 Norman Barrier, *The Sikhs and their literature: A guide to tracts, books and periodicals, 1849-1919* (New Delhi: Manohar Bk. Service, 1970), p. xxiv.

One of the successes of the early Singh Sabha movement was the establishment of the Khalsa College. So powerful was the urge for education in the community that a plea was made from the Golden Temple for Sikhs to contribute funds to the building of the college. The college was founded in 1892, and further *Khalsa* schools were created over the following years.

In 1902, the Chief Khalsa Diwan (CKD) was formed as a new umbrella organisation with the Singh Sabhas as affiliates, and with a new leadership. The CKD had adequate resources as much of the finance came from maharajas and *raises*, which allowed the CKD to have large numbers of workers. It also had the backing of some of the most important newspapers of the time such as *The Khalsa Advocate* and *The Khalsa Samachar*. The British also saw the CKD as a representative body for all Sikhs and CKD leaders also found themselves on the boards of government bodies such as legislative councils. However, not all accepted the CKD as the supreme body for all Sikhs and some Singh Sabhas resisted affiliation.

Although the CKD could never achieve its self-proclaimed status of being the principal representative body of Sikhs, it did achieve some notable successes. In 1905, the CKD was instrumental in getting idols removed from the Golden Temple, Amritsar, and in 1909, it drove the passing of the Anand Marriage Act which gave validity to the Sikh marriage ceremony. They also established the annual Sikh Educational Conference which commenced in 1908, attended by many thousands. The main shortcoming most attributed to the CKD was its tendency to seek too much favour from the British. They did little work to free Gurdwaras from British and *Mahant* control and were increasingly perceived to be weak by those involved in the Indian independence movements. By 1919, the CKD was alienated from the Sikh masses as it continued to agree with oppressive British policies, and detractors vied to dislodge the CKD from its leadership role.

The end of the 19th century and the beginning of the 20th century coincided with a Sikh intellectual renaissance. Teja Singh of Bhasaur became a prolific writer of religious and social reform pamphlets. Mohan Singh Vaid and Ditt Singh also provided much needed growth in Sikh intellectual journalism. Many Sikh newspapers were established at the beginning of the new century and although they had small circulations to begin with, they gave further voice to the cause of Sikh renaissance. The Punjabi language newspapers *The Khalsa Akhbar* (1883) and *The Khalsa Samachar* (1899) commenced printing and the English language newspaper *The Khalsa Advocate* debuted in 1901. All newspapers were monitored by the British on a regular basis and anti-British sentiment acted upon.

Tract Societies publishing historical and educational pamphlets also started to flourish across the Punjab. Current issues and critiques were popular tracts; with many including stories of brave Sikhs martyred for the cause of religion. Other tracts would share understanding of the Sikh scriptures and the teachings of the Gurus. The Khalsa Tract Society, founded in 1894 by Vir Singh, sold tracts by the thousand, as they were relatively cheap to produce. Vir Singh, who would become known as the 'Sixth River of the Punjab', was another prolific writer. In 1914, he completed the huge task of critically editing an important old Sikh historical text called the *Prachin Panth Prakash*. He believed that Sikhs had fallen from their high ideals and that by promoting stories of 18th century Sikh warriors and martyrs, contemporary Sikhs could be motivated to return to these forgotten ideals. Through his newspaper and association with the CKD, Vir Singh would be a proponent of Sikh recruitment into the British Indian army, as he felt that this was a means to return to those ideals. In fact, the (*Ghadar*) revolutionaries of

1914-15 would say that "the books and writings of Bhai Vir Singh inspired them to take action with the religious fervour of the Khalsa of old in a spirit of selfless devotion to the motherland."[8]

Thus by the turn of the 19th century and the beginning of the 20th, the Sikhs had many organisations and personalities vying to preserve Sikh orthodoxy and protect their faith from invasive elements. Many Sikhs now started to believe that their own survival and progression needed to be based on appropriate political representation. The Morley-Minto reforms of 1909 gave Muslims weighted representation in provinces in which they were the minority and Sikhs wanted to safeguard their interests with similar guarantees. In 1916, 50 percent of the seats were reserved for the Muslims of Punjab, but the Sikhs continued to be ignored.

Then certain events took place which would have a lasting effect on the British and 'loyal' Sikh ties. In 1913, the *Mahant* of the Rakabganj Gurdawara in Delhi, in disregard of Sikh sentiments, sold off a part of the Gurdwara land to the Government of India who, in turn, demolished a part of the outer wall to construct a new road following the decision to transfer the British Indian capital to Delhi. This resulted in a Sikh agitation; Harchand Singh of Lyallpur played a prominent role in the early stages of this affair. However, he was prevented from raising the issue at the Sikh Educational Conference at Jalandhar in April 1914. This was an example of the CKD bowing to the wishes of the British rather than those of their community. The outbreak of the Great War came at an opportune time. The Government decided to adjourn the decision until a later date, but the road was never built.

During the late 19th and early 20th centuries, Sikh soldiers fought colonial wars all over world, including Africa (Somaliland 1903-04), Burma (2nd Anglo-Burmese War 1852), Afghanistan (2nd Afghan War 1878-80), China (2nd Anglo-Chinese War 1860 and Boxer Rebellion 1900) and Tibet (1904). In 1897, on the North-West frontier a famous episode took place when a small band of the 36th Sikh Regiment took a stand against overwhelming odds on the Samana ridge at Saragarhi. Cut off from reinforcements they were attacked by 10,000 (estimates vary) Afghan tribesmen, the intrepid band of 21 Sikhs decided to fight it out to the bitter end. The outpost held out for many hours and the Sikhs fought desperately down to the last man. The tribesmen lost hundreds of men in the action, which is commemorated to this day, both in the United Kingdom and India.

Interestingly, Sikhs were never deployed to fight against 'whites' as part of a policy to secure European racial dominance and prestige. Thus, no Sikhs fought in the Boer Wars (1899-1902) in South Africa, although some served in Indian Medical units.

Many soldiers would decide to stay on after the war in such countries to pursue business and personal interests, to be subsequently joined by their families. The descendants of these Sikhs are still to be found in these countries to this day. During the period of 1860 to 1947, Sikhs found their way, sometimes in large numbers, to a long list of countries. Some went for job opportunities and others for a better life. The Land Alienation Act of 1900, which effectively cemented caste divisions (more divide and rule) in the Sikh community, may have also been a factor in Sikh emigration. Far Eastern countries such as the Malay States (present day Malaysia and Singapore) and China offered jobs such as policemen, watchmen and traders. Emigration further west would take the Sikhs to Canada, the USA and countries in Central and South

8 Gurcharan Singh Talib and Attar Singh (Eds), *Bhai Vir Singh: Life, times & works* (Chandigarh: Publication Bureau, Panjab University, 1973), p. 35.

America such as Mexico and Argentina. Sikhs would also find their way to East Africa, present day Kenya, Uganda and Tanzania, where they would be employed building railways for the British. Other Sikhs found futures in Burma, Australia, Fiji, Hong Kong, New Zealand, the Philippines, Thailand and Indonesia. Some even found places to live in Afghanistan. However, as soon as some of these doors opened to the Sikhs, some were closed.

Sikh emigration to North America and Canada in particular was popular in the early part of the 20th century. However, unlike the East Asian and African countries, the 'white' dominions were not so pleased to see such immigration, and there were anti-Indian riots in both Canada and the United States. As a reaction to increasing hostility and racism in North America, community activities for Sikhs started to centre around the newly formed Khalsa Diwan Societies in Vancouver in Canada and Stockton in the USA.

Jwala Singh and Har Dayal took on leadership roles and organised a new group called the 'Hindustani Workers of the Pacific Coast'. The group bought premises and started to print a weekly newspaper called the *Ghadar* (revolution), and thus the *Ghadar* party was born. Prompted by their experience of racism outside India, the party was vehemently anti-British and announced themselves as the 'Enemy of the British Government'. The party wrote articles in many languages, but many of the workers were Sikh and its largest issues were printed in *Gurmukhi*. The party propagated armed revolution and would take its cause back to India. Many articles became popular, such as *Ghadr-di-Gunj* (Echoes of Mutiny) and these sought to rouse the Indian nation to revolt against the British. Many articles appeared as songs or poems, and these appealed to Sikhs in particular. Kartar Singh Sarabha was an assistant editor and Harnam Singh Tundilat wrote many patriotic poems for the paper.

Laws were passed by the Canadian Government which were effectively aimed at halting Indian immigration. The would-be Indian immigrant would have to have a certain number of dollars and would need 'a ticket to travel in a continuous journey from their country of origin'. This law directly targeted Indians as there were no ships which travelled directly from India to Canada.

Gurdit Singh from Singapore was acutely aware of the regulations aimed at stopping Indian immigration to Canada. He chartered a ship called *Komagata Maru* to challenge and circumvent the 'continuous journey' regulations. The journey started from Hong Kong on the 4 April 1914. After picking up more passengers in Shanghai and Yokohama, the 376 passengers, of whom 340 were Sikhs, started their journey to Vancouver.

The *Komagata Maru* reached Vancouver in British Columbia on 23 May 1914 and, initially, they were not allowed to dock. Meetings were held by Canadian officials to decide the fate of the passengers. Weeks passed by in the stand-off. Legal arguments followed and it was decided to deny the right of entry. The marooned passengers took over the ship, and when a tug was deployed to tow the *Komagata Maru* out to sea, the desperate passengers fought back. The Government also sent in a navy ship and troops to deal with the escalating situation. Eventually twenty passengers were allowed to disembark and after some negotiation and the promise of provisions for the return journey, the *Komagata Maru* was sent back to Asia from whence it came. The ordeal of the passengers was far from over as the return journey was to be further complicated by the outbreak of the Great War.

The Sikh Soldier's Great War

Sikh soldiers and regiments fought all over the world during the Great War. They found themselves fighting the Germans on the Western Front, in parts of Africa and China, and fighting Germany's ally Turkey (the Ottoman Empire), in Mesopotamia (now Iraq), Persia (now Iran), and across today's Middle East. Many Sikh soldiers also defended the North-West frontier of India (now Pakistan), which was always a volatile region, as it continues to be to this day. The Sikh soldiers suffered great hardships across the different theatres of war. The 15th and 47th Sikhs were thrown into the freezing cold of northern France; the 14th Sikhs fell in large numbers at Gallipoli and hundreds were casualties in combat or fighting disease in Mesopotamia.

The flow of Sikh recruits from India increased year on year all through the war. Sikhs were to contribute 88,925 recruits during the Great War period in comparison to Punjabi Muslims 190,078 and Punjabi Hindus 83,515. This is notable as the Sikhs only formed just over 10 percent of the Punjab population. The Sikhs had been long recognised as a 'martial race' and were specifically targeted for recruitment. The 'martial races' theory dictated that certain Indian 'races' were more 'warlike' than others and would prove to be better soldiers. Each group 'had certain characteristics' and officers of the British Army believed strongly in this theory.

> One great feature with regard to the Sikh, who is one of the most warlike and powerful of Indian tribes, is the fact that he is never allowed to cut his hair or beard. This is the law of his caste. He rolls up his beard, no matter how long, and tucks it away under his ears. His hair, which is always washed with curds, is treated in the same manner. The Sikhs proved themselves a great fighting race in the Sikh War, and in some of their battles, though victory was said to be ours, in reality it was a draw. They come from the Punjab, the land of the five rivers, as it is generally described, and are an intellectual race, with a predilection for opium-eating, which enables them to overcome fatigue.[9]

Sikhs and Gurkhas were continually highlighted as being at the top of this tree, even though they did not make up the bulk of the Indian Army. Bravery and heroism became synonymous with the Sikh name. Examples would be recorded in British Officer memoirs such as the following from the Mesopotamian campaign:

> The desert around was dotted thick with fallen figures, some motionless in unnatural attitudes, others rolling about in agony and distress, a few walking, hobbling or staggering about. A particularly horrifying sight was one of our Sikh sepoys sitting on the ground and beckoning me to come over. The whole of his lower jaw had been shot clean away and the stump of his ragged tongue was hanging out. He indicated that he wanted a sip of water but he was not able to swallow.[10]

9 Cayley Calvert (Ed), 'Kitchener's Hospital for Indian Troops, Brighton', *Brighton and Hove and South Sussex Graphic*, 1:29 (July 1915), p 11.
10 Colonel W.C. Spackman, *Captured at Kut: Prisoner of the Turks* (Yorkshire: Pen & Sword, 2008), p. 45.

Again, this can be seen as part of a 'divide and rule' policy – in modern times this would be known more as 'racial profiling'. Tinged by racial superiority theories prevalent at the time, a British officer describes Sikhs thus:

> The ideal Sikh is the happy Sikh, the Sikh who is content with the place he occupies in his cosmos, who respects and believes in his superior officers, who does not consider himself unjustly treated, and who has received no injury to his self-esteem. For the virtuous ingredients in his composition are subject to reaction. When he fancies that he is wronged, he broods. The milk in him becomes gall. The "waters of life" stirred by steel, his baptismal draught, take on acid potency. "I'd rather command Sikhs than any other class of sepoy," a brigadier told me, and he had commanded every imaginable class of sepoys for twenty years, "but they must be happy Sikhs," he added. The brooding or intriguing Sikh is a nuisance and a danger.[11]

Indian soldiers were called *Sepoys* in the infantry, and *Sowars* in the cavalry, these were equivalent to British privates. The Indian officer ranks who held viceroy commissions (Jemadar and above), only held authority over Indian troops and were 'ranked' below all King's commissioned officers (See Appendix II).

Before the Great War the Indian Army were split into two types of unit, class regiments and class company regiments. Class regiments, such as the 47th Sikhs, were made up entirely of the same class. Class company regiments would have separate companies of the same class within the regiment, such as the 89th Punjabis. This recruiting policy would go further in trying to ensure that even the class was of the same caste. For example, some class regiments would be made up of *Jat* Sikhs only.

Sikhs also made up a significant proportion of the Imperial Service troops supplied by the Maharajas of the Punjab States. The Great War years would expose the Sikh soldiers to parts of the world that they had not seen before and to a type of warfare that they had never encountered previously; their lives would never be the same again…

11 Edmund Candler, *The Sepoy* (New Delhi: Lancer, 2008), p. 32.

1

All about France

Life and death are preordained, but he who has not seen the country of France, has seen nothing. It is as though he had never come in to this world. What more can I say?

The French people are extremely kind and friendly to Indians.

On seeing France I am satisfied that anyone who is without education is no better than an animal.

They respected us as we were regarded as the descendants of Maharaja Ranjit Singh, who had given high-positions to the French people in his army.

When the Indian troops of the Lahore and Meerut Divisions (See Appendix V) arrived in France in the winter of 1914, they were to confront one of the coldest winters on record in a country they had never seen before. Europe made a deep impression on the Sikh soldiers. Although they visited England, they spent much more time in France and many billeted with the French people. The character of the French people (who saw them as liberators) much impressed the Sikhs, especially the 'love' that they received from them. The Sikhs were also taken aback by the advanced culture that they saw the French people enjoying, from the beauty of Paris to the educational, scientific and agricultural achievement of the French people. In particular the Sikhs were impressed by French women, their hardiness in the face of the grim realities of war and the fact that they were educated. A Sikh Jemadar in 1917 said in a similar vein: "All credit to their courage! It gives me much pleasure, and I pray to the Guru to create similar courage in our women." This chapter relates the Sikh experience of France during the Great War years, and how Sikhs would appeal to relatives to make changes when they returned to the Punjab.

*****

> "I am well & pray ever for your welfare. My dear brother, this is a very fine country. They have an excellent way of doing things, & there is much beauty in the country. There is no doubt about it. Very many people come to see us, & one cannot tell the lord from the beggar. All are alike & they do everything with great intelligence and skill. They use dogs to drive their animals that is cattle & to extract butter from milk. They grind wheat & do everything by machinery, and thresh the straw, all by machinery. And they plough with horses. As for the shopkeepers, they are very honest & make no difference in their prices. Whether it be a child or a grown man, they ask the same price of

everyone. There is no theft or dishonesty. The shops remain open all day long and never a penny is stolen. And if a man commits theft they inflict a very severe punishment on him. They fix him alive & upright to a stake & fasten his hands with nails, & there he dies. So nobody commits theft. And the buildings that is the houses are very very fine indeed. Each house has at least six or seven storeys & the workmanship that they put in them is beyond all description. You may look at it all day & still not satisfy the desire of your heart to see. And they are very rich & full of intelligence. Even the children speak well. And they deal with one another in a very brotherly fashion. And there is no doubt of their cleanliness, they are very clean. And they eat with wonderful skill & daintiness. The boys & girls go to school from their earliest years to be educated, & there are many Indians here who are here for their education.

My dear brother, I have received a letter from home & after reading over the earlier letter my heart was filled with much happiness as to describe makes the earth hard & heavens high. (sic). My dear brother when I read the letter & heard all about the village I was quite overjoyed. My dear brother, they have been telling me that our dear brothers A & B have been killed in battle. I was sorely grieved for Havaldar A. I was wounded on the 31st October on the same day as C and D. So I came to the hospital where I have been completely cured. Havaldar A was killed in action on the 23rd of November. My dear brother, I must finish my letter. For here I am as a king, but the war is still going on. Hundreds & thousands of men are engaged & and it goes on day after day. This was is like the war which Hanuman made when he burnt the stones of (unintelligible). Men die in the same way & are wounded. There can be no confidence of life or of seeing again the dear children or of seeing you once more. For in a few days I shall go back to the war. When shall come the day when I shall see again my dear children? When shall I see you? Well, my brother, do not be anxious. We shall see what will come of it. My love to the dear children & greetings to all my friends. If I live I will write again."

From X.Y. a Sikh wounded in hospital at Milton to his brother in the Punjab. (Original in Urdu, dated the 18th January 1915).

*****

"I cannot write about the war, because we are not allowed. It is a strict order, & if any one writes about it, his letter is torn up & thrown away, so I do not write about it. The country is very fine, but it is very cold here. If it were not for the cold this country would be like Heaven. Otherwise it deserves praise. The Government makes the most excellent arrangements against the cold. It gives us very warm clothes. If it did not do so, every one would die of the cold, & what kind of battle would they fight then? No one has any clue to the language of this place. Even the British soldiers do not understand it. They call milk "doolee" and water "doolo" (du lait, & de l'eau). There is much comeliness in the country (i.e. the people are good-looking). The people dress themselves like the English. Of black men they think a great deal. No one keeps "parda" as we do. The country is a very open one (meaning that there is great freedom of intercourse). The ladies shake hands freely. They are not bashful about this. They do as the English do. Their houses are open & roofed. (sic). All the soldiers who have come from India find a lodging indoors. There are unused houses which belong to great kings. Of ornaments there are no traces (i.e. the women do not wear jewellery). The people here only know plain clothes. The great folk wear both fine and poor clothes."

From X.Y. a Sikh wounded & in hospital in France to his uncle at Jullundur in the Punjab. (Original in Gurmukhi, dated 27/1/15).

*****

"The memsahibs of this country do not cover the face, not only the old, but the young women. They have strange customs but intend no evil. They do not fear the bombs. Two were attending cattle behind our lines where the bombs were bursting. Bronn Sahib sent me to remove them from this peril. They not understanding, I pointed my 'Ruffle' as one who shoots, crying 'boom-boom' and shaking my head. At length, they crying 'Merci, merci' fled. In the cities they give us flowers and little flags, and offer us tobacco, not understanding the low of the Khalsa."

"The padshah (King) came to see the Indians all the way over the black water. He spoke with all, regardless of rank. It was not my fate to see the King, being in the trenches. I am told that though chosen by the All-Powerful to be seated on the throne, he does not hold himself distantly from the poorest. On the Sahib's barra-din (Christmas Day) he sent every Sepoy in the Army a gift. In Jai Singh's regiment all the English officer Sahibs save two, are dead or wounded. They wear turbans as we, but they never run a little ahead. A lieutenant has become a major; but every German that crosses our path is slain. Nathu Singh, Kishen Singh, Kanwar Singh of the village are dead. All is well here. I am well and happy to the Guru."

Sampuran Singh, ______'s Horse, letter to his Father, extracts from article, *The Khalsa Advocate*, Saturday, February 27, 1915.

*****

"You asked me to write and tell you about this country and say what are the best things that it produces. Reflect, my brother, and I will write down all the finest and most splendid things for you. First, unity: second, knowledge, or ability: third, obedience to orders: fourth, absence of jealousy with regard to women; fifth, the cleanliness of everything, in house, in person, in clothes, in DRESS. Throughout the country there is one style of dress with no caste distinctions. You cannot tell the prosperous rich from the poor. In the evening every young man goes for a walk. It is the same for men and women. Both men and women please themselves. They cannot forbid one another. That is the way of this country. Now I will write about the land and crops. The land is such that there is no level ground. It is all steep slopes and little hills. The soil is very poor and the crops nothing at all. I have seen no wheat anywhere. There is no sugar cane, nor melons, nor gram. There is barley, but only here and there. There is oats for the horses and plenty of grass. Rain is abundant and it is never hot at all. It is as cold as the month of Chet (March-April). They sleep indoors all the year round, and it is cold enough inside the house to use two blankets. There are plenty of vegetables, potatoes, cabbage, onions, and peas. These are the vegetables. The finest things produced are the sheep-dogs, the cats that churn the butter, horses that draw the plough, and the dogs that draw the carts. They make everything work. Without knowledge our country is blind … There is another thing that they do. They set cats to watch the fowls and use horses instead of oxen and motorcars instead of cars. All the office work is done by women, who also manage the post offices. If I see anything more, I will write and tell you about it. Everything here is dearer than in our country. What costs one rupee in India costs two here."

From Havaldar Surjan Singh, Guide's Infantry, now in hospital in England, to Jhimman Singh, in India. (Gurmukhi, 29/7/15).

*****

"If you were to see the general conditions of life here, you would be astounded. What can be done? The man whom God wishes to punish is born in India. This may be seen by comparison, but each man thinks his country and home's the best."

From Jit Singh, 6th Cavalry, serving in France, to Sirdar Harwant Singh, Ludhiana, Punjab, India. (Urdu, 10/8/15).

*****

"Will you please send with the watch in a parcel eight or nine rings, some of silver of superior make and some ordinary brass ones. The people here are always begging for keepsakes, and rings please them very much. It does not matter if they cost only a rupee and a half – only be sure to send them. They should be pretty to look at, whether silver or brass."

From Bishen Singh, 16th Cavalry attached 6th Cavalry, France, to Sirdar Amar Singh, Jullundur, India. (Gurmukhi, 25/10/15).

*****

"If I were to send you my photograph, I do not think you would recognise me, for I am in much better health than I was……..I am far better here in France than I used to be in India. The climate, and the food here are highly strength sustaining and health-giving."

From Kartar Singh, 6th Cavalry, France, to his father, Jullundur, Dt. Punjab, India. (Urdu, 11/12/15).

*****

"There is no news here worth writing, but perhaps you might like to hear how they deal with orphan children in this country. At this moment an orphan infant and a lad whose parents are lost are before me. So I will tell you about this, and I hope you will find it interesting. You know that the government of this country is a republic, that there is no individual king, but a person chosen to act as king for a fixed period. Every man, rich or poor, is required to study military arts and exercises, and to serve as a soldier for a specified period e.g. two years. In this period every man acquires a knowledge of military weapons and at a time of need, as at present, every male has to take his place on the field of battle. The government of the country brings up orphan boys and girls thus. At first they are made over to the charge of some women of the village or a neighbouring place. If the child is under three years of age, the government pays an allowance of eight francs (Rs. 5/-) a month for its keep. The amount rises by degrees to fourteen or twenty francs. So it goes on till the boy or girl is twelve years old, and in the meantime the same woman who has been put in charge of it is responsible for its education, behaviour and morals. After that it goes to the orphanage of its district where it receives an excellent education and is brought up in a manner surpassing that for the sons of rich men. So no one remains without knowledge and without profession and without skill because his parents died in his infancy. In a year's residence I have seen no one man or woman, young or old, not even a child, who could not read and write."

From Man Singh, 6th Cavalry, France, to Munshi Gopal Singh, School-master, Jhelum Dt. India. (Urdu, 13/12/15).

*****

"Besides this the skill and intelligence that are displayed here – I have nothing to add to my previous description. Wherever you look, there is the distilled essence of knowledge. A few days ago science produced here on the field of battle a new marvel – a noiseless gun. The gun goes off, but makes no sound. It is only when the projectile falls that it is known that the gun has been fired. No one can tell whence it came. Hail! Science that produces daily new marvels..................This it is that makes the difference between man and beast. Indeed the beasts of this land are better than ordinary inhabitants of your country."

From Bakshish Singh, serving with the 6th Cavalry, France, to Basant Singh, Student, Patiala, Punjab, India. (Urdu, 13/12/15).

*****

'News by postcard (1916). A historic 14 July. Stamp Paris 957. Our Indian allies, Opera Square.' (Avtar Singh Bahra collection)

*****

"I fold my hands and make petition before the true Guru and before God and before the government, that in our country these arrangements should be made. First, female infanticide should cease; second, jewellery should not be made; third, there should be no theft; fourth, knowledge should be acquired; and I hope that someday our government will achieve all this. And even as in Europe both before these terrible times and now too (this was the case) – I have seen France with my own eyes and can praise it with knowledge. For the people there live very good lives."

From Mula Singh, F.P.O. No.39, France, to Chanda Singh, Amritsar Dt., Punjab India. (Gurmukhi, 11/2/16).

*****

"Here it is very cold at present. It snows much. The little discomfort that we experience is due to the cold and rain. Otherwise the country is like heaven. It rains frequently. You are, no doubt, astonished at what I say and wonder how this country can be heaven. Listen to one little thing. Here no one drinks water. When they desire to drink, either at meals or at any other time, they drink juice of apples. So many apples are produced, that the people press the juice and store it in barrels, which they drink throughout the year. They let us have a bottle full for a 2 pice. All the men drink it. There is no prohibition, you may bring as much as you please inside the house. Barrels upon barrels are full of it. Moreover there are barns full of apples. If I return alive I will tell you all about this country. You will be staggered at all I shall tell you. It is a real heaven. There is plenty of milk, but only cow's milk. The people, however, drink very little milk. They milk the cows and they then extract the butter at the rate of a maund of milk in ten minutes. The skimmed milk they give to cows, calves, and pigs. The people are honest, there is no sign of theft. Goods to the value of lakhs of rupees lie in glass houses (i.e. houses that could easily be broken into). No one pays any regard to them. Grain, potatoes and such things, lie in the fields unguarded. In short the cat plays with pigeons and chickens, and the dog plays with the cat and tends the sheep, churns the butter, and draws a cart and guards it too. When a cow calves, they immediately take away the calf and do not let the cow see it. They rear it on skimmed milk. They milk the cow daily two or three times a day, without the calf being present. The cows in fact do not know whether they gave birth to a calf or not. It is a golden age."

From Bakhshish Singh, Sialkot Cavalry Brigade, to Sher Singh, Ferozpur, Punjab, India. (Gurmukhi, 27/2/16).

*****

"In this country dogs draw small carts and churn the milk. Ploughs are drawn by horses, horses draw wagons also, oxen are not used for these purposes. Cows are numerous and milk may be had for two annas a seer. There are no buffaloes in this country. All work is done scientifically. All (men women and children) are able to read and write. They speak and act with much intelligence, and are very well disposed towards us Indians. They are a truthful people. There is no theft, and they have no conception what dishonesty means. Our people here do not cast aside dishonestly and thieving. In short the association of the French people is much to be desired. We are most happy and comfortable here. We have never previously experienced such comfort, nor shall we do so in future. It is heavenly. No one knows what will happen hereafter. The country is splendid. I am unable to praise it sufficiently, it is so fine. Except for grain and millet, all other grains which are produced in our country are produced here. Potatoes are unlimited. Maize also is grown in small quantities, but no one eats it. All eat wheaten bread. In short the country is a paradise. There are such grand houses that a man is never tired of contemplating them. In these houses the beds for sleeping cost Rs.100/- each. There are no castes, all are one. It would be difficult to find another such country. It is cold for the 12 months a year. The climate is moist. It rains daily. In the winter it snows heavily. I cannot describe how heavily. We have nothing whatever to complain of. We have plenty to eat and each man has warm clothes costing Rs.100/-. We want for nothing. This much only we desire and pray for, that our King may be victorious."

From Lance Dafadar Sucha Singh, 6th Cavalry, France, to Balkishan, Ludhiana, Punjab, India. (Gurmukhi, 27/2/16).

*****

"Get the children (boys and girls) taught to read and write well. Here the teaching is obligatory. Men go to work daily, and it is the women who do all the letter writing at home owing to their having been compulsorily taught in their childhood."

From Sawar Sohan Singh, 19th Lancers, France, to Bhagat Singh, Amritsar, Punjab. (Gurmukhi, 28/2/16).

*****

"What are you doing about the land? Regarding the building of the house I wrote a few matters in my last letter now I write further details. Keep both these letters carefully till I return. The plan for a staircase to the upper story as followed in France is a good one. And the method of making stairs is easy. The method of ploughing adopted here is very simple. The man goes straight ahead, holding the handle of the plough with both hands on the level of his breast and throwing his weight slightly forward – under him is a wheel. All agricultural implements are made of iron. This is a great advantage as they do not break readily. All the instruments required by a man in connection with his work are kept in his house. He is not like we are. He has not got to go to the village a mile away if anything breaks. We never considered, as these people do, that all this work of mending could be done on the spot. There is no difficulty. All that is required is a cobblers awl and a leather cutter, with which to make large stitches in the leather. In our country we expect to regard leather as unclean and go to the village cobbler to have the work done. Unclean! Do we not handle the instrument afterwards and the leather sewn in it, and even drink water with the hand that had touched the leather!"

From k.d. Sher Singh, 30th Lancers, France, to Bishan Singh, Ludhiana, Punjab. (Urdu, 14/3/16).

*****

"This is a very nice country and very beautiful. The people are honourable, and treat each other well. They are always cleanly dressed and do not steal or defraud. The country is fertile, and produces everything except rice and sugarcane. We get very good cow's milk to drink. And Government also provides us with good and plentiful rations. We have no complaints and are very comfortable. We get good clothes, suitable for the climate, but the cold is intense. It rains every day - sometimes it snows."

From Sowar Harnam Singh, 3rd Skinner's Horse, France, to Barkat Shah, Patiala, Punjab. (Urdu, 15/3/16).

*****

"In this country the people are very particular about the cleanliness of their clothes and of their houses. On Sundays they do no work of any description whatever. They merely wear their best clothes and walk out on the roads, a man and a woman together. The cows give a great lot of milk. The people work by the clock (i.e. they have a fixed time for everything). Cocks (poultry) are very dear, costing about Rs. 2/8 or Rs. 3/-. Eggs are sold at 4 or 4½ annas a piece. There is one particular thing to mention and that is the people do not pilfer from each other, and they lie but little. There is one fixed price for everything, no second price is to be obtained by bargaining. Cash payment is required – credit is quite unknown."

From Sowar Sadhu Singh, Signal Troop, 8th Brigade, Head Quarters, Lucknow Cavalry Brigade, to Risaldar Kirpa Singh, 37th Lancers, Jallundar, Punjab. (Gurmukhi, 15/3/16).

*****

"Here all the male population has gone to war while the women do all the work instead of the men. It has snowed here for the past two days. The people treat us very well. They are all educated. Now the cold is less intense. The women do the work in precisely the same way as the men used to do it before the war. When we ask for anything the people take the trouble to get it and give it to us themselves. The French are fighting exclusively for their country and their race. None of the men are regular (i.e. professional) soldiers. When anyone dies, there is no weeping and lamentation (such as we have). The bereaved accept it as the will of God and keep silent."

From Risaldar Natha Singh, Ambala Cavalry Bde. France, to k.d. Sohail Singh, Amritsar, Punjab. (Gurmukhi, 16/3/16).

*****

"Send a phulkari (i.e. an embroidered cloth used as a table cover or a curtain) in a parcel. The people of one of the houses here have ministered much to me and I wish to give them a keepsake. They would not accept anything else."

From Jemadar Dalip Singh, Secundrabad Cavalry Brigade, France, to Teja Singh, Jallandhar, Punjab. (Urdu, 27/3/16).

*****

I will write you a little concerning this country of France which I have seen with my own eyes:

The people are full of knowledge, they rule themselves and take their enjoyment
They are neither deficient in intellect nor beauty.
They are like a garden on which the moon shines at night.
It is not possible sufficiently to praise this country, with the wide streets of its towns.
The people are like a garden of roses, some full bloom, others buds.
There is no apprehension about theft or robbery, no fear assails them when asleep.
They do not abstain from any kind of food, all things are lawful.
Labour is not regarded as derogatory, no one thinks labour above his dignity.
There are no thieves or beggars. If there should be any, they are very rare.
No one robs or defrauds, all do their work and take their enjoyment.
Read this letter and consider what there is of benefit and what of harm in this.
I pray to the Guru to bring together again, those who are now separated.
If I have made any mistakes, excuse me, since in Bhagat Singh the art of poetry is defective.
If it were otherwise then my poem would be like a string of pearls.
God alone is true, everything else is a sham.

From Bhagat Singh, Mhow Cavalry Brigade, France, to Hari Singh, Amritsar, India. (Gurmukhi, 28/3/16).

*****

"Do not entertain enmities and grudges among yourselves. I should like you to know that in this country I have not seen a single cucherry nor yet a quarrel. Every man goes on peaceably without quarrelling. There is no theft. The poorest man here is, to my mind, superior to our richest man. The people here are fond of working with their own hands and this is the duty of a man. He who does not recognise this is little better than an animal. When I survey this country I can assert without hesitation that a country where all the 'bandobast' is so excellent as it is here is fit to govern the world. May God grant that we may live always under the aegis of such a just King so that our fellow countrymen may always sing his praises."

From Ishar Singh, 6th Cavalry or 19th Lancers, France, to Sirdar Wariam Singh, Ferozpur, India. (Urdu, 12/4/16).

*****

"I am very fit indeed and the only thing I have to complain of is the separation from you. The people here show us more affection if possible than our own brothers. When we are transferred they weep and embrace us repeatedly. Every now and then we can't help thinking that they must have been our mothers in a former incarnation. You may lose your temper, but they, never. If any one of us gets angry they soothe us and appeal to us and if we do not respond they weep."

From Lance Dafadar Chandan Singh, 38th C.I. Horse, France, to Urudoh Singh, Lahore. (Urdu, 18/4/16).

*****

"The astonishing thing is this that whereas in France it rains daily, India is not the pleasure garden of God (i.e. It is dried up by reason of the drought). All this is the work of God. Here nothing exists which is harmful to the crops. Perhaps these people have somehow or other pleased God, or they are nearer to God or more firm in their faith (than we are). Whenever one thinks of the climate and the various other conditions of this country, India seems defective by comparison, and for this reason we feel ashamed when we are in the presence of those European people who have travelled in India and have become acquainted with our climate and manners and customs. I can certainly affirm that the soil of India is more fruitful than the soil of Europe. The cold is much less now, and the climate is becoming pleasant. Those men and animals (i.e. we) who are not accustomed to extreme cold, are now in better circumstances. Those who changed colour (i.e. suffered) through the cold, are now finding their conditions brightened. The signs of spring are everywhere except where the cruel hand of war has wrought destruction. From this it is clear that before the war the aspect of this country must have been very beautiful – a beauty which we were not destined to see. Now it is desirable that I should withdraw my hand from writing. The times are critical. In the future we can discuss all these matters at leisure."

From Sewa Singh, Sialkot Cavalry Brigade, France, to Dunna Singh, Hoshiarpur District, Punjab. (Urdu, 25/4/16).

*****

"We realised in the trenches this time that our shells play havoc with the enemy. The enemy's returns are feeble. It would appear that his ammunition is running short. We trust that our King will speedily gain the victory and defeat the enemy.........I again bring to your notice the custom prevailing in this country by which every child has two fathers – one is his real father and the other his religious father (i.e. his godfather) who has sworn in the church that on the death of the real father he will cherish and educate the child like his own. In this way you become Prem Singh second father, and on my death all his affairs will be regulated by you. I would be proud to fall in battle and especially on this occasion when I am serving my King in Europe."

From Lehna Singh, 18th Lancers, France, to Sirdar Sujan Singh, Hy. Magistrate, Kasur, Punjab. (Urdu, 25/4/16).

*****

"Life and death are preordained, but he who has not seen the country of France, has seen nothing. It is as though he had never come in to this world. What more can I say?"

From Bishan Singh, Marseilles, France, to L.D. Sawan Singh, 20th Deccan Horse, Neemuch, C.I. (Urdu, 30/4/16).

*****

"We have seen many kinds of countries and many kinds of people. There is no portion of the world left whose people we have not seen. Thus we have seen the power of God.

Religious mendicants and ascetics in India do much in their endeavour to find God, but they are unable to realise His power (as we have done).......In this country, the wheat will not be cut for 6 months yet. That is to say it will be cut in August. It is sown at the same time as we sow wheat in India. Grapes and apples are as plentiful in the country, as the Sanatha of the jungle (a common plant used for firewood, hedges and thatching in the Punjab). No one sells apples in the villages and farms. One can eat as many apples as one pleases without payment. This free fruit is a great convenience to us. In every village there is plenty of milk to be had. Buffaloes and camels are not to be found in this country. Cows are plentiful. The cows give more than 30 seers of milk each. Ploughs are drawn by horses. The plough used here, is much heavier than our plough. It is equivalent (in weight) to 10 of our ploughs. The two horses that draw the plough are the size of elephants. Every landowner in this country has plenty of land. Whether the land be hilly or flat, not a foot of it remains uncultivated. Ploughs work everywhere. The fields are not irrigated from wells or canals. At least it rains twice a week. Wood is very plentiful. There are no large forests, but each landowner has cultivated a little wood of his own. If he wants timber for house building, he can get it (from his plantation) without cost. They eat pigs, cows and horses here. When we are resting we stay in the houses of these people. They give us warm water to wash our face and hands. They warm our milk, tea and coffee. We sit in the room along with them, and warm our hands and feet before the fire. When we move on to some other place, the women mourn our departure as if we were relatives. They entertain us without fail with food at the time of departure. If you stay in a house for 3 or 4 weeks you are treated with as much affection as if you were a member of the house. There is plenty of pine here but there are no other trees here which are common to our country. Mangoes are not produced here. As regards corn, much wheat is grown but little maize. No pulse is grown, but peas are grown. The bread that is made is "double" (i.e. leavened bread). Sugar is made from a kind of radish. Sugarcane is not produced. There are few goats, but sheep in plenty. The value of a sheep is Rs. 35 or 36. Woollen garments are generally made here. Cotton is not produced."

From Diwan Singh, Sialkot Cavalry Brigade, France, to Arjan Das, Rawalpindi Dt., Punjab, India. (Urdu, 9/5/16).

*****

"Do not be at all anxious. Our Government has kept us so carefully and comfortably that out constant prayer to God is, that He will speedily give victory to our dear Government, and take us home rejoicing with flags waving. This country is very fine. Light rain falls frequently. The soil is so good that splendid crops are produced. We get milk in plenty. There are no buffaloes here. The houses are clean beyond description, and are surrounded by flowering shrubs and fruit bearing trees. The houses are so constructed as to afford the greatest degree of comfort and health. Most of the houses are constructed mainly of wood. And through and round each village whether small or large, roads go. It is all very pleasant and convenient. In our villages, no carts can enter, how much inconvenience do we not suffer, though building our houses so closely together! Horses are used to plough with, and crops are reaped by machinery. The reaping machine is such that as it cuts is also ties the corn into sheaves. We take great delight in watching these operations. There are only 4 months in the year, that is in the depth of winter, when green fodder is not obtainable. For the remaining 8 months the cattle stand knee deep in green pastures. The cows are milked three times daily with their calves separated from them. The quantity of milk under each cow is very great."

From Jewan Singh, 3rd Skinner's Horse, France, to Sirdar Hirchand Singh, Patiala State, Punjab. (Gurmukhi, 18/5/16).

*****

"I was talking to a wounded man from France who is in hospital here, the other day, and he told me all about France. I was so pleased to hear the way he praised France and all who come back say the same thing that if there is a beautiful and excellent country in the world it is France. The wounded who come back say they don't want to join their depots but to go back to the Expeditionary Force in France. The climate and the look of the country are such that once a foreigner has lived there he never wants to leave the country. They say that when a country is green, fertile and beautiful the inhabitants are sure to be nice people and this is the case with France. The French people are extremely kind and friendly to Indians, and my relatives here who have never been to the country are so attracted by the stories they hear, that they want to go there. Many people have got so fond of France that they have stopped writing home. I hear that our Allies have beaten down the Germans and that they are trying to get out of the conflict as best they can."

From Bishan Singh, Govt. High School, Quetta, to Jemadar Kartar Singh, 19th Lancers, France. (Urdu, 22/5/16).

*****

"The weather at the present time is very good. For the most part the sun is invisible, but when it comes out for a short time, we feel rather warm, because we always wear warm clothing. Cool clothing is not to be had here. No one wears it. The weather remains fine for 3 or 4 months then rain and snow come on. For this reason the people of the country wear hats, no one cares for turbans. Up to the present we are comfortable. God alone knows when this war will end. Up to the present time there is no hope. Our hearts long that God will speedily terminate it, so that we may return home. The climate of country does not suit us. I take "Fellowes Syrup" regularly. If I had not done so, I should certainly have been invalided to India, for some disease or other. Here, on account of the clouds, it is dark, inside, night and day. For this reason we work by electric light all day. The doors and windows of the houses are large and glazed. The interior of the houses is made of wood, but it does not appear to the eye to be so, as the wood work is beautifully finished. The ceiling is of wood – the floor also – as one walks one slips, because the floor is so clean and polished. The market places and roads are paved, and the houses are all built with lime or cement – none are built with clay. Houses are 5 and 6 and even 7 stories high. The cost of each house cannot have been less than 5 to 7 lakhs of rupees. We regard it all with astonishment."

From Balwant Singh, Clerk, Rouen, France, to Sirdar Jai Singh, Sialkot, Punjab, India. (Urdu, 28/5/16).

*****

"In this country there is no sugar-cane or cotton. They extract sugar from a species of carrot which is extensively cultivated. Grain here is as expensive proportionately as other things. Nevertheless I should be very pleased indeed to take up my permanent abode in this country. You ask "Why?" well, because here there is neither thieving nor lying. Further, whatever one man wants, even if the value thereof be only 2 pice, he can buy from another. If you want, say half a seer of milk, you can buy it from another person. Even though he may be a rich man he will not decline to sell you the milk. Again, if a woman goes by herself into the "jungle" no man will molest her. Also the people live well and dress well. Alas, my affection for my parents and brothers is very great, otherwise it would have been a "first class" arrangement. Well, if God grants me a continuance of life, I shall at any rate be able to think of this country after I return to India."

From Teja Singh, L.D., 9th Hodson's Horse, France, to Doctor Kesar Singh, Lyalpur District, Punjab, India. (Urdu, 29/5/16).

*****

"I am leaving France for another theatre of war, and therefore cannot go to England now. Of course many Indian Officers have been there, but I could not go on account of certain necessary reasons. I had to go there just next week, but now it is impossible, and so I cannot see Sir J.D. Smith. I am glad I have seen of France more than one can expect, and I am quite tired of all this now. Pray God I may soon return to India. France is the best country of all Europe and one can but only form the best idea of it. I have seen several big places of France, and I am so much attracted that I should like to come over here again sometime after the war. Anyhow I am sorry to leave it, but, if it were not for India."

From Sundar Singh, 30th Lancers, France, to Sardar Khazan Singh, Special Land Acquisition Officer, Delhi Province, India. (English, 15/6/16).

*****

"As you remark in your letter, Rouen cannot compare with Marseilles. I hope you will return to Marseilles. It is a portion of heaven. How beautiful are the hills about. La Valentine is a lovely and clean camp. While I was with "D. Force" I saw plenty of fighting, in fact I was present in all the fighting. At the commencement of operations the Cavalry frequently got good opportunities, and my Regiment did excellent work. Alas that we should have returned to India! Goodness knows for how long we shall remain absent from the war. I cannot describe to you how great fascination there is in fighting at the front. One experiences a feeling of exhilaration. He who has never been present in an action at the front, has seen very little indeed, in fact he has seen nothing. Do you think it would be possible for me to join you in France?"

From Kala Singh, Risaldar 16th Cavalry, Loralai, Baluchistan Agency, to Sheo Deo Singh, Risaldar 22nd Cavalry, Remount Depot, Rouen, France. (Urdu dated the 6th October, 1916).

*****

"You enquire about the price of things in France? Prices here have doubled since the war began, and entirely because of the war. All the men are entangled in the war, and the work of agriculture is carried out by the women and by the men who are physically unfit for the war. Wheat sells at 4lbs the rupee, ghi at Rs. ¼ per lb. Sugar at 2lbs per rupee. The price of all other commodities has risen proportionately in the same way. Milk for instance costs 6 annas a seer (quart)."

From Fateh Singh, Risaldar Major, 6th Cvy, France, to Yariam Singh, Ludhiana Dt., India. (Gurmukhi, 30/10/16).

*****

"You say you are always worried about me. I am so comfortable that I can hardly express my feelings. These good people take more care of us than ever our parents did. Parents sometimes get angry with their children and stop their dinner. Not so with these parents. They give us milk to drink every evening, dry our clothes and continually ask after our health. I cannot sufficiently praise their affection and I must say that no mother or wife or brother or sister has ever shown us such kindness. There is no anxiety and no discomfort; only one thing is lacking, your presence."

From Dafadar Chanda Singh, 38th Central India Horse, France, to Atur Singh, Lahore. (Urdu dated the 15th November, 1916).

*****

"The custom of this country is that when a child is 5 years old he is sent to school. For this reason I impress on you that, as soon as the "Little Uncle" is 5 years old, you should send him to school. These people (i.e. the French) appear to be superior to us solely because of education. Learning is a great benefit. Moreover the custom with us of having servants to do our menial work is profitless. These people themselves do their menial work with their own hands. They are not in the least ashamed of working. Our people are steeped to death in shame. If we were to do all our work ourselves we would reap much benefit both for ourselves and also for the Sircar."

From Hajura Singh, 38th Central India Horse, France to Sant Singh, Lahore District, Punjab, India. (Urdu dated the 5th December, 1916).

*****

"My father asks whether he should send Arup Singh to school or not. He should without fail, send him to school, because on seeing France I am satisfied that anyone who is without education is no better than an animal. In childhood up to the age of 15 years, a boy is unfitted for any kind of occupation, and after that age, even if he does not receive further education, it does not matter, as he will have received sufficient education to work with understanding. If the boy is not educated in his childhood, his years are wasted in play, and in later years he regrets that, in his childhood, he received no education."

From Khidmat Singh, 36th Jacob's Horse, France to Gurdit Singh, Lance Dafadar, 36th Jacob's Horse, Amballa, Punjab, India. (Urdu dated the 25th December, 1916).

*****

"I used to regard you as a shrewd and sensible woman; but now I find that you have no self- reliance. Look at the women of this country (France) how courageous they are, more so even than the men in our country. Their husbands are at the war, and they (the women) themselves manage all the work of cultivating the land and tending the cattle. They are quite independent of their husbands. If a woman's husband dies, she does not make her grief manifest, though she feels it in her heart. People are not aware from her manner that she is suffering. The work is done by the women to the same extent and as well as when the men did it. The health of the women remains good, they feed well, they labour well in every duty that has to be performed, and at all times they maintain a cheerful manner. One greatly admires their bravery. There are cases in which the enemy has captured houses and carried away some of the children. The mothers of the children however, do not weep and lament like the women of our country. Of course they grieve, but they do not allow themselves to be constantly absorbed in their grief. With courage and determination they so manage their houses, as to keep them in as good a condition as the houses of well-to-do people. All credit to their courage! It gives me much pleasure, and I pray to the Guru to create similar courage in our women. Courage apart, the people here do not lie and nobody hears of theft or violence. No boundary pillars are needed between fields of different owners. The people are wise, they sow in their own fields, whereas in our country, the boundary pillars are always being moved backwards and forwards. May the Guru deign to lead our people also into right ways."

From Jewan Singh, Jemadar 2nd Lancers, France to his wife, Gurdaspur District, Punjab, India. (Urdu dated the 20th January, 1917).

*****

"I shall be very pleased indeed, if you exert yourself to acquire learning, because in the present times learning is necessary for everyone, whether man or woman. It gives enlightenment in worldly affairs, and secures respect for its possessor from his family. For this reason you should be very solicitous as regards both education and health. You should not eat anything unwholesome, which might possibly make you ill. You should eat such things only as promote strength, for instance milk and butter. You should also differentiate between the hot season and the cold in the matter of dress. In this country the minimum age of men and women is 60 years, and the age of the majority is between 60 and 100 years. The reason for this is that the customs of the people, in regard to health, food and clothing are most sensible. And if by any chance anyone should contract an illness, immediate steps are taken to provide proper treatment for him. Procrastination in such a case, such as invariably followed in our country, is not permitted. Nor do the people act as we do in the matter of dress. If it is the height of summer we wear muslin, and if it is the depth of winter, we still wear muslin. Of course the result is that we readily contract sickness. In our country we eat bread made of millet flour and gram flour, and at the same time the butter pot remains hung up out of reach for safety! At least we smear the cakes with a greasy finger. The result is that the bread taken, sticks to one's throat, or gives rise to intestinal disturbance; sometimes even resulting in death. Women practice parsimony in food and clothing, in order that they may save enough money to buy a gold nose ornament, or to provide a silk embroidered shawl for their children's wedding ceremony. All these customs are very bad indeed, and especially the custom of wearing jewellery, in order to provide which, a person economises on the necessaries of life. Thus having become weakened through parsimony the person is carried off by some simple illness. My advice to you is to live well, and to dress in conformity with the seasons of the year. You should not spend a pice on jewellery, or on marriages or funerals. Have your children taught and do not adorn them with jewellery; thus shall you all sleep without fear of thieves, and you will save the lives of your children from the snatchers of jewellery."

From Kartar Singh, Kot Dafadar, 6th Cavalry (?) France, to his daughter, Rawal Pindi District, Punjab, India. (Gurmukhi dated the 28th January, 1917).

*****

"Fire falls upon us day and night. If I live we shall see about that. What a pity it is that our hearts are as black as our faces! If you were here to see this country you would be absolutely astonished. Beauty in perfection, sanitation in perfection, and no false shame between the sexes. Their hearts are like mirrors, and if it had not been for the kindness they had shown us, we never could have stood this country. Men, women and children they are all the same, all kindness and hospitality. If you all in India had hearts as pure as the people here there are many things which I could tell you of but as it is you could not understand them. We shall have nothing to do till April but lots of work then. We shan't be back in India for a long time yet."

From Jemadar Ghalla Singh, 19th Lancers or 6th Cavalry, France to Indar Singh, Ludhiana, India. (Urdu dated the 3rd February, 1917).

*****

"You wrote to me that we were in Paradise. Yes it is that same Paradise which you have seen. It is a fine country with a splendid climate. The weather worries us a bit but there never has been such cold since we came to France. But even then our men do not feel it as much as they did the first year. But after all there are things at home which you cannot get here. One's own hut is better than foreign palaces. There is nothing fresh about the war. We have been here a very long time and so everyone wants to see his dear ones again."

From Wardi Major Jivan Singh, 2nd Lancers, France to Dafadar Hetram, 2nd Lancers, Depot, Allahabad, India. (Urdu dated the 6th February, 1917).

*****

"My brother, this country of France is very well educated and the result is that every kind of enjoyment and advantage is to be found here. I will tell you about it if I am spared to come back. You must in your caste emphasise the necessity of every child, male or female going to school. You will not live to see the full results of this but one day the caste will reap wonderful advantage from it. If you can prevail upon the Manager of the Gurudwara at Nandhar to build a school do so at once and get hold of a really good teacher. If the Guru wills, we shall be able to start a really good system of education without payment. In France the boys and girls up to 13 pay no fees at all."

From Sher Singh, 20th Deccan Horse, France to Sirdar Risaldar Prem Singh, Haiderabad, India. (Urdu dated the 12th February, 1917).

*****

"I learn that one thousand rupees were spent on the marriage ceremony. Well, you were free to please yourself; but in this country no money at all is spent on marriage ceremonies, and we should follow this example."

From Kalyan Singh, 2nd Lancers, France to Bhagat Singh, Shahpur District, Punjab, India. (Gurmukhi dated the 5th March, 1917).

*****

"Death (of human beings) has become of as much account here as the death of an insect. The people here treat us better than our mothers treat their babies in India. Each morning the lady of the house in which we live, rises early and after warming water and making tea ready, she comes and wakes us. The money she has spent on us is more than a father and mother (in India) spends on their children. She has but one son who is 18 years old, and in fifteen days' time he has to go to the war."

From Nanak Singh, 6th Cavalry, France to Caur Singh, Jhelum District, Punjab, India. (Gurmukhi dated the 6th March, 1917).

*****

"Keep on praying to the Guru by whose grace we are still alive. Do not forget for a moment that we are in Europe, that country that surpasses all the countries of the world in beauty and pleasure. I am telling you the truth that I never think of India even in my dreams. Such pleasure and enjoyment I have never seen even in Persia."

From Gaula Singh, 38th Central India Horse, France to Asa Singh, Amritsar, India. (Urdu dated the 7th May, 1917).

*****

"This is the time that work is hard and we have to put up with all sorts of trouble in war, and lose our lives into the bargain. But the survivors forget all these hardships for France is such a fine country. If a man gets a days leave and visits any city all his worries are forgotten in the beautiful spectacle that meets his eye. If he lives he tastes enjoyment and if he dies, well, we have all got to die some day."

From Beant Singh, 6th Cavalry, France to Ram Singh, Kotah, Rajputana. (Urdu dated the 4th October, 1917).

*****

"I forgot to write last week because I was so busy building a house to live in. It is a beautiful little shanty built of wood and scrap iron. There are 25 beams in it which would have cost Rs. 15 to buy in India. My house is the best in the Brigade and I have a stove inside. I have made full arrangements against the cold as we expect to spend the winter out here and not in billets. My uncle came to see it and he said "You have had great practice in building huts and barracks". I said "When we go back to India if you and I don't hit it off with others at home we can leave them and build a little house for ourselves." We have been here for 3 months and I have spent all my time building and I have now made a palatial residence with a kitchen. The materials would have cost Rs. 200 to buy. If we march, all these things will have to be thrown away and at our next station we shall collect everything just as before. This is how we do it. I go out into the ruined villages and collect tables and chairs and everything that we need. Through God's goodness I am able to build a house in which I can really take pleasure and to build it for nothing."

From Jai Singh, 19th Lancers, or 6th Cavalry, France to Sundar Singh, Jhelum. (Urdu dated the 9th October, 1917).

*****

"When we think of home our hearts are sad. But for this we would be quite comfortable. The war is very different from other wars in comforts supplied. We have got accustomed to the cold and the Government arrangements for warding off the cold are splendid. Expensive warm clothing is given and long boots with several pairs of socks. We get also get warm pyjamas, coats, breeches and great coats. We are so glad that we do not feel the cold and we get rations of rum which keep the body warm. We also get comforters and gloves."

From Kartar Singh, 6th Cavalry, France to Ram Rakha, Jalandhar. (Urdu dated the 29th October, 1917).

*****

"I went to Paris on a week's leave. For a long time I had been anxious to see that city. It is now one and half years since I went to London. There is no doubt whatever that London is a great and wealthy city; but in my opinion it cannot compare with Paris in beauty and style and arrangement, and in roads and parks. I saw many famous buildings in Paris also historical edifices. I also obtained an introduction to gatherings of educated people. On one of these occasions I met a young girl of 19 years of age who was studying in the B.A. Class, and who could talk German, French and English fluently. I also met a man who knew 8 different languages, and I conversed with many learned Professors."

From Amar Singh, Risaldar, 18th Lancers, France to Mahtab Singh, Pensioned Risaldar, Patiala State, Punjab, India. (Gurmukhi dated the 30th December, 1917).

*****

"Do not worry yourself thinking as to how you are to marry the girls. I ask you why are girls brought into the world? Consider, both boys and girls are brought into the world, and if girls are neglected or killed off, these families that have boys had better kill them off too! For this reason both boys and girls should be kept, so that they may marry. Both are of the same value in God's eyes, and one should devote the same amount of care to their bringing up, and should treat them in precisely the same way. If you are afraid of the expense which marrying girls may entail my advice to you is to put away from you those customs of the Brahmins and barbers."

From Ishar Singh, 2nd Lancers, France to Jassu Singh, Ludhiana, India. (Gurmukhi dated the 4th March, 1918).

*****

"If God spares me to return I intend to start new customs. Look, in this country, rich and poor, high and low go to church together and worship, and there is no distinction between them there. In this country, moreover, people never spend money unnecessarily. In our country, the fools of people spend money for show and they ruin themselves over marriages and law suits. This is all due to ignorance. The very best custom in this country is that a man chooses his own wife, and a woman her husband and there are no disagreements and troubles after marriage. The same custom used to obtain in our country formerly; but later it was set aside by the intrigues of the Brahmins."

From Teja Singh, 2nd Lancers, France to Ganga Singh, Sialkot, Punjab, India. (Gurmukhi dated the 6th March, 1918).

*****

2

Faith in Guru and God

Since none of us fear death, the Guru has hardened our hearts to stone.

See how fiercely our Guru Govind Singh fought! So we must fight. To fight is the duty of heroes.

God's protection is everywhere, our hope is entirely in Him.

I have escaped twice or three times, but God knows what the future holds for me.

This chapter describes the Sikh soldier's belief in *Waheguru* (God) and how his fate was in '*His*' hands, how they envisaged their religion and what their ultimate fate would be. The soldiers would implore their Guru to bring an end to this war. A Sikh writing from the Kitchener Hospital in Brighton gives an example of this in April 1915, "When the holy Guru has cured me I shall return to the war for a third time. Do not be anxious. We must all be born and we must all die." The Censor linked these kinds of comments to fatalism and depression. However, the Sikh soldiers accepted their lot and many expected to be rewarded in this life or the afterlife for their sacrifices.

Some Sikh soldiers would reference stories from the Sikh Holy scriptures in relation to the predicament that they found themselves in. Others would break into poetry to describe how they were feeling or what they had experienced in the war. A song written by a Sikh in September 1915 includes the following couplet, "The cannon roar like thunder, the bullets fall like rain, and only the halt the maimed and the blind will ever see home again!" Again the Censor linked the breaking into of 'doggerel' poetry as signs of depression. However, the entire Sikh scriptures are written in poetry and Sikhs often used this medium to tell stories. Extracts from Sikh scriptures are included herein to indicate how the Sikh religion may have influenced the Sikh soldier's psyche.

The poetry also lauded the Sikh martial prowess in battle. Sikh soldiers would liken their fight to the battles won by the tenth Guru, Gobind Singh, others would say that the tenth Guru would be by their side in the midst of battle. Many believed that the British Raj had been ordained by the Guru (such prophecies thrived under British rule) and that fighting the Germans would "Illuminate the name of Guru Govind under the illustrious British flag." Letters from home also mentioned the same rewards for 'martyrdom', Chanda Singh, the *Granthi* of the 32nd Lancers in Delhi writes to a Lance Dafadar at the front, "If you die on the field of battle, you will find yourself at the feet of the Guru. You have been given a physical body in order that your soul may win this glory."

*****

"Tell my mother not to go wandering madly because her son, my brother, is dead. To be born & to die is God's order. Some day we must die, sooner or later, & if I die here, who will remember me? It is a fine thing to die far from home. A saint said this, & as he was a good man, it must be true."

From X.Y. a Sikh wounded & now in hospital at Brighton to his father. (Original in Gurmukhi, dated 18/1/15).

*****

"Till now I am well. We do not know what the Guru has in store for us in future. Once the Guru has saved me. Now I am ready to go to the war again. This battle will decide my fate. But the Guru is the master. May he bring me to my brothers again in safety. Keep on sending me letters for the present. Afterwards what does it matter? When I return to the trenches I shall leave a letter posted for you. After that do not hope for me."

From X.Y. a Sikh wounded in hospital at New Milton to his brother in the Punjab. (Original in Gurmukhi, dated 20/1/15).

*****

"I was wounded in the right hand in the inner finger two months ago & am now well in England. Do not worry. I pray in the house of the Guru that I may return to my country, but of this I have no knowledge. I have done loyal service once to the Government, & I am ready to do it again. But let it be that I am not sent back to the battle. The Guru has said it is right to fulfil one's oath of loyalty. I have done so devoutly. It is good to be loyal."

From X.Y. a Sikh wounded & in hospital at New Milton to his brother in the Punjab. (Original in Gurmukhi, dated 20/1/15).

*****

"I pray to the Guru that I may return to my home. I do not know for certain, but I expect so. For I was hit on my trigger finger, & the third part of it is cut off. So I hope that I shall return neither to the battle nor to the trench. I have twice escaped the bullet & am ready to do loyal service again. I am certain that I shall not die until I am again in my country. Since none of us fear death, the Guru has hardened our hearts to stone. Not one of us who went into battle took any thought of his home or his brothers. Every one of us repeated the name of the Guru. It is good for a man to die in battle in this way. He goes to Heaven. So all of us at that time kept in our hearts a prayer to the Guru. For those who die thus Heaven is completely fulfilled. Those who die in their village, they die among their children & brothers. For them Heaven is incomplete. At this time none of us cherish any earthly love. We shall all come home & then we shall enjoy such love. Whom God preserves He preserves in this manner, even as the Guru preserved the cat. The cat has had kittens in the potter's kiln. The potter comes and lights the kiln. Then the poor cat comes & sits beside the burning kiln. The potter says in his heart__"Why does this cat sit here?" He does not know that the cat has kittens there. The Kiln is red hot. Then the potter sees the kittens still alive. He is astonished. The pots are still unbaked. The potter marvels at the power of God. Thus if the Guru's will be to preserve me, he will preserve me. The battle is but beginning & men are dying like maggots. No one can count them … not in thousands of thousands. None can count them. They say that 1375 British Officers are gone & 35 of our Sirdars are killed & 29 wounded. On our side 57,000 died before the first of December, & of the Germans 450,000. The French & Belgians have suffered even more severely. Russia too has lost many soldiers."

From X.Y. a Sikh wounded & in hospital at New Milton to his brother at Amritsar in the Punjab. (Original in Gurmukhi, dated the 21st January 1915).

*****

"Who can turn aside the wishes of the Guru? Fighting is the work of brave men. The good sons of mothers are fighting. Do not think that I am fighting, but I have a great desire to return to it. You see in the end how the noble men will finish the war & how glorious their names will be. But, Oh Guru, it is an endless war & no man has found the end of it. I am well. Have no care for me."

From a Sikh, wounded in England to a friend in the Punjab. (Original in Urdu, dated 2/2/15).

*****

"And England is a very fine country too. The wounded Indian soldiers are being treated in England with such great care that my pen fails to describe it. We ought to give our lives for our kind Government. ____My brother, now is the opportunity for us to show our loyalty & we shall surely take it. A better or kind government will never give us. Choose either hand and you will find a sweet. If we fight & live, the kind government will give us a title, Raja or Bahadur. If we fight & die, we shall go to "surga" that is to say "behisht". I myself am ready for either course. For I am a son of Guru Govind Singh. My very life I will sacrifice for my king. May the Guru sanctify the words which my tongue has spoken."

("Surga" is the common Punjabi word for "heaven" which every Sikh would naturally use & know. The introduction of the explanatory term "behisht", which has the same meaning, but is an ???? word, suggests the idea that the letter may have been composed for the edification of the censor.)

From a Sikh now in hospital in England to a friend in India. (Original in Urdu, dated 9/2/15).

*****

Countless impose their will by force.
Countless cut-throats and murderers.
Countless sinners who pride themselves on sinning.

Guru Granth Sahib, Guru Nanak Dev Ji, Ang (Page) 4.

*****

"Be strong & fear not. Maintain a cheerful heart & do heroic deeds. Let not your courage fail, but show the spirit of a brave soldier. We shall not return to this life as men. This body must die & cannot live. You are wise & I need say no more. Trust in the everlasting God. Other hopes are vain."

From a Sikh in hospital at Brighton to his brother in the 58th Rifles in France. (Gurmukhi, dated 6/3/15).

*****

"So far as we are concerned the Germans have not yet been born, for we have not given our help to the Sirkar. But if the Guru takes us to France verily we shall slay the sinful Germans who have brought trouble to the Punjab".

From a Sepoy in the 23rd Sikh Pioneers in India to a friend in the 34th Sikh Pioneers, France. (Gurmukhi, dated 8/3/15).

*****

"I recovered from my wound and went back. Now I am wounded for a second time. When the holy Guru has cured me I shall return to the war for a third time. Do not be anxious. We must all be born and we must all die."

From Gudura Singh, Kitchener Hospital, Brighton, to his brother in India. (Gurmukhi, dated 8/4/15).

*****

"It is sad that we have all come to the war. Well, it is God's will. What must be, will be. Regrets lead nowhere."

From Hawaldar Rajmal Singh in hospital, New Milton, to Subedar Lal Singh 107th Pioneers, France. (Gurmukhi, dated 10/4/15).

*****

"There is much fighting and only a lucky man will return. This is not a war but the destruction of the whole world, and the world has already suffered much. There is no hope of peace. Do not write to me. If the Holy Guru preserves me I shall return home. Do not be anxious about me. I shall come to India. The corpses are piled six high upon each other. The German is very powerful, and of us there is nothing left. I cannot write about it for every harm possible has been done to us. xxxx The fire of the cannons and rifles is like rain. Where the shells fall darkness grows."

From Ratta Singh, 87th Punjabis in hospital, Brighton, to a friend in India. (Gurmukhi, dated 28/5/15).

*****

"Sewa Singh is going back to India in a month's time; give thanks upon thanks to the Holy Guru. In some villages there will be one man left, in others there is not one remaining. We three brothers have forsaken our little children to come here. The Holy Guru will preserve us."

From Makhan Singh, 47th Sikhs, Hospital, Brighton, to Sundar Singh, 38th C.I.H. (Gurmukhi, 16/8/15).

*****

The cruel German tyrant on Belgium laid his hand:
Patiala, Nabha, Russia, France and England bade him stand.
Came India to the rescue and Canada as well:
Teli and Turkey lent their men the German host to swell.*
And so the war is raging by sky and land and sea
And underneath the water; five kings are fighting three.
Praise to the men of Europe, the masters of machines,
With their flying-craft and their twelve-mile guns, their mines and their submarines.
And praise to the beasts of Europe who share the people's art;
To the cats that churn the butter, and the dog that draws the cart.
And horses speed the plough share and shops are faced with glass
And the rain it never ceases, and the fields are green with grass.
The cannon roar like thunder, the bullets fall like rain,
And only the halt the maimed and the blind will ever see home again!
*For we are all as kittens in the kilns of destiny***
Perchance the Guru may save us, but what will be will be!
We have eaten the salt of the Sirkar, before, when times were good:
Let us fight like valiant soldiers and pay the debt with our blood.
The Germans deal in numbers, the Frenchman has a trench,
And bodies are heaped upon bodies till all the air is a stench!
Bodies are heaped upon bodies like the stones in a river bed,
The trench is seven hundred miles long and who can count the dead?
Only potatoes and cabbage are grown upon English ground,
Some things you may do for a penny, but butter's a shilling a pound.

*The author meant Austria, which is confused with Australia.
**In the Sikh sacred books is a story how some kittens, hidden in a potter's kiln, were miraculously preserved by the Guru, while the potter was baking his pots.

A song written by a Sikh – September 1915.

*****

"I have returned to the regiment. A man who has been wounded is not forced to fight again. If a man wishes to do so of his own free will he is allowed to return only after signing a statement, but no one is compelled. I signed the statement and am here. Do not be anxious; for the old soldier has no fear – the Guru preserves him. Until death comes nothing can hurt him. Certainly we are fighting, and the battle is fierce, but the discomfort is not so great as that which men complain of in a frontier campaign against the Pathans. The government's arrangements are most complete, and the wounded are very well cared for. The arrangements are excellent. We Sikhs look on the war as a "tamasha". No doubt we risk our lives, - still, it is a "tamasha" nevertheless. We look to the Guru for victory. Our Emperor's strength grows from day to day. For every shell the Germans send us we send back twenty."

From L.N. Kesar Singh, 47th Sikhs, France, to a friend in India. (Gurmukhi, 18/9/15).

*****

The battle-drum beats in the sky of the mind; aim is taken, and the wound is inflicted.
The spiritual warriors enter the field of battle; now is the time to fight!
He alone is known as a spiritual hero, who fights in defence of religion.
He may be cut apart, piece by piece, but he never leaves the field of battle.

Guru Granth Sahib, Bhagat Kabir, Ang (Page) 1105.

*****

"On the 22nd of September the Emperor summoned me to his palace in London where he gave me a war medal for bravery. The Emperor was delighted with me. No one is allowed to enter the Emperor's palace. This boon was granted by the Great Guru. Your servant can do nothing by his own strength. God has done this for me."

From Jemadar Amar Singh, 9th Bhopal Infantry, Brighton, to Kaula Singh, Patiala, India. (Gurmukhi, dated 29/9/15).

*****

"The Guru will let us meet. If I die I go to Paradise. It is a fine thing to die in battle. We must honour him who feeds us. If our dear government is victorious we shall eat our fill! Our dear government's rule is very good and gracious. Let all you people pray with folded hands for our government's victory. India's name will be magnified. All our men must help – and help again. Such an opportunity comes but seldom. You will reap great rewards, if you help our dear government. See how fiercely our Guru Govind Singh fought! So we must fight. To fight is the duty of heroes. He who fights for the government will have great reward, - prizes, land, medals, distinctions, zaildaris, lambardaris, very great rewards. Such a chance will not come again. All our young men should enlist. Be lions, why sit like jackals? Now is the time. Soon the war will end and you will repent. Such an empire will not be offered you again."

From Hirnam Singh, 9th Bhopal Infantry, Hospital, Brighton, to Kapur Singh, Hoshiarpur, India. (Gurmukhi, dated 29/9/15).

*****

"What you were told about the war being over in three years is very short of the truth. This war will bring us to the end of the world and no one knows how long it will last. The news in the papers is all lies. All is in the hands of the Guru..............There is no one here to hear (my complaints). I am not allowed to write. The hope of returning soon is false. There is no saying what will happen. The Guru has the power, and if pity enters his heart he will put an end to the sufferings of all."

From Hukam Singh, S.A.S, Meerut C.C. Stn. France, to his wife in India. (Gurmukhi, 2/10/15).

*****

"If our dear Emperor wins we shall be well rewarded. We are certain that the Guru will grant the victory, for the enemy cannot drive the English Army from the position which it has taken. We believe that the Master will give us the victory in a short time. The enemy is behaving like a cowardly tyrant, not like a true King. To squirt acid, boiling water and blinding vapour is not bravery. The brave man fights with cannons and rifles."

From Kesar Singh, 47th Sikhs, France, to Hajara Singh, Nabha, India. (Gurmukhi, of 3/10/15).

*****

"I have bought 80 rupees worth of wheat and ghi which should last four or five months. By that time I expect there will be some result of all your sword play. You might have put your brave foot forward a bit. It's rather a disgrace for the Khalsa that the enemy has stood up to us so long. Put your best foot forward for our noble king, and be quick about defeating the foe, that all God's people may be at rest. We pray to God day and night that God will grant victory to our king. I am sitting behind and putting pressure on myself and friends. Well, you are showing your bravery with the sword, and I am praying. We will divide and enjoy the reward."

From a Sikh clerk in Somaliland, to Basant Singh, Clerk, in 47th Sikhs, France. (Dated 13/10/15). (No language stated).

*****

"It is true that everyman acts with a view to his own profit. May the Guru grant you promotion, for which you have left India to gain promotion and to show your bravery to our Emperor. Wherever he goes, no man can avoid what is written in his book of fate. So be fearless and have no care for your life when danger threatens the King."

From a Sikh in the P.W.D., Punjab, to a Sikh in the 12th Cavalry, attached 6th Cavalry, France. (Urdu, 15/12/15).

*****

"You ask me when we shall meet. I cannot say, for we do not know what is in the heart of the Holy Guru, and what he will do. We must obey his commands. He does what he thinks is right. We have had no joy in this world. We have had our turn of human incarnation, and we are doomed to the full series of transmigrations (before we are human again). (The meaning is "We have not been able to lead such a life in human shape as would entitle us to a second term of life as human beings. We must therefore go through all the prescribed 8,400,000 transmigrations before we return as men.)" We were accursed in that we had to leave our precious country. We do not know whether we shall see our land again. We have no certain hope. For from time to time we suffer catastrophes such as I cannot describe. We have spent a full year in France. It is a fine country. Nevertheless, so great are our troubles that we have no love of life, and we wonder if we shall ever taste its joy. What have we profited from our life? Who can bear the troubles that are come upon us? Yet we must face them."

From Asa Singh, F.P.O. 39, to Sohel Singh, 38th C.I.H., Agar, India. (Gurmukhi, 31/12/15).

*****

"A (Sikh) who, when he is to adopt any military journey, prays to his Satguru saying, that he is ordered to do so according to His will, and is now making over everything to Him to look after in his absence and when he goes off he cares not a bit for whatever he has left behind. Because a Sikh is brave and this slacken the bravery. In the military service I recite you the order of Pilla Guru Govind Singh Ji at the time of Chamkaur war which he fought against the bloody predacious Musalmans, his younger son when ordered to go and fight against gigantic Musalmans at the age of 7 years asked for a few drops of cold water to relinquish his thirst before he went on the field. My dear uncle, I let you know the words which our Pilla Sahib uttered for his darling. Go and fight bravely, your accounts have been transferred to the next world, there is nothing left for you here "Khalsa, make haste get out of the garhi." Now I hope you would have reached the conclusion. Before you left Amballa you had made over everything to your Satguru who is omnipresent. He is more, clever, wise and careful than all." Do your duty putting all your senses towards it. Revise Gurbani every morning when you get up and every night when you go to bed and before everything you begin to do. He is with you, when he will see you sticking with them. He will help you in all times."

From Sub-Inspector Kesar Singh, Phillaur, India, to Riss. Partab Singh, 30th Lancers, France. (English, 2/1/16).

*****

"Father dear, do not be in the least worried, for the Guru is always the defender and protector of our lives and bodies; and I fully hope that King will be victorious and that all our brotherhood will return singing the songs of Guru Gobind. I believe that this blessed day is now near at hand."

From Harnam Singh, (no regiment given), 2nd Sialkot Cavalry Brigade, France, to Sohan Singh, Amritsar, India. (Urdu, 13/1/16).

*****

O Lord grant me the boon,
that I may never deviate from doing a good deed.
That I shall not fear when I go into combat.
And with determination I will be victorious.
That I may teach myself this deed alone,
to speak only of Thy (Waheguru) praises.
And when the last days of my life come,
I may die in the might of the battlefield.

Guru Gobind Singh Ji, Dasam Granth.

*****

"As far as possible you must not be anxious about me, because I am a very fortunate person. God Almighty gave me birth in a good family and he favoured me further to this degree that he married me into a good family. While I was still quite young he blessed me with a daughter and three sons. When the necessity for earning my daily bread drew me to Europe, the same God granted me a meeting with all my best friends before I started. Then after parting from my relatives and friends I met you quite unexpectedly on 8/12/14 at Podejan (?) Station. Further on the voyage to Europe I saw on land and sea such wonderful things as I had never dreamed of, and when I reached Europe itself even stranger things came into view. The Europe that I speak of is that Europe which all people are longing to see. It is the "first Golden Age", in which all knowledge and beauty and wealth are found. In short the things from start to finish that are the best and most useful in the world are to be found in Europe, and those things which are not considered good enough for Europe, God has divided among the other quarters of the globe. Seeing all these wonderful things my heart turns away from the thought of leaving Europe."

From Kala Singh, Pavilion Hospital, Brighton, to Sardar Kesar Singh, I.O.M., Govind Garh, Punjab, India. (Gurmukhi, 14/1/16).

*****

"We are all thinking of you and this is our prayer in the presence of the Almighty, that the Guru may bring you back with victory. You must know that you are very fortunate in that you have got the chance to defend your country and serve the British government. You will remember that British rule was foretold by our true leader Tegh Bahadur, the ninth Guru. It was established in India for the protection and help of us Sikhs. It was on the voice of the Guru that the Eternal sent the English here. The blessing which this rule has brought to India are not concealed from you. The rise of the Sikhs is due solely to this power. But for this, the poor Sikhs would have brought their unhappy existence to an end in some crows' pond (sic). I shall be very pleased to hear of your valorous deeds. You are a brave soldier. Now is the time to display your manhood. Now is the time for loyalty. You are a true Sikh. By the Guru's order you must remember the promise of the Almighty, who said

"Recognise the hero in him who fights for his faith,
Though cut to pieces he will not quit his ground."

This war for the Sikhs is a religious war, because the war is directed against the rule which our Guru established."

From Eshar Singh, Inspector of Police, Punjab, India, to Jem. Jai Singh, 6th Cavalry, France. (Urdu, 19/1/16).

*****

"We must never forget that we have come to a far distant land to work for the British government, and God has given this opportunity of serving the King, and your son Atma Singh has also had this chance given to him. I hope that you are busy day and night in praying to God for us, and for the victory of the British Raj. May God speedily answer your petitions! We shall all sing His praises. This world is a transitory one and our days in it are few. We shall reap hereafter what we sow on earth. This is what we learn in the Granth and what the Sages teach us. If we do not follow their advice, we are working against God and you know well what the result of that will be. It is our duty to love God above our earthly father and mother, although what we owe to them we can never repay till the Day of Judgement."

From Dfdr. Jai Singh, Sialkot Cavalry Brigade, France, to Nand Singh, (Jagirdar), Jalandhar, India. (Urdu, 20/1/16).

*****

"Never be disturbed, Guru Govind is always ready to assist you. Consider how the four young sons of Guru Govind fought in the field of battle and were never disturbed in mind. Illuminate the name of Guru Govind under the illustrious British flag. Have no regards for your life when you are attacked or when you are attacking; the Guru is your guardian angel. If you uphold the honour of your mother, the King, God will reward you. You cannot be born again from your mother's womb. Your life is given once only, therefore do your duty well and do not bring any discredit on the Sikh name. It is written 'When you are in your mother's womb, God alone protects you. Now that you have attained to manhood, you must depend on your own wits.' Remember you are the follower of that Guru who enabled birds to kill the hawk. In fighting qualities one Sikh is the equal of 1¼ lakhs of other men. It is this that has illuminated the name of Sikh. The Guru will give victory to our King, and bring you back in safety. May George V, live in honour and glory as long as the sun shines on the earth."

From ---- ----. Rawal Pindi, Punjab, India to ____, France. (Urdu, 20th January, 1916).

*****

"Do not be alarmed. Keep your wits about you and do not be afraid of death. Death surely comes one day. If one dies in battle one's name is remembered (lit: "remains fixed") for many days. Rely on the Guru. We shall certainly meet again. Do not be despondent. It is not proper for you to write in this strain, because it makes me sad (lit: "makes my heart soft")."

From Jiwan Singh, 25th Punjabis, Bannu, N.W.F.P., to Hazara Singh, 30th Lancers, France. (Urdu, 30/1/16).

*****

"I presume that owing to your having gone to another sphere of action you have no leisure (to write). May the Guru give you success in the new field. If God gives you victory in this year, then those from whom you have been parted for so long, will again be blessed with the sight of you. I hope that you are well, and that you are meeting with the greatest fortitude the trials of the field, which I know to be almost without limit, and that you are upholding the honour of the British Raj by the sacrifice of your bodies and of your minds. May God bless your efforts."

From Fakir Singh, Lahore, Punjab, to Dafadar Dalip Singh, 30th Lancers, France. (Urdu, 31/1/16).

*****

"We believe God will give us a good opportunity (of distinguishing ourselves). When the enemy having left his trenches, our swift horses and our men full of spirit shall pursue them and take revenge on them for the evil deeds they have done. At present too, we go sometimes into the trenches and there we take some toll of the enemy; but our expectations are fixed on the coming days."

From Jem. Jai Singh, 6th Cavalry, France, to Sirdar Eshar Singh, Police Inspector, Lahore, Punjab. (Urdu and Gurmukhi, 25/2/16).

*****

"You say in the matter of Kesari's marriage you will wait a year (for my return). I feel confident that by that time the matter (i.e. the war) will be finished. It is the will of God. My destiny and the upheaval of the times has caused this disturbance (of settled plans). The youth of men in the army is being passed in anxiety and solitude, and in their old age they are caught in trouble. What a man does himself, for that there is no remedy. Without the will of God no alternative is available. If one becomes too anxious then one's courage is brought to blame."

From Sewa Singh, Sialkot Cavalry Brigade, France, to Jawahir Singh, Hoshiarpur, Punjab. (Urdu, 20/3/16).

*****

O Lord! Keep me now under Thy protection;
protect my disciples and destroy my enemies.

Guru Gobind Singh Ji, Dasam Granth.

*****

"I hear of certain promotions in the squadrons. Congratulate for me the recipients. The squadron has not yet had an opportunity of earning the highest promotions, still, progress in the path of good intention and bravery, and be second to none in the discharge of your duty to the illustrious Government. Loyalty is the very highest virtue, and our Lord Guru Gobind, himself, has said, that he is a true Sikh who trusts in God. Have faith in God then, and you will soon see victory secured to our King. The Germans have not started this war with any good object in view, but only for the purpose of shedding blood. There is a proverb to the effect that the greedy receive nothing. The time is near for them to receive the due reward of their evil doing, and for you, crowned with victory and honour, to return to your country and wear on your breasts the sign of your bravery."

From Gurdit Singh, Risaldar Major, 6th Cavalry, Sialkot, to Jemadar Ganda Singh, 6th Cavalry, France. (Urdu, 31/3/16).

*****

"Don't even mention the end of the work. God alone knows when it will end. No one has the foresight to say. This is not a fight. It is wholesale slaughter and destruction. May God bring peace speedily. This is my daily prayer."

From Balwant Singh, Rouen, to Sirdar Jai Singh, India. (Urdu, 4/4/16).

*****

The Sikh roars like a lion on the field of battle
And yields up his life as a sacrifice,
Whoever is fortunate enough to be born a Rajput
Never fears the foe in battle,
He gives up all thought of worldly pleasure
And dreams only of the battlefield,
He who dies on the field of battle,
His name never dies but lives in history;
He who fronts the foe boldly in battle
Has God for his protection;
Once a Sikh takes the sword in hand
He has only one aim, victory.

From Dafadar Natha Singh, 2nd Lancers, France, to Sowar Paran Singh, State Cavalry, Jhind, India. (Gurmukhi, 18/4/16).

*****

"Tell me whether any rumours about peace are current or not. If peace were to be made now, it would be a good thing. It is now nearly two years since the war began, during which time the war has gone on continuously without any definite result to either side. Now if God shows kindness it would be a blessing, because the continuance of the war means losses of various kinds. No one can tell what God means to do. The people of

India were decimated by the plague, and the European war has already taken heavy toll of lives. Nowadays not only in Europe, but also in Asia and Africa losses are constantly recurring. Now, truly, God might show mercy, but He is the Master and will do what He thinks fit."

From Bishan Singh, Persian Teacher Government High School, Quetta, Baluchistan Agency, India, to Jemadar Katar Singh, 18th Lancers, France. (Urdu, 24/4/16).

*****

"I see loyalty and bravery of your heart in every word of your letter. I pray "Sri Guru Maharaj" that he will further your good intention and carry them to favourable conclusion, and that a message of victory may soon reach us. May God cause the flag of our kind and just Government to flutter over the whole world, and may He make your names as illustrious as those of the great warriors Hanuman, Bhishna, Patama, and Arjan &c., as long as time lasts. I feel confident that the spirit which Guru Gobind Singh has implanted in the nature of all Sikhs, will be manifested in you, and that you will prove by your deeds the truth of his saying:

""When with one Sikh I fight a million enemies and with a (Sikh) sparrow I overcame a (enemy) hawk, then the whole world will see that I am Gobind Singh!" I feel that, in the same way you will pierce the rank of the enemy and overthrow him, and fulfil your loyal duty to our beloved Government."

From Lachmi Singh, Jindh State, Punjab, to Sirdar Katar Singh, Jemadar, 18th Lancers, France. (Urdu, 27/4/16).

*****

"You say that as the master of the garden is absent, it is falling into decay and ruin, and the parrots destroy the fruits. You are not to blame for this. It is two years since we were separated, and the trials which we undergo here, are far greater than those which trouble you. Where we are, the crash of guns is heard day and night, and more than gunshot we experience the bursting of bombs. May God help us. If He wishes that we should meet again, we shall meet, that is those of us whose fortune is good. Up to the present I am well. What you say, Kishen Kor (his wife) that the garden does not grow without the master is true. I indeed am a false master. The true master is God. If God's blessing is on the garden, He will not suffer it to decay. We go to the front for a fortnight, then we are relieved and remain behind for a fortnight. We write when we return from the front."

From Sundar Singh, 6th Cavalry, France, to Dedar Singh, Ludhiana, Dt., Punjab. (Gurmukhi, 23/5/16).

*****

"We are all well here. May the Guru preserve you all and enable you to destroy the enemy, and obtain fame. May you be victorious and may He bring you back soon. Work for the Sirkar and be true to your salt. Give my salutations to all the brotherhood.

I daresay you have great discomforts to face but bring fame to the Khalsa. If you are ever surrounded by the enemy don't surrender, but go on fighting to the last. If you die on the field of battle, you will find yourself at the feet of the Guru. You have been given a physical body in order that your soul may win this glory."

From Chanda Singh, Granthi, 32nd Lancers, Delhi, to Lance Dafadar Pritam Singh, 32nd Lancers, (attached 30th Lancers), France. (Gurmukhi, 23/5/16).

*****

"In this country it rains frequently. The climate is good. If I come back alive, I will tell you about it. All is in the hands of God. Except for Him we have no hope. May God bring peace into this terrible war of Kings. Except through peace there is no remedy. In this country all the able bodied men are engaged in the war. In the villages there are only women, children and old men."

From Sahib Singh, L.D., Sialkot Cavalry Bde., France, to Jeswant Singh, Rawal Pindi Dt., Punjab. (Urdu, 6/6/16).

*****

"You say that many men have returned home on leave from here. The reason is that they were wounded or very ill. By the blessing of God I have not had so much as a headache up till today. For what illness then can I return? I constantly pray God to keep me fit and well, for I do not desire to think of this mean thing (i.e. returning home while the war lasts). If you consider well, you will understand that when a man's fate comes, death reaches him, whether you close him up in an iron cage for safety, or hide him deep down in the earth. If then I am fated to die here, do you think that death will avoid me through fear of you? Such an idea is absurd. If am fated to live, I shall live even if I fall into a furnace. If, on the other hand, the tale of my days is accomplished, I cannot exist longer, whatever the circumstances may be. Look you! Puran Bhagat was fated to live, therefore he remained alive well for 12 years, and at the end of that time emerged again. Until today everyone remembers him. Therefore, if I am fated to live, there need be no anxiety on my account, even if the war lasts another 4 years. If my days are completed, then perhaps I may die tomorrow."

From Naubat Singh, Signal Troop, Sialkot Cavalry Brigade, France, to Mathra Singh, Rawal Pindi, Punjab, India. (Urdu, 21/7/16).

*****

If you desire to play this game of love with Me,
then step onto My Path with your head in hand.
When you place your feet on this Path,
give Me your head,
and do not pay any attention to public opinion.

Guru Granth Sahib, Guru Nanak Dev Ji, Ang (Page) 1412.

*****

"By the favour of God our Regiment has recently done work the like of which no other Cavalry Regiment has done in this war, and the fame thereof has spread all through the field of battle. So have brave and loyal a Regiment will be of service to the Sircar in many places, and the Sircar has become fully aware of its value. You will learn all details from the Fauji Akhbar which you read weekly. People say that the Germans are very brave, but we have seen with our own eyes that the Germans have no staying power. They are unequalled in deceit and devilry, but our just Government has given them such a taste of the fruits of treachery, that they will remember it as long as the world lasts. They are being punished daily, and by the grace of God our Sircar will soon obtain complete victory, and we shall then return to you."

From Sant Singh, 20th Deccan Horse, France, to Sirdar Bhagman Singh, Sirsa Dt., Punjab, India. (Gurmukhi, 10/8/16).

*****

"As to what you write about promotion, you know very well how promotion is got. Flattery is the way to get on but the Guru has not ordained that we should go in for flattery. Though seeing the success that flattery gains one is inclined to think that one should practice it, I for one will never recourse to it. But if you look far ahead you can realise that nothing really can be gained by it. What is written in your fate has to happen. Colonel Green commands and the Risaldar Major is Bhagga Singh. You can guess the sort of way things are being done. The Adjutant is Parnell Sahib. Well I am doing my work all right and everyone is kind enough to me but promotion is in the hands of the Guru. On 5th August Dafadar Hardatt Singh lost his foot through a bomb bursting and Lance Dafadar Dasaunda Singh was wounded in several places."

From Hazara Singh, 36th Jacob's Horse, France, to his mother, Ludhiana, Punjab. (Urdu, 14/8/16).

*****

"My "palace" at the present time is situated 2 yards below the surface of the ground and has an iron roof. It is very strong. When I am out on duty working, I see a perpetual shower of flowers (i.e. of shot and shell). We are very happy. Always have regard to what the Tenth Guru said and do not be anxious about me. The Guru is always with me."

"God's mercy rules on land and sea
Our sins are great, but Great is He
Vain are the devilish German tricks
On God our help our eyes we fix."

From Bachatar Singh, Jemadar, 6th Cavalry, France, to his son Hadeo Singh, Ludhiana Dt., Punjab. (Gurmukhi, 23/9/16).

*****

"I am tired of reading in the newspapers about the war. May God now give patience. "Educated men should not be killed, nor should religious mendicants". Looking at the conduct of the enlightened peoples of the world, it is clear that the above words of Guru Nanak are worthy to be written in letters of gold. All that is now being done by those peoples, is being done through the possession of worldly wealth. How many thousands of enlightened men are now engaged in the work of slaughter. The house that a man builds for himself is but an inn in which he passes a night and then goes on his journey. This itself shows the power of God. You write and say that day after day the enemy is being worsted. God grant that he may be speedily exhausted! In the newspapers is constantly being printed information about the fighting at Somme and Verdun. For two years we have been reading about these two places. The ground in these places, what with the digging of trenches and the havoc caused by shells must have turned upside down, and the inhabitants must either have been killed or driven away. Oh God, how great is thy power! Thou raisest up mountains out of the sea, and driest up rivers! Thou placest an ant on a throne, and crumblest an army into dirt! Millions of acres of populated land must have been devastated and the accumulated earnings of generations of men has been turned into ashes! Nowadays many "Doctors" have been sent to Mesopotamia. From Mesopotamia, Sirdars, doctors, and soldiers come home on leave. What! Do they not give you leave? The whole of the 16th Cavalry has returned. The news about local affairs is very slack, the war has made everything else slack. The cost of provisions &c increases daily. The price of hardware has doubled. Recruiting is carried on vigorously. The majority of the recruits come from the Punjab. Thank God the state of India is peaceful."

From Bhagwan Singh, Kashipur, Moradabad, U.P., India, to Naurang Singh, Sub. Asst. Surgeon., 19th Lancers, France. (Gurmukhi, 27/9/16).

*****

"We shall meet if God pleases. Everything is in His hands. If I am destined to drink the water of my well again and to gather fruit from my trees, then truly God will direct events accordingly. Let the sons of every mother join in prayer to God to bring about the end of the war saying to Him "Behold now the whole world is destroyed". The ending of the war (by man) is an extremely difficult task and there is no house out here (France) from which 4 or 6 sons have not gone to the war. We live in their houses and their women plough the land and drive wagons. Life for them is a matter of much difficulty."

From Atma Singh, 6th Cavalry, France to Huram Singh, Pensioned Havildar, Gujar Khan, Punjab, India. (Urdu dated the 2nd October, 1916).

*****

"As to getting leave, the men who get leave from Mesopotamia are near India and the climate etc. is exactly like India. We cannot possibly get leave for we are a very long way from home and the journey there and the return would take us two months. Don't worry about trifles like this. When it is God's will we shall quickly meet again."

From Sena Singh, 6th Cavalry, France, to Sahib Singh, Ludhiana. (Urdu, 5/10/16).

*****

"You write and accuse me of having told an untruth. My reply is that I never lie, because I am a Sikh of Guru Gobind Singh. The fact of the matter is that the life of the goat is in the hands of another, to keep or destroy as he thinks fit. What can the goat do? Well, if the goat's life is spared and we meet again all will be made clear. When the war is finished and peace is made we will return. We shall not return before. We have sworn to serve. It is not the way with Sikhs to run home on some pretence. It is only the white livered one who acts so. Until the war is finished it is our Guru's order to stand firm. The Guru's precept is that brave men show their bravery in the field of battle, while the cowards flee from the battlefield."

From Kesar Singh, 9th Hodson's Horse, att. 38th C.I. Horse, France, to Natha Singh, 1st Lancers, Jhalawar State. (Gurmukhi, 10/10/16).

*****

"May the Guru Ji protect you in soul and body just as when he gave you that vision two or three months ago of good Sikhs in the heavens. The Guru made them plainly visible."

From Gurbachan Singh, Amritsar to Dafadar Gurdyal Singh, 6th Cavalry, France. (Urdu dated the 22nd October, 1916).

*****

He alone is called a warrior, who is attached to the Lord's Love in this age.
Through the Perfect True Guru, he conquers his own soul,
and then everything comes under his control.

Guru Granth Sahib, Guru Arjan Dev Ji, Ang (Page) 679.

*****

"We got your three letters in the trenches. The reason for the delay was that a few of us are with the British Infantry in the trenches. Two of our men a Sikh and a Dogra were killed by a shell on the 29th October. Another Sikh belonging to the 6th Cavalry was also killed. What a glorious death! All three of them were seated washing their hands and faces and they did not even know that a shell had burst. They passed from life to death without knowing it. Don't be anxious at all. This is the best of all deaths. Keep on praying to the Guru who is the protector of our bodies and limbs."

From Nam Singh, Kishan Singh, Gurbachan Singh, A.P.O.H. 15 to Beant Singh, Jalandhar, India. (Urdu dated the 12th November 1916).

*****

"It is my custom, brave as I am, to stand in the field on battle and confront the enemy. There is no fear, for one day all must die."

From Man Singh, Ressaidar, 21st Cavalry attached 36th Jacob's Horse, France to Sirdar Khan, Jemadar, Base Remount Depot, Rouen, France (Urdu dated the 25th December, 1916).

*****

"Do not be in any way anxious, but at all times place your trust in the Guru and keep your heart firm. The Guru is continually looking after us and helping us. Our Sircar has made the very best arrangements for our safety in this war. In the front lines, the losses are very small and by the grace of God our Government is now four times as strong at the front and the enemy is being greatly pressed. At all times we are expectant of victory, and you should certainly pray for victory. We have no difficulties of any sort, in fact we are in great comfort."

From Chattar Singh, 6th Cavalry, France to Nawrang Singh, Pensioned Daffadar, Ludhiana District, Punjab, India. (Gurmukhi dated the 17th January 1917).

*****

"I cannot get leave, nor is there any other method by which I could come, until the war is over. There is absolutely no indication as to when I am likely to return, as there is no indication when the war will be over. By the kindness of the Guru my life has been preserved up to the present, and as long as I live I will continue to write, for you are to me as a father and a mother. I cannot write to you about my difficulties and trials, because it is forbidden to write about anything but our welfare. The orders are to the effect that, however much one may be suffering, one may only write and say that one is quite well and very happy, one is forbidden to write about one's trials and about the war."

From Dhan Singh, 6th Cavalry, France to Lahore Singh, Patiala State, Punjab, India. (Gurmukhi dated the 20th January 1917).

*****

"Your letter shows that you are very anxious about Sujan Singh and Dyal Singh and that your eyes are suffering from your anxiety and your teeth too. I am very worried about this. You are a wise man and trust in the Guru, then why be humbled in mind? You are always exhorting me to be brave, then do not be downhearted yourself. We are all together and very happy and comfortable. Instead of being anxious you should always be thanking the Guru for giving your family a chance of serving the King in Europe. We believe that the Guru will soon give victory to our King and that you will receive great izzat."

From Balwant Singh, 6th Cavalry, France to Janmeja Singh, Lyallpur. (Urdu dated the 25th February, 1917).

*****

"America is not fit to make war, nor will she do so. The Guru will give power to our Sircar and there is no need for the assistance of any other country. The Guru is already accomplishing much. On this side the Germans have been driven back two or three miles, and on that side we have taken Baghdad. It is all due to the grace of the Guru. There is some trouble in Russia. Well, let us see what the Guru will do."

From Jewan Singh, 38th Central India Horse, France to Bhagat Singh, Retired Subedar Major, Amritsar District, Punjab, India. (Gurmukhi dated the 24th March, 1917).

*****

"By the favour of the Guru the time is passing well. We have made many attacks but have not had any great opportunity to act only some small chances now and then. We have had a few casualties but God was gracious. The Germans have retreated many miles and we have captured many thousands of prisoners. We are advancing here in great style."

From Divan Singh, Wardi Major, 2nd Lancers, France to Sirdar Ajaib Singh, Wardi Major, 16th Cavalry, Loralai, India. (Urdu dated the 18th April, 1917).

*****

"I am very well indeed, don't be anxious in the least. God's protection is everywhere, our hope is entirely in Him. This world is a net and we are buffeted hither and thither. If you are caught in the net there is no use striking out and kicking right and left. You only damage your features, your wings, and your brains by trying to struggle. Endure passively whatever happens for no mortal can avoid his fate."

From Bhim Singh, 19th Lancers, France to Jawahir Singh, Hoshiarpur, India. (Urdu dated the 12th May, 1917).

*****

"You wrote about my coming on leave but you know well that I cannot come. I have often tried but it is not to be done. Don't trouble about my heart. It is like the heart of a tiger and I am not the least inclined to be worried. I learnt to endure hardships when I was a boy. As for the men who have got back to India it was in their fate and if it is in my fate I too shall get back there. You must be stout hearted as becomes a brave man and trust in God who looks after every living being. When you are in trouble, think of the good days which we have enjoyed and don't imagine that coming over here means death. No, death meets you everywhere, at home or aboard, in war or peace."

From Mehr Singh, 6th Cavalry, France to Makan Singh, Rawal Pindi. (Urdu dated the 21st May, 1917).

*****

"Why are you so despondent? You should steel your heart to endure these trying times bravely. God is displeased when you do otherwise. It is easy to be happy when times are bright, but he is a brave man who can keep his mind untroubled in the face of adversity. No doubt the times are very grave; but if one does not endure them bravely, he will get no help from God. The story is told of the son of Guru Gobind Singh, named Jhujhar Singh, who becoming mad with thirst returned from the battle to assuage his thirst. When he asked his father Guru Gobind Singh for water, he received the clear reply "The water which you are to drink is in with Ajit Singh" (the elder brother who was then lying dead on the battle field). Then Jujhar Singh came to his senses, and quickly returned to the battle field. The reason why Guru Gobind Singh reproved him in this way, was because he had turned his back on the enemy, and for this reason also he said to those around him:

'He alone is entitled to be called
Brave, who fights for right.
He may be cut into pieces but
He will never quit the battle field.'

Therefore have faith in God. He alone can help and protect you. There is no fruit in writing despondent letters to me, as I can do nothing to help you, the only effect produced is to make me unhappy on your account."

From Harjit Singh, Dhariwal, Punjab, India to Bhagwan Singh, Ressaidar, 19th Lancers, France. (Urdu dated the 6th June, 1917).

*****

"It is impossible to come on leave. If I were to try and get leave it would be foolishness on my part. There is no end to this war; which has caused so much loss to the whole world. Leaving aside the trials of the various armies engaged in the war, Kings themselves are involved in misfortune. For this reason you should have patience, and put up with the trials of this war. Our condition as fighting men here is such that we can look for help to no one but God."

From Seva Singh, 19th Lancers, France to Jowahir Singh, Hoshiarpur, Punjab, India. (Urdu dated the 14th July, 1917).

*****

"Our condition is like this. Some days it is very bad, so bad that hanging would be preferable. Some days it is enjoyable as though one were at a fair watching the sports. Some days it is such that we are enabled to pass weeks and even months in ease. Some days it is such that shells fly about grazing ones' bodies and we lie sleeping but by the grace of the Guru. We have passed through such days even in safety. There is no news about our return. I myself have no hope that I shall live to return; but if the Guru wills otherwise we shall meet."

From Udel Singh, 38th Central India Horse, France to Dil Singh, Ludhiana, Punjab, India. (Gurmukhi dated the 31st July, 1917).

*****

"There are rumours that the war is coming to an end. This all depends on the Guru. No one can say when the end will come. If our Government is victorious and the Germans are defeated I shall soon see you again. Through the kindness of the Guru another thing has happened. America has joined the war and peace must soon come now."

From Narain Singh, 18th Lancers, France to Bala Singh, Naini Tal. (Gurmukhi dated the 22nd August, 1917).

*****

Those who place their faith in the Lord's Name,
do not attach their consciousness to another.
Even if the entire earth were to be transformed into gold,
and given to them, without the Naam, they love nothing else.

Guru Granth Sahib, Guru Ram Das Ji, Ang (Page) 444.

*****

"As to what you write about our coming back, we have no idea whatever when that will be because God alone knows what will happen in this war. This is what they call in English a "World War". Everybody is either fighting or helping in the supply of provisions, transport and munitions and therefore all the peoples of all the countries are in the war. But we are all well and have no complaints and have all we wish to eat and drink. We believe that in the end the British will be victorious. God is our protector whether we are fighting or asleep in bed."

From Bishan Singh, 6th Cavalry, France to Ranjit Singh, Ludhiana. (Urdu dated the 30th August, 1917).

*****

"My son, you are indeed fortunate in that you have had the opportunity to discharge your debt of loyalty towards the Sircar. You are not far from us, you are the son of your country, and a ready sacrifice in her welfare. My hopes are fixed on you, and our King takes pride in being served by such as you. You are a hero of this great age. May the Guru keep you well and happy. You are under the protection of God. You are a hero, and the security of my life. Our Government relies on you. When Aurangzeb ruled over the land he desired to root out our race (Sikhs) root and branch. Today our King, ruler over the seven Kingdoms, is the protection of our race. His Armies have subjugated Baghdad. To you and to your fellows is due the honour of this achievement, and of the fact that the hearts blood of the Germans is being consumed. In the pride and joy that comes of all this, a little thing for me! We should send up unlimited thanks to Almighty God who has bestowed on us such honour and glory. Now I pray that God will speedily bring the day when your voice will be raised in the "Hurrah" of Victory, when you will feel the kisses of your mother, and be clasped in the arms of your wife, and when all of us being filled with happiness, will raise our voices in praise to our Government."

From Kishan Singh, Nabha State, Punjab, India to Gajan Singh, Veterinary Assistant, 18th Lancers, France. (Urdu dated the 2nd November, 1917).

*****

"Tell my wife she must learn to write to me in Gurmukhi for here all the girls are taught from their infancy. Our womenfolk are not equal in mind to the little girls here who are educated. When they marry they are able to teach their children and so it goes on. Bishan Singh must be sent to school and he must be also taught to worship the Guru. I have seen the wonderful work performed by the Guru and I feel more than ever devoted to Him. It is false to say that I have married here in this country."

From Gurdar Singh, 19th Lancers, France to his mother, Gurdaspur. (Urdu dated the 18th November, 1917).

*****

"On the 1st December at 8 o'clock we attacked the enemy's trenches on horseback. My horse was shot under me; but I reached the trench in safety. We drove the enemy out of the trenches; but he counterattacked us heavily twice. Our brave fellows drove him back with the bayonet on each occasion. Many of the enemy's men were also speared by our Regiment. The enemy's aeroplanes, flying not more than 200 yards over head, attacked us with bombs and machine guns. Nevertheless our Regiment held the trenches till they were relieved by the Infantry. We had losses and amongst them was our Colonel who was Kot Dafadar Sant Singh's best friend. Well, if I am destined to live I shall meet you again. If I were to write and tell you all the details of this battle the hairs on your body would stand on end. Those British officers, Sirdars and men who lost their lives in this battle have fulfilled their obligations. It is for such an occasion that each man, when he enlists swears on the Granth to be faithful, and it is therefore incumbent on us to fulfil our obligations towards the Government whose salt we eat. One's life is not for this world only. My father, you yourself fought for the Government in five wars and you were wounded in the Burma war. As a result of all the hardships you endured the Guru made you a Sirdar, while you fulfilled your obligations towards the Government and now live in ease on your pension. In like manner, I am fulfilling my obligations towards the Government and will continue to do so. Doubtless you will be gratified on reading this letter to learn that your son, even when he had his horse shot under him, did not show his back to the enemy; but at once fixed his bayonet on to his rifle and went into the enemy's trenches. Anyone who desires to be worthy of the salt he eats should not have any concern for his life. You will be pleased then when you read this letter and in reply will say "well done"!"

From Chattar Singh, 2nd Lancers, France to his father Hira Singh, Retired Jemadar, Jullundur District, Punjab, India. (Urdu dated the 6th December, 1917).

*****

"The Guru has forcibly taken Kartar Singh from me, I could do nothing for him, though I kept him constantly under my eye. It happened in this way, we were under very heavy shell fire, but had almost galloped through it when one fatal shell fell on us killing Kartar Singh and another outright and wounding several men. Do not be dismayed. Your son is a hero who has given his life for his King. He is not dead; he lives forever. He has gone straight to Paradise, because that is the reward of death in the field of battle in the service of the King. He has, in fact, achieved in an instant that which saints can only hope to secure after many years of trial. Earthly love is a small thing compared with the joys of Paradise."

From Jewan Singh, Resaidar, 2nd Lancers, France to Isar Singh, Gurdaspur District, Punjab, India. (Urdu dated the 10th December, 1917).

*****

"There is so much work just now that I cannot write about it nor are we allowed to do so. I am longing to see the old people but it is unlikely that God will grant our wish. The 2nd Lancers suffered a good deal. We were with them but God preserved us and we suffered but little. We are still ready for the work is going on."

From Sowar Tala Singh, 6th Cavalry, France to Bhopal Singh, Rawal Pindi. (Urdu dated the 13th December, 1917).

*****

"The news is that all our Cavalry Regiments are going to Basrah from France. I hope therefore to come soon, and hope to be with you in March. For the rest, all is in the hands of the Guru. When we board the ship I will write to you. We have today received orders to go to Basrah."

From Sohan Singh, 38th Central India Horse, France to Harnam Singh, Amritsar District, Punjab, India. (Gurmukhi dated the 22nd January, 1918).

*****

As is the will of Your command,
so do things happen.
Wherever You keep me,
there I go and stand.

Guru Granth Sahib, Guru Arjan Dev Ji, Ang (Page) 679.

*****

3

England and Hospitals

One Sikh goes as far as to apply to Brighton the famous Persian couplet inscribed on the walls of the Diwan Khas at Delhi, "If there be a paradise on earth, it is this."

England is a very fine country. The women are like fairies.

There are British soldiers posted as sentries all round the hospital who neither permit us to go out nor outsiders to come in. That is the kind of hospital we are in.

There is great hardship in the hospital now. The lame and the halt are being sent back to the front.

As the realities of modern trench warfare started to bite, Indian soldiers were being killed and injured in their thousands. Injured soldiers started to arrive by ship into Southampton by late 1914. Eventually there would be many hospitals used by the Indian soldiers and a depot was created for them at Milford-on-Sea. These hospitals were located in Brighton, Hampshire, Brockenhurst and Bournemouth in the south of England. The injured soldiers started to write letters home from England and, of course, these too would need to be censored.

The convalescing soldiers were visited by the King and Queen as well as other high profile visitors such as Austen Chamberlain and Lord Kitchener. These visits seemed to be much welcomed by the Indian troops and many wrote home about them. The Sikhs were particularly happy with the visits of the granddaughter of Maharaja Ranjit Singh, Princess Sophia Duleep Singh, daughter of the last Maharaja of Punjab. The Princess would spend time with the Sikh soldiers giving them gifts. She also volunteered as a nurse and raised funds for Indian soldiers. She would also have a letter from her to a Jemadar at the front examined by the Censor. However, the Censor cleared the letter as being harmless saying "she was just describing how she had entertained Sikhs at her house in Hampton Court." A Sikh Havildar in 1915 remarked about the granddaughters of Ranjit Singh after they had visited him, "To this day they speak Punjabi plainly." Princess Sophia would continue to be a remarkable woman and would play a role in the Suffragette movement in later years.

The treatment of the Indian soldiers was a perfect opportunity to engage in some positive publicity and propaganda. *The Indiaman*, 16 July 1915, had the following words to share: "On the upper balconies lay Sikh soldiers listening with rapt delight to their brethren chanting the verses from their Holy Book. In a tent beautiful with flowers a tall Sikh read the Granth, over which he waved a rod of white roses."

Sikh Gurdwara, monochrome photograph showing Sikh soldiers in a Gurdwara (a Sikh shrine) in the grounds of the Royal Pavilion. Taken during its use as an Indian military hospital 1915. (Royal Pavilion & Museums, Brighton & Hove)

The British were keen to show that the Sikhs were being treated well, religious rites were being respected and that they were able to visit other places in England like Buckingham Palace to receive medals. (Sikhs won a large amount of honours during the Great War, although no Sikh received a Victoria Cross). The Sikhs also visited museums and the houses of Parliament. Again the Sikh soldiers were impressed by the scale and grandeur of London. Although the picture painted of the Indian soldiers was of grateful soldiers who loved their King and their surroundings, all was not as it seemed.

One issue which concerned all classes was that injured soldiers that recovered were sent back to the front. A Sikh at the Convalescent Home, New Milton, describes his thoughts, "Everyman that recovers goes straight to the trenches. If a man is worthless they send him to India. Even if a man has only one finger in his left hand he goes to the firing line." Sikhs were very complimentary about the treatment received from British nurses, and there was uproar when in August 1915, British nurses were removed from some of the 'Indian' hospitals. After seeing the reality of the Western Front, many soldiers took the opportunity to tell relatives not to come: "____Singh is dead & we are utterly destroyed. None is left, neither fathers nor sons. Do not let Lait Singh come to the war." – warned a Sikh wounded and in hospital in England.

Convalescent Sikhs, monochrome photograph showing twelve Sikh soldiers posing outside the Royal Pavilion. Taken during Royal Pavilion's use as an Indian military hospital, 1915. (Royal Pavilion & Museums, Brighton & Hove)

Restrictions were placed on the Indian soldiers and there were probably many reasons for this. Interaction with British women was a constant fear as the British did not want European prestige tainted. The Sikh soldiers in particular were popular with the people of Brighton who saw them as exotic. "We have never seen such men. Only have we heard of them that they are the Sikhs of India who once fought against England." This interaction and socialising was monitored and soon Indian soldiers were not allowed to go into the towns without escorts. These restrictions became more apparent in the hospitals themselves, as a Sikh in July 1915 describes, "They do not allow us to go out of this hospital. There are guards of British soldiers set round the hospital and the place is enclosed with wire too." By September 1915, the situation had become worse and a Sikh of the 15th Sikhs lamented, "Here too we are in great discomfort. The sick in all the hospitals are gathered together and paraded. The men cry and moan but no one listens to them."

This chapter tells the story of the Sikh soldier's experience of the time they spent in hospitals in England, and their experience of English people and cities. By late 1915, the British decided to redeploy the Indian infantry to the Middle East. Most Indian soldiers were withdrawn from Europe, but the cavalry remained in France. As a result, Brighton's Indian hospitals gradually closed. The Pavilion was the last to close in January 1916.

*****

> The tremendous change that has been wrought by the war in the British attitude towards Indians in this country is a thing to marvel at.
>
> The tall, stalwart, be-turbanned, be-whiskered Sikhs, who not so very long ago attracted the rude notion of everyone, and about whom the street gamins made unseemly remarks as they followed them about in tormenting droves, now are considered to be the saviours of the Empire. Wherever they go they are respectfully saluted by the

populace. Not a few of the Englishmen and women who pass them in the street stop to shake hands with them and tell them what a relief it is to Britain to feel that the Sikhs are coming to their rescue.

For instance, two or three nights ago a large party of us Sikhs were walking in Shepherds Bush when some British Tommies stopped us and effusively talked with us as long as we could remain to listen to their praise of our soldierly race. On the tram car the other day, the conductor came up to me and said exultantly: "The Germans maybe playing mischief now, but you must wait until the Sikhs get after them. They will sing a different tune then."

The European War, By Saint Nihal Singh (extract), *The Khalsa Advocate*, Saturday, November 21, 1914.

*****

"I am in hospital & London is in Wilayat. I cannot describe the war, because 30,000 men have been destroyed & 20,000 more will be destroyed. Moreover the trench is 260 miles long. Further it rains without ceasing every day, & many men have been killed by the cold. Many have lost the half of a foot from the frost. The country is good, but in no country is there so much corn as in your country. ____has written to say that there is dysentery & now ____ writes that 128 men are dead. Moreover, India Milton New Hants & post a letter after seeing this address in Roman character (sic)

India's Troop
New Milton,
Hants."

From X.Y. a Sikh wounded in hospital at Milton to his brother at Jullundur in the Punjab. (Original in Gurmukhi, dated the 16/1/15).

*****

"Do not be anxious. If I die, you will profit greatly. For Government will give you a pension. Why should you worry? If I live, then Government will give us still more."

From X.Y. a Sikh wounded in hospital in England to his wife in India. (Original in Gurmukhi).

*****

"My brother & I are both here & all well. We do not know what comes next. Take good care of our home & be very careful. I have written to ____ to say that we are all well. If our lives are spared we shall meet again. Whatever is to be done is to be done by you (i.e. there will not be any one else left to look after things). Take great care of our home. And put your hand upon my son's head & promise that he shall be to you as your own. Give my greetings to ______ & to him who reads this letter. We are not allowed to write more."

From X.Y. a Sikh wounded in England to his brother in the Punjab. (Original in Urdu, dated the 18th January 1915).

*****

"We are very comfortable here & I get good food & plenty of milk. The cows here give nearly 20 seers of milk a day & are as big as buffaloes. The horses here are big & beautiful & and are used for ploughing. There are no buffaloes here, nor camels, only cattle. And the grain of the country consists of two kinds, oats & wheat. The people here grow great quantities of vegetables."

From X.Y. a Sikh wounded in England to a relative in the Jhind State. (Original in Urdu, dated 18/1/15).

*****

"As regards your request to me to send you a watch, this is what I have to say. They do not let me go outside this hospital at all, nor do they allow even the men of one's own village to come in to see one. There are British soldiers posted as sentries all round the hospital who neither permit us to go out nor outsiders to come in. That is the kind of hospital we are in. The babus in this place are of the kind that come to England for education, like Doctor Indar Singh. So it is impossible to arrange about the watch.

All the money I had is with you & ____ Singh. You know the facts. I have no money. ____ If I had I would arrange with some babu & send you the watch. ____ Singh too has left for India or I would borrow from him. I would never refuse you. My life itself is at your disposal. Take it if you will ___& what is there more than life? What can I do? If I could go out I could manage a theft or something like that. As it is nothing can be done. ____ As regards what you wrote about SOUVENIRS that I had a lot, there are three or four printed handkerchiefs, quite common things, & a comforter. I can send them or not as you wish. You wrote asking whether I was returning to the Punjab or going back to the trenches. I do not yet know for certain. If you will get me a hawaldar or a naik or a bugle-major (?) or if I can manage to become such, I will come at once. If not, I will never come. If no arrangement is possible ____ I cannot do it. Unless I am forced by an order I will do my very best to get out of it. But I shall act just as you tell me. I will come or not come, just as you write & tell me. I have told you how it has been with me. I said that I had the pain of heat (i.e. venereal disease) in my groin. If you & _____ Singh are in trouble certainly say that you are ill and have the pain in your groin. So you will come (here). Those who are ill in this way are certainly sent back to the Punjab."

From a Sikh in hospital to a friend serving with the regiment in France. (Original in Gurmukhi, dated 30/1/15).

*****

"Now I have seen the war I am very pleased. When we met the enemy hand to hand my heart exulted. The enemy suffered great loss & has now retreated. On our side are six kings; against us there is but one. How then can the enemy win?"

From a Sikh wounded & in hospital in England to his wife in the Punjab. (Original in Gurmukhi, dated 2/2/15).

*****

"A time of disaster has come. The young men are fighting. The guns are firing. The kings are looking on at the spectacle. (tamasha) Like dust in heaps the dead are lying before the trench. All of the __th except the depot are broken. Of the __th not a Sikh nor a Brahman nor any other is left. Jemadar ____ is a prisoner with the sepoys."

From a Sikh in hospital in England to his brother serving in a regiment in India. (Original in Gurmukhi, dated 9/2/15).

*****

"_____&______ have returned to India. Let me know when they arrive. Since the 10th of February I have returned to the trenches. (sic). For the wounded who recover to some extent are sent back there. My heart is very sorrowful. For _____&_____ have gone to their long home & ____ has returned to India. Therefore my heart is sorrowful."

The letter ends with a list of toys which he has sent for his children & of other presents which he has made, amongst them photographs of himself which he asks should be kept carefully to preserve his memory.

From a Sikh wounded & in hospital in England to his brother in India. (Original in Urdu, dated 10/2/15).

*****

"We are forbidden to write about the war. But it is a very tough job. For the rest you are a wise man & will understand."

From a Sikh wounded & in hospital in England to a Muhammadan armourer of his regiment in India. (Original in Urdu, dated 10/2/15).

*****

"This is not France where you can get two rupees for something worth a pice. On the contrary, England is a very hungry country & never gives anything for nothing. Many men have ordered watches from here costing 13 shillings. These watches go for a fortnight & then stop for ever. I do not know where I shall go from here. Perhaps I shall rejoin you. The government can send me where it pleases. I pray "Oh great Guru, who art my real king, send me not back to that place.""

From Sikh wounded & in hospital in England to a friend at the front. (Original in Gurmukhi, dated 12/2/15).

*****

"The board has not yet considered my case. When it does, it will be India or back to you. Repeat the name of the Guru & save yourself. Keep as much under cover as you can when you are at the telephone. Save your life. Take ____ aside & explain this to him. You are wise. There is no call for valour and nonsense of that sort. Keep in mind what I have written in this letter & do not tell any one."

From a Sikh wounded & now in hospital in England to a friend at the front. (Original in Urdu, dated 13/2/15).

*****

"Stay in the village and carry on the work as headman. Do not go anywhere else. Think over what I say & you will understand what I mean when I say "stay in the village.""

From a Sikh wounded & in hospital in England to a brother in India. (Original in Gurmukhi, dated 14/2/15).

*****

"I am using your envelope to answer your letter. To-day the 15th of February I summoned the Sahib who writes the petitions. He asked me how I was & this is what I told him.

I said that my father was an old man about 80 years of age, and that there were four men named Ranjit Singh son of Sohan, Indar Singh son of Hakim Singh, Arjan Singh son of Gangu, & Bhagat Singh son of Hanal, two of whom, Ranjit Singh & Indar Singh, caught my father, bound him, beat him soundly & robbed him of him of his gold ring. The other two who came behind were to kill him, but some passers-by rescued him. The four men then said "You have escaped this time. The next time we shall set dacoits on you, beat you to death & burn your house."

The Sahib told me not to worry. He would write a petition to the Deputy Commissioner who would arrange matters. _____Perhaps I shall go to India in a few days. But keep in mind what I have said about the petition. Tell no one."

From a Sikh wounded & in England to his brother in France. (Original in Urdu, dated 15/2/15).

*****

"There is much fighting. We have no news of it. England, France, Russia, Belgium, Japan. (sic). The English are very strong & will beat the Germans. Germany will give way. She has already retired thirty five miles. On the one side there are these five. On the other side there are few men."

From a Sikh in hospital in England to a friend in India. (Original in Gurmukhi, dated 16/2/15).

*****

"Everyman that recovers goes straight to the trenches. If a man is worthless they send him to India. Even if a man has only one finger in his left hand he goes to the firing line. The truth is we are all to be killed. We are sent to Aubassi (La Bassée) if we go at all, and not to any other place. We are all to be killed. Not a scrap of India is to be left. What I wrote in my last letter is true."

From a Sikh at the Convalescent Home, New Milton, 9th Bhopals, to a Sepoy in India. (Gurmukhi of 17/2/15).

*****

"My father & mother, brothers & sisters, you call those your sons & daughters who give you money. Those who do not you refuse to look upon & you even drag them before the law courts. Here the ladies (Meman) tend us who have been wounded as a mother tends her child. They pour milk into our mouths & our own parents, brothers & sisters, were we ill, would only give us water in a pot. There you see the brotherhood of religion, & here you see the brotherhood of the English who are kind to us without any further motive. The ladies even carry off our excreta, so kind are they, and whatsoever we have a liking for, they put it into our mouths. They wash our bed-clothes every week & massage our backs when they ache from lying in bed.

They put us in motor cars & take us through the city. When, at four o'clock, we go out from the hospital, the ladies of the city give us fruit. They say "We have never seen such men. Only have we heard of them that they are the Sikhs of India who once fought against England. Now do we see them with our own eyes as we see our sons." They cheer us for routing the Germans. Their kings say "Brothers, what manner of men are the Indians?" The government gives us envelopes every week. _____This is a devils' war. When will it end? If I recover, I shall not remain a soldier, but serve my parents who have food enough & to spare. (Military) service is great weariness. I shall browse on the grass at home & keep myself alive. I am wounded. The man who has lost a leg or an arm returns to India. My ankle is broken. I was hit twice. My life is safe, but my leg is useless."

From a Sikh in hospital in England to his father in the Punjab. (Gurmukhi, dated 20/2/15).

*****

"Brother, I may tell you nothing about the war. If I return I will tell you all about it. It is not a war of kings. The Germans capture & carry off French women (Meman) & cut off their breasts. We too do the same thing. The Belgian kingdom is wholly in the possession of the Germans. Flying ships sail over our heads. This is how the war goes on. Are you told the truth or do they tell you lies? Bombs are killing us & we are not accustomed to their use."

From a Sikh wounded & in England to a relative in India. (Gurmukhi, 24/2/15).

*****

"Any one here who certainly can never be fit for duty is after great difficulty sent back to India. But if a man can do even very little work, he is sent a second time into the trenches."

From a Sikh wounded & in England to his brother in Rangoon. (Gurmukhi, dated 26/2/15).

*****

"There are 160 hospitals in England & in each hospital there are 438 wounded men. There is no counting the number of wounded."

From a Sikh wounded & in hospital in England to a friend, an Indian officer of a regiment serving in India. (Gurmukhi, dated 26/2/15).

*****

"Further India has lost many men killed & wounded. Many of the English too have been killed & wounded. On our side are the (following) Rajas-: (1) India (2) England (3) Nabha (4) Patiala (5) Sangrur (Jhind) (7) Bhagsu (Dharamsala) (8) Baghar (Bikanir) (10) Farika (Africa) (11) Burmah (12) Belgium (13) France (14) Russia (15) Japan (16) Australia. Sixteen Rajas are fighting (for us). With the Germans are (2) Talia (i.e. Austria through a confusion with Australia) (3) Turkey. There are these three Rajas. We hope to beat the Germans. Further on both sides much damage has been done & there is no count of the number of men who have been killed & wounded. But there is a count of the Indians who have fallen & been wounded & are fighting. But of the men killed & wounded & still living in the other Rajas' armies there is no count because many villagers have died. When a shell falls in a village they are buried in the house by it.

Moreover the dead lie like chaff upon the threshing floor. What more can I say about the war? If I write the tears rise to my eyes. For the state of the parents of those who have fallen? Their parents & brethren are crying themselves to death. To die is all that the dead have left them to do."

From a Sikh wounded & in hospital in England to a friend in India. (Gurmukhi, dated 2/3/15).

*****

"I shall now give you a description of the war. A day will come when England & France & Belgium & Russia & Italy and India & Canada ___so many kings are on the English side___ will make an attack on Germany. Before May, there will be a charge & the charging host will rush like a dust-storm. No man will count their numbers, so great will be the battle line. Then there will be peace. Have no anxiety for me."

From a wounded Sikh in England to his uncle in India. (Gurmukhi, dated 5/3/15).

*****

"The fourth matter is this. You should not make a valiant effort to go into the firing-line. That is a very bad place indeed, so bad that I cannot describe it here. As far as possible arrange to remain behind. You can say to your double-company commander Sahibs "Huzur, my service has been very long. Please put me on some duty here." Many Indian officers with long service have been sent to Marseilles from the firing-line itself. My urgent advice to you is to arrange to stay in Marseilles."

From a wounded Sikh at Brockenhurst to a Subedar of the 34th Pioneers serving in France. (Urdu & Gurmukhi, dated 10/3/15).

*****

"The newspapers that they print tell lies. They do not contain news of us."

From a Sikh wounded & in hospital in England to his father in India. (Gurmukhi, dated 14/3/15).

*****

"You are our father now & are wise. I do not expect ever to meet you again. ____ Singh is dead & we are utterly destroyed. None is left, neither fathers nor sons. ___ Do not let Lait Singh come to the war. This is my most earnest injunction."

From a Sikh wounded & in hospital in England to his brother in the Punjab. (Urdu, dated 17/3/15).

*****

"I am delighted to hear that you are going to India. Do not wait a minute but go at once. On the 10th, 11th and 12th March there was a great battle. The Native Army (desi fauj) worked valiantly and took two miles of the enemy's line. The enemy suffered severely but our native losses were beyond measure. It is finished – vanished. What use is a reinforcement of 72 men? It is finished. You may take it as all over."

From an Indian Officer in the 15th Sikhs in Brighton to a Subedar. (Gurmukhi 17/3/15).

*****

"What is the truth of the report of our going back to India? What reason has so great a man as Wilcox Sahib to say what is not true?"

From a Sikh in Hospital in England to a friend at the front. (Gurmukhi of 25th March 1915).

*****

"The Sikhs did not turn even their noses. They were keen for the fight, and where one man fell, another from behind stood in his place. And we took pleasure in the battle."

From Bariam Singh, 47th Sikhs in hospital in England to his friend in India. (Gurmukhi, 31/3/15).

*****

"The Germans have asked for pardon from both France and Belgium. "But" he says "I shall not come to terms with the English." He is evacuating the whole country of Belgium. France is sitting quietly by and not attacking. Our people attack frequently. The battle began on the 10th of the 3rd month. The Germans are starving and gave themselves up – about a 1000 have come in. We hope that peace will be made in the fourth month. The water in the trenches in up to a man's waist. Take care, don't let anyone come here even by mistake."

From a Sikh in Hospital in Brighton to a Sepoy in the 67th Punjabis, Jhelum. (Gurmukhi, of 2/4/15).

*****

"This letter is written in great trouble. Read it with equal care, and mark its contents. We have done a deed and suffered Hell in our lifetime. We are helpless. God alone directs events. Diyal Singh, why dost thou weep? We have been wounded and come to England. Our religion (Dharm) is destroyed because we eat biscuits, which God gives. At the eighth watch (i.e. every 24 hours) we get one biscuit, as is written in our fate by God. We also get a glass of tea, which we drink as an "amrat" (amrit?) (i.e. to purge away all sin), as is written in our fate."

(The whole letter is written in a sort of poetry).
From Diyal Singh now in hospital at Brighton, to Hazura Singh, in India. (Gurmukhi, 20/4/15).

*****

"I have had an interview with the grand daughters of King Ranjit Singh. They gave me a memento, a pair of socks. They come to see Sikhs from time to time. To this day they speak Punjabi plainly, and I have sent the socks home by the hand of a friend as a memento."

From Havaldar Jass Singh, now in hospital in England to Bir Singh, 23rd Pioneers, Aden. (Gurmukhi, 21/4/15).

*****

"Do not be anxious about me. We are very well looked after. White soldiers are always beside our beds – day and night. We get very good food four times a day. We also get milk. Our Hospital is in the place where the King used to have his Throne. Every man is washed once in hot water. The King has given a strict order that no trouble is to be given to any black man in hospital. Men in hospital are tended like flowers, and the King and Queen sometimes come to visit them."

From Isar Singh, 59th Rifles in India, General Hospital, Brighton, to a friend in 30th Punjabis, India. (Gurmukhi, 1/5/15).

*****

"In the regiment we were not allowed to write any news. First an Indian Officer read the letter then the Double Company Commander, and if there was any news in it the letter was torn up and the writer punished. Now I am writing from hospital. The battle is very hard. Perhaps some men return to India. No one will come whole, but only after sacrificing a part of himself. The man who returns is very lucky. There is no hope of return. But I hope to come back. Not a man of our regiment remains – some are dead and some wounded. In this hospital we are well looked after and lack nothing. We are in great ease. In the trenches we underwent great hardship. Now we are in heaven and have forgotten our hardships."

From Birhar Singh, Havildar, 47th Sikhs, in hospital, Brighton, to a friend in India. (Gurmukhi of 6/5/15).

*****

"I have seen the King, his eldest son, and his daughter. The King asked me what regiment I was in. I said "the ninth". When was I wounded? I told him "the 28th of October". Was I willing to return to the front? I said "yes". Had I any complaint? "No". After saying this he went away. He had a Sahib with him who understood my language. The King was on horseback, so was the Sahib – there was no guard or anything of that kind. The King is very good. When I saluted he took off his hat to acknowledge the salute. I have seen the King's palace. It is very fine, full of churches and fortresses. The railways are 100 feet under the ground and the city is built on the top of them. They go under water also. They are well worth seeing."

From a Sikh in the 9th Bhopal Infantry, New Milton, to his brother in India. (Gurmukhi of 8/5/15).

*****

"A wounded man is told by everyone that he is lucky, because no one can escape altogether in this war, which is a desperate war. I did not tell you about the war before but I can do so now I am in hospital. I cannot write to you about everything for that would be a long story, but I shall tell you all if the Guru takes me home again. This war has done our people great damage. When the fight begins one man does not recognise another. Not a man in our regiment is left. Some are killed, others wounded. Only a few of the wounded die. The German King is very powerful. When there is a new invention it is he who first puts it into practice. The English copy it when they see it. The German King is very clever. He is the master, the English are his disciples."

From Bishen Singh, in hospital in England to a friend in India. (Gurmukhi dated 14/5/15).

*****

"In Europe there is much lust but nothing of the nature of modesty. The result of the fighting is that corpses grow as thick as straw in watered wheat. If I wrote all day I could not tell you what my eyes have seen. The 47th Sikhs now consist of reservists of the 35th 87th and 31st and the 36th. 200 rifles have come from the 35th and 47th (? reservists).

Of a total of 2800 there remain now 96. All this is true. The Lahore and Meerut Divisions are in France. We do not know about the others. No one is in the 47th."

From Jagat Singh, 47th Sikhs at Brighton to a friend in India. (Gurmukhi of 16th May 1915).

*****

"If the true God grants me life on this occasion I shall see you again some day. If not, I cannot help it. Had I known anything of the facts I should have come and met you there. I thought that reservists were not going to fight, but I was deceived. I was sure that our regiment was not at the war and that if we were sent anywhere it would be to China where the regiment was. Our sepoys petitioned the Officer commanding the depot to be sent there. This was not granted, and we could not refuse to come here to the war, for the British Government was paying us for work in just such a difficulty. We are men of very little understanding, for since a reservist sepoy fights for just two rupees just as the man who draws a hundred rupees."

From Indar Singh, Company B, 47th Sikhs, Military Depot, Milford-on-sea to a friend in India. (Urdu, of 18/5/15).

*****

"Here there are many pears of the kind you have in your garden. They encounter our people on our walks and we sit down and enjoy them. Then we are put in jail."

From a Sikh in Hospital, Brighton, to a friend in the Punjab. (Gurmukhi, dated 7th June 1915).

*****

"The place we call Paradise is this country. There is no glare and no dust and no darkness. Fairies are the people of this country. The shopkeepers and the buyers are all women. There men have nothing to do with this. Sometimes the sun shines, but with moderate heat only. It rains every second day. The sea is all around. There is little cultivation. Everyone is in the same kind of service. The land is sufficient only to keep numbers of bullocks, horses, cows, sheep and pigs. There is not one house that is not built of bricks or masonry. All the houses are alike. The storm of death is raging."

From Jagat Singh, 47th Sikhs, Hospital, Brighton, to his brother in India. (Gurmukhi, of 16/6/15).

*****

"Moreover some wounded and sick will escape from this country. Very few will return well and sound. The regiments have been filled four times each and even then there is no one left. I was wounded in Belgium in the trenches. There is a hill called Number 60. You can see it on the map. Here a stiff battle was fought. 22000 attacked. 18000 died. 4000 remained. The roads ran blood."

From Bhagwan Singh in hospital, Brighton, to Basant Singh, 32nd Pioneers, Sialkot. (Gurmukhi dated 19/6/15).

*****

"We are in England but are treated like convicts. Every day we go to take the air but a European Sergeant and an Indian Babu accompany us."

From Naik Narain Singh, No.8 A. Indian General Hospital, Mont Dore, Bournemouth, to a friend in India. (Urdu, 22/6/15).

*****

"The people pay us great respect. Ladies old and young kiss our hands and take us home and feed us with fruit etc. People who have been in India are not so kind unless they belong to the Army. Those who are in the Army are good. Now our Government will be victorious. The Germans are not so strong as popular opinion in India supposed them to be at first."

From Subedar Ram Singh, Pavilion, Brighton, to a friend in India. (Gurmukhi, dated 29/6/15).

*****

"After describing France in the usual manner (no camels nor buffaloes, the women like "mem-sahibs" etc) the writer says "The people are very affectionate and our men are being ruined.""

From Budh Singh, No.3483, Kitchener's General Hospital, Brighton, to a friend in India. (Gurmukhi, 8/7/15).

*****

"The hopes by which we people were led to come here have not been fulfilled in the least. This Commanding Officer has not done anything for any of our havaldars or other Indian Officers, in spite of great efforts to persuade him."

From Havaldar Amar Singh, Pavilion Hospital, Brighton, to a Sepoy in the 30th Punjabis. (Gurmukhi of 10/7/15).

*****

"Every evening the youths one and all go to the town where women meet them. The women have no modesty but walk with the men who please them most. Marriage is by choice. Already there are five women, and after the war it is expected that there will be ten women for every man. Everyone who goes to the closet in town pays 4 pice, and the charge for using the urinal in four pice, and a pound of butter costs twelve annas."

From Surjan Singh in hospital Brighton to his friend in India. (Gurmukhi of 18/7/15). (In describing England the writer concludes).

*****

"They take great care of us here such as no one else could take except a man's mother, not even his wife. If a man falls sick at home and remains ill for a month the whole household grows weary of his illness, but these people don't grow weary. The arrangements for our food are very good, because men have been selected from the regiment to look after it and every man is served by his caste-fellows. First we suffered because the trenches were ill made, but now they are very strong and there are no losses in the trenches and no hardship. Much rain falls and if you dig down a little way in the ground you come upon water. It is very cold but we have plenty of clothing and get good rations. Our regiment has got the better of all the other regiments as they agreed to eat biscuits and European bread, but our regiment refused. So now we get "ata", and the other regiments get biscuits and bad at that. People told us that there was no "ata" in this country and we should have to eat biscuits, but where there are inhabitants there "ata" must be obtainable. Besides, there are plenty of mills."

From Bir Singh, 55th Rifles, now in hospital in England, to Gunga Singh, same regiment at Kohat in India. (Gurmukhi, 17th July 1915).

*****

"You mentioned that there were two Sikhs of Subr. Kala Singh's village in the 57th Rifles and asked about them. I will tell you. One of them is dead, and the other has got eight years imprisonment. The reason for his imprisonment was that he fired and wounded himself. A white man (gora) caught him, and so he was sentenced. He did this when he came to leave the Subr. (sic). After he had left him he did not go back to the regiment but wounded himself and got into the motor car. The motor car driver said "You have just gone away from here. Why have you come back so quickly?" ----- ---- Get some medicine from the babu and send it to me, some stuff that will make me ill. When I get back something may turn up. There is no use in my staying on."

(It appears from the letter that both the writer's sons in India are recently dead.)
From Mangul Singh in hospital at Barton to Jemdr. Bhur Singh, in India. (regiment not mentioned). (Gurmukhi, 20/7/15).

*****

"Do not be anxious about the punishment. A wounded man from the depot has told me that an order has been sent to the Indian Depot cancelling the punishment order. It is a very good thing that the punishment has been remitted. But you must not be at fault. The Government of course can do as it likes. God sees all things."

From Arjan Singh, 47th Sikhs, Indian Convalescent Home, England, to Arjan Singh, 35th Sikhs, attached 47th Sikhs, serving in France. (Urdu, 20/7/15).

*****

"I am very much annoyed because the officers here are very bad. The work which they give me here to do, if I were to do it, could not be accomplished day and night. I came here to serve as a soldier, but they threaten me with severe punishment. I have written to the officer commanding the 47th Sikhs to say that I want to come away from my present task. I do not care for death. We all have to go to the Great King's Palace. For death I do not care. But I will not stand being spoken to by Babus in a way that pierces a soldier's heart. It is worse than bullets. I will tell you the rest in another letter."

From Ward Orderly Diwan Singh, in hospital in England, to Bir Singh, 47th Sikh Rifles, serving in France. (Gurmukhi, 24th July 1915).

*****

"They do not allow us to go out of this hospital. There are guards of British soldiers set round the hospital and the place is enclosed with wire too. They give us plenty to eat."

From Bhan Singh, wounded in hospital in England, to Bhagat Singh, 51st Sikhs, serving in Egypt. (Gurmukhi, 28th July 1915).

*****

"When this letter reaches you in the month of Katik, I shall be back at the front. You wrote to me saying "When you come to the Punjab, write to me, I shall be at Amballa." But it is not my fate to come to the Punjab. The medical board has sent me back to the firing line, and I am not coming to the Punjab. I am going to France. I have no expectation of ever seeing you again, but while there is life there is hope."

From Das Mul Singh, in hospital in England, to Bakhshish Singh in India. (No language/date stated).

*****

"My ceaseless prayer is that the Holy Guru may never show you this war. I cannot tell you about it, it will be for the best for you if you remain drilling recruits in India."

From Bishen Singh, hospital, Brighton, to Chanan Singh, 34th Pioneers, Ambala. (Urdu, 4/8/15).

*****

"I have often written to you that it is my privilege to fight. I have no fear of death and am returning to the trenches a second time of my own free will. I am very well, although my arm is a little weak, and am fit for work."

From Chet Singh at Milton-on-sea, to a friend in India. (Gurmukhi, 7/8/15).

*****

"As regards what you write about the 9th and 125th Regiments, these battalions have gone. General Wilcox has sent then back saying these two regiments are not fit to fight. They have not done well in France. Kehar Singh has written saying they were perhaps going back to India and that there is nothing now to be done on the Canal. Now hear about this place. Bread is baked on gas stoves etc etc etc. When we arrived there were no arrangements for us Sikhs but now by the Guru's kindness a Gurdwara has been built and twice daily a fine service is celebrated in it. Every Sunday there is a meeting which many Sikhs attend. Prayers are offered and many sacred texts read. There are seven Granth Sahibs." (Sikh Scriptures)

From Balwant Singh, K.I.H Brighton, to Jemadar Ishar Singh, 21st Punjabis, Peshawar. (Gurmukhi, 11/8/15).

*****

"Formerly we used to go into the town, but the men began to misbehave badly and we were stopped from going. Now only the sick go to the town. If anyone climbs a wall and stays out he gets a dozen lashes. We are let out into the town once a month – and then only two or three men with two or three white soldiers. For this we have only ourselves to thank, for had those rascals not misbehaved we should still be allowed to go out every day. In the days when there was no restriction, two or three men used to spend a couple of nights or more in the town. They were given a dozen lashes, but this did not prevent them from behaving as before. So the present rule was enforced."

From Tulsi Ram, Asst. Storekeeper, Kitchener Indian Hospital, Brighton, to a friend in Peshawar. (Gurmukhi, 12/8/15).

*****

"I am lying here half killed by gas. For this there is no remedy. About three ounces of blood came from the mouth and there is vomiting with pain. The liver burns and the temperature rises to 104 degrees. I have escaped with my life, or, rather, I have been born again. x x x Many Emperors have come here. Three or four Kings are together, but their strength avails nothing."

From Hari Singh, hospital, Brighton, to a friend in India. (Gurmukhi, 18/8/15).

*****

"Here too we are in great discomfort. The sick in all the hospitals are gathered together and paraded. The men cry and moan but no one listens to them."

From Rur Singh, 15th Sikhs, K.I.G.H., Brighton, to Basant Singh, 15th Sikhs, Marseilles. (Gurmukhi, 5/9/15).

*****

"This is the Lord Roberts of the Indian Army. He died of the cold. He was old and came to see the Army in France."

From a Sikh at Brighton to a friend in India. (Gurmukhi on the back of a picture postcard (Lord Roberts)).

*****

"Here there is nothing new, nor have I heard any news. You probably know that we have parades twice a day, morning and evening. We can say nothing. The sick are much worried and harassed."

From a Sikh in Kitchener Indian Hospital, Brighton, to a friend in the Convalescent Camp, Boulogne. (Gurmukhi, 16/9/15).

*****

"England is a very fine country. The women are like fairies. I cannot describe them, so excessively beautiful are they. Now, in truth, let me die; I have seen many things. Now nothing troubles me. Here there are many good things. If you want any, let me know. First there are fine glasses which enable one to count the bones in one's body, even when dressed. Another shows a man's face beautiful although it be ugly. Another enlarges a man's face, if it be small. Also there are very good rings, also there is a mechanical lamp which shines in the dark. What shall I bring you? I cannot count all the things. The country is very good............."

From Hirnam Singh, 9th Bhopal Infantry, Hospital, Brighton, to Kapur Singh, Hoshiarpur, India. (Gurmukhi, dated 29/9/15).

*****

"On the 14th the Emperor gave me two medals. He decorated me with his own hands in his palace in London. An account of it has been published with a photograph in all the papers. By mistake only one medal was mentioned but I was given two. The occasion did me very great honour. They treat me with great respect in London. I am always given a motor car in which I go to see the famous places. All this is by the grace of God, and the favour of our Captain of our company and the (good work) of the company itself. And I was only a poor Jat! My thoughts are now very much towards my company and I pray always to the Guru for its welfare."

From Sub.Major Sundar Singh, Brighton, to Hav. Basant Singh, 1st Sappers and Miners, France. (Gurmukhi, 19/10/15).

*****

"In London there is in a museum a copy of the Granth Sahib (Sikh Scriptures) of the tenth Guru. It is placed open in a cupboard. The sight saddened my heart for it is lying on the ground and not open upon a stand of any kind."

From Kehar Singh, S.A.S., Brighton, to Indar Singh, S.A.S. Hospital Ship (?) Gascon, Southampton. (Urdu, 21/10/15).

*****

"As regards your advice to me to stay where I am – if I am made ward orderly they will pass me as fit and send me to France very quickly. The rule these doctors follow is to put on some duty here any man who is lame or has a useless hand, and then, after a month, to write him down as a malingerer and pack him off to France. The very dust of which we are made is corrupted. They even punish a man for going lame. My brother, I cannot get rid of my lameness, but they are not sending me to India. Our Major is a good man, so I am willing to rejoin. The doctor of the place I go to, wherever it be, is sure to send me to India. I am not being made ward orderly."

From Ram Singh, K.I.H. Brighton, to Jam. Dhola Singh, 47th Sikhs, France. (Gurmukhi, 21/10/15).

*****

"I have been wounded and am in hospital in England. The bullet hit me in my left shoulder but I was not damaged badly. My arm is strong again. You say that wounded men have returned with pensions – well – that rests with the Guru to decide. If it be my fate, I shall return to my life in India. If not, then there is no hope, unless the war ends, of my ever coming home, for those who recover from their wounds are sent back to the war."

From Balwant Singh, 47th Sikhs, Brighton, to a friend in India. (Gurmukhi, 24/10/15).

*****

"You wrote telling me not to return but to remain here. I have no choice to stay here. We have to do what we are told. I have no longing to return. Meanwhile I hope that I shall eventually go back to India. Medical Boards are held at very many places, but the doctors here are civilians and they do not know that a lame man cannot march with a regiment. All these doctors do is cure the wound and after a day or two report the man fit for the trenches. The completely useless men return to India. From Marseilles however a great many men are sent to India. It is certain that I shall not get rid of my lameness, for the bullet hit me in the ankle which makes it difficult for me (to walk). It is painful to put on my boots and there is also some swelling."

From Ram Singh, 47th Sikhs, Brighton to a Sikh in the 47th Sikhs, France. (Gurmukhi, 26/10/15).

*****

"I will return to you in a few days. There is great hardship in the hospital now. The lame and the halt are being sent back to the front. Who will let me go back to India?"

From Sher Singh, Milford, to Hav. Kehr Singh, 34th Pioneers, France. (Gurmukhi, 29/10/15).

*****

"There is great hardship in the hospital. (Only) those who are (quite) unfit to work go back to India. Even the wounded they are most reluctant to allow to return to India. There is nothing else to be anxious about."

From Sher Singh, Milford, to Hav. Keth Singh, 34th Pioneers. (Gurmukhi, 3/11/15).

*****

"Government has given orders that no one is to trouble the wife and children of a man on service, nor his father either. I am being troubled by a transgression of the government orders."

From Kehr Singh, Brighton, to Ram Singh, Ferozepore. (Gurmukhi, 4/11/15).

*****

"Your humble servant has got the bahaduri medal. On it is written "For Distinguished Service". There is no money attached to it, but it is a great distinction and every officer who sees it is exceedingly pleased. They say if I go back to the front I shall get a military cross. I am not afraid of dying, but my hand is no use, and even a letter is very difficult to write."

From Nk. Mit Singh, 47th Sikhs, Brighton, to Subedar Bhan Singh, 47th Sikhs, Marseille. (Gurmukhi, 7/11/15).

*****

"There is a Sikh church in each hospital. Sirdar Buta Singh, has sent us a large number of "Granth Sahibs" (scriptures), and we are very happy in our hospitals. Services are held just as in India. Government has made excellent arrangements for the sick and wounded. There is no trouble of any kind. We pass our days in joyful ease while government showers benefits upon us. We bless God continually and pray for his bounty."

From Ranjit Singh, 38th C.I.H., York Place Hospital, Brighton, to a friend in India. (Gurmukhi, 10/11/15).

*****

"Your obedient servant begs to represent that he has fifteen years' service; that he has performed his duties faithfully and that he has put in a year and a half in the trenches. He was wounded on one occasion and was obliged against his will to go to hospital. He did not go to hospital for his own ends. He has suffered very severely. Then he served again in the trenches and was again severely wounded on the 25th September. Now one of his juniors in the regiment has been promoted to Jemadar, a man who has never even seen the trenches. For the rest, your honour has full power. If your honour sends for your servant, he can come. He is in perfect health again. If your honour wishes to bestow on him the rank (of Jemadar) please send for him. If not, be pleased to send a reply to this letter. Your servant has come from his country to fight and to win promotion, and not to sit in hospital. Your servant has now quite recovered."

From Hav. Budh Singh, 58th Rifles, Indian Convalescent Home, New Milton, to the Officer Commanding 58th Rifles. (Urdu, 8/12/15).

*****

"This hospital is six hours distant (from Brighton). It is very cold. There are 24 beds, 16 doors and 18 windows. It is very windy. There is no fireplace. We are not given milk. Only a few of the sick get milk. The board sits twice a week. We have three blankets over us. It is very cold. We have to call the nurses "mother", and the European soldiers "Orderly Sahib" – if we do not we are reported. The five Brighton hospitals are good. The others are not good. We are not given soap. We got nothing. There is a good "Gurdwara" (Sikh Church). Our ward orderlies are black men. A Major is in command. Under him are lady nurses, as in China."

From Sepoy Ranga Singh, 124th Bilochis, Lady Hardinge Hospital, Brockenhurst, to L.N. Jagandur Singh, 35th Sikhs, Dome Hospital, Brighton. (Gurmukhi, 30/12/15).

*****

"Do not write to me here again, for I am off directly and hope to see you soon. For the Guru has been very gracious to me. This is all due to him and to the kindness of the Doctor Sahib. Do not let it worry you at all, but, my friend, I really do not want to leave this place and come back to India, because this country of our King is a very beautiful one and all the people are learned. My salaams to all."

From Jagindra Singh, 58th Rifles, K.I.H., Brighton, to Sardar Sabha Singh, Ludhiana, India. (Urdu, 11/1/16).

*****

Picnic party photograph depicting a large mixed group of civilians and wounded Indian soldiers posing for the camera at The Kitchener Hospital, 1915. (Royal Pavilion & Museums, Brighton & Hove)

*****

"You will be pleased to hear that on the 5th of this month the king himself invested me with the D.C.M. at Buckingham Palace. I expect you have read about it in the papers. I have now come back from London, but I am going there again with about twenty-six other Indian officers on the 11th of this month. We are going to present a farewell address to the King. I hope that I shall read it."

From Sub. Sher Singh, Ind. Conval. Home, Barton, to Babu Gurcharan Singh, Lahore. (Urdu, 9/2/16).

*****

"And my friend, this is a photo of our King's granddaughter. He who was King of the Sikhs Ranjit Singh. She has distributed her photo amongst Sikh brethren at the depot (Milford) in the evening of the 23rd Feby. at 5 o'clock."

Written on the back of a photo of a lady signed Sophia A. Duleep Singh, 1916.
From Kartar Singh, 15th Sikhs, Milford-on-sea, to Gurdit Singh, Rae-Wind, Punjab. (Gurmukhi, 24/2/16).

*****

"I have already, I think, told you something about my visit to England. To see such a large city and so fine a country properly, one week is quite insufficient. It is impossible to state in this small letter, the impression left on my mind by the magnificent buildings that I saw, and the evidence of the great power of England. If I live to return, I will tell you all about it."

From Hira Singh, Risaldar Major, 30th Lancers, France, to Sirdar Sant Singh, Intelligence Branch, Kennedy Lodge, Simla, India. (Urdu, 24/5/16).

*****

"I must write and give you a brief account of my trip to England. The first day I visited the Museum and in the afternoon some of the leading shops. The managers of some of these get as much as 75,000 rupees a year. In the afternoon of the next day I went to tea with the Secretary of State for India and he gave us an excellent little entertainment after tea. The little daughter of the Secretary of State, about 11 years old helped us to tea. The next day we visited His Majesty and saw the investiture of officers who had distinguished themselves in this war. Then the King expressed his pleasure at seeing us and ordered the Royal stables to be shown to us. We saw 84 saddle and harness horses and several motors. We also saw a little carriage used by Queen Victoria in her childhood and also a little two-wheeled donkey buggy in which she used to drive. There was also a four-wheeled carriage used by King George III in 1781 made entirely of wood which cost a lakh of rupees. In the afternoon we saw the Houses of Parliament. One room there is 400 years old and the body of Edward VII lay in state there for four days. It is called Westminster Hall. Next day we saw Hampton Court Palace. There is a magnificent Garden there with a vine 150 years old which bears 2000 bunches of grapes. Thence we went to the house of the daughter of Maharaja Ranjit Singh who gave us tea and coffee, and expressed her pleasure at seeing us. She also gave us "Khir" and we stayed for an hour and a half. Thence we went to the Aviary, and saw many wonderful things, among them a tortoise 200 years old and a snake which swallows a goat whole every month and takes a month to digest it. We also saw the reindeer which is used for ploughing and whose milk is drunk. We went to Sheffield the next day and inspected the factories. The managers were very kind and took us all over the place and explained everything. Sheffield is 14 hours from London. The next day we rode in the Park for 4 hours. There are thousands of chairs for visitors and arrangements for eating and drinking. We then went to Madam Tussauds and saw many interesting wax figures including a Russian soldier 8.5 feet tall, and General Tom Thumb only 3 feet 3 inches high. The Duke of Wellington who conquered at Waterloo has more medals than anyone has ever had. In the afternoon we went to the Theatre and saw dancing by a French girl who is said to be celebrated all over the world. The next day we went to Portsmouth and on board a submarine which dived with us and we had a look through the periscope. The next day we visited Windsor Castle and the King's cattle belonging to his home farm."

From Risaldar Mul Singh, 30th Lancers, France, to Risaldar Major Bahadur Singh, Depot, 30th Lancers, India. (Urdu, 16/6/16).

*****

"What am I to say about Valait (London). It is a very big city and very beautiful. The shops and factories are worked entirely by women. Seeing this I was very delighted because the women were aiding the Sircar. Consider the condition of our women in India! This is due to a lack of education, and to nothing else."

From Hazura Singh, Jemadar, 38th Central India Horse, France to Lall Singh, Ferozepore District, Punjab, India. (Urdu dated the 16th February, 1917).

*****

4

Loyalty and the King Emperor

We came to defeat the King's enemies. They are not yet defeated.

For eighteen years I have eaten salt at the hand of our Emperor and now I shall repay him with my loyalty.

We are known to be a military people and loyalty is our fundamental principle.

Here lies the martyr Sikh Guru, who prophesied the advent of the British in India.

One multi-faceted part of the Sikh soldier's story of the Great War was loyalty. The creation of this loyalty and how this transpired is described in this chapter. The Sikh soldier when swearing an oath on the *Guru Granth Sahib* on enlistment was also required to swear allegiance and loyalty to the British. The King became an almost mythical figure at the zenith of Empire. Many Sikh soldiers mentioned being loyal to a King that they had no real knowledge of. One of the methods used to engender such loyalty were references to Sikh scriptures. Verses were extracted and their meanings manipulated to make them useful to the British cause. So a particular verse using what might be described as 'war' or 'battle' based references were used and propagated to the Sikhs in their literal meanings, rather than the original thought which was more the 'battle' of the mind. Further in other revered Sikh works where the English translation referenced the word 'master' – it was used in the context that the British were the master rather than *Waheguru*. Many such manipulations of the Sikh scriptures occurred during the British period.

To allow this to happen the British needed certain Sikhs to become collaborators for the Raj. Such sycophant Sikhs were unfortunately readily available, including some Sikh Maharajas and certain aristocratic families who would supply wealth and propaganda to their British overlords to ensure that their privileged positions would be maintained. This favour would manifest itself in many ways; manpower through the supply of Imperial Service troops, speeches made at massive *durbars* exhorting co-religionists to fight for the British as the 'Sikh religion required them to do!' In fact, some Maharajas would go to great lengths to highlight their loyalty.

Some, if not all, of the newspaper editors would be very pro-British, encouraging Sikhs to fight. Many rural Sikhs were at this point illiterate and these articles would be read aloud in villages, backed up by the alleged references to religion. Letters from Sikh soldiers further emphasised how these messages must have been well spread. Stating messages such as, "I congratulate you on having given full proof of your loyalty & fidelity to the King & shown no regard for your life." Many Sikh soldiers also believed that by showing loyalty to the British in their time of need would bring benefits after the war. Indeed, land grants did become commonplace but not all such promises would be kept.

Messages from Sikhs at the front would again be a powerful propaganda tool for the British. Many newspapers would carry stories sent from Sikh soldiers about German or Turkish brutality. Although propaganda, these stories would shed light on the life of that particular soldier. Even the fabled Rudyard Kipling was drafted in by British Intelligence officers in 1917 to write fictitious letters from Indian soldiers as a means of engendering further loyalty to the British crown.

Newspapers written in *Gurmukhi* would make their way to the soldiers at the various fronts. These newspapers such as the *Akhbar-i-Jung* and *Fauji Akhbar* would become very popular with the soldiers who would also write articles for them. The majority of these articles would be pro-British, and generally spoke about how the Sikhs were fighting for their religion and that the British were pro-Sikh.

The British, through the Indian Soldiers Fund wanted to ensure that the Indian soldiers did not have much to complain about, which may have created dissension. Food for the different religious groups was catered for by separate kitchens. Sikhs were supplied coconut oil for their hair and many religious articles were sent to the front. Some of these articles such as three thousand *Kara's* were shipped from Sheffield. These articles 'were made under the supervision of Sirdar Basheshar Singh, son of the Prime Minister of Patiala.' Three hundred 'handsome' copies of the *Guru Granth Sahib* were supplied along with other 'books suitable for the spiritual needs of the Sikhs.' These included "1100 *Panj Granthi's*, 1200 *Nit Nem's*, 168 *Guru Updesh's*, 10 *Janam Sakhi's*, 200 *Sachcha Sauda's* and 500 *Japji Sahib's*."[1]

The Sikhs in their letters mention the arrangements made by the Government, as they believed it to be, on several occasions. These include comments such as "Among all the nations engaged in this war, the arrangements of our King are the best" are commonplace. Many of the Sikh soldiers came from impoverished backgrounds and many stated "It was the duty of the Sikhs to serve their Government loyally and faithfully." These 'comforts' enjoyed by the Sikh troops also created loyalty to the British on a large scale. This led to poems being written from the front lauding the King Emperor. Proclamations of loyalty also came from Sikh organisations all over the world, from London to India to the Malay States.

*****

> "I was distressed to hear that you had been wounded. But God will have pity. Keep your thoughts fixed on the Almighty & show your loyalty to the Government & to King George V. It is every man's duty to fulfil his obligations towards God, by rendering the dues of loyalty to his King. If in rendering the dues of loyalty he must yield his life, let him be ready to make even that sacrifice. It is acceptable in the sight of God, that a man pays the due of loyalty to his King. God grant you life & happiness. Those heroes who have added lustre to the services of their country & King, let them offer this prayer before God, that victory may be the portion of their King, & let them show the whole world how brave the people of India can be.

1 British Library: L/MIL/5/828/1, Reports of the Censor of Indian Mails.

The final prayer of this humble one before God Almighty is this that God may make bright the heroes of Hindustan in the eyes of the world & with his healing hand may soften the sufferings of the wounded & restore them to health, so that they may go back to the field of battle & render the dues of loyalty to their King of peace, the King of kings, George V, & secure victory for him."

From X.Y. writing from Gobind Garh in the Punjab to a Jemadar in the 34th Sikh Pioneers now serving in France. (Original in Urdu).

*****

"Sir,
We are fully conscious of the pressure of work on the department at present, but at the same time we realise the importance of our mission. Therefore, we beg to trouble you to kindly arrange an interview for us with His Majesty's Secretary of State for India, at the earliest opportunity.
We wish: -

1. To express the sentiments of the Sikhs in the British Isles, arising out of the present crisis.
2. To put forward a few very important suggestions in connection with the complicated position of the Sikhs in Canada; and all along the Pacific Coast; resulting from the question of Hindu immigration to Canada; and aggravated by the undesirable influence there.

Requesting your due attention.
To the Political Aide-de-Camp
To the Secretary of State for India."

The Khalsa Jatha, British Isles, London. 79, Sinclair Road, West Kensington, 17th August 1914. Signed, Basheshar Singh, Sant Singh and Teja Singh Randhawa, Hon Secty; Khalsa Jatha.

*****

"Your letter reached me. It was as if you had come yourself. A thousand thousand thanks to our Guru who has stretched out his hand to preserve you from this terrible war. I congratulate you on having given full proof of your loyalty & fidelity to the King & shown no regard for your life. If you get a high place from the Government & much honour & exaltation, your life will be a source of pride to your family & kinsmen."

From a relative in India to a Sikh Subedar. The letter is addressed to a hospital in England. (Original in Urdu, dated 15/12/14).

*****

Three generations of soldiers from one Sikh family. (Courtesy of the Council of the National Army Museum, London)

*****

"I have had no letter from you, but from what I see in the papers you are busy fighting all the while & have no time to write. You who are serving in France have got a fine chance. Do your duty bravely for your King ... God bless him___& sacrifice your lives for him, if need be."

From X.Y. a sepoy in the 29th Punjabis serving in East Africa to a relative in the 47th Sikhs serving in France. (Original in Urdu).

*****

"Brother I fell ill with pneumonia & have come away from the war. In this country it rains a great deal, always night & day it rains. So pneumonia is very rife. Now I am quite well & there is no occasion for any kind of anxiety. I am in Wilayat___ every kindness. If any of us is wounded, or is otherwise ill, Government or someone else always treats him very kindly. Our Government takes great care of us, & we too will be loyal & fight. You must give the Government all the help it requires. Now look you my brother our father the King-Emperor of India needs us & any of us who refuses to help him in his need should be counted amongst the most polluted sinners. It is our first duty to show our loyal gratitude to Government."

From X.Y. a Sikh wounded in England to his brother at Amritsar. (Original in Gurmukhi, dated the 15th January 1915).

*****

1. Arise, awake Oh warriors, this is not the time for sleep.
The enemies are thundering over our heads, take up your arms.
Buckle on the five arms, and take your swords in hand.
Let rifles be on your shoulders and daggers tied round your waist.
You have to fight for your King, who is our "Sarkar".

2. The warrior Singh Sardars fight like mad lions.
The earth trembles when they assault.
From Egypt to China, they have made a name, Oh friend.
Sons of Guru, brave Sikhs, should thunder on the battlefield.
Sympathisers of the Emperor, heroes can they lag behind.

3. Rajputs and Gurkhas, who are great warriors,
Should arise and be prepared, as they eat the King's salt.
Oh Muslims and Pathans, who have lion-like figures.
Oh Brahmans, Hindus and other lakhs of sons of Bharia.
Girdle up your loins and proceed across the seas.

4. There is a war in Europe, where millions fight.
The Germans intoxicated with pride, are proud of their armies.
With the help of their ally they are menacing others.
If any one speaks to them of reasons they turn a deaf ear.
With greed for more land, they are causing a massacre of humanity.

5. George our King, who is full of dignity and magnanimity.
Had told the tyrants to keep peace of mind and explained.
"When justice could be done by the pen, why should we use arrows."
But the Germans intoxicated with pride, would not listen even to the advice of their Lord.
They attacked the weak and wanted to crush them.

6. Russia told them not to do so much 'Zulum'.
France also warned them to fear God.
Our King asked them to rest assured, he would settle all disputes.
They should meet and talk over the matter.
But the tyrants declared; we want this not, fight if you have valour.

7. Like a shameless person they attacked one with whom they had no cause of enmity and wanted to crush him.
Seeing Belgium powerless, they ran over her head.
They devastate the country of the weak, this is tyranny.
They commit. But brave sons of Belgium. You are adored in the four "Yugas".

8. Our King, having seen such an extreme injustice being done.
Drew at last from the scabbard his blade of victory.
One has to keep his word and stand by his friend, even at the loss of thousands of lives.
If once we take any one under our protection, we should never forsake him again.
The word of a man can not be broken, although women may do so thousands of times.

9. The Germans are cheats of the world and friend of necessity.
They pin no faith in promises or agreements.
They write treaties and then tear them away like a scrap of paper.
How can we trust such a nation of swankers.
They kill their own friends, and relatives in order to serve their own purpose.

10. They have caused havoc in Europe and they do not allow anyone to live in peace.
They have amassed a large army through "Zulum".
And devastated the country, lakhs of people are being killed by guns.
God will certainly destroy such tyrants and murderers.

11. To efface tyranny "Dharma" therefore fights -
Our King to uphold the right or religion.
William is the Daryodhan of the Kaliyuga and like Krishna (King) George supports the "Dharma".
Oh God, grant victory so that the bells and gongs may ring incessantly.

12. If there be such a King, hero of the Dharma as ours and his subject sacrifice -
Their lives, they are sure to go to "Swarga" (heaven).
Arise, Oh heroes, and warriors draw out your swords, this is the time to serve our King and it will never come again.
Oh Indians, advance forward and shine like the sun.

13. This is the time to prove your love of the Government and a lover's ambition is to die like a moth on a candle.
To love his King is a Sikh's religion and to crush the enemies of his King is his practice.
A warrior always engenders the love of his beloved to the end.

14. Arise, Oh warrior Sikhs, go across the seas; our brothers are already there and it is our turn now.
Shout cries of "Fateh" after conquering the Germans.
British flag will, certainly predominate, when Satguru and his Khalsas are at the back.

15. Come out Oh Handsome youths, brave and robust.
Buckle on the five arms and transform yourselves into sarkar's nice soldiers.
Do not love this life, every one in the world is to die one day.
If you serve your King, you would have done "duty of life".
There is no death better than one on the battlefield.
"Warrior is he who fights for (Dharma) duty and who would rather die being cut to pieces – than leave the field" (Tenth Guru).

16. To efface the "Zulum" is religion. This is the command of the Guru.
The Germans are great tyrants, efface their existence from the world.
You receive your succour from your Guru and the Great Russians and French are at your back.
All are enemies of the tyrants and want to stop the tyranny.
Roar, Oh, brave lions, and advance to the fight.
Blessed is the mother who bears forth a brave son.
Who goes to the field and either dies fighting or returns home victorious.
If mother be a lioness, she gives birth to a lion.
She lulls her baby with lullabies of war and her son grows up to be a brave "Singh".

17. Oh Singhs – leave the ploughs now and fetch the swords.
You have drunk the "Amrita" (nectar) of sword, now keep honour of the sword.
Let lakhs of you be recruited, to thunder in the battlefield.
The lions do not sit in the cultivated field, they show best in vast Arenas (Jungles).
Roar in the battlefields which are the retreats of the Singhs.

18. Go, my friends, do not love your homes, we have to obey command of the Guru, to serve our King.
We will be great in the world when our King is great.
The order of the Guru is "Deg-Teg and Fateh" (Hospitality, Sword and Victory).
Hari Buddh prays, may the Sarkar be victorious.

Translation of a Poem named "HALLI-DI-WAR." (By Bawa Budh Singh, Executive Engineer).
The Khalsa Advocate, Saturday, January 23, 1915.

*****

A Call to Duty

Cowards die many times before their deaths;
The valiant never taste of death but once.
W. SHAKESPEARE.

'The Mahabharata' of Europe is still going on, the most terrible war the world has ever known is still raging without showing the least sign of it being stopped soon. Both the parties are using the engines of destruction and ruin, the gods of which are still unsatisfied and work incessantly to slake their thirst for blood.

The Western civilisation has defeated in own purpose and has produced men who are killing one another. The whole of the world is today in a life and death struggles for liberty and honour and it is a question of the existence of certain States and Nations.

Our brethren are fighting in Belgium, France, Egypt and wherever their services are required, side by side with the troops of the allies and are reported to be doing excellent work to the utmost joy and satisfaction of those whose lot has been to remain behind in the land of five rivers, offering prayers to the Almighty Father for the success of the British arms, favourable issue of the war and the speedy return of the brethren to their homes – the sweet homes, like which there is no other place.

We are quite sure that the blood our brethren are shedding, in receiving the martyrdom for this noble cause, will not fail to be the seed of the church of 'Liberty', 'Peace', 'Honour' and 'Glory'.

When will the demon of war order a retreat? When will the god of destruction call halt to this carnage? Are the common questions of the day. The eyes of some of the believers are turned towards that 'Fountain of Love' which was seen five centuries back. They are waiting and waiting very anxiously, with the hearts beating and eyes wide open, the arrival of our Nanak with his white flag of 'All Peace'. If anyone can save humanity at this critical time it must be Nanak – The Guru in whose eyes Hindus and Muslims, Christians and Jews, Brahmans and 'Shudars', high and low, poor and peer are the same – the Sat Guru who preached the Gospel of Righteousness and Brotherhood of man. Had the world cared for his teachings, it would never met with such a hard lot, and even now if it pays a little attention to them, this great struggle with all the horrible consequences that come in its train, can be brought to a standstill – but, no, the world is hankering after money and matter and displaying an energy in reducing the flowers of the nations to dust and ashes and thus coming to the conclusion that only the fittest should survive. It is deaf to the teachings of Baba Nanak and takes pleasure in witnessing this bloody scene and has, with inward satisfaction, turned its eyes towards that great centre of activity and field of 'Death'.

The utter disregard of the teachings of the Gurus has brought us to such a strait, but yet it is not too late, while the beastly passions are still at their height let us try to act upon their teachings and instructions and find out what were their views regarding the war. Our Gurus were all in all for peace and courted it with all their might, they did not engage themselves in war for the sake of gaining political power and ruling over the kingdom, and the wars were not of their seeking and they always played a defensive part in the struggles in which they were obliged to enter. The following Swaya of Guru Gobind Singh shows clearly what his views regarding the political power, says he –

"If such Emperors were to march and conquer all the countries beating all kinds of drums.

If herds of beautiful elephants were to trumpet loudly and if thousands of horses of royal breed were to neigh there.

Although Emperors whether past, present or future, cannot be counted by anyone.

Yet without worshipping the Name of God; they must go to their final home (of death) empty handed."

But this does not mean that we should ignore his mission. He had come into the world to resist tyranny and rescue the world from the yoke of oppression. He himself has said –

"Understand ye! All pious people, I am born for this purpose – spreading the Sikh creed, raising the saints and rooting out all evil-doers."

Gentle readers! Are not the Germans evil-doers, have they not massacred and troubled thousands of innocent children and harmless women?

Then why are the lions still here, how long will the followers of Guru Gobind Singh let them do these evil deeds? According to the Divine Command –

"Spread here and there the reign of virtue
Arrest and punish the tyrants and evil-doers."

Guru Gobind Singh's sole object was to save the world from sins and sufferings. Khalsa Ji, are you fulfilling the mission of Guru Gobind Singh?

In order to achieve this noble object the Saviour administered the sacred Sikh baptism unto his followers and turned them into a real military nation. 'Amrita' was the machine that turned out such brave Sikhs who made our Saviour say –

"I will have the sparrows, hunt the hawks,
Then and there the world will call me Gobind Singh."

Our Gurus and martyrs did not attach the value to death which we do, they had realised fully well the following verse of Bhagat Kabir –

"Warrior is he who fights for (Dharma) duty, and he would rather die being cut into pieces, than leave the field."

Guru Gobind infused such spirit into his Sikhs that they became a shield to the weak and poor against the tyrants, says he –

"Blessed are those in the world on whose lips rests the name of the Lord and in whose mind dwells the idea of War".

"This mortal body does not last long, sit-test thou then in the boat of eternal fame and goest across the ocean of this World."

O True Sikhs! This is the time to serve your King and this golden chance to show what you are, will never come again. How beautifully has been said -

"If a woman is to give birth, she should bear generous and brave men, otherwise the woman should remain barren to save her honour."

He asked his Sikhs to be true to the salt very emphatically in the following words –

"Be loyal to your Sovereign; leave death and life in the hands of God. He who deserteth his master in the battlefield shall be dishonoured here and thrown into the hell hereafter."

The worst sin, the meanest crime for a Sikh is to run away from the field, the ideal was reached when he said –

"The vultures do not touch the corpse of a wretch, who foresaketh his master in the battlefield, and this is worth its weight in gold."

Oh Khalsa Ji! Awake arise; and prove yourselves the worthy sons of the 'Lord of the White Hawk'.

What does it matter; if you face the odds; you are the sons of the one who made a single Sikh fight hundreds of thousands. The tyrants are before you and it is now your duty to uphold the traditions of your ancestors.

Do not forget that you are fighting for the sake of glory and righteousness; you have entered the struggle for the sake of All-loving and beloved George, who is our Sarkar; and we are quite sure the foe will take to the heels when they hear your fine old and proud war cry of "Siri Wahi Guru Ji ka Khalsa, Siri Wahi Guru Ji ki Fateh."

Girdle up your lions, brace up your minds, buckle on your arms, take out your rifles, draw out your swords and thunder on the battlefield.

Those of you who cannot possibly do it, help your officers in all the ways and shake off the foundation of false rumours.

But you fresh blood! Do not lag behind, see the recruiting officers, get your names enlisted and then say hello to Germany – where the tyrants await you to receive their punishment. And while you are in the field, bear in mind that you are there for the white race of which Guru Tegh Bahadur spoke and do not fail to repeat –

"Cauldron (charity), Sword, Victory and Unhesitating Patronage are obtained from Nanak, Guru Gobind Singh."

Balwant Singh Chatrath, III Master, Khalsa High School, Chalwal, Distt. Jehlum, 10-2-15.

Guru Gobind Singh and the War, By Balwant Singh, *The Khalsa Advocate*, Saturday, February 27, 1915.

*****

"The prophetic prescience of our Holy Guru Sri Guru Tegh Bahadur, and how gloriously it was fulfilled to the letter in due course, is now too well-known to the educated world to call for discussion here. It attracted the attention of the Press in 1903, when a Sikh prayer was held in the honour of the late King Edward's Coronation Durbar, and attended by the Sikh Maharajas, Rajas, Reises, respectables and masses at Sees Ganj Delhi, the very spot where the 9th Guru fell martyr to the cause of piety and peace. Then again in 1911, in honour of the auspicious occasion of the Coronation Durbar of His present Most Gracious Majesty, King Emperor George, a magnificent Sikh Procession and Prayer was held at Delhi, which in its pomp and splendour far surpassed the function of 1903. As on the front wall of the Sees Ganj Temple, the centre of the celebrations, were emblazoned the words, 'Here lies the martyr Sikh Guru, who prophesied the advent of the British in India', they attracted the attention of each and every passerby from His Excellency the Viceroy down to an ordinary official and individual. They were also noted by the representatives of the Foreign Press, and most probably by the agent of Reuter too, and have been referred to in the official accounts of the Durbar. It is, therefore, needless to say that the prophecy of the 9th Guru became a most interesting topic in those days, being talked over and discussed everywhere as such. Those fond of research went to the documentary evidence on which this wonderful information was based and its oldness satisfied everyone as to its unquestionable authenticity, so much that our present popular Viceroy and Governor-General, His Excellency Lord Hardinge of Penshurst, referred to it in his Delhi State Entry Durbar speech in 1912 saying that the great 'Sikh prophet' foretold the approach of 'an empire greater than the great Moghul'. History has the following account in that connection:

One day as Guru Tegh Bahadur was in the top story of his prison, the Emperor Aurangzeb thought he saw him looking towards the South in the direction of the Imperial zenana. He was sent for the next day and charged with this great breach of oriental etiquette and propriety. The Guru replied, 'Emperor Aurangzeb, I was on the top story of my prison, but I was not looking at thy private apartment or at thy queens. I was looking in the direction of the Europeans who are coming from beyond the seas to tear down thy 'Pardas' and destroy thine Empire. The writers state that these words became the battle cry of the Sikhs in the assault on the mutineers in Delhi in 1857, under John Nicolson, and that thus the prophecy of the 9th Guru was gloriously fulfilled. – The Sikh Religion by Macauliffe, preface as well as Volume IV, quoting the Suraj Parkash, which is the oldest work on Sikh History.

As we have already said, the prophecy of Sri Guru Tegh Bahadur has now become well known throughout the civilised world; but what his illustrious son and successor, the 10th Guru, foretold about this blessed Raj is known only to those selected few who are thoroughly acquainted with the Sikh history, and have carefully scrutinized the Sikh annals; and we are afraid that among the European writers few except the late Mr. Macauliffe ever knew of it. And the most interesting feature is that Sri Guru Tegh Bahadur simply prophesised the advent of the British Nation in India, whereas Sri Guru Gobind Singh foretold about the British rule and did so more than once. To wit, referring to the prophecy of his Divine Father, he said to his inquisitive Sikhs, 'Then shall the English come and their glory increase', while 'the glory of the Turks shall fade away'. (Sikh Religion by Macauliffe Volume V, Page 107, based on Suraj Parkash, Rut III, Chapter 37). Again when Bir Singh, Madan Singh, a Rajput chief, and Sham Singh visited the Guru, the last named pointed out to him that the Muhammadans and Hindus were very numerous, and how could the Sikhs who were a few contend against, much less hope to obtain Empire, the Guru replied:

What God willeth shall take place. When the army of the Turks cometh, my Sikhs shall strike steel on steel. The Khalsa shall be partners in present and future bliss, tranquillity, meditation, virtue and divine knowledge. Then shall the English come, and joined by the Khalsa rule as well in the East as in the West. The holy Baba Nanak shall bestow all wealth upon them. The English shall possess great power and by force of arms take possession of many principalities. The combined armies of the English and the Sikhs shall be very powerful as long as they rule with united councils. The Empire of the English shall vastly increase, and they shall in every way attain prosperity. Wherever they take their armies they shall conquer and bestow thrones on those who assist them. 'Then in every house shall be wealth, in every house happiness, in every house rejoicing, in every house religion, in every house learning and in every house a woman.' Can there be a clearer and more definite apocalypse than this? The 10th Guru not only foretells the advent of the British, but also explicitly forecasts what the Sikhs will do in association with them, not only in India or Asia but also in France, Germany and Italy, and explains, about two centuries before, the blessings of the present humane rule viz., wealth, happiness, rejoicing, religion, learning, etc. And how completely this prophecy has been fulfilled, has been witnessed even by children in this present age of trade, peace, justice, reform and education. That the valiant sons of the Great Guru are now fighting in the west under the blessed British Flag, has certainly given the finishing touch to the beauty with which the prescience has been fulfilled up to date.

Sceptics may point out that this is a mere story concocted by the late Mr. Macauliffe. But they will be perfectly satisfied when they know that Mr. Macauliffe did not add a single word to what he culled from the Suraj Parkash on the subject, as that great work being older than the English rule in the Punjab, none can venture to doubt the veracity of its version. Its author, Bhai Santokh Singh was born in 1825 A.D. or say 90 years ago, when the Sikh monarchy under Maharaja Ranjit Singh being in its fullest swing, none could even dream of the English so much prospering and the Sikhs fighting under their flag. The Sikhs rather fought against the English, a score of years after that, and it was a dozen years after that still (i.e. in 1857) that they joined them against the mutineers. There can, therefore, be not a shadow of doubt as to the truth of the statement being unchallengeable throughout, and every Sikh and admirer of the 10 Gurus should feel proud that Sri Guru Tegh Bahadur foretold the advent of the British and Guru Kalgidhar forecast their work in India, over a century and a half before they actually became a paramount power."

Guru Gobind Singh's Prophecy about the British Rule, *The Khalsa Advocate*, Saturday, June 26, 1915.

*****

Sir, I have the honour to request that the attached letter may be forwarded to the Editor of the "Akbar-i-Jung" for the favour of publishing. I have the honour to be Sir, Your obedient servant, Subadar Major, 107th Pioneers.

"From Baba Gundit Singh to the praiseworthy, bright faced, pure bodied and God's dear Pashanara Singh. May God grant you His Name, Sikhi belief and a bath in Siri Amritsar (i.e. in the Golden Temple in Amritsar which is supposed to contain sanctified water and which is one of the most famous temples of the Sikhs in the Punjab). Siri Wahaguru ji Ka Khalsa, Siri Wahaguru ji Ki fatah. (This phrase is peculiar to the Sikhs and the nearest approach in English are the words – Good morning, Good evening, Good night and Good-bye). The news is that dear Dhian Singh died on the 2nd of Wasakh, Sanmat 1972. That was God's will. One may worry if an unhappenable thing should happen. Nanak says that nothing in this world is immortal. Dear friend your letter to hand and I was very glad to have it. Please be patient. God is everybody's protection. Love God (because) he is the only Helper. If you think that there be a sacrifice in battle, then two things are attained. First your Emperor, whose grain you have been eating, would be faithfully served. Secondly, by sacrificing you will attain (your) salvation. Friend, do not be disheartened but roar like a lion and serve the Government faithfully, because the Government is pleased with one who serves his Master with money, body, heart and soul, and this God is pleased with him also because he has performed his duty well. And always make this prayer – Oh! God may the British Government always smile and be happy. The salvation for which the saints, sanasis etc., undergo such a lot of trouble and pains is quickly obtained in the battlefield. Every hero, that is killed in battle, obtains salvation. So be brave. God will help you. Keep God in mind.

Bhai Gian Singh sends his kind regards to all the Khalsae, Baba Harnam Singh, Ajit Singh, and Jugat Singh, all send their kind regards. Bebe ji also sends her kind regards.

Please write a letter quickly how you are getting on.

Siri Wahaguru ji Ka Khalsa siri Wahaguru ji Ki fateh."

Bhai Gian Singh, Santpura Bawian. 13th Jeth Sanmat 1972.

N.B. The words in brackets are the translator's additions to make the sentence intelligible to explain the meanings of the words vaguely used in the letter.

From Subadar Major Jath Singh, 107th Pioneers, Gurmukhi, 29.6.15. Translation.

*****

The A, B, C of War

A is **A**ngry **A**ustria sending to Servia an ultimatum of War,
B is the **B**rave **B**elgium bruised under **B**abe-killers' wheel of Car;
C is the **C**rown Prince of Germany away with his troops back,
D are the **D**iffident enemies that pluck and energy lack;
E are the feeling **E**nglish with cause noble and righteous their,
F are the **F**rench **F**ighting a **F**ight hard, **F**urious and **F**air;
G is **G**ermany down with her Krupp and Shell,
H are the **H**ungry **H**uns to soon find their way to hell;
I is the late joining **I**taly with her war material and crew complete,
J is **J**ocose and **J**ubilant **J**ap lately on enemy inflicted a defeat;
K is the unhappy **K**hedive with Turks who lost his fame,
L is **L**ouvain a standing stain in Kaiser's fair name;
M is German **M**ilitarism the aim of allies all,
N is the **N**aval warfare wherein the Kaiser sees his fall;
O is the **O**ttomon Empire overcome by ruinous ill-advice,
P are the **P**russian Guards taken prisoners by Russian sepoys;
Q is the **Q**ueer Turk not alive to his own profit and gain,
R is the **R**ussian **R**esistance well known to Germany's pain;
S is our **S**ailor-King **S**olace to the wounded **S**ikh **S**tout;
T are the civilised **T**respassers that Hague convention scout;
U is the whole **U**niverse hard complaining of German cruelty,
V is the **V**ictory in store for British arms with suriety;
W is Mr. **W**ilson **W**orking his **W**ay for a reasonable course,
X is the '**X**traordinary gas that seems to be the last resource;
Y are the **Y**east lovers in fear of **Y**eomanry **Y**elping,
Z are the **Z**eppelin raids disserviceable far from helping.

By Mr. Harbhajan Singh, English Master, Khalsa High School, Gujranwala.
The Khalsa Advocate, Saturday, July 10, 1915.

*****

Religious books for brothers in the front

"The Secretary Khalsa Jatha London informs us that there is still a good number of copies of Sri Guru Granth Sahib in the hospitals at the front, but that copies of the Sacha Sauda and Panj Granthi Gutkas (booklets) are badly wanted there. Though the Chief Khalsa Diwan has so far been able to send two hundred Panj Granthi Gutkas to the front, but more still are urgently wanted. So, those brothers who desire to send any number of these gutkas may kindly post the same to the office of the Chief Khalsa Diwan, which will most gladly comply with their instructions at once. Cash remittances received for the purpose will be utilised in purchasing the gutkas."

Rai Bahadur Sardar Sadhu Singh, Joint Secretary Chief Khalsa Diwan writes (extract). *The Khalsa Advocate*, Saturday, September 18, 1915.

*****

"Please find out about a man called Faujdar Singh of the 1st section – I do not know his number – and let me know. I have heard that on the 11/4/15 when we were coming here he, if he is the Faujdar of my village, ran off somewhere. Write and tell me where he is now, and find out from him his name and number and send them to me. Send him many Fatehs from me and tell him "If you had to do this (i.e. desert) afterwards, were you dragged by force to enlist by any one?" Tell him that Bahadur Singh (the writer) No.378 and Hakin Singh, No.890 are together in this country and there is no cause for anxiety. Let him do his duty to the government with all his heart. Give him my address, so that he may send me a card. If he will do so, I will answer."

From Bahadur Singh, 35th Sikhs attached 47th Sikhs, serving in France, to Kishan Singh, 35th Sikhs, Rawal Pindi, India. (Urdu, 22/10/15).

*****

The King of England wired to us "You must go tonight"
Valiant men of India, you must know how to fight
Take the Erpree trenches, take Hill Sixty-two,
Let Lahore Division show what it can do!"
Off we march as quickly as our feet can go!
See us in the morning opposite the foe!
Fix up a machine gun! We may run away!
All alone it can eat up a regiment a day!
Is a silly German there? Kill him with a bumb,*
All around, above the ground, hear the bullets hum!
See, the foe is falling back, See, we take the trench!
All the world shouts "India!" now Belgians, Germans, French!
Every day the airships play, sailing through the sky
Roundabout and roundabout, shooting as they fly.
Now they spy us where we lie, home they turn again.
Soon the monster German shells pour on us like rain.
Great shells wander twenty miles seeking out their mark,

Roaring madly in their rush, maxim bullets bark.
Little shells sing softly while they run along,
*(Flocks of Kulan** flying now sing the same soft song!)*
Peace? The word is never heard, for Great God has sworn
That a million widows first, must their children mourn.
I, the poet, Gurdit Singh, very closely see,
Such a war can never, never, never, be!

*Pronounced to rhyme with "hum".
** Cranes.
From a Sikh – Poem in Gurmukhi, dated 19/11/15.

*****

I have received a letter from a friend and shall feel obliged if you will kindly publish it in your esteemed paper (Akbar-i-Jung) the following few lines which I have extracted from it.

"May God keep you well and safe and that you may return to India. It is my humble prayer that the flag of victory of our King Emperor may remain unfurled for ever. It is my firm faith that our King Emperor will be victorious in the war because His Majesty did not enter it from any personal motive but in order to save a weak kingdom. God always helps such kings. You should fight without fear and return to India when the victory is won.

May God always grant victory to our King Emperor. Let us all utter this prayer from our true hearts.

His Majesty has conferred such a blessing of peace upon us that a wolf and a lamb can meet together. They all pray that God may always grant victory to our King Emperor. His Majesty has given us free education and has thus extorted a prayer from our hearts for His Majesty's victory.

The Germans have entered the field against our King Emperor, but they have suffered defeats which have compelled them to say that God may always grant victory to our King Emperor. When all the kings of the time seek the protection of His Majesty's power, how can the Germans help saying that the victory will be of our King Emperor's. Our prayer to the All Merciful God is that He may always grant victory to our Emperor King George V."

Letter without date from Punjab Singh, 59th Rifles.

*****

"Dear one, remembering you in my heart is very sad. But what can be done? Through the force of necessity we have had to submit to these trials. Reading the Sikh history I find that the Sikhs are a warlike people, who in order to protect and elevate their honour have shed their blood freely in the past and are shedding it as freely now. In the future too, they will continue freely to shed their blood to support the honour of the British government. My dear one, you are also a Sikh, and war has ever been the occupation of our family. For this reason it is incumbent on you to serve with bravery in the present war … My dear one, the affairs of the world go on; we eat and drink and sleep. Nevertheless my heart is rent with anguish at the thought of the trials and dangers that beset you, and I know that, at the same time, your heart feels intensely the continued separation from your dear ones."

From --- Schoolmaster, Khalsa School, Sayyad, Rawal Pindi, to Sowar Awtar Singh, 30th Lancers, France. (Urdu, 24/11/15).

*****

I shall feel obliged if you would kindly arrange to publish the following news in one of the issues of your esteemed paper:

"The Sikh officers and soldiers of the 4th Cavalry held a religious meeting on the 16th July, lasting four hours. The Sikh officers and men of the 15th 47th and 59th Infantries as well as those of the 6th Cavalry had been permitted by their respective Commanding Officers to attend and took part in the meeting. We are much thankful to these Commanding Officers who had so kindly permitted their men to join in the gathering.

At first Dr. Mosl Chand Sharma of the 4th Cavalry delivered a lecture on religion. He explained the principles of a true religion. The audience was very pleased with his lecture. He was followed by Lance Aaih Bota Singh of the 47th Sikhs who spoke on the grandeur and nobility of the Sikh religion. In the course of his lecture he also emphasised that in accordance with the orders of their Gurus it was the duty of the Sikhs to serve their Government loyally and faithfully, that they would never get such a rare opportunity to do so as the present one.

All the people assembled received this statement with great enthusiasm. Captain Hills (the name is not readable) who was present at the meeting remarked that the Sikhs were great loyal soldiers of the Government and constituted their right hand. Then a special prayer was made for the victory of our Government in the present war. After this prayer the usual concluding prayer of the meeting was said and the people dispersed taking kara parshad (a pudding which Sikhs distribute to all present at a religious meeting), and thanking the Government for their kindness.

If there not be room in the Gurmukhi paper, arrangements may kindly be made to publish the letter in the Urdu paper."

The above letter is counter-signed by Rasaldar Sindar Singh.
Letter without date (in Gurmukhi) from Kot Dafadar Bishan Singh, 4th Cavalry on service in France.

*****

A message from brothers in the front

"As we came on active service to this far distant foreign land in the days of severe winter and rain and especially those of a horribly bloody World War we never for a moment expected to bear all those comforts which we are now enjoying along with our other Indian brothers. It is not my intention to go into all those details and make the letter a lengthy one, but in order to bring to the kind and revered notice of our enthusiastic brothers in India, the simple yet beautifully furnished Gurudwara, that has been so very kindly erected by our great and magnanimous Commanding Officer Colonel Bamfield I.M.S., a real Karmyogin, just and ever pains taking for the welfare and uplifting of all those entrusted to his care. He has been equally popular among the Indians and as well as the higher official circle. We find in him a staunch supporter of all our religious ideas and observances and so we have come to keep our implicit faith in him and offer him our cordial respect for the benefits he is always doing on us.

When we got here well settled in a very magnificent and spacious French building, a Military Training School for officers and got easy time, we had held some Jormelas in this hospital on the auspicious occasion of the birth of some of our Gurus.

In the meantime we were very fortunate to hear from the O.C. that he was going to erect a mosque for the Mohammedans and a Gurudwara for the Sikhs, which words he at once fulfilled. It was built in the month of July 1915, and since then most of our brothers are regularly attending it throughout the whole of the day.

By the kind permission of the Colonel one man has been especially detailed as a Granthi. We hold Jormelas (religious meetings) every Amawasya and Purnmashi, do prepare Karaparasd and distribute among all of the men of the staff also.

The joy we feel from prayers, meditations, and reading Granth Sahib etc., is really far superior to that experience in India and it is mainly due to the more earnestness and purification of the heart which were the natural outcome of our intensely self-sacrificing duty.

It is owing to this that our egoism has much vanished, our low thinking and living or yielding to any such temptation has given way to a simple, enduring, firm, noble and generous mode of life.

It is also removing selfishness in our hearts and filling them with love, unity and a strong sense of duty. Our brothers who come to our Gurudwara for prayers etc. at time also offer before the Granth Sahib their humble pies. This money was collected and as now amounted to a decent sum we wish to send to the following institutions as mentioned below:-

Rupees 90 for Kanya Maha Vidyalaya, Ferozepore, and Rupees 75 for Sikh Orphanage, Amritsar.

The only thing we now wish is to die a heroic death in the cause of our most beloved Emperor, King George V and thus leave a perpetual memory of our actions for the great future historians to record it in their works."

Jemadar Adjutant Chanda Singh, Man Singh Ahluwalia, Hospital Store Keeper, Lahore Indian General Hospital. Montreuil, Boulogne Base, France, 1st December 1915. *The Khalsa Advocate*, Saturday, February 5, 1916.

*****

"Do not be anxious about me. For eighteen years I have eaten salt at the hand of our Emperor and now I shall repay him with my loyalty. Now is my opportunity. The man who at this time does his duty by the government with absolute loyalty need have no fear for the future … It would be difficult to find another government so good as ours, under which no man is harassed."

From Jan Phuman Singh, 31st Punjabis, attached 47th Sikhs, to a friend in India. (Gurmukhi, 1/12/15).

*****

"Now my advice to you is this. In the service of the Sirkar do not leave to tomorrow the work that should be done today. Do today's work today, so that you may gain advancement, and also make a good impression on others. The orders that are given to you to carry out, fulfil them in the readiest way and give up frequenting the bazaar. Do not follow advice which would, in the least degree, produce bad results. There are many people who give unsound advice solely with the intention of bringing discredit on the person to whom the advice was given."

From Dfdr. Dalip Singh, Sialkot Cavalry Brigade, France, to Lance Dafadar Sawan Singh, 20th Deccan Horse, Neemuch, Central India. (Urdu, 7/1/16).

*****

"I cannot tell you anything that has happened recently, as we are forbidden to say anything. If I am spared, I shall enjoy life again one day. I am quite well. I am waiting and thinking continually of the blessed day which shall bring victory to our King, and a happy meeting with my friends at home. If I die, it will be better than living, and if I am spared, I shall taste the joys of life. It is our duty to serve our government loyally, and we are going to do that. The rest is in the hands of God."

From Dfdr. Basant Singh, Sialkot Cavalry Brigade, France, to Sirdar Ujagar Singh, Veterinary Graduate, Allahabad, India. (Urdu, 22/1/16).

*****

"My dear friend, this is our constant wish that our king may soon obtain victory. It is not my voice alone (which speaks so) but that of the whole Sikh tribe down to the young children. Because there is probably no single Sikh, who has not some relation or friend at the war. How then can they be at ease? If we have patience, then it is based on this alone, that in the first place, the Sircar takes such care of its sepoys, and they have every comfort. Rations &c are given in full measure. They have no hardships. In the second place we know full well, all of us, that in the end, victory will be on our side. Moreover, according to our religious principles, you are taking part in honourable work, and you are fulfilling your duty when you share in this work. In short our consolation lies in this, that we are performing our duty. Our brothers (at the front) do, of course, have trials and difficulties; but they bear them as heroes."

From Sahib Singh, Sub-Inspector Police, Nabha State, Punjab, to Jemadar Kartar Singh, 18th Lancers, France. (Urdu, 4/2/16).

*****

"Give this letter to Captain Kehr Singh of Sarupa. Say to him 'Have it read out to the people. Read out to the people whatever the King wrote. For the rest, as they please, but they ought to give all the help they can. You are number one of the village. You are a Captain. You have taken advantage from the house of the government. All is known to you. Now is the time.' Write and tell me (when this has been done)."

From Kunda Singh, No.448, 47th Sikhs, Indian Military Depot, Milford-on-sea, to Bachhattar Singh, Ludhiana, Dt., India. (Gurmukhi, 6/2/16 – forwarding a copy of the King's message).

*****

"Both of us, brothers, are well, and we are grateful to our Government, who have made such excellent arrangements for us. We want for nothing. Among all the nations engaged in this war, the arrangements of our King are the best. Everything goes up to the trenches, rations, goats, spirits. Cooks are present in the trenches……..From many sides our artillery is raining shot and shell, and thousands of the enemy are killed and taken prisoners daily. We feel certain that in a short time our Government will secure the victory. Our Allies, the French, have a gun, so large that it takes a shell 6 maunds in weight, and we have some of the same kind. When a shell is fired at the enemies trenches it literally wipes them out. We used to hear before, but now we have seen with our own eyes, that there is no King the equal of our King. It is incumbent on you people to do all you can to help our King."

From Kartar Singh, 36th Jacob's Horse, France, to Indar Singh, Lyalpur, Punjab. (Urdu, 13/3/16).

*****

"We are very comfortable. We get plenty of rations and clothes. Those who on some pretence or another remained behind (in India) did not act loyally towards the Government. They will understand what they have done at the time when we return to India. They will see medals on our breast, and will be envious. At the present time, men with short service succeed in getting promotion to Naik and Dafadar."

From Hira Singh, 35th attached 36th Cavalry, France, to K.D. Bhara Singh, Depot 35th Cavalry, Dehra Ismail Khan, N.W.F.P., India. (Gurmukhi, 13/3/16).

*****

Let me send you a few lines of poetry about our King:

Let the world see your deeds, soldiers of India!
Britain is ours and we're all for Britain
Let German ears ring with this, soldiers of India!
Strike like brave warriors, make the foe listen
Show them what valour is, soldiers of India!
Like the heroes of Bharat, trample the foe down
Make streams of blood flow, soldiers of India!

After long years, comes your chance of a battle
Show them what stuff you are made of, soldiers of India!
Flame springs from your hearts, love of your country
Spread the fire far and wide, soldiers of India!
Germans so full of plans, clever and subtle
Down to the dust with them, soldiers of India!
May God preserve our King.

From Ajaib Singh, Amritsar, to Nar Singh, 38th C.I. Horse, France. (Urdu, 15/3/16).

*****

Let me send you a few lines of poetry:

An Ode to the Sword

O fire of loyalty O flame of faith
O Sword of India the world has worshipped you
Fate has given a chance to test the enemy
Lovers of peace kept the sword sheathed
But drew when innocent blood was shed.
God gave the opportunity to the rusty sword
It flashed from its scabbard and showed its metal
It must make German blood flow
Even in their City of Berlin
It had been thirsty for blood for many a day
Skill with the sword was India's birth right
Loyalty they drank with their mother's milk
They fought in Europe and won renown
They had to fulfil their destiny
And smite German heads from their trunks
Thanks to the King who has given us this chance
To show that Indian bravery is no old wives' tale
This was our bounden duty and no favour
To shed our blood for King George Panjam.

From Diwan Chand, Clerk, 17th Mule Corps, to Sowar Aurung Singh, 11th Lancers, attached 19th Lancers, France. (Urdu, 22/3/16).

*****

"What Gurdit Singh told you is doubtless true, because I am very far and in no circumstances can I come to you till our King has obtained victory. Moreover, to come before victory is secured would be unlawful for me, because it is the duty of a subject to die (if necessary) for his King."

From L.D. Ishar Singh, 36th Jacob's Horse, France, to Ishar Singh, Gurdaspur, Punjab. (Urdu, 31/3/16).

*****

"Those subjects of the British Government who have served in this war, will, together with their families, certainly be remembered by the Government as to the fulfilment of their rights. This Government of ours is a very just and humane one. We are indeed fortunate in that we are covered by the shadow of the British Government, and we hope that that shadow will remain over us till the end of time. Also the late Viceroy, Lord Hardinge, left for England in the beginning of April. In his place the new Viceroy, Lord Chelmsford, assumed office, on 4th April. The viceroyalty of Lord Hardinge was very beneficial for the people, let us see what favours the new viceroy will give to the poor subjects of India. We hear that he also is a very right and high-minded person. This inauspicious war started in the late Viceroy's term of office, and may God terminate the war in the new Viceroy's time, and give our Government the victory and confound their enemies. Write and tell me how far Verdun is from Paris. It appears from the newspapers that the enemy is making heavy attacks there, and not succeeding returns crestfallen to his own trenches. Our allies are very brave and strong and it is difficult for the enemy to stand up against them. He hits recklessly right and left, but he has not the strength to establish himself firmly in one spot and fight from there."

From Bishan Singh, Quetta, Baluchistan Agency, India, to Jemadar Kartar Singh, 18th Lancers, France. (Urdu, 10/4/16).

*****

"It is expected that the finish of the war will come quickly. The arrangements of our King in this country are excellent and a very large Army has been assembled. We fully expect that victory will be for our King. The Germans are now very weak."

From Jewan Singh, Sialkot Cavalry Brigade, France, to Narinjan Singh, Jhelum District, Punjab. (Urdu, 29/4/16).

*****

Now up and show them, O men of Hindustan
Overthrow the Germans, O men of Hindustan
You are "Birtanias" and "Birtania" is yours
Tell that to the Germans, O men of Hindustan
Show them your might so that they will admit it
India's lionhearted cast down the enemy
Spread wide the river of blood, O men of Hindustan
After long years, your day has come,
Show them your prowess, O men of Hindustan
From your hearts let the flame of patriotism arise
Let the fire of it scorch and burn the enemy.
Mingle the prowess of the Germans with the dust
Hurl them below, O men of Hindustan
May God give victory to George the Fifth
And utterly destroy the Germans

From Indar Singh, Dhariwal, Punjab, India, to Ganesha Singh, 35th Sindh Horse, attached 36th Jacob's Horse, France. (Urdu, 11/6/16).

*****

"Do the King's work well and be faithful. It is the order if the Guru that one should be faithful to the person whose salt one eats, and this is the time for us to do all that is possible for the King."

From Fauja Singh, Dafadar, 9th Hodson's Horse, France, to Teja Singh, Dafadar, 10th Lancers, Lolarai, Baluchistan Agency, India. (Gurmukhi, 25/7/16).

*****

"Our King's army has made an assault on the enemy which in violence and intensity has even surpassed the assault on Verdun. Our army has captured many very strong trenches and positions, and taken a considerable number of prisoners. The enemy has now grown weak and it is expected that our King will soon obtain victory."

From Lakha Singh, Risaldar, 18th Lancers, France, to Sirdar Sajjan Singh, Hony. Magistrate, Lahore, Punjab. (Urdu, 25/7/16).

*****

The Call to Arms

"Dear Khalsa Ji, - it is two full years today since this terrible war of unprecedented severity and magnitude was inflicted upon the world by the unprincipled aggressiveness of the Central Powers of Europe. The loss of money, material and life which has occurred during this period of strife is not easy to comprehend.

Some of you may possibly ask the question why Our Emperor took part in this war in which the British Empire was not primarily concerned. Kings and Nations have responsibilities on their shoulders for the maintenance of equilibrium even outside their own dominions and the preservation of the rights of the weak is one of the noble duties of the great and small, according to the commands of the Great Guru viz.,

Brave is he who fights for the weak;
Who is cut down to pieces but never leaves the field.

Our Emperor has nobly intervened in this war of aggression as the champion of the cause of righteousness to protest against the Central Powers' mercilessly trampling the independence of the small Belgian Kingdom and disposing, as waste paper, the solemn treaties on which international obligations of the two countries were founded. The righteousness of the cause espoused by our noble Emperor has aroused the whole-hearted sympathy of the British nation which has laid aside all mutual differences of opinion and is striving, as with one soul, to achieve the end for which the Emperor has unsheathed his sword.

No less has His Majesty had the support of his millions of subjects in India and the other overseas dominions.

The spirit of sincere love and deep loyalty exhibited by the Indians in general and the Sikhs in particular, during this crisis, is too well-known to need any demonstration from me. You are all aware how the Princes and people of India have, at this juncture ungrudgingly sacrificed their kith and kin on the battlefield in the service of their King-Emperor, besides subscribing their mite in money towards the equipment of our armies and the noble objects connected with the alleviation of suffering caused by this inevitable war. Our wishes for the victory of Our Emperor have been constant and sincere. We are, therefore, supporting Our Emperor with our body and soul (Tan, Man and Dhan).

This outburst of genuine attachment is an indication of how the British Government has endeared itself to our hearts and how it has inspired us with feelings of deep love and sentiments of unalloyed loyalty. It is laid down in our daily morning prayer by Guru Nanak Sahib that "by the conquest of mind you conquer the world," meaning that he who has won the affection of the people of this world can best govern it. The success attending mere conquest with the sword is but transitory. The conquest of the hearts of the people by love, on the other hand, creates everlasting affection and attachment.

The celebrated Indian poet Brind observed:

There is no other tie stronger than that of love.
The humble bee pierces through a wooden bank.
But lies idly imprisoned in the lotus leaves
And does not try and come out of them.

No wonder then that whichever country comes once under British protection, its people deem it a God sent blessing and always pray for its continuance, for British rule is based upon principles of unflinching justice and righteousness and is characterised with sympathy and solicitude for the welfare of the people, which inevitably results in peace, prosperity and happiness.

The mutual attachment between the ruler and the ruled is growing daily, as is evidenced at every occasion when it is put to the test. The feelings of attachment to our King-Emperor's Government are universal, being shared equally by prince and peasant, but there are special reasons for my particularly sincere devotion and unbounded love for His Majesty's sacred throne.

Firstly, the Guru who called the Phulkian House his own house also blessed the English nation to save India from the clutches of misrule and tyranny. It follows that the House designated by the Guru as his own should be linked by ties of unequalled attachment to the Rulers of this country, who are administering it in accordance with his blessings.

Secondly, the great Queen Victoria of happy memory granted the rulers of Patiala the exalted and endearing title of "Farzandi-i-Khas Daulat-i-Englishia" thus consolidating the intimate relations existing between this House and the British Crown. This honour is unique; so is the devotion of the Patiala House to the British Government.

Thirdly, the brave Sikh nation, to whom I am proud to belong and which looks upon me as its leader, regards it as one of the most important principles of its faith to unstintingly shed its blood for the honour of the British Flag.

The Khalsa has not only avowed this truth but has always given practical proof of it whenever the chance has arisen or an opportunity has offered itself. The history of the dark days of the Mutiny, the Frontier wars, and of the war in Egypt, South Africa and China afford ample illustration of what I say. The exploits of the Sikh soldiers have resounded all over the world and monuments like those of Saragarhi are inspiring records of what they have done for their beloved King.

The present war is no less an index of the gallant deeds of the Khalsa than past records. Even with your exalted ideas of the services rendered in the Military lines by your brethren, I am sure you will be surprised to hear of the part which the Sikhs have played in this war. The Sikh population of India numbers 3 million out of a total population of 330 million. In other words, it represents slightly over 9 per thousand of total population. But out of the total Indian Army of 1,77,00 as many as 36,000 or over 203 per thousand are Sikhs, all on active service. So also against a total of 127,000 Indian recruits who have been enlisted from August 1914 to March 1916, 22,000 or over 173 per thousand are Sikhs.

And what is more, as many as 342 out of the total 1,355 military honours conferred since the beginning of the war i.e. more than one fourth, have gone to the Sikhs. You have doubtless heard of the conspicuous gallantry displayed by the 14th Sikhs at Gallipoli and the 15th Sikhs in the operations against the Senussi Arabs. Is this not good testimony of the deeds of the valiant Khalsa? I need hardly mention that all my regular Imperial Service Troops are serving at the front and are being maintained by me at full strength. But I wish to express here my satisfaction at this splendid manner in which my subjects have responded to my call for recruits in the British Army. You will be glad to know that of the 36,000 Sikhs on active service 5,000 belong to the Patiala State, which furnishes a total of 5861 combatants of all religions. Of the Indian States, Patiala stands first in the number of combatants supplied to the armed forces.

One of the sublime teachings of our Guru Father is unflinching loyalty to the ruler and implicit obedience to his orders. The Sikhs cannot forget the words:

He who is impertinent to his master, is put to great shame
and
None should bear arms against his rulers.

It was due to the teachings like these that when some misguided emigrants divorced from Sikh teachings and traditions and under the influence of the wicked enemies of our faith, returned to India with an evil purpose, they were openly disclaimed by the Sikhs and handed up even by their own relatives to receive the punishment which they deserved. I was well pleased to see how my co-religionists stood against these fools, who had allowed themselves to be duped by interested parties, and helped the Government in nipping their mischievous propaganda in the bud. This was just what I expected.

The Great Guru has proscribed it as one of the rules of life of the Sikhs to remain thoroughly loyal to their master and to sacrifice even their lives for him thus:

Be loyal to your sovereign:
Leave death and life in the hands of God,
He who forsaketh his master in the battle,
Shall be dishonoured here and condemned hereafter
The vultures, knowing him to be disloyal.
Will not touch but spurn his flesh.
He shall not go to heaven hereafter nor obtain glory here,
Abundant disgrace shall light upon his head
Be assured of this that human birth shall be profitable to him.
Who loseth his life with his face to the foe,
For all the drops of blood that fall from his body
So many years shall he enjoy in the company of his God.

(10th Guru Guruvilas).

How can they who have received the baptism of the sword be afraid of death? On the contrary they always pray in the following words of the Tenth Guru, to die fighting against the enemy.

I am the son of a brave man, not a Brahmin.
How can I perform austerities?
How can I turn my attention to Thee
O Lord and forsake domestic affairs?
Now be pleased to grant me the boon I
Crave with clasped hands
That when the end of my life cometh,
I may die fighting in the mighty battle.

(10th Guru's 24th Avataras).

At Abchal Nagar, when the Great Guru was on the point of leaving this earthly frame, he solemnly advised his followers as follows:

Practice the art of war:
Be gallant and bravely face the foe!
You will gain all the worldly wealth,
Enjoy yourself and let others enjoy it;
Die in the battlefield and enter the gates of heaven!
To enjoy all bliss there.

(Suraj Parkash).

The Sikhs who believe and act according to the above teachings, feel confident that the victory of their Governments is the victory of their faith, totally identifying themselves with the British rule and the progress and prosperity thereof.

Khalsaji, it is true that the war has caused terrific loss of life and is still taking a heavy toll. I know many of my Khalsa brethren are in mourning and they have my sincere sympathy. But these are sacrifices in a great and noble cause and according to the teachings of our holy Guru which I have just cited, the soldiers dying on the battlefield may have gone to heaven. This satisfaction should bring proud succour to those they have left behind making them, feel proud that a member of their family has sacrificed his life in the service of their Emperor in a righteous cause and on the path of religion. You should look at the manner in which the brave British citizens are sending millions to the battlefield and the way in which those at home are calmly and patiently bearing the losses which the furious warfare entails. This should be a solace and an encouragement to such of us, as have been hard hit. Many brave soldiers and statesman, the pride of their nation, have departed from this world leaving gaps which can hardly be filled. Such men cannot come back to guide us by their wisdom and experience and we are the poorer for their loss. Many of them were our personal friends. The greatest of them all, a hero of heroes and a statesman of statesmen was the late Earl Kitchener of Khartoum. His loss, although a national one, is felt by us all more keenly because he was so well known in this country for his genial sympathy with the military races and for his towering personality, and was loved and admired particularly by the hardy Sikh soldiers.

But are all these valuable lives lost in vain? Is nothing to come out of the precious blood which is being so unstintingly shed? No, we must get what we desire. These sacrifices in the right cause are sure to bring into this world of ours a lasting peace. According to our Guru "the warrior's wrath is aroused when an arrow strikes him," so these sacrifices have roused the ire of all righteous men. The powers of darkness shall now be hurled down for ever from their pinnacle of foolish pride and made confidence, those who boasted of their might shall be crushed and awakened to the unpleasant truth that it is right that conquers and not might. These wonderful sacrifices must end for all time, the trampling of the liberties of weak nations; blind lust for power and unbridled ambition for aggrandisement shall find a permanent check. I am glad to say that, by Guru's grace, the time for such a consummation is not far off. Every day is bringing us closer to it.

You might perhaps want to know why with the enormous resources at His Majesty's command our Emperor has not succeeded so far in crushing the enemy. The cause is not far to seek. The powers of darkness which flourish by deceit and treachery always embarrass the righteous in the beginning for the former secretly prepare the material for mischief while the righteous, by their unsuspicious nature, are not prepared to counteract when the evily disposed choose to spring a surprise upon them. Such machinations succeed for a time but their end is inevitably disastrous to the aggressors. That is exactly what happened in the present case. We regarded everyone as our friend and had no evil intentions against anyone. We followed a policy of mutual trust and did not amass war material, for we did not seek war, nor did we poison the minds of our people against any other country with a view to dupe them into supporting an unjustified war. On the contrary our enemy had for a long time been secretly devoting all his energies to preparing men and material for a protracted war on an unprecedented scale.

Our enemy having the resources of science at his disposal, his preparations were not of a nature to be lightly dealt with. Our first object, therefore, was to stem the tide of his onslaught, while we gained time to prepare our material, in turn, which, thank God, is now ready. He lost command of the seas long ago, most of his colonial possessions have been conquered by the Allies and we are already beginning to see him losing ground daily in the main theatre of war. He is being hemmed in on all sides and held in a vice like grip which it will be impossible for him to break through. The pressure, though slow, is steady and continuous. The noose we have thrown round his neck has been sufficiently tightened even for our obstinate enemy to be filled with the fear of our approaching success, a success of which we never had the slightest doubt. It therefore, behoves us to exert ourselves to the utmost to hasten the approach of that glorious day by helping the Government in every possible manner with men, money and our moral support. It is only in this way that our earnest desire for a speedy victory can be fulfilled.

On an anniversary we generally pray for many happy returns of the auspicious day, but on this second anniversary of the war, we very sincerely pray before the Guru that it might end before the third year is over, and that instead of gathering here next time for a war anniversary you may be invited to celebrate the glorious victory of the British Arms.

I thank you, gentlemen, for the trouble you have taken in coming here in such trying weather. I feel much obliged to you for your kindness in accepting my invitation to hear what I had to say to you.

Dear Khalsaji, I have given you the trouble in order that I may deliver you a message concerning our duty in this struggle. I hope you will carry it back to your homes and spread it among the Sikhs in all parts of the country. I earnestly wish that you and through you all the Indians generally and the Sikhs in particular should take it to heart and act accordingly because in the spirit of the teaching of our holy Gurus whom I have already quoted in the early part of my speech, my message to you is:-

"It is our bounden duty to try our utmost for the victory of our King-Emperor and never to think of peace until the enemy has been completely worsted and a permanent peace secured for the coming generations. Let our enthusiasm to support our armies with an unlimited number of men with money and with other necessary material, run high. Let our efforts in this direction be continuous and incessant and let them not slacken in the least till the desired goal is reached. Let us pray daily before the Akal Purkh, with hearts pure and sincere, for the final and speedy success of the British Government."

Let us even now, all with one accord, pray before the Almighty that the armies of King George be victorious in every field of battle. May the love and loyalty of the Gurus own house to British government ever increase! May the Khalsa nation, in remembering the blessings of the great Guru ever support the British Flag in all climes and countries! May our armies come home victorious from the various fronts and may we share with them their joy and pride for the noble and gallant deeds faithfully performed in pursuance of their duty:

Wah Guruji ka Khalsa
Sri Wah Guruji ki Fateh."

Speech by H.H. the Maharaja of Patiala, on the second anniversary celebration at Patiala, 5th August 1916.

*****

Indian Army officers and Maharaja Bhupinder Singh of Patiala inspecting a railway gun, 1918. (Courtesy of the Council of the National Army Museum, London)

*****

"We all the Sikhs assembled here on the occasion of the Dedication of the Sikh Temple, take this opportunity to express our deep feelings of loyalty to the British Crown.

We are a small nation forming one-hundredth of a total of 330 million of the Indian people; yet though we are small in number we form one-fifth of the British Indian Army, overwhelmingly out of proportion to our numbers, and our services to Britain have been considerable.

The Sikhs have fought shoulder to shoulder with the British troops, and unsparingly shed their blood for the British cause in Afghanistan, Burma, Egypt, China and Persia. While Britain has not forgotten the part played by Sikhs in the suppression of the Indian Mutiny. We are known to be a military people and loyalty is our fundamental principle.

Coming to more recent events our brothers, true to the words of the Great Gurus, are bravely facing the foe in every part of the field in this World War and are leaving the question of life and death in the hands of God. In Gallipoli, the 14th Sikh Regiment, though greatly thinned in their ranks, stood their ground so nobly that they won the admiration of all the allies. While the 36th and 15th Regiments did gloriously, one in the reduction of Kia Chow and the other in France."

The Sikhs in Negri Sembilan.
Gurudwara, Seremban, 7th August 1916.

Extract from Sikh Loyal Address Negri Sembilan.

*****

"I am hopeful through the favour of the Guru that victory is at hand from what I have seen. I am sure that very soon the Germans will throw away their weapons. The prisoners who have been taken say that it will be very difficult for Germany to stand now that the heavy artillery of the British us doing so much execution. The prisoners also say that there will be a retreat soon, and that they recognise we are too brave for them. The side which has justice for its motto will succeed in getting its rafts to the opposite bank. Britain's role hitherto has been to help the innocent and to punish the sinner. Therefore, my brother it is every man's duty to sacrifice his life and property for our King until the British Flag waves in Berlin. I am confident that we shall be victorious this year and will join our friends in India."

From Santa Singh, 20th Deccan Horse, France, to Dafadar Harnam Singh, 21st Cavalry, Frontier Force, Lahore. (Gurmukhi, 19/8/16).

*****

"By the favour of the Sircar, the war has no bad effect in India. India rejoices when she hears of the brave deeds of the thousands of her sons at the front. We look forward with pleasurable anticipation to the time when the fruit will be secured for all the blood that the brave warriors of India have shed – namely when our King George the Vth will gain the victory, and the Germans will taste to the dregs the bitterness and humiliation of defeat. May God bring that day quickly!"

From Jawala Singh, Jhelum, Punjab, to Bishen Singh, Jemadar, 19th Lancers, France. (Gurmukhi, 18/9/16).

*****

"Do not be concerned about me. I am quite well and happy, but pray God to give speedy victory to our King and his allies, so that we may return home. In this way only can the object for which we came here be secured, and our honour be increased. Thereafter, we can live in honour under the banner of our King. Do not be anxious, I say. The sons of many mothers have come to the war, and it is for the sons of warriors to fight for victory. It is a matter of gratitude that we are today having an opportunity to serve our King. Even a dog does not eat a human corpse; why then should one set store on what happens to one's body? If a man serves his King now with his soul and body, he will live happily and be honoured for the rest of his life; but if he does evil now towards his King, he will reap his just reward when the war is over. Do not be concerned about me. I have need of nothing. The Sircar provides for us solicitously as a mother does for her child, or a merchant does for his horse."

From ___, ___ Lancers attached ___ Horse, France to ___, Ludhiana District, Punjab, India. (Gurmukhi, 21st December 1916).

*****

"I hear that everyone's pay has been raised since January 1st. I have read the details in the papers, and free rations have been given and pensions increased. I am indeed grateful to the British Government and pray morning and evening for their victory."

From Atwar Singh, Medical Hostel, Agra to Jemadar Bharpur Singh, 2nd Lancers, France. (Urdu dated the 8th January 1917).

*****

"This country is too fine for me to describe it. The people are lovable and are all owners of property. Every tree in the country is either good for flower or fruit. It is the image of paradise. I have seen Paris on leave and if I return I will tell you about it. I am unable to write anything. I am now about to go to England on 10 days leave to see the country. Do not be concerned at all about us. We are all well and happy and have nothing whatever to disturb us and we have no concern for our lives. We are ready to serve our Government, day and night, because we shall never again have such an opportunity to prove our loyalty. The only thing that disturbs us occasionally is love for you which draws us in your direction. Further, life and death are in the hands of God."

From Pal Singh, Jemadar, 38th Central India Horse, France to Sher Singh, Kot Dafadar, Amritsar District, Punjab, India. (Gurmukhi dated the 9th January, 1917).

*****

O educated Punjabis! Dally not.
O matriculates and graduates! Go to the front.
Show your bravery by raising a Double Company.
Kill the wicked Germans and reach Berlin.

Poem, *The Khalsa Samachar* (Amritsar), 18th January 1917.

*****

"As a New Year's greeting, the King has sent his picture to each and every man serving in the Army here. May God grant long life to the generous Sovereign who has deigned to think of his humblest soldiers."

From Balwant Singh, 19th Lancers, France to Sundar Singh, Amritsar District, Punjab, India. (Urdu dated the 21st January 1917).

*****

"We, the Sikhs in the Straits Settlements and Federated Malay States, assembled here on the occasion of the First Sikh Union Day beg to approach you with an address expressing our deep sense of loyalty to the King-Emperor and our willingness to help His Majesty's Government at all times and in all possible ways.

In the year 1868, a handful of Sikhs came to this country as policemen; and the treatment accorded to us by the Government was so liberal that we have grown to be seventy thousand in number, who are employed in various capacities as policemen, soldiers, clerks, merchants, contractors and planters.

Though we are not rich in money, we possess loyalty to Britain in abundance. We are proud to say that we have supplied more soldiers to the British Army than any other nation of the same size; and we have not hesitated, at any time since the Indian mutiny, to spill our blood for the British cause in whatever place there was need of our service.

Coming to more recent events, during the mutiny at Singapore, when the 5th Light Infantry revolted, the Sikhs, true to their Gurus and their words, stood firmly by the side of their English Officers and never wavered from their oath of allegiance nor ceased to pursue the rebels, till the mutiny was put down.

We beg to remain, Sir, His Majesty's Most loyal subjects, The Sikhs of S.S. and F.M.S."

Police Barracks, Gurudwara, Singapore, 4th February 1917.

Extract from Sikh Loyal Address Singapore, 4th February 1917.

*****

"Your servant has been in the field for two years and 4 months. He desires that a sum of Rs. 5 may be remitted monthly to the Sircar, out of his savings, for the "War Fund" as long as the war lasts. If your servant's savings are not sufficient for this purpose, the monthly instalment should be taken from the Rs. 10 allotted by him as family allowance, the balance of Rs. 5 being sent to his family. You should not think that his family will be displeased with this arrangement. They will raise no objection."

From Channan Singh, 19th Lancers, France to the Officer Commanding, Depot 19th Lancers, Sialkot, Punjab, India. (Urdu dated the 14th February 1917).

*****

"I have received your letter and am greatly pleased to hear that even on "field service" our "brothers" (co-religionists) have been celebrating the birthday of our Guru Sahib. Thanks, a thousand thanks, to the Government under whose rule, not only we, but the members of every sect are able to observe fittingly their holy days. May the Guru ever keep over our heads the shadow of this great King."

From Budha Singh, Sirdar Bahadur, Batala, Punjab, India to Amar Singh, Resaldar Major, C.I. Horse, France. (Urdu dated the 23rd February 1917).

*****

"In every house in the Punjab, prayers are offered up daily for victory to our Government and the people are joyfully subscribing to the Government war loan, and are eagerly enlisting in the Army. The eyes and thoughts of all the people are turned in eager expectation to that day when our Government having obtained complete victory, peace and plenty, will return to the land. May God speedily grant the realization of the wishes of the people. It is a well-known saying that "God speaks through the voice of the people."

From Sadhu Singh, Ferozepore District, Punjab, India to Hazura Singh, Machine Gun Squadron, Secunderabad Cavalry Brigade, France. (Urdu date the 16th April 1917).

*****

"Be loyal and hardworking. This incarnation will never come again, so be useful to your king. I am ready to do anything I can to help you and am willing if necessary to give my life. I am prepared to give 3/4ths of all I possess to the Government and live on what is left. Write and tell me what you think; Shall I be right in so doing or not? In your first letter you said "now is the time for you to help." I am ready, for I am very happy and comfortable under the British Raj. For this reason my family and I pray every morning when we rise that the British Raj may endure for ever."

From Bhugwan Singh, Gujrat, Punjab to Lance Daffadar Santa Singh, 21st Cavalry, Frontier Force. (Gurmukhi dated the 27th April 1917).

*****

For months we have remained comfortably in billets
Your own eyes have seen what comfort was provided for us.
After two hours drill a day, we wandered about at will
Kicking about footballs and having tugs of war
Leaping about like lusty lions
For the great Sircar has nourished us like children
For two years and a half our Sircar has been engaging the enemy
Now the opportunity has come for which we have been nourished by the Sircar.
And it is our duty to do our bit in the field of battle.
Without any thought of comfort or discomfort
Having full confidence in God
We must now discharge our debt of loyalty to the Sircar in accordance with the teachings of the Guru.
Becoming one in heart and soul with England
Let us engage the enemy and smite him hard.
Life and death are in the hands of God
Therefore let us have no fear.
It is commendable to give one's life in war for the sake of loyalty.

From Mehar Singh, 38th Central India Horse, France to Bhan Singh, Lyallpur District, Punjab, India. (Gurmukhi dated the 6th May 1917).

*****

"In the present great European conflict the Sikhs in every part of the World have contributed their quota of loyal services to the Crown, and we beg you to assure His Majesty's Government that we, as citizens of the Empire, shall continue to perform all duties devolving upon us to the utmost of our ability.

The British Raj has been a godsend to India, for apart from the beneficence of His rule, we, the Sikhs are bound religiously to honour His name and uphold and maintain His cause, because his advent and rule was predicted by our Great and Holy Guru Sri Guru Tegh Bahadur Sahib, two centuries ago, at the time of his martyrdom.

We may be forgiven a feeling of pride and elation in recalling the fact that the Sikhs fought under the British Flag during the Indian Mutiny of 1857, when the Sikh Chiefs then formed the 1st Punjab Cavalry, whose exploits and deeds of daring in the British Cause were far famed, and as a result of the services then rendered by them there originated the famous phrase "Punjab Saved India."

Signed for and on behalf of the Sikh Community of Kelantan by the President, Vice President, and Secretary of the Khalsa Diwan, Kelantan.

Sawan Singh, Jemadar, President. Bhagat Singh, Jemadar, Vice President. J.S. Bhagwan Singh, Secretary.

Kota Bharu, Kelantan, May 1917.

Sikh Loyal Address Kota Bharu, Kelantan, May 1917.

*****

"Pray continually for the welfare of our King. The Guru has said the "King" should rule so that the subjects may live in safety. The King is the protector of his subjects and it is incumbent on us therefore to pray for his welfare, so that he may in return provide for the welfare of his subjects."

From Lakha Singh, Dafadar, H.Q., 5th Cavalry Division, France to Bhajan Singh, Ludhiana, Punjab, India. (Gurmukhi dated the 2nd June 1917).

*****

"We get everything here that we are accustomed to get in India. Plenty of milk, sugar, ghi, oranges and grapes. Every day the forces of our King continue to advance, and we expect that our King will soon secure complete victory and that we shall return victorious to our Native Land. The Germans are now much exhausted and can do no harm whatever to our King's Army, whereas our King's Army inflicts heavy losses on them daily. What I tell you is the literal truth and if any one says anything to the contrary, he is a liar. I know what I am writing as I have seen it with my own eyes. The Germans are reduced to misery. They have nothing left to eat, whereas our King gives each soldier even more rations of every kind than before. He also uses much ammunition and consequently the loss of life amongst the troops is very small."

From Chaman Singh, 19th Lancers, France to Mangal Singh, Montgomery District, Punjab, India. (Urdu dated the 5th June 1917).

*****

"We are thousands of miles away from Hindustan, how then can we come on leave? Only those people go on leave who are fighting in countries near to Hindustan. Our constant prayer is that God will speedily give victory to our King, so that we may return in honour. Tell my father with due respect, that he should not allow himself to be anxious. There are thousands of men here, besides myself who are fighting for their country, and to do so is our bounden duty. It would not be the act of a true man to turn his face away from this country until our King has obtained victory."

From Basawa Singh, 6th Cavalry, France to Sirdar Ganda Singh, Sialkot District, Punjab, India. (Urdu dated the 23rd June 1917).

*****

"You and Bhagwan Singh ought to give all the aid you possibly can in the war to the Deputy Commissioner direct. Don't think that you will have to pay a large sum. Whatever you give will be remembered in the history of the family as an effort to help the Government and you will be respected for it by the officers after the war. But at this time, do not think of what you are going to get out of it but give all the money, cattle and garis that you can spare as a return for the protection of Government and for the King. The Government has given me two medals, one for Distinguished Conduct and the other for valour which carries with it an extra rupee a day. Government and the officers are particularly kind to me although everyone is fighting like me."

From Risaldar Kalil Singh, 20th Deccan Horse, France to Sirdar Hazara Singh, Lyallpur, Punjab. (Urdu dated the 9th July 1917).

*****

"I am not afraid either to live or die. This is all in God's hands. I have escaped hitherto from a rain of shells and bombs and I believe it will be the same in the future. If He has laid down that my work shall lie in the midst of such a blazing fire I shall go on doing it with His help. There are two points to note in this. The first is that God has ordained my career and the second is that loyalty to the King compels me to serve him and to be true to my salt. I am sure victory is at hand, and we shall soon return to our native land. The enemy's condition is very bad and it is difficult for him to preserve his life. He is surrounded on every side and you will soon hear of a glorious victory being won. He will soon be crushed under foot for the condition of our Army and that of our allies is improving day by day. No one fears death. If a demand is made for a volunteer to go ahead, a thousand offer. The evil deeds of the German have excited universal indignation. He utterly destroyed all the towns and villages and blew up the roads and cut down the fruit trees and has burnt everything. He has seized and taken the civilian inhabitants. This is a not a royal way of waging war. Our Government's behaviour is of a very different kind. It is that of a real King."

From Risaldar Dyal Singh, 6th Cavalry, France to Chuni Lal, Cambelpur, Punjab. (Urdu dated the 14th July 1917).

*****

"Do not be at all anxious about me. God is the Master. May He keep our King well and prosperous. Our duty is to serve our King with loyalty and steadfastness, be it ever so long before we return. What other opportunity shall we have of serving him? Remember this."

From Gurmukh Singh, 36th Jacob's Horse, France to Dafadar Lal Singh, 16th Cavalry, Loralai. (Urdu dated the 28th July 1917).

*****

"His majesty King George V visited his Army in France on July 13th. He came in a motor with his staff. 130 of our regiment went to meet him including 16 English and Indian officers. His Majesty looked at all of us with a smiling face. We formed lines on both sides of the road.

I see that the lumberdar is asking you for Rs. 200 for the War Loan. Do not give him a penny. I have myself subscribed Rs. 200 so do not be taken in by the lumberdar. If he has anything to say let him say it to me who have been fighting for 3 years. I do not need any exhortation from him to do my duty. I have been serving the King with mind, body and property and he has no right to worry you. If he says anything more let me know."

From Ressaidar Ganda Singh, 6th Cavalry, France to Gobind Sahai, Pind Dadan Khan, Jhelum. (Urdu dated the 30th July,1917).

*****

"The winter has commenced here, and the snow which causes much discomfort, is about to arrive. Bravo the sentry, who in the service of his King stands at his post, unmoved in spite of wind and cold, until he is relieved in due course! If, at such a time his mother should see her son standing there, in spite of heart rending shell and machine gun fire, she would instantly press her hands over her heart. Fortunate indeed are those parents whose sons have come to this war and are taking part in it. It is fitting that such sons should be born to their parents, otherwise they are useless. I daily call on the name of my brother, Arjan Singh, who testified to his loyalty with his life."

From Chattar Singh, Lance Dafadar, 2nd Lancers, France to Hira Singh, Jullundur, Punjab, India. (Urdu dated the 15th October 1917).

*****

TO BASRA HO!

Khalsa march to Basra ho!
Stop the lurking German foe.
Germany did cruel deeds in haste
And in her greed laid countries waste
Want only drove out people from homes
Catch by the ear these German drones
Khalsa march to Basra ho!
Push back the lurking German foe.
Many a child shot with guns
In sight of mothers killed their sons.
So many died of sheer wants
Stop stop the savages in their haunts.
Khalsa march to Basra ho!
Drive back the lurking German foe.

Belgium did she loot and plunder
Smote her worse than lightning thunder
Pity nor mercy did she show
Advance and goat-like kill this foe
Khalsa march to Basra ho!
And smite the lurking German foe.
All solemn treaties she forgot
Burnt towns and cities caring naught,
Drove peaceful people to jungles low,
Go kill the battering ram like foe
Khalsa march to Basra ho!
And smash the lurking German foe.
Sank ships and showed such brutal joy,
Property worth million they did destroy
Perjuring and plotting are their great feats,
Go Khalsa kill these sneaking cheats
Khalsa march to Basra ho!
And shatter the lurking German foe.
From long designs of War had she
Had she her eyes Oh India on thee!
Thirsty was she for Indian blood
But her cunning Curzon understood.
Khalsa march to Basra ho!
And destroy this lurking German foe.
Of her legions she is proud,
Hides evil intent and boasts aloud,
Cruel is she and fit for old nick,
Her swollen stomach deserves a kick
Khalsa march to Basra ho!
Strike hard the lurking German foe.
By terrible onslaughts make her cry
"Oh Grandma! Come, help, or else I die!"
A decisive victory you must gain
Let Teutons feel the Sikh Chakra's main.
Khalsa march to Basra ho!
Lay prostrate the lurking German foe.
Force her to humbly own defeats
Right in the midst of Berlin streets
Then Khalsa shout out "Sat Sri Akal"
By gallant deeds win applause from all.
Khalsa march to Basra ho!
And kill the lurking German foe.
Bring joy to Britain ever more
Great glory and honours for you in store
Reises and Jagirdars ye soldiers shall be

Changed troubles and strife in wealth and glee
Khalsa march to Basra ho!
Wipe off the lurking German foe.

By T.S., *The Khalsa Advocate*, Saturday, October 27, 1917.

*****

"It is very difficult for me to come. Make your own arrangements for the wedding and don't wait for me. We have not the slightest idea when we shall get back. Till our Emperor King George V is victorious, we will not come back nor do we want to do so."

From Gopal Singh, 19th Lancers or 6th Cavalry, France to Gurmukh Singh, Montgomery, Punjab. (Urdu dated the 29th October 1917).

*****

"As regards leave I desire to say that until my King has secured victory, we do not intend to avail ourselves of leave. Don't worry about my marriage. If I live to return, it can be arranged in due course. Rikha Singh is willing to enlist, and you should arrange for him to be enlisted because it is of the highest importance to help the Sircar in this emergency."

From Rur Singh, 36th Jacob's Horse, France to Jawala Singh, Karnal District, Punjab, India. (Gurmukhi dated the 24th January 1918).

*****

And so Teja Singh, now a full-fledged solider, went back to Phul Narbala with his back as straight as a spear and with his chest stuck out like a "Pahlwan". What happened there I do not know, but certain it is that he came back proudly a month later with two of his friends, who were so impressed by Teja Singh's altered appearance, and by his tales of the fine life in the Regiment that they could not rest till they had also enlisted. They both received the reward of fifty rupees, and they wisely did as Teja Singh had done before, namely to send the money home to their parents to help in the upkeep in their homes.

The Commanding Officer was very pleased with Teja Singh for having brought two recruits. "I am very pleased with you," he said; "Since you have come here you have always done your work well, and you have learnt to read and write, and now you have helped the Government in bringing two recruits. As your work is so good I shall certainly make you into a drill instructor."

There is not much more to be told. The Commanding Officer was as good as his word; Teja Singh started his training as a drill instructor that very day, and such was his industry that he learned his new work in less than two months.

And then came the proudest day of his life! Reading the Regimental orders one evening he suddenly came across his own name. What was this?

"The Commanding Officer is pleased to make the following appointment: "To be a Lance-Naik and to be employed as a drill instructor" ... No. 2742 Sepoy Teja Singh."

Teja Singh, on reading this, did not know whether he stood on his head or his heels. The first thing he did was to ask his Commanding Officer for a few days leave so that he could go back to his village and show himself to old Gujar Singh. This was readily granted, and a few days later he and his old friend Kehr Singh, who had also obtained leave, both arrived at their old home. How proud was old Gujar Singh! "It is no surprise to me," he said; "I knew you were good enough to be made a Non-Commissioned Officer. Am I not an old soldier! Do I not know who will make a good soldier and who will not?"

That evening the old man sat in his little courtyard with Teja Singh, Kehr Singh and Atma Singh round him. He told them old, old tales of the time of Ranjit Singh, and no one listened more attentively than Teja Singh, now a soldier himself. But all good times must come to an end, and before long the old man began to yawn. "Before sleeping" he said, "Listen to me, Teja Singh, my son. Had it not been for the help you have always given me every month, I would have starved this year, and so would Atma Singh. The rain failed and our crops came to nothing. By doing this you proved yourself a good kind boy. Now let an old soldier advise you; you have made a good start, and are already a Non-Commissioned Officer. If you continue as you have begun, you will certainly be a Jemadar before long. It rests with you, and with you alone. Always remember you are a Sikh, and that a Sikh is a man to whom honour and good name are worth more than all else in the world. Honour God and the King.... the English King who has given us peace in all the land......obey your officers, do your best in everything you do. That is all I can say; I who am an old soldier tell you this."

I am sorry to have to say that all the last part of the old man's speech was wasted on Teja Singh. He had long ago fallen asleep, and was now dreaming of the coming Hockey tournament in his Regiment, in which, in his dream, he scored 95 goals!

Teja Singh Khalsa joins the army. Government of India, Simla, 1918. (Extract).

*****

5

The Western Front

Corpses lay at every step & the blood ran in little rivers.

We hear the Germans talking in their trenches and the Germans hear us talking in ours.

In the trench the snow rises from the feet to the neck & the feet & hands are frost-bitten.

The enemy's bullets scorch our heroes, while machine guns and cannons spread their shot upon us.

There is no hope that I will see you again. For we are as grain that is flung a second time into the oven, & life does not come out of it.

This chapter concerns the experiences of the Sikh soldier on the Western Front and how they reacted to the war situation. The Lahore Division was the first Indian contingent to reach France and included the 15th and 47th Sikh regiments. They were thrown into battle quickly and fought in the First Battle of Ypres in October 1914.

The reality of full-on trench and mechanical warfare was an eye opening experience for many of the Sikh sepoys. Many commented on the cannons, machine guns and artillery fire. "Many who were met by the cannons blast have passed silently beyond, as one sails away in a ship", remarked a Sikh Risaldar Major.

Trench warfare was very harsh, and the terrible cold, snow and rain prayed on the soldier's morale and well-being. The water could get over knee deep in some trenches, and lice would be a constant concern. "Work in the trenches is very severe for the water was up to the waist in January and February, with cold like that of Kashmir and rain continually falling", said a Sikh Havildar. The cold got so bad that frost bite would take hold, with some soldiers starting to wear three pairs of socks as protection while huddling together under blankets.

As the battles started to rage, many soldiers felt that the 'black' (Indian) soldiers were being put in the front of the line to protect the British soldiers. The Lahore Division lost many men in the first few months on the Western Front. As the casualty tolls started to increase, the soldiers felt that the war was becoming the "destruction of India". Sikh soldiers were also involved in the Second battle of Ypres which was the first battle in which the Germans used poison gas as a weapon. "They used the smoke which brings about madness and everyone becomes insane on account of it", explained a Sikh recovering in the Indian General Hospital in Brighton.

The battles left deep impressions on the Sikh soldiers. On many occasions, the war would be at its most brutal during hand to hand fighting in trenches or villages in France. Sikh soldiers enjoyed this type of warfare as they could see their enemy, which they preferred to a war of big guns. Stories of Sikh fighting prowess and ferocity spread amongst the Germans, with rumours that the Sikhs did not take prisoners. A Sikh soldier recalls: "On being captured and being searched a German prisoner thought the men were looking for a soft place to put the bayonet in; he wept bitterly and the Sepoys tried to comfort him with "Daro mat jawan, daro mat." (Don't be afraid, young fellow)."[1]

Many Sikhs commented on the strength of the Germans and the war machines that had been deployed by both sides. "Flying ships sail over the trenches like birds", commented one Sikh soldier. The magnitude of the warfare and the different types of guns, artillery and shells left the Indian soldiers in awe of European scientific knowledge. The speed of firing is underlined by a Sikh solider at the Somme, "The fire of the machine guns and artillery is so rapid that one cannot keep time with it even by chattering one's teeth."

The Sikh soldiers wanted to share their experiences with kin and comrades through letters. They, by now, were well aware of the censorship and many Indian soldiers tried and many succeeded in evading the censorship. The Censor himself observed that a 'fulsome' letter from Sikhs at the front has got through to the London press. "Till then we had been able, in accordance with orders, to stop all communications from Indian soldiers intended for the English press." – remarked the Censor in September 1915. With the censorship in mind, 'secret' or 'coded' writing became more frequent. Letters were written by Sikh soldiers in cipher trying to explain the predicament that they found themselves in. The censorship was able to pick up on the less subtle code, but there were many that would have got through unnoticed. Soldiers also used the French postal service as a way of getting round the system and again letters must have got through.

Postcard of troops of a Sikh regiment marching down a road lined with trees, France 1914. (Courtesy of the Council of the National Army Museum, London)

1 Anon, *47th Sikhs war record: the Great War, 1914-1918* (Chippenham: Picton Publishing, 1992), p. 31.

The Indian soldiers were said to be very close to their British Officers and the Commander of the Indian forces on the Western Front, James Willcocks, in his memoirs, states "for no argument decked in rhetoric will alter the fact, that you can NEVER replace the British officer in the Indian Army."[2] However, in nearly all the letters sent by Sikh soldiers that were recorded by the censorship, there is literally no mention of their British Officers; only a handful and mostly when they had been killed or in relation to pay. This seems strange taking into account Willcock's assertion. Also, there is no direct mention of British soldiers who fought side by side with the Sikhs; there are, however, a couple of instances where French soldiers are mentioned.

There are numerous mentions of Indian soldiers by British soldiers to be found. A soldier from the 'Black Watch' serving with Indian regiments gives a simple but powerful insight into the world which people from different sides of the Empire had been thrown.

> We of the Black Watch got on with these (Indian) soldiers by sheer force of comradeship, unaided by any but the most rudimentary form of exchange of ideas. We had been warned at the beginning not to attempt to fraternize with Indians. We were told, officially, that they were queer fellows, and we could not hope to understand them. Moreover, we had heard, though not officially, the old story that the only way to make an Indian respect you was to treat him roughly. We never did that. As we passed Gurkhas, Sikhs, Jats and Punjabis we greeted them just as we did the Tigers of Leicester, or the Devil-may-cares of the Connaught Rangers. "Teek, Johnny," said we, "but Allyman no bon" ("Well done, Indian soldiers. The Germans are no good"). The Indians would reply: "Black Watch teek. Black Watch dam good." All would smile very happily.[3]

Sikh soldiers were involved in nearly all the high profile battles on the Western Front during the Great War, from the First and Second battles of Ypres, to the battles of Neuve Chapelle (See Map 1), Loos, the Somme and Cambrai. There were large numbers of casualties and many Indian soldiers were taken as prisoners of war. Letters were also received from these prisoners of war. Most POWs were treated well by the Germans in Europe (in contrast to East Africa), hoping that the Indian soldiers would swap sides. The Germans also used the *Ghadar* newspaper as a tool to support this. Letters from Sikh POWs generally told of their welfare and included requests for money. Desertion was not very common among Indian soldiers on the Western Front, and even less amongst Sikhs. In the first fourteen months there were only two recorded cases of Sikhs deserting to the Germans, in comparison to 36 other Indians.[4]

When the Indian soldiers were not involved in fighting, there was time to take part in sports competitions and shows far from the front. Sikh soldiers wrote letters home discussing prizes they had won in inter-regimental competitions, including sports such as football, wrestling, Tug of War and running. (Sikhs had already quickly embraced hockey when it was introduced into the Indian Army at the beginning of the 20th century). The Horse Shows particularly impressed English officers who, in their letters home, described the trick riding of the Indian Cavalry as

2 James Willcocks, *With the Indians in France* (London: Constable and Company Ltd, 1920), p. 344.

3 William Linton Andrews, *Haunting Years, The Commentaries of a War Territorial* (London: Hutchinson & Co, undated), p. 65.

4 Gordon Corrigan, *Sepoys in the Trenches: The Indian Corps on the Western Front 1914-15* (Gloucestershire: Spellmount, 2006), p. 194.

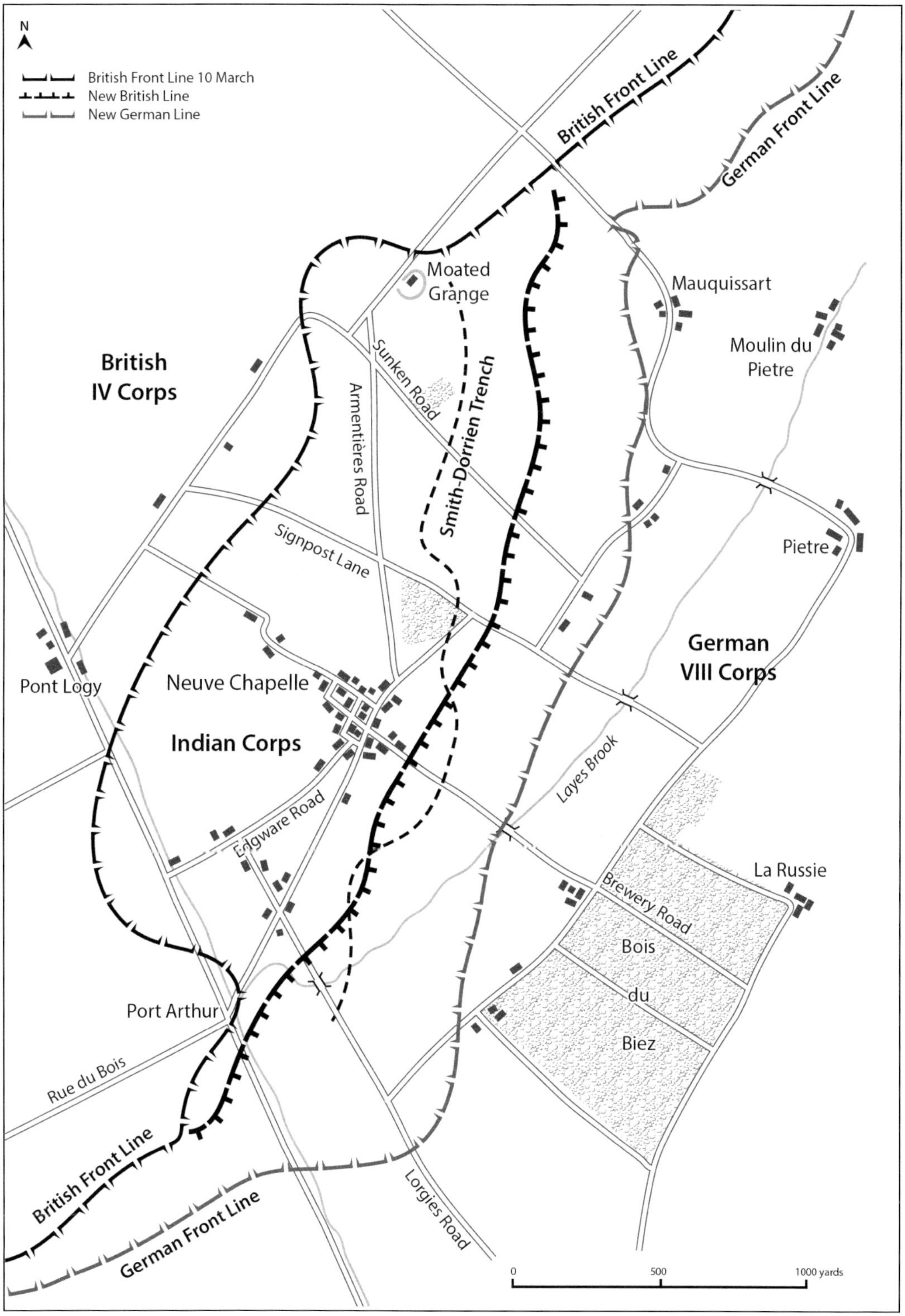

Map 1: Neuve Chapelle, March 1915.

a combination of 'Olympics and the Delhi Durbar'. Sikhs would also be allowed to celebrate important religious festivals, such as the birthday of Guru Nanak. Religious ceremonies would take place and the *Guru Granth Sahib* would be carried from village to village in processions.

A few things in relation to Sikhs grabbed the Censor's attention during the war on the Western Front. Firstly, he noted in one of his reports in November 1915 regarding some medical cures used on Sikhs: "Their dislike for this form of electrical treatment induced certain Sikhs the other day to send a postcard to Lord Kitchener in which they complained that electrical treatment had the effect of turning them into women!" Sikhs were noted to also be uneasy about wearing steel helmets. The Censor was asked to ascertain whether Sikhs were willing to wear the new helmets. In a report in June 1916, the Censor said, "I had a confidential talk on Sunday on board the channel boat with a Sikh Risaldar returning from London and he told me that the general opinion was that whether with or without a *pagri* of any size or shape whatever, their use was forbidden by the Sikh religion, and that this view had been accepted by Officers commanding." As Sikhs spent so much time billeted in French towns and villages, it was highly likely that they would become more friendly with the locals. In a report in December 1916, the Censor related that "For months not a day elapsed without at least one letter and frequently two passing through this office from French women addressed to this man and as we never saw any of his replies it was clear that he was evading the censorship by posting letters in the French P.O."

Several other things fascinated and amazed the Sikh soldiers on the Western Front. "We see all the preparations that are being made and are astonished. The material of war is beyond computation." Sikhs were able to fight alongside French and French African colonial troops and British Empire troops from all over the world such as Canada, Australia and South Africa. They would also encounter people from China and Vietnam on the Western Front. Censored letters also exist of a Sikh Soldier who had enlisted in the Canadian Forces and had been sent to the Western Front.

Sights such as observation balloons and aeroplanes were mentioned often in Sikh letters. A further amazing sight would have been a Sikh called Hardit Singh Malik who flew for the Royal Flying Corps (RFC) during the Great War. This Oxford student, who was originally denied the opportunity to fly for the RFC due to his race, wrote to his brother on his decision to join the RFC in 1916:

> For I do believe that a man is all the better for having been tested in the forge of modern warfare and having been brought face to face with the elemental problems is fitter to live like a man, when all this war and the talk of war is over.
>
> There is of course the risk, but then the risk is not to be magnified. There are millions of human beings running the same risks today and surely one is not fit to live if one is not ready to face death and smile. Besides, we Sikhs have a great fighting tradition and we should not make too much fuss about death. I am not so foolish as to think of nothing. Naturally, one take's one's precautions – all possible precautions – against death for the sake of those who are left behind, but you, being a religious man, will I think, agree with me when I say that one should utterly despise death and scorn it.[5]

5 Hardit Singh Malik, *A little work, a little play: the autobiography of H.S. Malik* (New Delhi: Bookwise India, 2009), p. 66.

Malik flew over the Western Front in 1917 in his Sopwith Camel and was responsible for bringing down German planes. He later flew over Italy too and secured more kills. Malik was one of the lucky ones and returned to India after the war.

Although rations and warm clothing became more readily available by the end of 1916, the cold was a constant concern for the Sikh soldier. As one of them observed, "Today is lovely with a bright sun. The strongest sun here is about equal to our weakest sun."

Ultimately, the British decided to withdraw all Indian forces (the Infantry re-embarked at the end of 1915) from the Western Front in March 1918 and they were transferred to fight the Turks across the Middle East. The Sikh soldiers would take with them tales of digging trenches at night, seeing the mutilation of hundreds of men and horses and "the cannons are such that they throw a shell weighing twelve maunds (1008 lbs) which destroys the earth five hundred paces round about where it falls." Of the terrible suffering from the cold, which itself claimed its victims and the horrible deep mud. With all this first hand witnessing of destruction of humans and land on a massive scale, a Sikh soldier described the carnage as "The war of today is a strange and wonderful thing!"

*****

1914

"If it be the will of God I shall someday tell you the whole story. In the mean time I write thus much. On the 28th October in the evening, while in the act of charging, I was wounded by the enemy's machine gun. My company suffered heavy loss & inflicted the same upon the enemy, many of whom were taken prisoner & many killed. Before this too we had heavy fighting & our troops had proved their fidelity to Government, so that our renown was very great. Well, when I was wounded I came to England & many men of the Indian troops have come to England. Now I am all right again. My wound healed very quickly. The fighting is still going on just the same. I hope we shall soon be victorious. ______ So you are all well & happy, but our brothers who are in the trenches have endured sufferings beyond the power of words to describe. When God grants me to see you again, I will tell you the whole story. I think you will not believe what I tell you ____ of the fighting of our ships & of our fights with the bayonet. I have seen such sights that my wits are still amazed. You generally read the newspapers, but I put very little faith in what is told in the papers. _____ The hospital in which I am was formerly a big hotel. The arrangements are excellent, & I am absolutely comfortable in every way.

At first I was at Brockenhurst which was near Mr Lieut. - Governor Dane's house. He used to come and see us. & the King & Queen came. Lord Curzon came too & other officers of high estate come & they look after us very well."

From ____ a non-commissioned officer of the 47th Sikhs to ____ Sirdar Bahadur & E.A.C. at Amritsar. (Original in Urdu).

*****

Photograph of first camp of Indian troops, Western Front 1914. (Courtesy of the Council of the National Army Museum, London)

*****

1915

"I was hit by a bomb. Now I am quite well again. I am not yet dead I am alive. I do not expect to survive. So long as I live, I hope, while there is breath in the lamp. (sic). ____ Men are dying in hundreds of thousands. If I die, what then? If my arm did not pain me, I should write a long letter. What shall I say about the war? Every king in the world is fighting. Where the battle is there are so many corpses lie that a man cannot walk."

From X.Y. a Sikh wounded in England to a friend at Raiwind in India. (Original in Gurmukhi, dated 15/1/15.)

*****

"Teja Singh & Sundar Singh have been killed by bullets. Ladda Singh has been wounded by a bullet in the leg. My advice to you is that you must not allow any of our people to enlist. For think over this. Here it is freshly noised that four or five men are killed by one ball. ____ Some of the balls weigh ten pounds (800lbs). The corpses lie as thick as ??? in the jungle. With one shot we kill 20 or 25 of them & they do the same with us. The big guns fire a ball twenty miles. There are several other matters about which I cannot write. Our war is against the German Emperor. The English ladies ("meman") love me. ______ I expect to come in about a month. ______ Now I have learnt what kind of thing (military) service is. If I return alive I shall serve you as well as I can. For here there is not one hour's certainty."

From a Sikh wounded & in Milford in England to his father in the Punjab. (Original in Gurmukhi, dated 22/1/15.)

*****

"The war is very heavy & hard. There is little rifle fire, it is a battle of cannon & machine guns. When there is a battle the guns fire hard. The machine guns go on motor cars. The German guns are very cruel. But now the English guns are being used which are far stronger & heavier than those & are much more cruel. The artillery fire upon trenches is especially severe. A lucky man escapes & a very lucky man will meet his brothers again. Countless cannon & machine guns are firing. Think of this carefully & understand what I say. In the trench the snow rises from the feet to the neck & the feet & hands are frost-bitten. Every one will be distressed by the snow & the snow is most distressing. It rains & snows day & night. The sun is never seen. But God's will is being done. Braziers burn in the trenches & one gets as much liquor as one wants to drink, as a protection against the cold. On the 18th day of the twelfth month, the 15th 47th the 59th & the 9th, these four regiments were surrounded. They formed a square & fought hard. There were seven brigades of the enemy around them. Both sides lost heavily. No regiment came to our aid. _____A French officer of artillery came & saluted the General saying he would relieve the troops with pleasure. For, he said, India has come to help us. So the French batteries & the guns were turned aslant & the big batteries behind were warned & fire was opened on the enemy's reserves. Many German were killed & the four regiments were released. On the 24th day of the twelfth month there was a very fierce fight. The whole line advanced & the enemy's guns roasted our regiments even as grain is parched. On all sides men were fighting with sword & bayonet. Corpses lay at every step & the blood ran in little rivers. From the 18th to the 25th in this week many men died. 892 hawaldars died & 87 sirdars & many Sahibs. There was no counting the sepoys. Of these about a lakh died. This was the loss in one week. Since we arrived, the Lahore & Meerut Divisions have been constantly fighting. They came 72,000 strong. Of these 42,000 have been killed & wounded. They are killed. The other divisions are sitting behind. The commander of the Lahore Division says that until both divisions are killed the third division will not join in. 1942000 Germans have been killed & wounded. On either side is there any weakness. When the fight is decided there will be peace. Meanwhile, regiments are being annihilated. _____The German says in letters & newspapers "If any king had German shells & French guns & the Indian army he would rule the world." The Indians have not left their trenches. The men have given their lives where they stood, and the whole might of Germany sits beaten. Our King says that he is keeping India & will have his kingdom again."

From a Sikh wounded in England to a friend in India. (Original in Gurmukhi, dated 29/1/15).

*****

"I have come wounded to England. The bullet is in my arm. There is much to talk of, my brother. Fortunate indeed is he who returns alive from this war. The man whose leg or arm is cut (off) does not go again into battle. But he who recovers from his wound goes back to fight. There are four lakhs of Indians in this war. My brother, this is no war. It is the "Parlo" (the final destruction of the world). A whole world is being killed. If I return alive I shall tell you much. If I end, what is there to tell."

From a Sikh wounded & in hospital in England to his brother in the Punjab. (Original in Gurmukhi, dated 3/2/15).

*****

"We all arrived on the 1st February at Marseilles, and the men of the regiment that had arrived before us are also in Marseilles. All the reinforcements for all the regiments come to Marseilles and are sent on from here to the front. The front is 1200 miles from here. When any regiment of infantry or cavalry falls below strength reinforcements are sent from here. I have written to you before, but I could not give you any news in those letters because the letters written here have to be produced before an officer and we are forbidden to say anything about the war or where we are. If any such information is given the letter is torn up. But I am sending this letter by hand via Bombay where it will be posted and forwarded to you. Those men are returned to the Punjab who have eighteen years' service upwards, or whose health is poor. The fighting is now not so violent as it was said to be at first. Its violence began to decline from the day on which our Punjab brothers joined in the fray. The cold is the greatest hardship. It is so severe that a man can neither open hands nor feet and it rains every day. The sun is never seen. We are all well fed. We get each man twelve "chittaks" "ata", one and a half of "gur", and the same amount of "ghi" every day. Meat we get twice a week, and rum. I cannot tell you anything about the city. If you were to put the whole of Pind Dadan Khan on one side, and one house of this place on the other, they would be equal. The money here is different. It is French money. But France is one thousand miles away and the fighting is beyond France. We have no definite orders about going forward. As soon as orders come we are sent forward by train. The English and the women of this place are very pleased to see us, like opening flowers. They shake hands with our men when they disembark and attempt to feed them from their pocket. There is much immorality here which I could not describe if I were to write for a year. There are people here of all degrees and they are of the same colour and complexion as our English from England (it is possible that this sentence really bears the opposite meaning). London is thirty-six hours from here by rail. if I live I will certainly go to see London at the end of the war … He will be a very fortunate man who returns to his country and his home in safety. I have had a larger issue of clothing here than I got in Delhi. When we go to the front we take with us only the clothes that we stand up in and two blankets and a waterproof sheet. All the rest are left behind here in charge of the government.

The place at the other end where the armies are camped is ten miles from the trenches. The troops are changed every twenty four hours, and each regiment takes its turn once a week. When they go they are fresh and fit. When they return they are senseless and drowned with rain. Warm clothing heated by a machine is out ready for them and the men are shut up in a warm house. After four or five hours they come back to their senses. Every man wears three pairs of socks and warm boots. But even so it appears their hands and feet sometimes fall off. Nowadays, there is snow a foot deep or even more. The rain never ceases. It is said that there will be a great attack at the end of March. As God wills so it will be. Do not be nervous but whatever is fated will happen to me. There is no use in being nervous. People invent many false rumours. It takes 40 days for a letter to reach you, but here we have time to write and envelopes are given to us as many as we want. Do not have any sort of anxiety till the war is at an end. Guns, machine guns and weapons of all kinds are not be reckoned here. But here there are only 2000 men. All the rest have gone forward. The Germans are very frightened of our men but they (the Germans) are sturdy fellows. Several times they have displayed the white flag and then attacked, but now we know their tricks and have taken many of them prisoner. Spread this news everywhere because this is the only letter that I can send you."

From Nanak Singh, 4th Cavalry, written from Marseilles Depot, and sent by hand to India whence it has been returned to the military from the Dead Letter Office. (Urdu, 15/2/15).

*****

"This is a good war. Here we are near the sea and the Germans are extended to the east almost as far as Hindustan; but against them the English and other nations are drawn up in increasing numbers, so that they cannot now move further into the lands they cover."

"The bombs first broke down the mud wall in front, destroying many; the trenches were rendered nearly flat. Sardul Singh was killed by the wind of one without being hit. Then the Germans came in great numbers and we slew them. One or two fell into the trench. Outside they were lying, one on top of the other, so high that we could not see for the corpses. At night, they came again filling the sky with lightings - a kind of magic the secret of which they possess. Again we slew all. They have too many machines, and these are too cunningly contrived. Otherwise, they are not equal to the Sikhs. They are slow with the bayonet, and move heavily. Often, they have no fear."

"I was for a long time outside a village named Festu-Shah where there is always much fighting, and there is a tree on which hang pieces of the soldiers of different nations, all blown into the air by bombs and mines. You may see Indian turbans there and different kinds of caps and boots."

Sampuran Singh, ______'s Horse, letter to his Father, extracts from article, *The Khalsa Advocate*, Saturday, February 27, 1915.

*****

"The war is a very stubborn business. When we arrived we came in motor cars to the trenches. At that time there was no organisation at all on our side. The trenches were full of water. Now arrangements have been made & we get spells of rest. We remain only twelve days in the trenches & then come away for a rest. The Germans seem to be weakening a little."

From a Sikh in a cavalry regiment serving in France to a friend at Loralai. (Gurmukhi, dated 6/3/15).

*****

"No one here says that he will return to India. Even the English do not speak thus, but they say that every man will be killed. They say that the war will only begin next month & that what has already passed is nothing. They also say that in any case the Germans will destroy all us of us utterly. When the Germans attacked Russia, they drove her back. For they are very powerful. We are now in the same trenches in which we were at the beginning."

From a Sikh in hospital at Brighton to his mother in the Punjab. (Gurmukhi, dated 7/3/15).

*****

Neuve Chapelle

"On the 9th March the "Lord Sahib" who commands the Indian Armies came & announced that as the Lahore & Meerut Divisions had both done good work & had suffered heavily, & as the new army had been completed & had arrived from England, our King-Emperor, God bless him, had sanctioned the return of these two divisions to India, where they would arrive in about two months' time. Our regiment is in the Lahore Division. If this announcement is true, we should arrive in India by the end of May. But we do not know the real facts. Rumour has it that the war will be over in June. Since the 10th March there has been very heavy fighting. The enemy has been driven back four miles. Our regiment is in front of all the rest & has lost heavily. On the 15th it will retire from the firing line & after that, we expect, it will not go forward again but return to India. But only a very few men will be left. On the 10th another British officer joined us. He has been wounded. Three Indian officers have been killed & six wounded. We do not know as yet for certain the number of men killed or wounded, but there must be about two hundred of them. For the rest if it be true about our return to India, I will send you a line."

From a sepoy in the 47th Sikhs to a friend, a railway guard, at Gujranwala in the Punjab. (Urdu, dated 13/3/15).

*****

"I rejoined the regiment of the 15th. Since then we have had three turns of fighting. Once we fought for six days, the second time for twelve, & now since the 10th we have been engaged in a great battle. At first the enemy were in some places two hundred yards from us, in others three hundred, & in others one hundred yards & over against them were we. We killed them & they killed us. Now we have begun to advance & have beaten the enemy well back. In these last two days our people have driven the enemy far back & have taken about 3000 prisoners. Of course we lost heavily, but we also inflicted heavy loss on the enemy & we are in possession of three covering trenches. The enemy are now very frightened. When our men without a thought for their own dear lives & in loyalty to our dear government reach the enemy's trenches, the Germans in fear throw down their rifles & come running towards us with their hands up. Now we hope that victory is very near. I expect that you will see your son very soon.

Our losses have been great, but we died doing good work. On the 11th and 12th our losses alone were a captain killed, six British officers wounded, three Indian officers killed & six wounded, & many men were killed. My dear Sirdar, our dear army has earned great honour for the way in which it has come to France & fought. Our regiment is the first among all our regiments. Of course you do not know, but not only have we not tarnished our name, but we have added lustre to it. We can get nothing out of fighting; all the honour is for you. The advantage all goes to the "civil". You must remember us & recommend us. We cannot open our mouths on our own behalf, for this is our rule that forbids our speaking for ourselves. It is a pity that while our army has been doing such fine work, fighting against cold & water, & causing great loss to the enemy, the newspaper men have slept and have said nothing about it."

From a Sikh Officer of the 47th to his father, an honorary magistrate of the Lahore District, Punjab. (Gurmukhi, dated 13/3/15).

*****

"Further since the 10th March severe fighting has begun again. Our regiment is in front of all the others & has driven back the enemy five miles. But it has suffered heavily. You will have heard of this through the D.A.G.. Further General Willcocks Sahib Bahadur has issued an order that the Lahore & Meerut Divisions, these two, will go back to India in a month or two, because they have done very well and suffered very heavily. The King's sanction to this has come & there will be no more drafts from India. If this is true, we shall reach India by the end of May, if we live. ____If this is true, our fate is good; if not, we must rest in hope."

From a Sikh in the 47th now in France to a friend in India. (Urdu, dated 14/3/15).

*****

"We then went into the trenches again, where our regiment suffered severely __ one Sahib & three Indian officers with 24 of other ranks were killed. Seventy-two rank & file are missing, 230 N.C.O.s & men were wounded & six Sahibs & six Indian officers. Kesar Singh has gone to hospital wounded a second time. His first wound was slight & so he recovered quickly. I do not know where he is wounded this time but I hear that his wound is not severe. I have told you before that Harnam Singh is a prisoner. When the war is over, he will be free & will return to India. It is said that the Germans treat the Indian prisoners with honour & respect & give them proper food & drink & look after them carefully. The losses which I have mentioned were incurred in two days, the 11th and 12th March. Now the regiment is back from the trenches in billets & we hope to return to India in May or June."

From Makhan Singh of the 47th Sikhs to a friend in India. (Urdu, dated 19/3/15).

*****

"You proposed to enlist and come to France. (You are lucky because you did not). Perhaps someone may escape from this war. On the 10th, 11th and 12th, the Meerut Division made an attack and won a great victory. We took three trenches, wounded 600 and killed 400. (Then follows a list of killed and wounded) I cannot write all the names. A splinter of shell hit me. I am well again. The German guns throw a huge shell which digs a hole in the ground 35 feet wide and 14 feet deep. My brother such a war will not be again, nor has such a war been before. It is Mahabharat, the death of the Punjab. I have written this letter by stealth. It is true. Now perhaps the new army of 10 lakhs from England will relieve us. The Poona and Lucknow Divisions will come here. Only the lucky man will return. Then the Lahore Division attacked and destroyed three German lines. 400 men were killed and an advance was made of 2 miles. The Artillery fired for 35 minutes. The guns fired for 500 rounds "rapid". The attack was made on a breadth of 4 miles. Perhaps the newspapers will describe it. It is true. The English also suffered heavily. They put the black men (Kalian Admian) in front and the second line is of white soldiers. Of complete regiments only 400 or 200 are left. We black men suffered heavily. They put us in front. We took 12 German Officers including a General. The distance between them and us is 200 yards, sometimes 100 yards. Very many in each Division were wounded. 200 Germans were taken prisoners. On the 27th of February, a mossulman Company deserted to the Germans. What more can I write? Here they are promoting Sepoys to be Officers."

From a Sepoy at the front – 107th Pioneers to a Sepoy in India. (Gurmukhi 23rd March 1915).

*****

"My brother Johan Singh was hit on the hand the first night. He died on the 27th of Kalik. The Doctor declared he had shot himself, and the Doctor had him killed. You must not volunteer for service here. On no account must you come. x x x x. Perhaps the Germans will be beaten. They attacked in three lines. Two lines were blown away. The Gurkhas wounded many with their kukris. When the guns fire the Germans willingly surrender x x x x. The Germans are professors of war. They are fine (lit. heavy) men x x x. When the Brigade attacks, the Gurkhas and Sikhs go first and the white troops are put in the second line. No one asks about the dead x x x . Those who fight against Turkey need have no fear. The Germans have sent their own Officers to Turkey. The Mems work hard in the field. We call them Mems in our country. They plough and roll the land xx. The firing line stretches for 250 (miles) x x x. Many guns are firing, many bullets flying. Many bombs are bursting. At night they send up star shells. Air ships give information. Subedar _____ has become 'Major' and 'Bahadur'. Send him a card and mention me."

From the same Sepoy to a (? retired) Indian Officer of the 128th Pioneers in India. (Gurmukhi of 23/3/15).

This letter is much the same as the last. The following extracts are peculiar to it.

*****

"In Europe our bodies are suffering great hardships, but God has saved my life. The Guru can preserve us in flames of fire. He will preserve us in this world of trouble. Then we shall return to the Punjab – if not, who knows where our future lies, here or elsewhere. This is the will of God Almighty. What is written in our destiny must be. When you write let me know if the wounded arrive in India. What do you think of the war in India? Is there fighting in Waziristan or not? We have heard that the fort beyond Peshawar has been taken by the people of Tirah and that the Waziris have occupied the country beyond Bahnu. Write and tell us the truth. Now hear what is happening to us. On the 9th March the General told the Lahore and Meerut Divisions that they were to make a grand attack and glorify the name of the Punjab throughout Europe. The attack came off on the 10th at 7 o'clock in the morning. We fix bayonets and look towards the enemy. The enemy trenches are two yards off (sic). They have been well built. In front is barbed wire and we are not expected to attack here. With a shout to our Guru we hurl ourselves forward. The enemy's bullets scorch our heroes, while machine guns and cannons spread their shot upon us. We leap the wire entanglements and overwhelm the enemy, killing some and capturing the rest. On the 10th we captured 1650 Germans and took four lines of trenches defending the city of La Bassée. Here from the beginning the enemy have been very strong. On the 10th and 12th we took 2 miles of enemy position. Next day, at 5 o'clock, the Germans attacked in eight lines. There was fine fighting on the battlefield. Eight lines of the enemy were destroyed. We also suffered great losses in killed and wounded. On that day no one took thought of his friend, and the slightly wounded man made his way back himself. If severely wounded a man lay out in the battlefield. When the sun set in the evening the rain began to fall. The wounded were picked up and sent back. The enemy attacked fiercely but were beaten back with great loss. We did not give up our trenches but pressed the enemy hard. They could not recapture their lost lines. From the 10th to the 25th the Germans lost 70613 men. In the hospital it is rumoured that the remnants of five or six regiments will be returned to India. Only the strong man sees the battle and he will never during his life forget its taste. Those who returned to India wounded early in the war have not seen the real battle. Some lucky men have returned to India without having known the taste of battle. They returned smiling to their country. Now only the lame and halt with one leg only and broken bones are sent home. No sound man can return. You will say "you have not told me about the battle". Well, I can't describe it – so many are killed and wounded. Please write and say if any more regiments are coming here. Here in England two pounds of flour cost one rupee (16 pence). Everything is dear. The German arrangements for war are good. They have many machine guns. Their little bomb guns throw bombs to a distance of 500 yards, and they spray vitriol acid which burns our clothes and dries up our bodies. At night they send up star shells, and also make light with electricity (searchlights). The war is a great sight at night. Here cannons are firing, there machine guns, here and there bright lights, there bombs hurl through the air. Bullets fly day and night incessantly drinking the blood of heroes."

From a Sepoy in the 59th Rifles in hospital in England to his brother in India. (Gurmukhi, 5/4/15).

*****

"On the 10th and 12th of March there was a great battle and the regiment lost heavily. Now there are only 100 sound men left. Many have been killed and many wounded. Before this we got a reinforcement of 35 men which brought the regiment to full strength, but now we are reduced to 100 men all told. So the regiment has twice suffered heavily. In the charge on the 12th we took many prisoners and I was wounded. My luck has been very good for I have been wounded twice, first on the 18th of October soon after we arrived. Twice the Guru has preserved me beyond all expectation. Twice a bullet has hit me and twice I have escaped. If the Guru is still kind I may see my brothers again. It will be a day of great fortune. Here we have suffered heavily."

From Pala Singh, 47th Sikhs to a Sepoy of 24th Punjabis in (?) the East. (Gurmukhi of 6/4/15).

*****

"The fighting grows fiercer day by day. This is no war, but the destruction of India. Those of the wounded who are not fit for duty are sent back to India. All the rest are sent back to the trenches. The ground of the field of battle is full of uproar. If you dig but a little depth, water exudes. We have great trouble in digging the trenches. I hope that we shall win, but I shall not be there to see. Have no anxiety about me. As long as I live, I will go on sending you letters."

From Badan Singh a Sikh serving in France with a detachment of the 27th Light Cavalry to a friend at Secunderabad in Southern India. (Urdu, dated 17/3/15).

*****

"I am now about to return to the trenches. There is no hope that I will see you again. For we are as grain that is flung a second time into the oven, & life does not come out of it."

From a Sikh at the front line to his father in India. (Gurmukhi, dated 17/3/15).

*****

"On the 4th day of the English month we captured six score men, among whom two or four turned out to be 'Mems' (women)."

From a Sikh in Hospital in England to his brother of the 45th Sikhs in India. (Gurmukhi of 24th March 1915).

*****

"When you people drove us out of the cantonment [Kohat?] you killed us all. Until now God has preserved us but there is no hope of anyone of us returning to India. This is no war but the destruction of the world."

From a Sikh Sepoy in France to a friend at Kohat, India. (Urdu of 26/3/15).

*****

"I am not allowed to write about the war. But it is true that only the very lucky man can escape to India. As a man picks up a handful of roasted grain and flings it back on the oven (so we are being sent back to fight). Only the crippled and blind, those with one limb and unfit for work are sent back to India."

From a Sikh at the front to a friend in India. (Gurmukhi of 28/3/15).

*****

"We hear that the Lahore and Meerut Divisions are retiring to India. Be sure to let me know if this is true or a lie. Tell me about the regiment and the company. If a man is wounded but not dead, write his name, and if he is wounded put "1" after his name. If he is dead put 2 after his name, and below write that so and so sends his greeting. If you write this way, no one can catch you. Otherwise the letter is torn up."

From Naik Sarwan Singh, 59th Rifles, in hospital, Brighton, to Dun Singh, a Sepoy, 59th Rifles. (Gurmukhi of 7/4/15). Letter sent through letter box, stamped.

*****

"We attacked in the third month and multitudes were killed. The throne of the German King is 70 miles behind the trenches. India is much further off. The Germans retreat every day. Russia is a long way behind. Many German women are fighting, and we have caught many of them and put them in prison. The German war is very hard. We have taken many German cannons and machine guns. There is no rumour of peace."

From Ganga Singh in hospital, Brighton, to L.Naik Bur Singh 45th Sikhs, India. (Gurmukhi of 8/4/15).

*****

"I cannot tell you what is happening here. But you can understand this – a man who returns to the Punjab is one who has died and is born again."

From Mansa Singh, 34th Sikh Pioneers, to his uncle in India. (Gurmukhi dated 12/4/15).

*****

"The German is very strong. His ships sail the clouds and drop shells from the sky; his mines dig up the earth, and his hidden craft strike below the sea. Bombs and blinding acid are thrown from his trenches which are only 100 or 50 yards from ours. He has countless machine guns which kill the whole firing line when in attack. When he attacks we kill his men. The dead lie in heaps. England is full of wounded. No man can return to the Punjab whole. Only the broken limbed can go back. The regiments that came first are finished – here and there a man remains. Reinforcements have twice and three times brought them up to strength, but straightaway they were used up. The German is very strong."

From Giyan Singh at Indian Artillery Depot, Milford-on-Sea, to his brother in India. (Gurmukhi, dated 15/4/15).

*****

"At one time or another the seed, however it may be sown, springs up in the blade. Now the soldiers are all contented and grateful, for letters come continually from their homes saying that their pay for January and February has been received. Our fellows are engaged in work all day, and ready at all times with their loins girded, and making forced marches, but like exercises with the left hand (i.e. that can be performed with ease). Work in the trenches is very severe for the water was up to the waist in January and February, with cold like that of Kashmir and rain continually falling; snow also coming down but when the guns fire they say "Brave soldiers, I am your helper, advance without fear, your enemy cannot make you turn a hair".

The machine guns say "Brave youths, be not anxious for your flanks I am responsible for them, if any foe should cast an angry glance in your direction, I will pull out his eyes and rend his heart in pieces". If we have so much aid, that the guns take care of our wings, the machine guns of our flanks and the xxxxx of our rifles pushes us to the front, what remains in the future? Victory to all when the roll is called. Our good allies the French and our own Government are everywhere victorious, and the enemy grows weaker day by day, and the arrival of our reinforcements increases day by day. There is fighting above the ground, and trenches below the ground; there are flying ships (i.e. aeroplanes) in the air, and battleships in the sea. There are hundreds of miles of front, and the fighting is carried on with much crashing and ingenuity. Our good squadron Commander made our squadron fight against the enemy with much skill and heroism, as the General said when he had a regimental order published."

From Havildar Ganda Singh to Lance Dfdr. Thakur Singh, Cavalry, Sialkot. (Urdu, 19/4/15).

*****

Second Battle of Ypres

"Fifteen hundred wounded have come here – up to the 27th April. No wounded have come from the attacks of the 25th and 26th. What you read in the newspapers is all untrue. We also get the papers but 10 parts of their contents are lies and only one part is true. The Germans have retaken the trenches they lost. Now they have invented a bomb containing acid. Their old bombs were not so dreadful. They used to explode about 15 seconds after being thrown and the men beside whom they fell used to throw them back and wound the first thrower. The new bombs explode in the air and the light shows up the men and the enemy directs his grenades and machine guns accordingly. Thus much damage is caused. France has become frightened for herself and has retired 7 miles, Belgium has retired 7 ½ miles, and Russia 6 miles. The English have retired 1 1/2 miles. I believe that there will be a great loss. Germany has given a clear order that she will destroy any ship left on the sea. She declares that her rations are being stopped and she will shut her enemies' latrines. She is to begin her blockade from the air on the 15th May. At present the weather is so cold that the oil in the airships freezes at a height. Her ships fly great distances. But the British airships do not reach even the German supports. Do not show this letter to everyone. It has reached you with great difficulty."

From Dharm Singh, Ward Orderly, 2594, Section A, 1st Division, Indian Kitchener's Hospital, Brighton. (Gurmukhi, 30/4/15). To Naik Bakshi Singh, 1905 A Company, 72nd Punjabis, Peshawar.

*****

"The battle is being carried on very bitterly. In the Lahore Division only 300 men are left. Some are dead, some wounded. The Division is finished. Think of it – in taking 50 yards of German trench 50,000 men are killed. When we attack they direct a terrific fire on us – thousands of men die daily. It looks as if not a single man can remain alive on either side – then (when none is left) there will be peace.

When the Germans attack they are killed in the same way. For us men it is a bad state of affairs here. Only those return from the battlefield who are slightly wounded. No one else is carried off. Even Sahibs are not lifted away. The battle ground resounds with cries."

From Isar Singh, 59th Rifles in India, General Hospital, Brighton, to a friend in 30th Punjabis, India. (Gurmukhi, 1/5/15).

*****

"L.K.A.M. These letters begin four words. I cannot tell you more." (The words are Lakhan Kroran Admi Margaye, i.e. Hundreds of thousands and tens of millions of men have died)."

From a Sikh in Hospital, England, to a friend in India. (Gurmukhi, 8/5/15).

*****

"After the battle of the 10th to 13th March there remain 200 men in each regiment – the rest were killed or wounded. Then came the battle of the 26th of April. In it the whole of the Lahore Division was destroyed. There are 30 or 40 men left in each regiment – the rest are killed or wounded. Only the crippled men or the man with pneumonia will return to India – no one else – all the others will be killed. No men are left in India. Understand what this war is."

From Hardit Singh in hospital, Brighton, to a brother in India. (Gurmukhi, 16/5/15).

*****

"The war is still very hard and thousands of men are killed and wounded. At present the sides are equally matched and peace will come when they stop fighting. Neither can win. For the enemy is a heroic King. If England had not helped France he would by now have captured all Belgium and France. But he fears the Indian armies and he does not attack their trenches, but attacks at other points. When the Indians attack they capture the enemy trenches but they lose very heavily. The enemy has now returned four or five miles. He held a town where he kept his stores. There was a station in it from where he supplied the trenches. We have captured this town. He will now be in distress. Flying ships sail over the trenches like birds, and were the fear of death not ever present it would be a fine show (tamasha). In France the dogs churn butter, horses wash clothes and cats sit beside the milk without drinking it. Everything is well worth seeing. I cannot describe how kind the people of England are to us."

From Isar Singh, Hospital, Brighton, to a friend in India. (Urdu of 22/5/15).

*****

"I cannot write about what happens here. You must understand me. The black pepper has been finished and the red pepper is being finished. Do not send the rest of the black pepper which is left in India. It cannot be digested here. The red pepper is very useful."

From Kahil Singh (? in Hospital) Boulogne, to Arjan Singh, 25th Infantry, Jhelum, India. (Gurmukhi of 27/5/15).

*****

"We hope that the Lahore Division and the Meerut Division will go to the Suez Canal this month. They met in France on the 23rd of October 1914. Now they will be relieved. They have each made a great name. In every regiment of these divisions, 200 or 300 have been going every week (into the trenches). In this way so long a time has passed (without their complete destruction). I cannot describe the storm here, nor could you realise it. We are now just where we were when we joined in the fight. Neither side can move. But there is heavy fighting. If anyone escapes home from the storm he will tell you about it. Since the 10th of March the fighting has been fierce until now. Shells weighing 700 and 800 pounds fly hither and thither and there is no counting the bombs."

From Jagat Singh, 47th Sikhs in hospital, Brighton, to his friend in India. (Gurmukhi, 10/6/15).

*****

"The black pepper is finished but there is much red pepper. Keep the black pepper carefully."

From Narain Singh, in hospital Brighton, to his brother in India. (Gurmukhi, of 14/6/15).

*****

"I was wounded on the 9th May. I got two bullets in my right arm. I was taken to hospital, thence to England ... At the first attack we lost a very large number of men and gained nothing. With difficulty we took one trench. Then the enemy began to attack. They used the smoke which brings about madness and everyone becomes insane on account of it. Also they squirt acid, which sets fire to our clothes and men die of burns. It is a very bad state of affairs. Our regiment with reinforcements was 1700 strong with 39 Indian Officers. What is left you can see from this letter."

From Rustom Singh, (regiment not stated) Indian General Hospital Brighton, to Lance Naik Amr Singh, 29th Punjabis, British East Africa, 15th June 1915. (Language not stated).

*****

"We all of us send you our Salaams and honoured Sir we are in great need of money. Please arrange that the Government send some money. Also we have no clothes. We are not allowed to say anything."

To Officer Commanding 47th Sikhs
From
No. 1340 Sepoy Baryam Singh
No. 432 Sepoy Dayal Singh
No. 1918 Sepoy Vir Singh
No. 2281 Sepoy Arjan Singh
47th Sikhs.

Message from Sikhs at Zossen, POW camp in Germany. Dated 15th June 1915.

*****

"Airships are such that they travel 100 miles in an hour. They sail at a height of 7 miles. This war is not one of rifles. We do not know how it is going. Here we cannot say whether we shall return alive or wounded or if we shall die."

Letter in cipher code from Basant Singh, 15th Sikhs to his brother in India, 17/6/15.

*****

"I hear that the birds have eaten all the millet grain and there is nothing left but the empty ears."

From Basant Singh, No.2575, F.P.O. 14 to a brother in the 93rd Infantry, India. (Gurmukhi, dated June 1915).

*****

"Here there is heavy firing. The strength of the Germans is great. Attacks are frequent. The regiment lives in the trenches. There is no counting the numbers of dead."

Cipher enclosure to Gurmukhi letter from Sant Singh, Brighton, to Bishen Singh, India. (Address not legible, 16/7/15).

*****

"Many sons of mothers, brothers of sisters and brothers of mothers have been lying dead for a whole year on the field of battle. A year has passed and there they lie. He who sees them for the first time says that there is no place left empty. All the ground is covered with corpses. So many corpses are there and all have perished in forty seconds. As a man climbs a plum tree and shakes down the plums, they fall and lie in heaps. So are men here fallen. There is no turn. They too are children of mothers."

From Santa Singh, now in hospital at Barton, to his mother in India. (Gurmukhi, 20/7/15).

*****

"No doubt one's life is in danger every SECOND, but the spectacle is such as has never been seen in this life. Here flying ships of various kinds are manoeuvring overhead and dropping bombs. Hundreds of kinds of guns are firing. Here MAXIM GUNS are being discharged, there bombs are being thrown by hand. The whole sky is ringing with the noise of pistols and rifles. In some places the scoundrel Germans are using poisonous gas and liquid fire upon us. Elsewhere the flying craft are fighting a battle amongst themselves. Life or Death, my dear Nihal Singh, is in the hand of the Guru, but this fight will not be forgotten till the day of judgement. Now our government has put forward so many guns, that if each were to fire two rounds a day, I expect 100,000 rounds would be expended daily. Each round costs, I believe, Rs.1000. So think how great is the expenditure."

From Subr. Sohan Singh, 15th Sikhs, now in hospital (K.I.H.) at Brighton to Havaldar Nihal Singh, 19th Infantry, Quetta. (Urdu, 29/7/15).

*****

"To the person who examines this letter. Please cut out what is unnecessary and do not destroy the letter."

From Teja Singh, serving in France to Dfdr. Bhagat Singh, 13th Lancers Risalpur, India. (Urdu, 6/8/15).

*****

"There is no hope of the war ending. I expect it will go on for one or two years, unless there is peace. But there is no hope of peace. This war was not begun by any human power, and no human power can stop it."

From Gur Dyal Singh at Marseilles, to Har Sant Singh in India. (Urdu, 14/8/15).

*****

"While we are sitting in the trenches the bullets from rifles and machine guns do not reach us. The trenches are of bags. Many shells and bombs fall into the trenches. These wound a great many men, but kill few. Every man carries 200 rounds. Our trenches are from 100 to 400 yards from the German lines. The latter distance is where there is no room in the (original) trenches (which are full of dead). The corpses of men killed in attacks cannot be removed. We hear the Germans talking in their trenches and the Germans hear us talking in ours. We dig in the trenches at night. The clothes we started in were all taken from us at Marseilles, where we were given fresh uniforms. We are always in uniform and ready. We each have an overcoat and a blanket, and no other clothes. In this country grapes grow in the fields like wheat at home. Pears and apples are as common as mangoes. Potatoes, radishes, carrots, cabbage and beans, of these there is a great harvest here. Everything is very dear. The only cattle are horses and cows. The wheat is being cut now. There is no spring crop. There is ice and snow. We are not allowed to write in plain letters. Lice swarm and the trenches are very uncomfortable. In the trenches they play "plate pianos" (phono-graphs). We read the letter from Bhag Singh to Bhagat Singh by smoking it (warming it). If you send me his address I shall write to him."

From Benta Singh, 57th Rifles in France, to Ratan Singh, 28th Punjabis, Colombo. (Gurmukhi cipher code of 30th August 1915).

*****

"They do not allow us to write any news. Could we do so we should give you all the facts. Understand this that what happened to Jamadar Sharif is going to happen again. (Presumably Jamadar Sharif died in action). We live alongside of him still, and sometimes we push them (dead bodies) aside to make room for ourselves. Anyone who is "bacha o'd" (saved), we call a "bachha" (boy). In one spot 7000 lie at "attention" like Jamadar Sharif, and there are other places like this. We stopped nowhere but came straight to this spot."

From Atma Singh, 57th Rifles, France, to Nanak Singh, 28th Punjabis, Colombo. (Gurmukhi, 31/8/15).

*****

"I am not allowed to write more fully. You know our circumstances – the horror of the funeral pyre –

> "The plantain leaf beside the thorn
> Has but to move and it is torn"

Our bodies are the plantain leaf. What a good thing it is that you are in Colombo and Dharm Singh is at home."

From Nand Singh, 57th Rifles, France, to Bhula Singh, 28th Punjabis, Colombo. (Gurmukhi, 31/8/15).

*****

"You can draw your own conclusion from what I wrote to Nanak. It is with reason that the greybeards call the winning wrestler "Bacha" ("Boy" – there is a pun here between "Bacha" = "boy" and "Bacha" = escaped, from "Bachna" to escape). If you go wrestling with your friends, wrestle carefully and save your legs and arms."

From Uttam Singh, with 57th Rifles in France to Shib Singh, 28th Punjabis, Colombo. (Gurmukhi of 1/9/15).

*****

"If you play hockey and such games, play carefully so as not to get hurt. The fisher who examines his net to see what fishes are looking at it finds it difficult to live. We all see that is going on and we are helpless. We are like men who have been lifted away from the well at Mangalwala and left on the sandhills of Taliawala in Jeth or Har*. If God is kind we shall meet again."

* The well, always under or near shady trees, is naturally often the only place where villagers can gather to sit and talk in relative comfort. Jeth and Har – the middle of May to the middle of July.

From Uttam Singh, with 57th Rifles in France to Fauja Singh, 28th Punjabis, Colombo. (Gurmukhi of 2/9/15).

*****

"I am very well. I am an orderly to a French Sahib, who only speaks English. I always remain with him. Whatever there is to show to our men, the Sahib explains to me in English. I explain it to them. I have nothing to do with anyone but him, nor do I go anywhere (without him). I am in great comfort. If there is an (occasional) annoyance, why, so there is at home. Do not be in any way anxious. I am in no hardship. In short, for sleep, and food and drink and everything else I am so well off that I cannot describe my advantages."

From Harnam Singh, 4th Cavalry, serving in France, to Sher Singh, Municipal Police, Shanghai, China. (Urdu, 4/9/15).

*****

"A draft of Punjabis consisting of 200 men has arrived. We have met them all. The Sub. Major's brother Dildar Khan, who had just been made Jemadar when he came, is dead. He was killed in the trenches on the 26/8/15 two days after he first went into the trenches. When he was hit, the men with him all ran away and he remained lying out at night. Next day a man went and fastened a rope to his foot and the others pulled him in. All the rest are well."

From Sub. Tota Singh, 124th Baluchis attached 47th Sikhs to Bhaga Khan, Clerk, 124th Baluchis, Quetta, India. (Urdu, 11/9/15).

*****

"Since the first of this month we have been in the trenches. As yet we do not know when we are going to rest. Firing from both sides goes on continually. Yesterday evening one of our guns brought down a German AEROPLANE like a bird. One of its wings was completely broken (by the shot) and it fell like a kite from a great height to the ground. It landed about 300 yards behind the enemy's firing line in our neighbourhood. If it had fallen between the lines, we should certainly have carried it off. Of the Punjabi Double Company I have only seen Hav. Sher Dil and Allahbad. For since they came there has been no opportunity to meet. You have heard about the two Punjabi Jemadars – one killed and the other wounded. On the day we came into the trenches and for two days after we suffered great discomfort from the rain. Since then the weather has been fine and there has been no discomfort. When (a regiment) has been into the trenches at one point it never goes there again. They always find some new place to show it."

From Bhagwan Singh, serving with the 47th Sikhs in France, to Naik Abdul Hakim Khan, Q.M. Clerk, 124th Baluchis, Quetta. (Urdu, 12/9/15).

*****

"We are still in Marseilles. The news of the war is thoroughly bad. Below I write the signs which will give you news when we go forward (to the front). For our letters are examined.

The signs are as follows:
I The fighting is very mild.
II The fighting is moderately severe.
III Attacks and counter-attacks.
IV Heavy losses.

B = ILL.
J = bullet.
M = dead."
(The letters B, J and M were letters from the Gurmukhi alphabet).

From Mela Singh, 25th Cavalry (attached 4th Cavalry) Marseilles, to Magar Singh, Lyallpur, Punjab. (Urdu, 26/9/15).

*****

"On the 25th we attacked. Our brigade took six trenches from the Germans, but afterwards the supports did not reach us and we had to retire. In our two companies we lost 25 killed and 60 wounded, and four missing. My brother, no one will come away alive from the war unless he be crippled, or peace be declared, and there is no sign of peace. As we are forbidden to write news I have written this with great difficulty." (Follows a reference to a code – not at present intelligible).

From Pertab Singh, 69th Punjabis, France, to Charan Singh, Hoshiarpur, India. (Gurmukhi, 28/9/15).

*****

"What you say in your letter about not being disloyal to the Emperor, and it being the religion of Sikhs to die fighting the foe – all that you say is true. But if only you yourself could be here and see for yourself! Any shrivelled charas-sodden fellow can fire the gun and kill a score of us at our food in the kitchen. Ships sail the sky like kites. Wherever you look, machine guns and cannon begin to shoot, and bombs fly out which kill every man they hit. The earth is mined and filled with powder; when men walk upon it the powder is lit and up go the men! There is no fighting face to face. Guns massacre regiments sitting ten miles off. Put swords or pikes or staves in our hands, and the enemy over against us with like arms, then indeed we should show you how to fight face to face! But if no one faces us what can we do? No one stands up to fight us. Everyone sits in a burrow underground. They fight in the sky, on the sea in battleships (manabar jahaz), under the earth in mines. My friend, a man who fights upon the ground can hardly escape. You tell us to fight face with the foe. Die we must – but alas! Not facing the foe! My friend, the cannons are such that they throw a shell weighing twelve maunds (1008 lbs) which destroys the earth five hundred paces round about where it falls."

From a Sikh, F.P.O.13 to Mahant Partab Das, Patiala. (Gurmukhi, 18/10/15).

*****

"When the battle is at its height who will say goodbye and go forward to fight? In front of us the Germans ply their bombs. Who will come to show their prowess? The machine guns rattle; who will go boldly forward? Who goes will never return. See it if you like and consider it. Many mothers' sons are dying whose brothers and sisters are far away. What Wazir Singh says is true. I never tell a lie."

"We are 11,000 miles apart. Meeting is impossible … I will write the whole story whether anyone is angered thereby or not. We are forbidden to write; I have written and sent it by hand, and posted it in some post office. If it reached an Indian officer, he will be pleased to see it. We are very well and happy. Do not worry about us.

(Prose) We are now fifty miles behind the firing line and live in houses in the villages and drink fresh milk. We want for nothing and the men and women are very fond of us. We are certainly in danger of being killed, but we never saw such comfort before. Such a country it is, I say in my heart, let the war not stop for two years. We live in such a country; we have clothes without count. If you want any more after one month you only have to take them. The cold in this country is intense. For this reason people are in much distress; and in this country horses work machines with their feet, dogs churn milk, cats watch the milk and pigeons carry letters. We see these things ourselves. We are forbidden to write anything save that we are well and happy. I wrote to you about promotion, and the Major Sahib told me off severely and tore up the letter. I am very fond of writing. The troop officer first reads and looks at the letters then everyone hears them and then they are closed and the letters you send are all read out in front of the troop officer and then given to us. I have posted this letter with the greatest difficulty. I do not know whether you will get it or not."

From Wazir Singh, in France, attached 29th Lancers, to a Rissaldar, in India, 31st Lancers at Kohat. (Gurmukhi, 30/10/15). (Verse)

*****

"You told me to tell you if I was comfortable or uncomfortable. You ought to understand, does a man who is another's servant ever live in comfort? You are a sensible person."

From Sub. Hukam Singh, 34th Pioneers, France, to Karm Singh, Gujrat. (Gurmukhi, 1915).

*****

"And what you say about the letters being very slow in arriving, now I know what that is. Any letter in which anything superfluous is written, is torn up and thrown away. If they were not thrown away you would get them all. That is why you have got so few letters."

From Hukam Singh, 57th Rifles, to Ralla Singh, 28th P.I., Colombo. (Gurmukhi, 4/11/15).

*****

"Do not wait too long for me. When my meat and drink is fated to be in Hindustan I shall surely come. In a few days we shall go back from the firing line. We hear from people that we shall be in our homes by Christmas. But see what our great Guru wishes. No official order is out about it, but it is the common rumour that white troops have come to take our place. The Indian troops will have a holiday for the whole winter. I expect to see you by Christmas. It depends on the fighting; everything cannot be done by the appointed time, as necessities must of course be given consideration. If heavy fighting started here, who would let us go? Accordingly I cannot give you any certain news."

From Basant Singh, 47th Sikhs, to Pal Singh, Jullundur. (Urdu, 6/11/15).

*****

"If I live we shall meet. Otherwise whatever God wishes to do we must accept. Here the state of affairs is that one cannot depend on anything from one minute to another. One cannot foretell what may happen in a single minute."

From Ganda Singh, 69th Punjabis, France, to Munshi Ram, Patwari. (Urdu, 13/11/15).

*****

"My friends, dates are not produced in this country. They grow in Arabia, Persia, and Egypt. Here, however, we have an abundance of rosy apples and pears. If you wish for some, make and send an indent, it will surely be complied with. But remember that they are so icy cold that I myself cannot touch them, although I much desire them, since I am troubled with rheumatism. Tell Bakshi about the apples and pears … You will no doubt be glad to hear that from 1.11.15 I have been promoted to Havildar. Promotions in fact go begging here – there are few left to give them to – but still I am thankful to my officers."

From Ram Singh, Rouen, France. A.G.'s Office, to Sirdar Khundan Singh, Clerk, 128th Pioneers, Egypt. (Urdu, 13/11/15).

*****

"Tell me also what is the colour of the envelopes in which my letters reach you – white or green. I am anxious to know this, for I have a suspicion that the envelope is changed on its journey. I always send you green envelopes in which it is forbidden to say more than is necessary."

From Indar Singh, F.P.O.11 to Sundar Singh, 55th Rifles, Kohat. (Gurmukhi, 7/12/15).

*****

"The cold here is excessive. Here are two stories about it. One day three or four of us signallers were working at the telegraph and telephone. When the message we were at was finished, a Jat added through the wire "If this cold continues for another month or two we shall leave the earth with pleasure." When I think of this story or hear it told as a joke – I laugh aloud. The second story is that on the 19th of November I began writing a letter and found that the ink was frozen in the inkstand. I broke the inkpot, took out the ice, melted it over a fire and wrote the letter to you with the melted ink."

From Signaller Nattha Singh, 30th Lancers, France, to Dfdr. Wazir Singh, 7th Lancers, Force "D". (Gurmukhi, 8/12/15).

*****

"When we make an attack, the Germans do not let us advance. Where one man (of them?) is killed, ten of (our?) dead bodies lie on top of him. The Germans are very stout fellows. They put everyone to flight. The French too are full of fight. We have left France and gone to fight in Egypt. There are no Indians left in France. The positions in France are very strong, and cannot be broken. Neither the Germans nor ourselves can advance. (Both sides) sit in the trenches. What more can I write?"

From Balwant Singh, Marseilles, France, to Nk. Tek Singh, 87th Punjabis, D.I.Khan, India. (Gurmukhi, 24/12/15).

*****

"We have heard that all the (Indian) Cavalry regiments which have come to fight in France are to go to Persia, because here there is no scope for cavalry fighting. Ever since they came they have fought only as infantry. If they go to Persia, they will suffer heavy loss. If they have to go, they will leave this country of France for Persia in the month of January."

From Nanak Singh, 9th Hodson's Horse, France, to Munshi Tulsi Das, Treasurer, Punjab Bank, Nowshera, India. (Urdu, 26/12/15).

*****

"I am well and hearty and a prisoner in Germany. Let me know all home news and if you can, send me money as I am very hard up. Lance Naik Bhan Singh sends his salaams, also Sipahi No. 2807 Chetan Singh."

From Sipahi No. 3508 Chamir Singh, 54th Sikhs, attached 58th Rifles (Zossen) to Naik Asa Singh, 54th Sikhs attached 58th Rifles. (Urdu dated the 28th December 1915 – post mark 1st February 1916).

*****

1916

"This week there has been a football match between our regiment and the 9th. The 9th won by two goals. This is an excellent country. We have heard that there has been some loss (i.e. in the 16th). Write and tell me all about it. We mean to live and die in this country. Live and die – that is what we intend to do. We have no intention of returning to India. It is our very good fortune that our lives should be spent for the government. They are in the Guru's keeping. He must take them some time, but on the part of the government generosity and devotion to its subjects will remain. If the Guru takes that which is in his keeping, I write to you again, do not think that I am sad. You must conclude from the appearance of my letter that there is simply a difference of place for me. Whether here or there all the men of Hassanpur are well and happy … You wrote in an earlier letter that I seemed depressed, and you could see it from my letter. No, my dear Sirdar, even if the war lasts ten years, I do not mean to die or be depressed. When the victory comes I mean to live in this country. I never dream of India. My heart is quite estranged from it."

From Natha Singh, F.P.O.19, France, to Riss. Hoshiar Singh, 16th Cavalry, I.E.F. 'D'. (Urdu, 11/1/16).

*****

"Now listen. We have been fighting for fourteen months, and the fighting has been very fierce. I have been in every fight and have fought with great valour. Our people have exalted the name of our country. When the order comes that the enemy is advancing in our direction, as a tiger advances upon his prey, (we stand to) and with fine spirit knock the senses out of him. Our troops have been accounted the stoutest of all the troops. At this time they are in such heart that they would slay the tiger unarmed. (Every man) fighting with his heroic brethren becomes himself a hero. It was my very good fortune to be engaged in this war. We shall never get such another chance to exalt the name of race, country, ancestors, parents, village and brothers, and to prove our loyalty to the government. I hope we shall renew our Sikh chronicles. Do not be distressed.

Fighting and war are the Sikhs' pap. Such hardships come upon brave men. What is fated must be endured. I pray to God to give us a chance to meet the foe face to face and make a sacrifice. To die in battle is a noble fate. I expect we shall get our chance. It is a fine death to draw two or three breaths only after being hit. It is not good to die painfully. There will never be such another fierce fight nor such arrangements made. Food and clothing, all is the best; there is no shortage. Motors convey rations right up to the trenches. When we go to the trenches we go in such spirits as to the wedding of a younger brother, or like boys to the fair of Chapai. We go singing as we march and care nothing that we are going to die. The fighting is strange – on the ground, under the ground, in the sky and in the sea, everywhere. This is rightly called the war of kings. It is the work of men of great intelligence. We have seen many things of which we cannot write. If we return alive, I will tell you all about it."

From Signaller Kartar Singh, (?) 6th Cavalry, France, to Kunar Khan, Ludhiana Dt., India. (Gurmukhi, 22/1/16).

*****

"This morning we had a dismounted parade in full marching order. Usually we have one twice a week. To-day we marched nine miles in about three hours. As we went we all laughed, and jumped and joked and sang songs and hymns marching along. Washdev Singh and I were together and we had a fine talk and many rumours. All the men of this country from 18 to 48 have been taken to fight. Today we met a fellow of about forty years of age. We asked him why he was not at the front. He said he could not go, because he had too many children. He had five sons and two daughters. Here it is the rule that fathers of five children are excused from military service. They remain at home to look after their children."

From Jem. Man Singh, 6th Cavalry, France, to Riss-Major Gurdit Singh, Rawalpindi Dt., India. (Urdu, 27/1/16).

*****

"My hand is now quite all right. It is my intention if the war ends, to return home with all the honour that is due to me. But to make an end of this business has now become very difficult for God. (It has spread to) far places, to the ends of the earth. But for this, my heart yearns for my brothers and my country, and I ponder whether I shall now go home or not. But my heart has no answer to this question. Here I have several times, in fact very often, seen in a dream Baba Dhanpat, of Madikala, who passed away in our temple. Another man comes with him. These two come especially to see me. I am astounded why they continue to appear over and over again to me. I am in a very far country and do not remember them, but still they appear to me in times of difficulty."

From Dfdr. Diwan Singh, 6th Cavalry, France, to Diwan Chand, Rawal Pindi Dt., India. (Urdu, 30/1/16).

*****

"I missed most of my post from different places when I was in hospital no doubt, as the post and nearly all other arrangements were worst. I must say I prefer to commit suicide than to be admitted into any hospital whatsoever, it may be in England, France or anywhere..........I had gone down a lot when I was in hospital on account of a wound and being starved I must say. Oh, I will talk to you about the hospital trouble when I will meet you personally."

From Riss. Mokand Singh, Camp La Barasee, Marseilles, France, to Captain Bakhtawar Singh, Patiala Lancers, Egypt. (English, 31/1/16).

*****

"What you heard, that we were leaving France and going elsewhere, has proved false. All who were to go have gone. If hereafter we receive orders to go, I will let you know. My dear Harnam Singh, people tell me that last year the cold here was intense, but now it is not worse than the Punjab. We had a few days' snow, but it ceased. Sometimes we have hoar-frost and then it is very cold; otherwise the cold is nothing. We have at present nothing to do. We are better off than in cantonments. Matches are fixed to take place between the regiments, at tug-of-war, wrestling, football and running. We are the winners at football in our division. In the second division the 9th have won. We are to play them. I will let you know who wins. I went to pass the machine gun school. There Rissaldar Kehr Singh's squadron was engaged and he used to come and see me every day. He is working better now, but still takes far too much liquor. He sometimes comes to see me in the regiment too. The orders here are that on Sunday any man may go to any other regiments to see his friends, if he likes. I have not heard anything of Sardar Bachan Singh for some time. If you have any news of him, keep me informed of his welfare. As for the war – read the papers. What is written in them is quite true. Think now, if the Germans have been unable to do us any harm in a year and a half, what can they do now? Our government has very boldly set the enemy's teeth on edge, and for some years after this war, he will have some difficulty in recovering his senses. He will never regain the power which he has now. Our government's intentions are honest. It always helps the weak. (The German) thought to secure in his power all the small kings, but since his teeth have been set on edge, he has sat down in silence.

My dear Sir, this country, through the excellence of education, has reached (its) pitch (of advancement). But for its knowledge, it would not even have been as good as India. For India is a fine country. Everything is produced there. But for lack of knowledge, it would fall short of no other country."

From Hazura Singh, F.P.O. No.39, France, to Sirdar Harnam Singh, 11th Lancers, Delhi, India. (Urdu, 7/2/16).

*****

"I have won Rs.200 /- by wrestling. I had a bout with a man of the Guides' Cavalry who came to our regiment. And now I have to wrestle in the division. The man who wins will get Rs.500 /- and a glass. In the same way there are rewards in all the competitions viz: - (1) wrestling, (2) tug-of-war, (3) running, (4) wrestling on horseback, (5) football. These are the five games. I have won three bouts of wrestling and three are left. It will be decided on the 20th February. I will tell you all about it."

From Sowar Bhaga Singh, 38th C.I.Horse, France, to Kaku Singh, 8th Cavalry, Jhansi, India. (Gurmukhi, 11/2/16).

*****

Postcard, *Illustrated War News*, 7 October 1914. (Avtar Singh Bahra collection)

*****

"You ask me to tell you something (about the war). My friend, you must know that no one, even those as highly placed as great generals, know (what is happening). How then, my friend, is a humble sepoy to know! That which you tell me as having heard, well doubtless you did hear it; but I know nothing about it. I cannot write an untruth. What I hear or know that I write to you of my own accord without being asked. There is no advantage in telling an untruth. What I have already written, you may accept without any doubt or misgiving."

From Ganda Singh, 9th Cavalry Brigade, France, to Naik Mansa Singh, 53rd Sikhs, Jullundur, Punjab. (Gurmukhi, 20/2/16).

*****

"I write a letter to each of you every week. What am I to do if you do not receive them? This is all due to the carelessness of the Post Office officials, who lose the letters of men who have come to the war, as readily as if they were pieces of waste paper. When these postal officials deal thus with our letters (that is the letters of men stationed in hospitals) then what must they not do with the letters of poor sepoys? Even when letters are accurately and clearly addressed, they are knocked about from place to place. A letter sent to me by Subedar Ishar Singh in November was not delivered to me till 10th March. The address on the letter was as clearly written as a row of pearls! Yet it was not delivered to me till the 5th month! This is a sample of the carelessness of the Post Office officials!"

From Dharm Singh, Indian Hospital, Rouen, to Dr. Sarmukh Singh, Hospital Assistant, Simoor State, Nahan, Punjab. (No language, No date).

*****

"You say that you have heard that the entire Indian Army has left France. This is not so. The infantry have left but the Cavalry is still upholding the honour of the Government here. By the grace of God the Cavalry are flourishing like fields of sarson (rape seed) in the Spring. At the present time much rain and snow are falling and consequently the cold is very severe. The snow accumulates all day … Sirdar Buta Singh of Rawalpindi has sent a copy of the Granth (Sikh Bible). He has conferred a great favour on us, since we can have worship celebrated during our sojourn in a foreign land."

From Mohan Singh, 6th Cavalry, France, to Sardarni Bishan Devi, Lyalpur, Punjab. (Urdu, 25/2/16).

*****

"For two months no remounts have come for us. We got seven shiploads – 3000 horses – from India. Now all the horses that come from India are sent to Egypt, for this reason we have received no remounts for a long time. We have here about 1500 sick &c horses. It is believed that some of these will go to the front from here, and some to Egypt. This matter is under consideration, when it is settled I will let you know."

From Rissaldar R.S.H. Singh, Remount Depot, Marseilles, to Dfdr. Budh Singh, Gujrat, Punjab. (Urdu, 28/2/16).

*****

"I write you a letter practically every week. Consider, why do not the letters reach you? I cannot myself suggest the reason. Consider the matter in your own mind. No doubt you will find the reason."

(Note: The writer no doubt has in his mind either the operation of the censorship or the danger of submarines).

From Budh Singh, Sialkot Cavalry Bde., France, to Bishen Singh, Rawal Pindi, Punjab. (Urdu, 6/3/16).

*****

"If I were permitted to write about the ladies what should I write? Moreover it is not permitted to write on such a subject. I am an officer's orderly. The ladies said "Have the photograph taken because we are going to England." I have done nothing wrong. It was only a matter of affection. They were very kind to me."

From Ganda Singh, 38th C.I. Horse, France, to Bahadur Singh, Lahore. (Gurmukhi, 7/3/16).

*****

"Do not ever concern yourself about my safety. You know full well that when a man becomes a soldier, he on the first day of service offers his life as a sacrifice to the Government. His head is sold and purchased on the first day. Therefore have no concern for me even inadvertently and go on doing your own work to the best of your ability."

From Kartar Singh, 6th Cavalry, France, to Ram Rakha, Jullundur, Punjab. (Urdu, 7/3/16).

*****

"It happened on the 13th March. Some of the men in the Musalman Squadron were practising bomb throwing. One of the men had a bomb in his hand ready to throw. When the bomb exploded 9 men were injured by the explosion. One died at 8 o'clock yesterday morning. The British officer Captain Bennett [?] was seriously hurt, and there is no hope of his recovery. A Jemadar and two men are also seriously hurt. The remaining four are fit for work. This calamity has cast a shadow over the regiment. Captain Bennett (?) was a very kind hearted and honourable gentleman. I feel so sad about it all that I can write no more today."

From Kehar Singh, 3rd Skinner's Horse, France, to Sirdar Harnam Singh, Rupar, Punjab. (Urdu, 15/3/16).

*****

"We had a tug of war on the 19th with Jacob's Horse in which we scored a decisive victory. The British officers were very pleased and General Leader with his own hand presented the prizes and we got 30 francs. The 29th Lancers and the 38th C.I. Horse had a wrestling match on foot in which the latter won. They got 70 francs. Then the 2nd Lancers and the 29th Lancers had a wrestling match on horseback. The 2nd won and got 30 francs. The regiment is in excellent condition."

From Jit Singh, 19th Lancers, France, to Risaldar Major Abdul Aziz, 19th Lancers, Marseilles. (Urdu, 21/3/16).

*****

"I have written you many letters but you have never answered one of them. I am very hard up indeed for money and want a Khaki turban. Mind you send me money without fail. Many men are getting money and why cannot you send me some? If you do not choose to send it you must do as you like. If you have not got the money get it deducted from my pay. I am very well. Do not be anxious about me. The following men of my regiment are with me:

299 Pala Singh Havildar
1479 Lance Dafadar Ishar Singh
2081 Sipahi Mal Singh
Mana (Mahomedan) stretcher bearer
Kidi Khan.

Nika Singh Havildar is wounded and in hospital. I have not seen him. I hope he will soon be well. Sipahi 1173 Rajan Singh is also with me. He belongs to the 66th Punjabis. Malla Singh No.627 of the 76th Punjabis is with me too."

From Lala Singh, Havildar, 82nd Punjabis attached 58th Rifles, Zossen, Berlin to Jemadar Deva Singh, 82nd Punjabis (Gurmukhi without date, Postmark Zossen dated the 21st March 1916).

*****

"There is a big 'maidan' close by us where we exercise. It was covered with crops but Government took it up for a training ground. We are all in houses but the horses are outside. The horses are not in good condition at all owing to their being outside in all this cold and wet … What you say is true, but the only person who can form a true opinion about military service is the man who has done it. It sounds very fine to be in the Army but there are drawbacks. First of all you have to be ready at any moment; secondly, you have to take orders from men whom you would not think of employing as labourers in your own village, and thirdly, you have much more inconvenience to put up with than in your own home. There may be honour (izzat) to be won in the Army but after all it is nothing when compared to one's family pride."

From Indar Singh 18th Lancers, France, to Sirdar Dasounda Singh, Amballa, India. (Urdu, 19/4/16).

*****

"I wrote to you before for a warm shirt and a warm vest, also £2 in cash. I write again to remind you about this. Please send the things and money without fail. We get very little pay here, and I am very much in need."

From Sharm Singh, Dafadar, Sialkot Cavalry Brigade, France, to Sirdar Sohan Singh, Gujranwala District, Punjab. (Gurmukhi, 3/5/16).

*****

"Now listen to the details of this war. This war commenced on the 27th July 1914 and it is now the 6th May 1916. Since the day it commenced it has been increasing. It never decreased by so much as a grain of mustard seed. No one knows for certain when it will end, but the great ones think that it will probably end in 1918, even they do not know for certain. On our side the following countries are fighting, France, Belgium, Russia, Portugal, Italy, England and Serbia. On the other side Germany, Austria, Turkey, Bulgaria and Montenegro. Our side however, is the stronger. Where we are there is no work for cavalry at present. We merely do our ordinary drill or when it is necessary to give the infantry rest, we go into the trenches, or where the enemy may be exerting unusual pressure, we go as reserves to prevent the enemy from breaking through. Now hear about the climate of this country. The cold is not severe at present, but it is as cold as it is in India during January. The direction of the wind at present is from the East but the sky remains cloudy. No one can sleep outside or without a quilt. It rains 10 or 12 times a week in the winter and 3 or 4 times a week in the summer. The hot weather (summer) is hot merely in name. As a matter of fact it is colder than the winter in India. Some of the crops are sown in the autumn. At the present time such crops having emerged from the snow are 3 or 4 inches in height. The rest of the crops are being sown now. Both crops will be reaped in the autumn. All the reaping is done by machines, nothing is done by hand, nor could it be done. Some of the draught and ploughing work is done by horses. The country is hilly and gravelly. It is sometimes 400 feet high and sometimes 400ft low. In short it is a hilly country and for this reason it is impossible for the war to end quickly. Such a war has never been and never will be again.......As much as I am permitted to write I have written – for the rest all is well."

From Hazura Singh, Signalling Troop, Sialkot Cavalry Bde., France, to Sirdar Kirtar Singh, Ludhiana Dt., Punjab. (Urdu, 8/5/16).

*****

"I am on that front where there is fierce fighting and the enemy is being pushed back. For a long time there was a savage conflict at Verdun, and many French and Germans have been killed, but our forces are strong in every way."

From Bishan Singh, 19th Lancers, France, to Arjan Singh, Jallandar. (Urdu, 24/5/16).

*****

"Be so kind as to reply quickly to my letters. No doubt what you say is true. Since I have been two years in this country, you have become tired writing so many letters and it is not your fault that you are tired, since the whole world is exhausted. How long can one be expected to write letters? Usually one month or two months, or even a year, but there is no limit to the time that we have to stay here, and for how long can one expect to be remembered? But I hope that on reading this letter, you will act on it."

From Bishan Singh, 18th Lancers, France, to Harnam Singh, Signaller, 39th C.I. Horse, Guna, India. (Gurmukhi, 6/6/16).

*****

"On the 16th June there was a great assembly held in the 38th C.I. Horse to mourn for Lord Kitchener. There was a long service, and the Guru's prayer for the dead was read aloud."

From Mishan Singh, Sowar, 6th Cavalry, France, to Ishar Singh, Pensioner, Rawal Pindi, India. (Urdu, 18/6/16).

*****

"Russia has made a great impression on Austria. Austria had brought great pressure to bear on Italy; but now through the effort made by the Russians, the one who was in the act of despoiling the other, has in his turn been despoiled. Russia has entered Austria to a depth of 18 miles. 1½ lakhs of Austrian prisoners have been made, and we hear that the Austrian killed and wounded number 5 lakhs. If one or two more victories of this kind were obtained, complete victory would certainly be secured at an early date."

From Bishan Singh, Sialkot Cavalry Brigade, France, to Peshawar Singh, Risaldar, 19th Lancers, Sialkot, Punjab. (Urdu, 20/6/16).

*****

"My letter has been delayed because we went into the trenches. We went on the 18th June and returned on the 29th. It was very trying there, as it rains every day and there are consequently many puddles in the trenches and constant danger of bullets, bombs and shells from above. We have to eke out an existence in such places. The enemy's trenches are about 50 yards away. We believe that our Government will succeed. The arrangements of the Sircar are excellent. We receive our rations punctually without fail. Dalip Singh's Regiment has gone to either Mesopotamia or Egypt. I don't know which. The 36th Jacob's Horse are with us here, about a mile away."

From Tara Singh, 6th Cavalry, France, to Gulwant Singh, Ludhiana Dt., Punjab, India. (Urdu, 4/7/16).

*****

"The fighting continues. Our Sircar has taken about 20,000 prisoners. The wounded and dead are beyond count. The fighting is very severe indeed. Many French villages which the enemy had taken originally have been recovered. It is hoped that the enemy will now speedily be driven out of France and Belgium. Our Government is very fortunate, for although we are near the enemy, still we are able to drill as if on parade, and to engage in sports and other amusements."

From Sundar Singh, Risaldar, 18th Lancers, France, to Sirdar Hira Singh, Risaldar, Cantonment Magistrates' Office, Rawal Pindi, Punjab. (Urdu, 10/7/16).

*****

"I am very glad to get a chance of seeing some fighting. The air fighting in particular is a most interesting spectacle. They flit hither and thither like pigeons. The firework displays are very fine, so magnificent indeed that it is no light thing to endure them. But the Guru has given his brave men such souls that the rain of shells does not affect them. The happy feature of the present day is that our benignant Government is everywhere in the ascendant and the adversary is getting daily weaker."

From Huzura Singh, 20th Deccan Horse, France, to M. Sadho Singh, Firozpur. (Urdu, 11/7/16).

*****

"I have not written you for some time, as we are in the jungle. A great general attack is going on. The show is a great one as Russia, and England are smashing up the Germans. Most of the fighting is being done by the Infantry and Artillery. It is a great spectacle and great numbers of the enemy have been captured. The fighting is going on in the sky, on the earth, and under the earth. It is a fight of the greatest skill, strength and bravery. Such a fight is rarely vouchsafed to anyone. If I am spared I will tell you all about it and if I die, why that is better still."

From Risaldar Sundar Singh, 18th Lancers, attached H.Q. Staff, 2nd Cavalry Division, France, to Sundar Avtar Singh, Chiefs College Lahore, India. (Urdu, 17/7/16).

*****

"Today the Cavalry attacked and achieved a great success. The enemy appears to be somewhat weakened. The matter will now be settled quickly. On the other side the Russians are pressing him, and on this side we and the French are pressing him. On both sides he is giving ground."

From Jewan Singh, Jemadar, 2nd Lancers, France, to Sirdar Bhagat Singh Bahadur, Subedar Major (retired) Amritsar Dt., Punjab, India. (Gurmukhi, 17/7/16).

*****

"On the 14th July, Harnam Singh was very slightly wounded in the right thigh by a bullet. He will rejoin in a few days. Kidar Singh and Budh Singh were killed. The Guru Sahib showed his favour on us that day, for the bullets were falling as hail falls in a storm. The enemy was pushed back 1½ miles, and left countless dead behind him. At the present time the artillery bombardment on both sides is very severe, and the shells fall near us, nevertheless we are expecting to advance with great eagerness. On that day 1000 Germans, including 3 Generals, were taken prisoners. Every day the enemy gives ground."

From Hazura Singh, 20th Deccan Horse, France, to Sirdar Sundar Singh, Gujranwala, Punjab, India. (Urdu, 18/7/16).

*****

"I herewith send your honour a translation of an "epithet" written by me on the death of His Excellency, Lord Kitchener. Though it is not very well written or translated, yet I hope your honour would like to read it."

1. Suddenly has disappeared Lord Kitchener, our great hero.
Where has he gone, Our great Hero?
2. A trusted leader of the Armies was that soldier.
Where has he gone our great Hero?
3. Biggest General in the world was he,
To that height had reached, Our great Hero.
4. All around and everywhere we see Armies of Kitchener,
This is one of the works which he did, Our great Hero.
5. In every quarter are engaged the Armies of Kitchener,
Beaten the enemy have they, those men of our Great Hero.
6. As the War Lord he came to see us,
And told the soldiers, our great Hero.
7. "Drive the enemy back"!
He made this scheme, Our Great Hero.
8. Having given this order,
Filled all the Armies with enthusiasm, Our Great Hero.
9. From the small army in the beginning of the war,
He increased to the present extent, Our Great Hero.
10. Having called Indian troops for service in Europe,
He has given them this honour, Our Great Hero.
11. He was an example of the Military heroes,
And has left it for all, Our Great Hero.
12. War always very busy,
He showed all to be doing something always, Our Great Hero.
13. His loss will never be forgotten,
The disappearance of Our Great Hero.
14. Was going on duty when "death" called him,
He was drowned, went in the sea, Our Great Hero.
15. Oh North Sea! Hear me,
Rests in thy laps our Great Hero.
16. Keep him in rest, Our Great Friend,
Who has gone to sleep in thy bed, Our Great Hero.
17. Oh Ajiz! Pray for the great soul,
Who has left us and was a Great Hero.

From Teja Singh, Dafadar, 2nd Lancers, France, to Major A.N.Scott, Depot, 2nd Lancers, Saugor, C.P., India. (English, 21/7/16).

*****

"The Khalsa nowadays join the Gurbani Prem, and the Grunth is carried in procession through the entire village, and is shown to all Sikhs in the Cavalry. Now at the front.

One man is so efficient in reciting the Grunth, that he is employed on that duty alone. Prayer meetings are constantly held, and our Sircar give us every opportunity for holding them. At the present time the fortunes of our Sircar in the fighting are very high. It is impossible to praise this country sufficiently, because the people are so high minded and truthful. There is never any fraud or dissension, or untruthfulness amongst them. They are very kind and helpful towards each other. And what is the root of it all? Knowledge and learning. And why are our people defective? Because of our ignorance. My friends exert yourselves. Learning and knowledge are essential things."

From Harnam Singh, Resaidar, 6th Cavalry, France, to Gurdial Singh, Ludhiana Dt., Punjab, India. (Urdu, 21/7/16).

*****

Somme Campaign

"At the present time the war has reached a degree of violence, which it is impossible to conceive. The number of thousands of shots per second fired by the artillery cannot be counted, and as regards rifle fire it would be quite impossible to estimate the intensity of it. When it rains there are a few spots here and there, perhaps, which the moisture fails to touch, but not even the smallest portion of the surface of the ground has escaped damage by rifle, bomb, and shell fire. If you were to estimate five shots on every square inch of ground you would not be far out of the mark. The enemy is now giving ground. His losses have been enormous. The fire of the machine guns and artillery is so rapid that one cannot keep time with it even by chattering one's teeth. The work of our brave men is worthy to be seen. One forgets the achievements of Bonaparte when one sees what our men have done. How our heroes have gone forward, quite regardless of life and crushed the head of the enemy on the ground! Battalion after battalion follow their music, filled with enthusiasm, just as a snake dances to the pipe of the charmer and darts forward to strike. Such intoxicating music has never been played before. Battalions go forward with even step, steadily and firmly, just as an elephant moves along the road swaying slightly from side to side, to show the worth of their valour. Truly even from the enemy's lips they must have wrung applause. Thousands of heroes have arisen in this war as brave and illustrious as was Bonaparte. Even the heavens do not cease from shedding tears on our warriors, so great is their valour. Hail Europe! From time immemorial the fame of your valour has been spread over the whole world! What in truth can I write and tell you about this war. Things are being done here which stagger the on looking world. Alas the regulations prevent me from writing more fully, otherwise I would write you a volume of details, the perusal of which would inflame your soul."

From Gajan Singh, 18th Lancers, France, to Sirdar Harbans Singh, Ludhiana Dt. Punjab. (Urdu, 25/7/16).

*****

"We are now in the trenches and are fighting with great courage. We have now come to understand what this war is. We do not wish the war to stop yet, we want it to continue. In our village (in India) the fair is held once a year only, here there is a continuous fair. There are many beautiful things to see and fruits to eat. You will have to use much persuasion if you wish us to return. At the present time the war is about a quarter finished. We have still three quarters to accomplish. We are not afraid to die, we have come through some very trying times safely. When we return we will tell you everything. We see men of all nations here, and we have seen all the countries. Formerly those people who had been to China used to come and boast of what they had seen and done. Now we have seen all the countries and we shall never again let the China people come and sit on our doorstep (and boast). You will understand (our worth) when we return with rows of medals on our breasts. Heretofore a "one medal man" has been accustomed to swagger amongst us, even though his medal was pinned on to a shirt of coarse home spun cloth. We shall experience very many and grave difficulties here, but we shall surmount them all and return victorious, even if it takes us one hundred years to succeed."

From Sham Singh, 6th Cavalry, France, to Kehar Singh, Ludhiana Dt., Punjab, India. (Gurmukhi, 30/7/16).

*****

"We are very keen on the fighting and do not be anxious about us. We hope the war will soon be over as day by day the enemy is being crushed. The guns fire all day like the thunder in Sawan. The heaven and earth are indistinguishable and at night there is a regular Diwali festival. There are thousands of men and thousands of different kinds of fighting, on the earth, in the nether regions, on the sea, and under the sea and in the air. This fight is being waged with the greatest ability. It is a very difficult war but the arrangements are marvellous. The shells are passing over our heads as we sit in the trenches but there is no danger. After ten days we get relieved and then after ten days rest we come back again. We are full of fight and ready to do our bit as long as the war lasts. We are fortunate men to have been able to join in the great war. We will do our best to uphold the family traditions and the reputation of our tribe."

From Bakhtawar Singh, 6th Cavalry, France, to Gugar Singh, Lyallpur, India. (Urdu, 23/8/16).

*****

"At the present time we are 5 or 6 miles behind the trenches. Night and day we hear the sound of the guns. Sometimes the firing is so intense that the sound of the guns does not cease for a single minute. Aeroplanes circle above our heads and make observations of the enemy's position from afar. Sometimes enemy aeroplanes come to observe us and reach to a point above our heads. Then our anti-aircraft guns bombard them and drive them back. When we see the shells bursting all round an enemy aeroplane we think it great fun. Sometimes our aeroplanes drop bombs on the enemy's troops, and in spite of gun fire return to our lines. Our men frequently go to dig trenches, but thanks to the favour of the Guru we have not suffered any losses."

From Hazara Singh, 36th Jacob's Horse, France, to his mother, Ludhiana, Punjab, India. (Gurmukhi, 26/8/16).

*****

"I am off for a Cavalry attack on the enemy on the 15th September. It is quite impossible that I should return alive because a Cavalry charge is a very terrible affair and therefore I want to clear up several things which are weighing on my heart at present. Firstly, the sharp things you have written to me have not annoyed me. Don't be grieved at my death because I shall die arms in hand wearing the warrior's clothes. This is the most happy death that anyone can die. I am very sorry that I have not been able to discharge my obligations towards my family because God has called me already. Well, never mind you must forgive me. I have abandoned to you all my worldly possessions which you must make use of without hesitation. Don't worry your grandparents after I am gone. Give my love to my parents and tell them not to grieve as we must all die someday. Indeed this day of death is an occasion for rejoicing."

From Jemadar Indar Singh, F.P.O. 42, France, to Chattar Singh, Ludhiana, India. (Urdu, 15/9/16).

*****

"It is not true that I have been wounded. I was working in the trenches when a shell fell and I was buried in the rubbish. I was insensible and was taken to the hospital where I remained for a week and I am now back again all right at my work. I am perfectly well and not wounded at all. By the grace of the Guru, our King will soon be victorious. The German soldiers cannot fight at all. They throw away their arms and are made prisoners at once. We have made a very large number of prisoners and taken a lot of ground."

From Lance-Dafadar Phula Singh, 35th Scinde Horse attached 36th Jacob's Horse, to Dafadar Puran Singh, 35th Scinde Horse, Jabalpur. (Urdu, 25/9/16).

*****

"The fight is going on with great violence. The ground is covered with corpses and no one touches them. For this reason, the number of dead and wounded lying out in the open is beyond description. Shells and bombs fall in showers. There is no word of when our Indian Cavalry will return to India. I hope we shall not return till the end of the war. The war will last at least two years more and even after then no one can say when it will finish."

From Hazara Singh, 6th Cavalry, France, to Kehr Singh, Ludhiana, India. (Urdu, 7/10/16).

*****

"After you left, our regiment had some hot work. Our losses were slight, 60 casualties, out of which 16 were killed. More than 100 horses were wounded and 25 of these died. Out of my squadron 6 men were killed and 16 wounded, 12 horses were killed and 33 wounded. The action continued from 6pm on 16th July till 4am next morning, when we were relieved by infantry. The whole night we were fighting and making trenches. Subsequently the British Army gained many successes. From 1st July to 30th Septr. the British Army alone has made more than 26,000 prisoners and has captured many guns and much ammunition and material."

From Prem Singh, Risaldar Major, 20th Deccan Horse, France, to Rurh Singh, Ressaidar, 30th Lancers, Peshawar, N.W.F.P. (Urdu, 9/10/16).

*****

"D Squadron made an attack and lost 3 men killed and 7 wounded. 30 horses were killed and 40 wounded. They got the order to seek the village of Thiepval near Martinsast which is on the other side of the trenches. When they got there firing began. They dismounted and took shelter but there was no sufficient cover for the horses which suffered accordingly. But they did not abandon their position until the infantry came up. Then they retired when night came on. They worked hard but gained only a little advantage. But it is proverbially difficult to fill an empty cask with water by scooping it up with one's hands. But this is our idea and it seems rather a laughable one."

From Seva Singh, Sialkot Brigade Signal Troop, France, to Dafadar Lahora Singh, 19th Lancers, Depot, Sialkot, India. (Urdu, 14/10/16).

*****

"Our conditions here are similar to those during Camps of exercise in India. This is the first occasion on which we have lived in tents during two years (except Marseilles and Orleans). Nevertheless we are comfortable, since our camp is situated near villages a few miles behind the fighting line, and we can get everything we require. In the first place our requirements are practically all satisfied by the Government ration, but if we require anything else, it can be purchased. It is only occasionally when we are required to go near the fighting line that we cannot purchase these rations; but we always return to Camp after a few days. Up to the present time we have had no opportunity to fight as Cavalry. Occasionally we have gone to the front as infantry. We fully expect, however, that someday an opportunity will come for us to fight as Cavalry."

From Jai Singh, Jemadar, 6th Cavalry, France, to Sirdar Singh, Sub Inspector of Police, Hoshiarpur, India. (Gurmukhi, 27/7/16).

*****

Postcard, 'Camp Hindou', Western Front 1914. (Avtar Singh Bahra collection)

*****

"The 20th Deccan Horse have done more praiseworthy work in this war than any other regiment. Nor is it likely that any other regiment will do better work. Troop B has become famous. You will have learnt all about it no doubt, from the Fauji Akhbar. We expect that after the present strenuous time is past (it will not last long) we shall attain comparative ease. The Germans are very artful and resourceful but those who are in the right always attain success while treachery only attains transitory success. By the help of God, victory will soon be secured to our King."

From Santa Singh, 20th Deccan Horse, France, to Kartar Singh, L.D., 21st Cavalry, F.F. Lahore, India. (Gurmukhi, 4/8/16).

*****

"I am often in the firing line. I go with each party that goes forward with machine guns, or bombs, or telephones or with the night patrol. I am going strong so don't be anxious about me. Our trenches are from 50 to 100 yards distant from the enemy. At night we come out into the open and work for eight hours. At that time there is considerable danger. The war is certain to end in October. All arrangements have been made."

From Kartar Singh, Sialkot Cavalry Bde. France, to Mota Singh, Risaldar, Sangrur, Imperial Service Lancers, Punjab, India. (Gurmukhi, 6/8/16).

*****

Postcard, *Illustrated War News*, 4 November 1914. (Avtar Singh Bahra collection)

*****

"Although there is danger ahead, our whole force remains happy as it if were celebrating a wedding. Right into the trenches there are various kinds of music and songs are sung. We do not fear death. Those whose fate has come leave us. Do not be anxious about us, we are quite happy. We are anxious about you, simply because you are far from our eyes. Perhaps in November we shall return to you."

From Rulla Singh, Jemadar, 6th Cavalry, France, to Sahilla Singh, Ludhiana Dt., Punjab, India. (Urdu, 7/8/16).

*****

"Just look at the English! They spend their lives in far off countries and they appreciate knowledge. As for us, we are like spiders which do not like to leave their web, and just like them we are unwilling to leave our village's boundaries. A man gets experience by travelling in other countries and cities and you can't get that by sitting in your house. I am more comfortable here that I ever was in cantonments, and therefore you should not talk nonsense."

From Lance Dafadar Chaudra Singh, 2nd Lancers, France, to Harchand Singh, Hissar, India. (Urdu, 9/8/16).

*****

"In future, instead of letters, you will receive from me cards printed in Gurmukhi. The issue of green envelopes has been discontinued and letters on white envelopes are read before being sent on. Nothing may be written on the printed card but signature and date. If anything else be written the card is torn up. The cannons roar and the airships fly overhead, but notwithstanding all the stress and turmoil, the Sircar gives us suitable opportunities for the performance of our religious ceremonies. For this favour we are all thankful, and are strengthened in courage."

From Kehar Singh, (?) 19th Lancers, France, to Ram Singh, Ludhiana, Dt., Punjab, India. (Gurmukhi, 13/8/16).

*****

"I am writing in a big building in a town the name of which I cannot mention. On one side, the town has been laid in ruins, but the other three sides are standing. Occasionally the enemy sends a shell into the town. From above aeroplanes drop bombs. In the night star shells are fired from both sides. In the day one does one's work, but at night one moves about. The inhabitants except for a very few, have fled from this dangerous place. The charm of the place is that it is not more than three miles from where the fighting is taking place. A market is held in the town and occasionally shells fall there."

From Naurang Singh, 19th Lancers, France, to Bhola Singh, P.W.D., Kashipur, Nain Tal, U.P., India. (Gurmukhi, 27/8/16).

*****

"Sometimes we are so hard put to it that we don't get food for five days. In fact our troubles are at times so great that it is impossible for me to find words to describe them. I used to write to you every week before but I cannot write regularly. If you don't hear from me don't be anxious......Before I used to get green envelopes. Now we don't get them and that is why our letters are delayed. Now we have to use white envelopes and our letters are read first by the Indian officer and then by the British Officer. Consequently we are unable to write about our private matters."

From Karam Singh, Sowar, 6th Cavalry, France, to Ladha Singh, Sialkot Dt., Punjab. (Urdu, 24/9/16).

*****

"I am quite well and hope you too are so with all your family. I received your two letters dated 18/8/16 and 8/9/16 during the last three weeks but I regret owing to the regiment having gone to the front I could not write to you. Hope you will kindly excuse me. We were in bivouac behind the firing line and there was heavy rain for three days. There was too much mud in our camp but by the kindness of Waheguru, the rains stopped and fine weather came on. We could not get a chance to be in touch with the enemy. We are progressing on our front day by day. A dismounted party of our regiment was separated some days ago. They had got a chance to see our Army attacking the Germans. They tell us that as soon as the Germans see our men attacking upon them they at once throw their arms and cry "comrade" "comrade".

There were only four casualties amongst our party i.e. 1 man killed and 3 wounded; all of "D" squadron.

B. Nihal Singh had a narrow escape from an accident while he was walking with the Wardi Major of his regiment who was shot by an office orderly of the same regiment. The orderly was also shot afterwards by the sentence of a F.G.C.M."

From Hazara Singh, 36th Jacob's Horse, France, to Jemadar Man Singh, Depot, 36th Jacob's Horse, Ambala. (English, 4/10/16).

*****

"Our life here which God has designed for us reminds me of the parrot's nest in a branch overhanging a tank. When a storm comes, the branch sways and dips in the pond and comes up again. So we sometimes sleep on spring beds and live in comfortable houses and at other times we sleep on the ground in the middle of the mud."

From Risaldar Ganda Singh, 6th Cavalry, France, to Munshi Kalwant Rai, Shahpur, India. (Urdu, 5/10/16).

*****

"You say you intend to write to Suka Singh (prisoner of war?) Well, I have already sent him a letter, which has perhaps reached him. You cannot send him a letter because any letter sent to him must be written in the French language and letters written in any other language will fail to reach him. Besides you could not tell him everything, since one is allowed to write a letter of four lines only, and in such a small space one can only say that we are well and trust he is the same. Consequently I had written him a letter asking about his welfare, but up to the present I have received no answer. I expect it will take a very long time for a reply to come, because it must naturally take a long time for letters to come from or enter into the enemy's country."

From Hazara Singh, 36th Jacob's Horse, France, to Tara Singh, Patiala State, Punjab. (Gurmukhi, 5/10/16).

*****

"There is no information yet as to how long the war will last, but there is no hope that it will end shortly. We see all the preparations that are being made and are astonished. The material of war is beyond computation. Whatever one requires is supplied without fail. There are hundreds of thousands of men and horses and millions of money are spent per day. Still we get fresh rations every day, and we suffer no inconvenience for want of anything. The arrangements of our King are better than the arrangements of the other Kings. Rations and clothes are supplied in plenty. Half the time is past and half remains to be gone through. If I get through it safely, I will meet you, but if not, well, what does it matter? I have eaten the salt of the Sircar for many days."

From Jewan Singh, L.D., Signal Troop, Sialkot Cvy. Bde., France, to Hari Singh, Jhelum Dt., Punjab. (Urdu, 16/10/16).

*****

"You are right in supposing that the Germans are being trampled underfoot. The day is at hand when the tyrant will receive the reward of his villainies and the ideas he had of world domination will be scattered far and wide and his dream of playing the part of Napoleon will be dissipated. The time is near when the echoes of the victory of dear India will be heard, and we, wearing the insignia and medals which are the reward of bravery, will be restored to the bosom of our beloved mother India. I am very proud to think that I have been accorded the privilege of sharing in this great war."

From Kartar Singh, 18 K.G.O. Lancers, France, to Sirdar Sahib Singh, Nabha, India. (Urdu, 28/10/16).

*****

"I got your letter in the trenches. Two of our men belonging to the 6th Cavalry and a Jemadar and a Naik of the 36th departed bravely from among us for ever. Three more of the 36th and one of the 29th were wounded. Last night our patrol brought in 5 Germans, our 3 machine guns and heavy artillery also pounded the Germans. It was a wonderful spectacle and makes one worship God. The Germans are weakening day by day. We shall soon return victorious."

From Bishan Singh, 19th Lancers, France to Babu Achar Ram, Depot Sialkot, 19th Lancers, India. (Urdu dated the 8th November 1916).

*****

"On the 9th November Sri Nanak Guruji's birthday was celebrated with great splendour, and we all enjoyed ourselves very much and food was distributed. To-day in the Base Depot we consecrated a temple to the Guru ji. Don't forget this."

From Risaldar Tawan Singh, 38th Central India Horse, Base Depot, France to Risaldar Amar Singh, 38th Central India Horse, France. (Urdu dated 10th November, 1916).

*****

"Indur Ram Singh and Jat Ram left for India to-day, one on pension and one on leave. The officers treated them with great "izzat". The General sent his motor car to take them to the railway station and Colonel and Major Rowcroft with an escort of seven Sowars went to the station to see them off."

From Antar Singh, 9th Hodson's Horse to Sirdar Takht Singh, Sargodha, Punjab. (Urdu dated 15th November 1916).

*****

Canadian Sikh Soldier

"I believe this war will soon be decided. You know that there is frost in parts of Europe. What can I say? The frost or rain falls every day and the mud is beyond description and the war is terrible. The Germans are war weary and I could write a lot about their bad condition but time will not allow. On the 13th & 14th November 3000 to 4000 prisoners were brought into the trenches. In two days the British Army made all these prisoners and the French made 3000. The treacherous German is however very hard to convince that he is beaten. I am hopeful that he will soon be crushed."

From Private Waryam Singh, 38th or 58th Battalion, Canadian Expeditionary Force to Indar Singh, Kapurthala, India. (Gurmukhi dated the 18th November 1916).

*****

"I should like to tell you about what happened on November 18th, but I am not allowed to write. I can only give you some idea of what happened. On the 4th November there was a big fight, and much hand to hand fighting took place and many prisoners were taken. The dead were countless. Shells and bullets were falling like rain and one's body trembled to see what was going on. But when the order came to advance and take the enemy's trench it was wonderful how we all forgot the danger and were filled with extraordinary resolution. We went over like men walking in a procession at a Fair and shouting when we seized the trench and took the enemy prisoners. I didn't think of our safety at all but felt that the Guru Maharaj was fighting in me. He is great and it is thanks to Him that I was able to do all I did. Pray to Him whenever you pray that He may deliver us all in times of danger and bring us back again to you. When we took the trenches some of the enemy escaped and some were taken. The dead were countless. The bravery which we showed that day was the admiration of the British soldiers. After the fight they asked me how it was that I was so utterly regardless of the danger."

From Private Waryam Singh, C. Co., 9th Platoon, 38th Battalion, Canadian Expeditionary Force, to Wazir Singh, Kapurthala, India. (Gurmukhi dated the 23rd November 1916).

*****

"There is another thing that I wish to tell you, though the telling is profitless. He is a fool who says anything in his own praise, so forgive me. I do not tell to exalt myself, but simply by way of relating an experience. It concerns the condition of affairs in the house in which we are billeted when we are resting. You know that in every house there are children and sisters, and you know also that the behaviours of soldiers in uncertain. In a hundred there are about 5 really good men, the rest are very indifferent, whatever the class from which they come. One day hearing their coarse badinage and seeing their drinking to excess of intoxicant liquors, I could not restrain myself, and told them that it was not seemly for them to behave in this way, adding that they should pass the days honourably. In fact I reproached them well. The officers and everyone else know that I never touch strong drink, and live cleanly, and for this reason my comrades listened to me and acted in my advice. Consequently the people of the house thereafter treated me with much consideration and respect."

From Wariam Singh, Private 58th Battalion, Canadian Expeditionary Force, France to Indar Singh, Patiala State, Punjab, India. (Gurmukhi dated the 11th December 1916).

*****

"We are in winter quarters but parties are sent out for trench digging and machine gun work. We took one machine gun in to the trenches and we did great execution and gained a reputation in the Brigade. Jemadar Ghulam Khwaja and Lance Dafadar Rahmat Khan were killed."

From Hazria Singh, 36th Jacob's Horse, France to Sirdar Gurdit Singh, Pay Dafadar, Depot, 36th Jacob's Horse, Umballa, India. (Urdu dated the 25th November, 1916).

*****

"The applications for leave for some few men have been accepted; but there is nothing definite as to when they will get the leave. Moreover it is still uncertain whether leave will really be given. Perhaps it is merely mentioned (as being probable) in order to calm our hearts."

From Chattar Singh, 19th Lancers, France to Naurang Singh, Pensioned Dafadar, Ludhiana District, Punjab. (Gurmukhi dated the 28th November 1916).

*****

"Yesterday I returned from the trenches with my squadron (machine gun) after an absence of one month and seven days. When I came to the horses I heard from Didan Singh that 5 per cent of the men will be allowed to go on leave. Our machine guns will in a few days be manned by British soldiers and we shall return to the regiment. Our machine gun squadron did praiseworthy work in the trenches and it is expected that my name amongst others has been entered in dispatches. Let us see what comes of it. The Regiment is distant from me, about 9 miles. It is right on the sea shore and far away. I don't know the reason for this."

From Bishan Singh, Jemadar, 19th Lancers, France to Sundar Singh, Treasurer, Depot 19th Lancers, Sialkot, Punjab, India. (Urdu dated the 30th November 1916).

*****

"Veterinary Assistant Chattar Singh was deprived of his Kot Daffadar's rank, because he wrote to a Frenchman and posted the letter in the French post office. He went away ill for a time, and when he returned, he wrote another letter in the same way and was caught. The result is that he has lost his Daffadar's rank also."

From Teja Singh, Lance Dafadar, 9th Hodson's Horse, France to Sirdar Balwant Singh, Lansdowne, Gujranwala District, Punjab, India. (Urdu dated the 12th December, 1916).

*****

"During the last 5 days the French have captured 284 German Officers and 11,103 men as prisoners, and are daily progressing more and more. This is the answer to the German peace note, which he has sent to the Allies."

From Hazara Singh, Lucknow Cavalry Brigade (unit not stated) France to Sher Singh, Sub-Overseer, P.W.D., Burma, India. (English dated the 20th December 1916).

*****

1917

"I wrote to you about my leave, but it has been postponed for the present as the road to India by sea is unsafe. It is very dangerous and for this reason men are not allowed to travel. I will let you know later on what happens. From the 1st January 1917 increase of pay has been ordained: Rs. 20 a month to Risaldars and Risaidars, Rs. 30 to Risaldar Majors, Rs. 10 to Jemadars and Rs. 2 to Dafadars and Rs. 1 to Lance Dafadars. This good news was read out to the Indian Forces on New Year's Day."

From Risaldar Ganda Singh, 6th Cavalry, France to Hakumat Rai, Shahpur, India. (Urdu dated the 8th January, 1917).

*****

"When leave was sanctioned my name was entered in the first list; but now there is much danger on the sea, and leave is closed till another order is issued. After March leave cannot be reopened, because then the "reaping of the spring crops" (i.e. the spring offensive) will commence. All your letters reach me, except when the (mail) steamer is sunk, then they do not come."

From Masthan Singh, Dafadar, 38th Central India Horse, France to Daya Singh, Maler Kotla State, Punjab, India. (Gurmukhi dated the 23rd January 1917).

*****

"Since 18th January snow has been falling and the ice is so strong that the sun never affects it and the frost is terrible at nights. No water is to be got except from wells, and that is frozen in half an hour, either inside or outside. The ground is like stone and many men have died at night from the cold. The roofs are frozen like blocks of stone and you could drive a carriage over them. The people say there has not been such cold for 28 years and the Zemindars cannot do any agricultural work outside and if this state of things continue for two or three months there will be a famine. It is God's will; no one knows what will happen. I am helpless but I wish I could fly away at night in a dream and see you. The whole world is in distress like me. Who can say what God may choose to do! As to the war we all believe that it will end in the summer."

From Kaka Singh, 38th Central India Horse, Mhow Cavalry Brigade to Niranjan Singh, Ludhiana, India. (Gurmukhi dated the 5th February 1917).

*****

"It is impossible to get leave. It is a question of war. It is no doubt true that the men with this force have domestic affairs so urgent that I can't find words to express my meaning and their people at home are being much worried by their neighbours. I am absolutely hopeless and helpless. Some men were granted leave but it is all knocked on the head now. Do your best to quiet the people in my father-in-laws house for they are at their wits end when they think of the position of the young women and fear for their izzat."

From Jemadar Bishan Singh, 6th Cavalry, France to Babu Pohlu Ram, Hoshiarpur, India. (Urdu dated the 14th February 1917).

*****

"Bhai Bhargun Singh has joined the Mesopotamian Army which is doing a good advance and making a lot of Turkish prisoners. I saw in today's paper that our army is about 14 miles from Baghdad. I hope soon we will be able to bring peace with victory as the enemy is now starving. Our Almighty God will help us in every way."

From Jemadar Bahadur Singh, 36th Jacob's Horse or 29th Lancers, to Nandhin Singh, Lahore, India. (English dated the 10th March 1917).

*****

"At the present time the fighting is being waged very fiercely, and we are advancing continuously, while the Germans are returning completely crestfallen. Our Cavalry had a reading of the Grunth, two miles behind the firing line."

From Bishen Singh, Ressaidar, 19th Lancers, France to Budha Singh, Pensioned Risaldar Major, Amritsar, Punjab, India. (Urdu dated the 4th April 1917).

*****

"We are all well here. Today there has been a heavy snow fall and it is bitterly cold. The mud is very deep and it gives us a great deal of trouble. We are very busy and I have hardly the time to write at all and have no arrangements for writing. Here no one takes any money for anything. Beautiful chairs which noblemen used to sit on are being broken up for pegs for the horses."

From Man Singh, Jemadar, 6th Cavalry, France to Risaldar Major, Depot, 6th Cavalry, Sialkot, India. (Urdu dated the 8th April 1917).

*****

"It is very cold still, with rain and snow. We are camped in the open near the Front and we shall soon destroy the tyrant and gain victory for our King. The German is ignorant, brutal, savage and a wild animal. The villages which we have taken from them contain nothing but burnt and demolished houses, trees cut down and broken furniture and roads destroyed. This is the act of a wild beast."

From N.S. Bhai, I.M.S., P.O. No.7, France, to M. Nawab Din, Jullundur City. (Urdu dated the 24th April 1917).

*****

"The operation of seeding the ground is being prosecuted with greatest vigour. The work is very heavy and the oxen are getting fatigued because where the work is being done there was no shelter for them from the sun, and besides the soil was very wet and soft so that they sank in it to their knees."

(This is intended to be descriptive of the recent operation at the front).

From Jagat Singh, 38th Central India Horse, France to Magar Singh, 38th Central India Horse attached 18th Lancers, Marseilles, France. (Gurmukhi dated the 29th April 1917).

*****

"The war of today is a strange and wonderful thing. When the day is fine, combats in the air are numerous, if not balloons, in which observers sit, mount up for observation to a height of 2 or 3 miles. Thus any movement of troops that takes place by the enemy is immediately known. The contending troops on either side were sheltered in trenches and 'dug outs'. Some of the latter being 50 feet underground. But the German 'dug outs', which were made strong with cement and were very deep, have been completely destroyed by our guns and the enemy had to evacuate them and retire in some places to a distance of 15 miles. Some of the positions evacuated by the enemy were strongly defended by line upon line of barbed wire to a depth of 30 yards and a height of 4 feet."

From Bagga Singh, Jemadar, 19th Cavalry [?] France to Dasvanda Singh, Pleader, Ludhiana, Punjab, India. (Gurmukhi dated the 1st May 1917).

*****

"Today is lovely with a bright sun. The strongest sun here is about equal to our weakest sun but it is an astounding thing that after being so long in a cold climate we feel even this little amount of sun. Just imagine how we shall feel the sun when we get back to India. Today we are perspiring and thirsty. I have come out with a party to graze horses and are camped in a very fine abandoned grove. No one knows where the driver is or who he is. We feel miserable to see the shattered houses all around. There is a fine house here which has been apparently spared by both parties and when I go upon the roof I can see no one but a few Indians nor is there any sign of cattle or of cultivation, only a waste of trenches and wire overgrown with grass over which our poor tired horses have to walk. Here and there are the graves of gallant youths who have died for their country and God has crossed their graves with wild flowers. These are heroes who gave their lives to drive out the tyrant German."

From Jemadar Man Singh, 6th Cavalry, France to Shyam Singh, Sargodha, India. (Urdu dated the 8th May 1917).

*****

"I do not venture to praise you; but truly you deserve praise on account of your intelligence, since you have introduced an excellent arrangement for us. It has often happened that, owing to the British Officer being very busy and also to my own negligence, my correspondence has ceased. Now, however, through the favour which you have conferred on us (by the introduction of Multiple Green envelopes) correspondence has been made easy. Since many letters can be sent under one envelope. Well done! Most excellent! The other hidden things (of the censorship?) are known to the whole Army."

From Ganda Singh, Ressaidar, 6th Cavalry, France to His Honour the Censor, France. (Urdu dated the 9th May 1917).

*****

"Our Sircar Bahadur is progressing daily. The country which our Calvary now occupies has been brutally devastated by the tyrant Germans. All the fruit trees have been cut down (you must read of it in the papers). We can get nothing, not even milk in the villages for the Germans have carried off the cattle and the women."

From Prem Singh, Risaldar, 9th Hodson's Horse, France to Hony. Capt. Mir Jaffar Khan, Risaldar Major, Zaida, Peshawar District, N.W.F.P., India. (Urdu dated the 13th May 1917).

*****

"I was late in writing because we were in the trenches and did not get back till 18th April. We shall soon go into the trenches on foot as infantry and do not know how long we shall have to stay. As to your pressing me to come on leave you ought to realise that I would not stay a day in this country of my own free will. We are praying God that that day may soon come when we shall clasp your feet again. We believe that victory is near at hand because the Germans are weakening day by day and countless prisoners are being taken while our forces are increasing continually. We shall soon be back in India beating the drums of victory."

From Lance Dafadar Sant Singh, 6th Cavalry, France to his mother, Rae Bareilly, U.P., India. (Urdu dated the 14th May 1917).

*****

"This year we are being called upon to fight in the trenches not as Cavalry. It is a matter for satisfaction. Full satisfaction will only be enjoyed when, having beaten the enemy, we chase him to Berlin. The enemy has been driven very far back this year."

From Lakha Singh, 9th Hodson's Horse, France to Sujjan Singh, Risaldar, 4th Bullock Corps, Poona, India. (Urdu dated the 17th May 1917).

*****

"A meeting was held in London when some new members were appointed to the Council. H.H. Sir Pertab Singh and a Sirdar from each of the Regiments were there, and a shield was presented to them from the members of Parliament, which on the close of the war is to be deposited in Delhi as a memento of the war."

From Ishar Singh, 34th Poona Horse, France to Man Singh, Subedar Major, 29th Punjabis, Rawal Pindi, Punjab, India. (Urdu dated the 19th May 1917).

*****

"I hear that the 15th Lancers were exclusively a Mahomedan regiment but that they are being strengthened by the introduction of a Sikh Squadron. This is good and the Guru should help in this."

From Jemadar Jai Singh, 6th Cavalry, France to Risaldar Kirpal Singh, 2nd Camel Corps, Baluchistan. (Urdu dated the 21st May 1917).

*****

"I am writing from the jungle where there are no villages. All the houses have been destroyed by the enemy. It is the hot season now, so we are out in the open. There is a big Canal and we live on the banks and shall stay there for two months. The Germans have gone a long way back."

From Tulshi Singh, 6th Cavalry, France to Munshi Mothi Ram, Parathpur, Rajputana. (Urdu dated the 26th May 1917).

*****

"I had no time to answer your last letter. I am now spending a portion of my precious time in writing this. At this moment every engine of war is uttering its sweet voice and I am sitting in a water hole writing to you. I have committed my life to God. I have just been binding up a sowar who has been hit in the head and whose brain is protruding, but all wounded as he was, his pluck was praiseworthy for he called for his rifle and asked to be allowed to go on ahead. This shows how the conduct of a beloved Government has affected the hearts of their soldiers. This soldier cared nothing about life but his one thought was victory. This is true that the weakness of the enemy inspires us with hope of victory. Our Aeroplanes, Cannons, Machine guns, Lewis guns prevent the enemy from raising his head. If he fires one, we give him 100 shells back. May God soon give us victory."

From Risaldar Daya Singh, 29th Lancers, France to Bhagwan Das, Rawalpindi. (Urdu dated the 30th May, 1917).

*****

Battle of Messines

"The enemy is retiring, and we keep on pressing on after him, either on foot or on horseback, as the opportunity offers. At present we are on foot in the trenches, because the weather is favourable. We are going strong. We can hear the enemy conversing and they can hear us. The enemy has lost half his strength and we are confident of victory. We are nearing the boundary of his territory and when we reach it the fighting will become more severe. The fight is a kind of entertainment. On one side a river of blood is flowing, while 200 yards in the rear of it, bands are playing. No one pays a thought to the killed or wounded, and no one has any fear of death. It is as though everyone were strolling through a fair."

From Kartar Singh, 38th Central India Horse, France to Balwant Singh, Patiala State, Punjab, India. (Gurmukhi dated the 8th June 1917).

*****

"I have been in the trenches since the 22nd May. The Germans are now losing strength and are giving ground daily. The British, Indian and French forces are advancing, and countless German prisoners have been made and are being made. The sight here is a truly wonderful one. Night and day, the big guns, machine guns and rifles are fired. Some are wounded – some killed, though in my regiment the casualties have been few. The end of all of this is not in sight at present, because all the Kings are engaged in the war. We expect that the Germans will be defeated; but one cannot say when that will happen as it appears certain that this war will last a very long time. There is no prospect whatever of peace, till one side or the other has been completely defeated. If we are alive then, the Indian Cavalry Regiments will probably be returned to India, after they have completed three years' service here or they will be relieved by other regiments coming from India. Time after time you reproach me about not coming on leave. Do you think that I delight in undergoing hardships and risking my life? If you think that I purposely avoid coming on leave, you are quite mistaken."

From Sant Singh, 2nd Lancers, France to Mahadeo Singh, Rae Bareilly, U.P., India. (Urdu dated the 8th June 1917).

*****

"My regiment is doing duty in the trenches like infantry. Up to the present we have not had many casualties, and other regiments have fared in the same way. Our British and Indian forces are getting the upper hand and the enemy gives ground daily. The French too are driving the enemy back. The German is so great a tyrant that whenever he has to retire from a town, he sets it on fire and carries the inhabitants away with him. This is great tyranny; but we hope soon to give the German his just reward. His country will be destroyed in the same way. Neither the British nor the French will be content till they have entered Berlin."

From Sant Singh, 2nd Lancers, France to Madho Singh, Rae Bareilly, U.P., India. (Urdu dated the 14th June 1917).

*****

"We are experiencing very great hardships at the present time. We are advancing daily, sometimes one mile, sometimes two. All night we work, and we go to sleep at dawn. The towns which we take are found to be burnt by the enemy, who also cuts down all the trees. He also destroys the roads and the bridges and puts poison into the water. Thus our hardships are at present beyond expression."

From Hazura Singh, 19th Lancers [?] France to his mother, Ludhiana District, Punjab, India. (Urdu dated the 8th June 1917).

*****

"The bullets fall here in the same profusion as fireworks at the marriage of a rich man's son. We will not return till we have penetrated into Germany and exploded our fireworks there. Our lust for battle is not yet satisfied. For 3 years we have experienced many trials and fought in various ways; but the real fighting will commence when we begin to burn their houses and break open their doors and despoil their goods. Then the end will be in sight. It will come, about the completion of the third year – not before. Never mind, even if the war lasts ten years, we shall leave our mark here. If we die, no matter – if we survive, no matter; but to die in battle is a glorious end. It is not well to die in one's bed wrapped up in a blanket. Better a bullet and then oblivion in ten minutes."

From Kartar Singh, 38th Central India Horse, France to Jhaman Singh, Lyallpur District, Punjab, India. (Gurmukhi dated the 8th June 1917).

*****

"There is a matter which I am very loth to write about which has inflicted a great stain on us but I feel obliged to tell you about it, because official notice is sure to reach the Depot. Sowar Sham Singh and Ram Singh on the 30th were tried by Court Martial for not relieving each other on sentry duty and leaving the place without any sentry. They were sentenced to be shot, but this punishment is generally commuted to one of a year's imprisonment. These two men have disgraced the caste and the Squadron."

From Man Singh, 6th Cavalry, France to Sirdar Gurdatt Singh, Risaldar Major, 6th Cavalry, Depot, Sialkot. (Urdu dated the 9th June 1917).

*****

"The enemy is retiring daily. The arrangements of our Government are very good. We are stinted for nothing, we get everything in plenty. Clean, fresh, water is brought for us from the rear. In fact at the present time the Government has thrown wide the doors of the treasury, and those men are liars who sitting at home, spoke to the contrary. I do not suppose that there are any such now, since many wounded have returned and have doubtless described exactly how matters are here."

From Ganda Singh, Ressaidar, 6th Cavalry, France to Hakumat Rai, Shahpur District, Punjab, India. (Urdu dated the 12th June 1917).

*****

"We are getting on all right up to date, thanks to God's care as to food and drink we have no cares whatever. I will give you an example. You remember the ghee we used to get on bread and about which we used to quarrel with grandmother when she did not give us enough. Well we get such a supply of that that when any one comes to see me I give him two or three seers without hesitation. If a friend comes we use about 15 tins of it and another 15 tins of Gur. This all comes out of our ration. We have only two or three hours of work and then I get on my cycle and go out for a round. The officers are very pleased with us just now."

From Dafadar Tar Singh, 19th Lancers, France to Budh Singh, Rawalpindi. (Urdu dated the 20th June 1917).

*****

"There is a great difference between the fighting now and what it was. The Germans have retreated and the Americans have arrived. The horses have plenty of grazing on grass and lucerne in the villages which the Germans used to occupy."

From Risaldar Harnam Singh, 6th Cavalry, France to Udai Chand, Depot, Sialkot. (Urdu dated the 2nd July 1917).

*****

"What news can I give you but the following:

> Many bridegrooms whose thoughts were with their brides have passed away.
> Many other men have struggled with death like fluttering pigeons.
> Their widows are weeping, since nothing but sorrow remains for them on earth.
> Many who were met by the cannons blast have passed silently beyond, as one sails away in a ship."

From Amar Singh, Risaldar Major, 38th Central India Horse, France to Lal Singh, Dafadar, Amritsar District, Punjab, India. (Gurmukhi, dated the 17th July 1917).

*****

"You say I ought to come on leave because many others are coming. You forget that they are only 3 days' journey by sea and we have 5 days of rail and 25 days of sea if the ship travels fast. You seem to have the idea that our life out here is just as if we were in cantonments. This is a great mistake. We have such discomfort to put up with that I cannot put it on paper for we have not only to fight but to do such work as we have never done at home. I am longing to see you again and the children but I have little hope of it as this is a very fierce combat. Fire rains all day and night and my turn may come any moment."

From Dafadar Tara Singh, 6th Cavalry, France to Chaudhuri Ishar Singh, Hoshiarpur. (Urdu dated the 13th August 1917).

*****

"Do not be anxious because we are very comfortable here and the Government treats us with the greatest consideration. Even the King and the Queen (who is a real Princess) came here four times to see us. They asked all the men if they had any complaint to make about anything at their homes and they all said "No". The Colonel asks us all every month whether we have any trouble at home and if any one says he has, the Colonel sends on his petition to the Deputy Commissioner who decides satisfactorily."

From Chattar Singh, 19th Lancers or 6th Cavalry to Harnam Singh, Gurdaspur. (Urdu dated the 17th August 1917).

*****

"I am in a place just now entirely destitute of trees from which the enemy has retreated. He demolished all the villages before he left and destroyed the railway station. They say that he carried off everything that was valuable and broke up the rest. We have rescued 22 villages from them. The Germans are retreating and we are advancing. They are much weaker than they were."

From Harnam Singh, 6th Cavalry, France to Karam Singh, Ludhiana, Punjab. (Gurmukhi dated the 25th August 1917).

*****

"Ever since March we have been visiting the trenches. The war is at its height and every day four or five attacks take place. We are working on foot day and night and you know what we suffer. There is no need for me to write. We get plenty of rations, the trouble is that that we are always in uniform and get no time to sleep, and as for bathing, we never can think of it. The lice are crawling over us. Our hearts are failing us because of the length of the war. All the rest of our force has been transferred and we have no hope of leave. We are weak and the war is long because it is only this year that our Government has advanced. It is a great fight and we advance every day and we shall conquer but it will take five or six years."

From Kartar Singh, 6th Cavalry, France to Risaldar Moti Singh, Sangrur. (Urdu dated the 25th August 1917).

*****

"The fourth year of the war has begun and the combatants are still fighting with firm feet. If any one advances in the day, double the advance is made by the other party at night. They are all fighting now most cleverly having profited by their experiences. For this reason there is no end to the war. We have recovered from the Germans since March about one fourth of the land they took and it is now in the possession of our French friends. The villainy of the enemy is shown by the way in which he has burnt down or blown up the finest houses. He has cut down all the trees from the most valuable to the smallest bush. He has burnt everything from the noble's palace to the peasant's hut. When one looks at the terrible state of the country, one longs to slay the enemy at once but it is alas impossible. It is a war of Kings."

From Hazura Singh, 6th Cavalry, France to Bisambar Das, Lucknow. (Urdu dated the 26th August 1917).

*****

"Until the war ceases we have no hope. No leave is given to the Cavalry units in France, nor are they relieved. Those who have served their full time are pensioned, and if I live till then, I will return on pension in October 1918. Here we are required to do every kind of war work. This war is terrible. Nothing like it has happened before. The 4th year of war has commenced, and the strength of our King has increased greatly since the beginning. No one knows when this war will end; but the appearances are that it will last another four years at least. Shot and shell fall day and night and we move amongst them constantly. For three years we have slept on the ground and walked in puddles. We have endured heat and cold, and are kept constantly on the alert. On top of this, our homes are ruined and our children wander from door to door. It will be a propitious day for me when I return to greet you and to see my children again."

From Tara Singh, Dafadar, 6th Cavalry, France to Hukam Singh, Montgomery District, Punjab, India. (Urdu dated the 10th September, 1917).

*****

"The cold here is so intense that one's hand and feet become numbed. In December and January, goodness knows what it will be like. The trials of the "field" are very severe. If I live to return, I will never even mention military service again."

From Anatar Singh, Supply Agent, Amballa Cavalry Field Ambulance, France to Gurmukh Singh, Campbellpur District, Punjab. (Gurmukhi dated the 16th October 1917).

*****

"At the present time the arrangements for food are excellent. In the morning at 7 o'clock we get tea and biscuits; at noon we get bread and vegetable curry with condiments and jam. At 3 p.m. we get tea and biscuits. At night we get bread and meat or fish, vinegar, onions and spirits. In short we get plenty of sustaining food. We are also given sufficient warm clothing. Government always makes the best arrangements for our comforts. The wants of each religion and caste are considered. We are at present in that bit of the country from which the enemy retreated after having suffered defeat. For that reason the soil is untilled and un-peopled; but there are signs that it will become inhabited again shortly. The cold is not very great and it rains occasionally only. The strength of our Army increases daily and we shall never suffer defeat."

From Tara Singh, 6th Cavalry, France to Kartar Singh, Rawal Pindi District, Punjab, India. (Urdu dated the 7th December 1917).

*****

Battle of Cambrai

"This is the first time we have been called upon to fight as Cavalry in our 3 years' field service. Our regiment was at the forefront of the attack and my squadron. Thanks be to God the attack was made with the utmost bravery and it achieved splendid results. The fury of our charge and the ardour of our war cries so alarmed the enemy that he left his trenches and fled. At first we were assailed by machine gun fire like a rain storm from left to right, and afterwards from the front but how could the cowardly Germans stand before an onslaught of the braves of the Khalsa! This credit is not due to us but to the Guru, through whose favour we speared many of the routed enemy on our lances and brought back many prisoners. On our return, celebrated Generals came and congratulated our Regiment. Our losses were light. 2 British officers and 2 Rajput Sirdars were killed and some sowars. Our brave Colonel Turner was also killed. Alas!"

From Jewan Singh, Ressaidar, 2nd Lancers, France to Bhagat Singh, Pensioned Subedar Major, Amritsar District, Punjab, India. (Gurmukhi dated the 10th December 1917).

*****

"We were given a special job to do which has gained a great name for the Regiment. We had losses, but they are small when compared with the results secured. In this affair our Colonel Corbyn was killed. It is much to be regretted. You will be delighted to know that your troop was in the forefront and that I was in command of it. We took numerous machine guns from the enemy and 50 prisoners. I hope to go on leave to Paris shortly and there get rid of the cold and fatigue which have laid hold on me during the trying times of the past few days. What am I to say to you about leave to India? This year, no mention has been made about such leave. Some Sirdars of another regiment raised the question of leave to India this winter; but up to this day no answer has been given to them. I do not expect that we shall return till the war is ended."

From Amar Singh, Risaldar, 18th Lancers, France to Mahtab Singh, Patiala State, Punjab, India. (Gurmukhi dated the 13th December 1917).

*****

"Several of our men have gone on leave but I cannot come as I have not served long enough. Moreover, as I am always thinking of the Guru's teaching, it is all the same to me what country I am in. It is possible to meet in correspondence and by exchange of photographs. Do not worry about me for I am not coming back until either victory is won or peace is made in some way. I think victory is near but if not I am confident of getting back in March or April."

From Jemadar Rala Singh, 6th Cavalry, France to Harnam Singh, Ludhiana. (Urdu dated the 22nd December 1917).

*****

"It is very cold and there is about 2 feet of snow and ice everywhere. The arrangements are splendid, good rations for everybody and an issue of rum daily, and plenty of good clothing. We want for nothing except a sight of you and the warmth of our own country."

From Bishan Singh, 6th Cavalry, France to Sher Singh, Shahpur. (Urdu dated the 23rd December 1917).

*****

1918

"It is the winter and sometimes it rains and sometimes is bitterly cold. But our King has made admirable arrangements for our clothing and for the protection of our feet. There is no discomfort of any kind, but what can one do when the rain is excessive? But in war hardships and comforts must alike be accepted."

From Dyal Singh, 19th Lancers, France to Teja Singh, Lyallpur. (Urdu dated the 14th January 1918).

*****

"The news is that all our Cavalry Regiments are going to Basrah from France. I hope therefore to come soon, and hope to be with you in March. For the rest, all is in the hands of the Guru. When we board the ship I will write to you. We have today received orders to go to Basrah."

From Sohan Singh, 38th Central India Horse, France to Harnam Singh, Amritsar District, Punjab, India. (Gurmukhi dated the 22nd January 1918).

*****

"In regard to what you write to the effect that if I do not come on leave soon you will telegraph. I would remark that you are an educated man, whereas women have not much sense and you should therefore explain to them that it is not proper that they should write, time after time, in this way. Where is the man who does not desire to go to his home? This is an occasion when it is incumbent that we should serve the Sircar body and soul. I am not like those men who return home invalided. If God is gracious and I live through this, I will return in good time. Tell them to be patient and keep a good heart."

From Phala Singh, Lance Dafadar, 35th Sind Horse attached 38th Central India Horse, France to Rur Singh, Amritsar District, India. (Urdu dated the 8th February 1918).

*****

6

World War Sikh

The misery which we are enduring here is as great as the comfort we enjoyed in France.

The Sikhs are good to see in the mornings combing their long black hair: in this setting it puts one in the mind of the Spartans before Thermopylae.

Some men of ours are in the besieged force, 20 in number. They have eaten their horses and mules.

The Masuds are giving the Sircar much trouble on the frontier. For this reason the Sircar has collected a considerable force here.

This part of the country which is the part near Damascus is very beautiful. There are quantities of grapes and pomegranates and all kinds of fruit.

Sikh soldiers would fight in all the major theatres of the Great War. Indeed, Indian Expeditionary Forces A through G, were sent to fight in France (A), East Africa (B&C), Mesopotamia (D), the Middle East (E), Egypt (F) and Gallipoli (G). Fortunately, many of the events in these so called 'side-shows' would form the content of letters to and from Sikh soldiers on the Western Front, and thus would come to the attention of the Censor and are described in this chapter. Letters would also be received from Sikhs who had ventured further afield all over the world.

Sikhs fought against the Germans in Tsingtao, China, in a joint British and Japanese venture in 1914, relieving the Germans of one of their Far East colonial possessions. British interests were also protected on the North-West frontier of India, where fierce tribes such as the Mohmands and Mahsuds had never really been subdued. 1915 was a particularly difficult time on the North-West frontier for the Indian army. Regular Intelligence summaries showed that '4,000 Hindustani fanatics had occupied the Ambeyla Pass', 'a Mullah had raised his standard at Shabkadr' and a week later reports arrived advising 'a 15,000-strong force was gathering in Swat' and that in the Upper Swat valley 'all the tribes had agreed to fight'.[1]

The North-West frontier was just as important then (as it is today), with regular concerns that the Germans were trying to seduce the Amir of Afghanistan to turn his attentions to India.

1 Peter Stanley, *Die in Battle, Do not Despair: The Indians on Gallipoli, 1915* (Solihull: Helion & Company, 2015), p. 235.

This force was further supported by Sikh troops in Baluchistan, ensuring that German agents could not infiltrate through these areas. The Persian campaign was a complex one, mainly there to protect British oil interests in the region, it also faced local tribal disturbances, a Persian mutiny, and in the end activities against the Bolsheviks during the Russian Civil War.[2]

Sikh troops wrote to friends and relatives describing their experiences and the hostile environments they encountered. According to the Censor, German agents were also active in China (Hankow) trying to seduce Indians. Many Sikhs lived and worked in Hong Kong and the Censor noted that "many of these Sikhs who took refuge in Gurdwaras were wanted by the police!"

In the war against the Ottoman Empire of the Turks, large numbers of Sikh soldiers fought in Mesopotamia (modern day Iraq, created as a consequence of the Great War). The Mesopotamia campaign (See Map 2) had many targets including the protection of British interests in and around the region and ensuring the Arabs and Turks did not come together as one force. The campaign was a muddled one, although ultimately successful when the British entered Baghdad in March 1917.

There were a huge number of Indian troops deployed in this theatre of war (588,717 to October 31, 1918)[3], including thousands of Sikhs. The campaign was initially successful with the capture of the strategically important Basra. It was then decided to try and capture the prized city of Baghdad. However, errors were made after the battle of Ctesiphon that resulted in a retreat to Kut-al-Amara. Surrounded by the Turks, a siege lasting many months transpired. A Sikh soldier describes the event, "I was for 5 months amongst the besieged in Kut. When we were starved out we had to put up a white flag" and "the trials which we underwent are beyond description." Thousands died during the siege and in captivity at the hands of the Turks.

There was also evidence of particular maltreatment of Sikhs by their Turkish captors. Sepoy No. 799, Ujagar Singh of the 45th Sikhs told of his experience at the hands of the Turks:

> After the attack of the 36th and 45th Sikhs on the 1st of February last, I was wounded and taken prisoner, after a small party of about twenty or twenty-five of us had been completely surrounded, and no help was forthcoming from the rear.
>
> Those of us who could walk were taken back along a communication trench to the Tigris, being first of all stripped of our uniform, boots, watches, and money, etc. The Turks murdered all our wounded who could not walk. I saw this with my own eyes; they bayonetted Subadar Ram Singh as he lay wounded, but the other names I cannot give as I did not personally know the men. We were then taken across the Tigris in 'bellums' to some huts north of Kut-el-Amara, which appeared to be some general's headquarters. We slept in one of the huts that night, locked in and under escort.[4]

The Mesopotamia campaign was particularly harsh with a British officer stating in a letter to England, "that in the course of two years in Mesopotamia he had experienced all the ten

2 Narinder Singh Dhesi, *Sikh Soldier, Volume Three, Policing the Empire* (East Sussex: Naval & Military Press, undated), p. 222.
3 Government of India, *India's Contribution to the Great War* (Calcutta: Superintendent of Government Printing, 1923), pp. 96-7.
4 Lieut-Colonel R.H. Anderson, *Regimental History of the 45th Rattray's Sikhs during the Great War and after 1914-1921* (East Sussex: Naval & Military Press reprint of 1925 edition), p. 236.

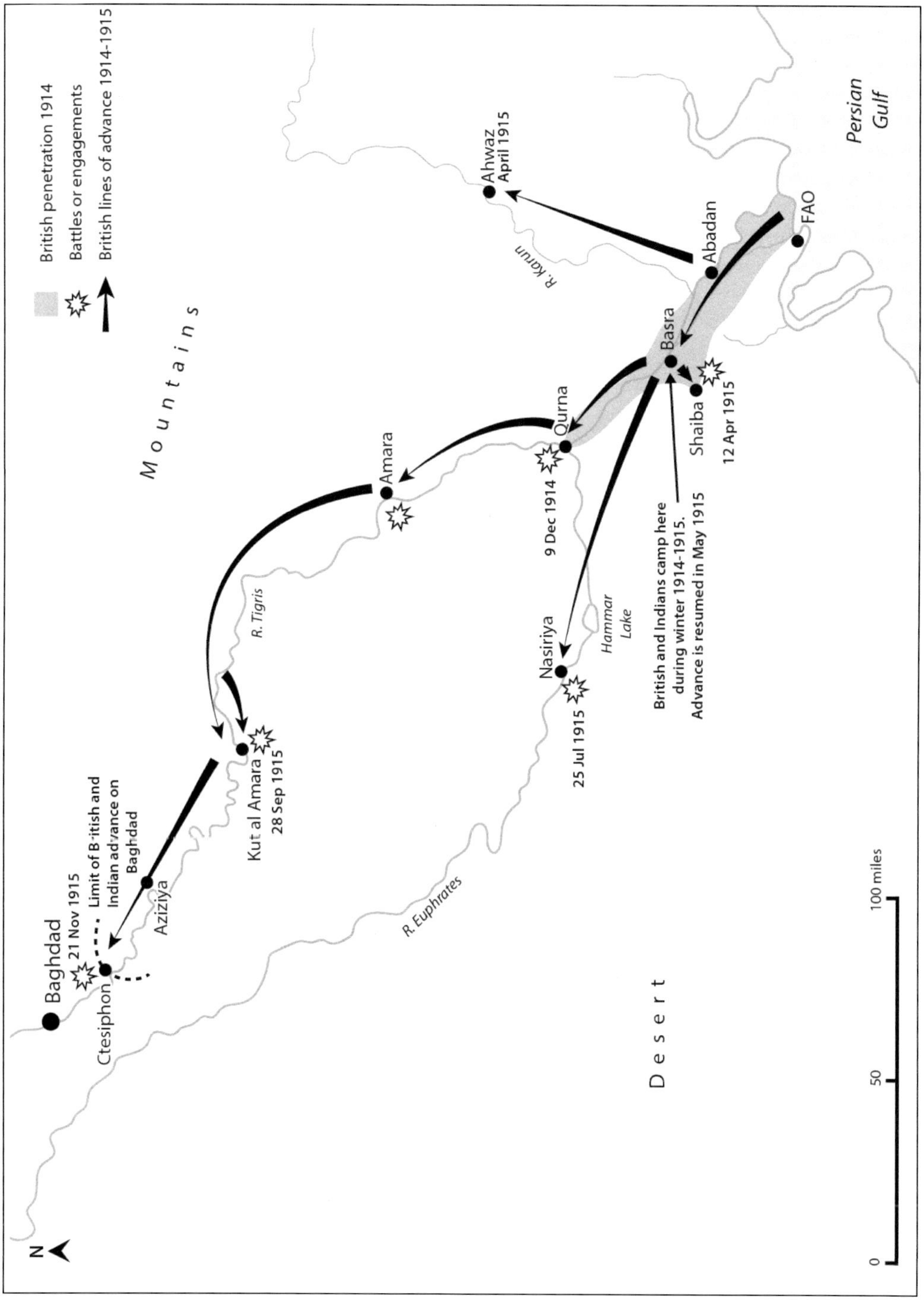

Map 2: Mesopotamian Campaign, 1914-15.

plagues of Egypt, except the death of the first-born!"[5] There were many issues which affected the soldiers. Apart from the fighting itself, there were inadequate arrangements for food and for the treatment and transport of the wounded, which led to terrible suffering and disease taking its toll on the soldiers.

The desert heat was in complete contrast to the freezing cold of France. The soldiers often took on long marches in heat topping 120 degrees Fahrenheit. Soldiers died on their feet from heat stroke; sandstorms, flies and mirages made the conditions unbearable. The local Arabs also caused major concern as they would customarily treat the defeated side badly. So one day, the Arabs would be friendly but the next day become scavengers and strip belongings from dying soldiers.

The retreat from Kut-al-Amara would be reversed eventually by 1917 but the loss of life and suffering was tremendous. The Sikhs would rejoice in this victory and were very happy to be able to see the place in Baghdad which was visited by Guru Nanak. Petitions and requests were also put to the British command to build Gurdwaras in the conquered country as the Sikhs had spilt so much blood here.

The 14th Sikhs fought valiantly at the disastrous campaign of Gallipoli in 1915 and lost many of its men in the battles of Krithia, Gully Ravine and Sari Bair, while leaving behind trenches named after them such as 'Sikh Street'. Sikhs along with Gurkhas fought alongside their British, French, Australian and New Zealand Army Corps (ANZAC) comrades. Many of the interactions with Sikh soldiers were recorded by ANZAC soldiers in their personal diaries and the majority showed positive and inquisitive relations. Sikh toughness in battle impressed many of the ANZACs and the Indians were most complementary of the Australian troops encountered at Gallipoli, mostly due to the fact that they treated them as equals.

Sikh soldiers Gallipoli Peninsula 1915. (Courtesy of the Council of the National Army Museum, London)

5 Colonel N. Ogle and Lieut. Colonel H.W. Johnston, *History of the 1st Battalion 2nd Punjab Regiment: Late 67th Punjabis and originally the Madras Infantry, 1761-1928* (East Sussex: Naval & Military Press 2014 reprint of 1928 edition), p. 35.

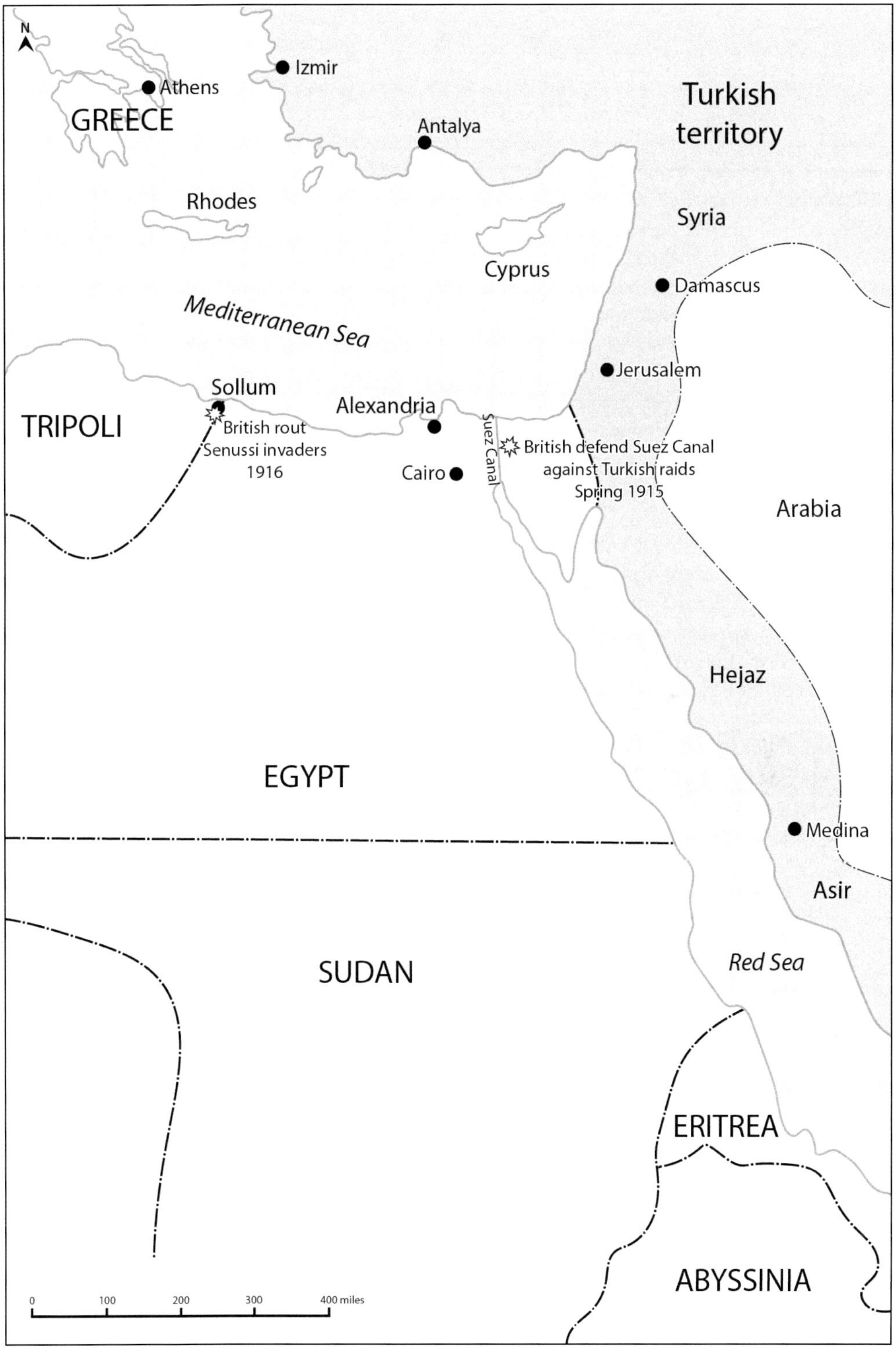

Map 3: Egypt, 1914-16.

Sikh soldiers fought in the defence of the Suez Canal against the Turks in early 1915 (See Map 3) and Malay State Guides protected Aden at the same time. The 15th Sikhs would fight in the Egyptian/Libyan desert against Senussi tribesmen in 1916. The 23rd Sikh Pioneers fought against Dervishes in Somaliland at Shimber Berris in early 1915. Sikhs also fell in the Salonica (modern day Greece) campaign in 1916. The East African campaign was ill-fated, opening with a failure to capture the port of Tanga in November 1914 (See Map 4), where many Sikhs fought in the Imperial Service troops (including the Kapurthala and Jind infantries) provided by the Punjab States. The campaign was a disaster and went on for most of the war period as the Germans fought a guerrilla war against the British army. The Germans in East Africa were accused of being particularly cruel to British and Indian POWs. Near the end of the war, Sikh soldiers found themselves fighting on many fronts including Palestine, the cavalry having success in the battle of Megiddo. Letters from Sikh soldiers sent from Port Said described the locations and events as they saw them.

Sikh soldiers were stationed as part of the Malay State Guides and 36th Sikhs regiment in Singapore when the 'Singapore Mutiny' broke out in February 1915. Muslim troops of the 5th Light Infantry had mutinied and shot some British officers as they believed they were being sent to fight fellow Muslims. The mutineers did not trust the Sikh soldiers as they considered them to be likely to be loyal to the British. They were mostly correct in this assertion although a small number of Sikhs were given prison sentences as a result of the mutiny. Many Sikhs gave evidence against the mutineers and those statements about the events were recorded in the official enquiry into the incident.

Letters were arriving from all over the world to the Western Front. Letters arriving from Canada and the USA were particularly scrutinised due to possible links to the *Ghadar* movement. Other more harmless letters arrived describing distant countries that Sikhs had settled in. Sikhs living in other countries were also joining their armies to fight in the war such as Canada (including a Buckham Singh and a Waryam Singh and others), Australia (including a Gurbhachan Singh and a Sarn Singh and others), New Zealand (including a Jagt Singh and a Sham Singh) and even the USA (including a Bhagat Singh).

*****

China Deployment

> "The English have suffered severely. Nothing is put into the LOOS (news), but we get to know a good deal from day to day. The German ship Emden has sunk forty English ships near this land, & she is sinking all the seventy English ships of war. She (Germany) has not been much damaged although she gets little help. The English have eight kings helping them, the Germans three. We hear our king has been taken prisoner. Germany said that if she were paid a lakh of rupees by five o'clock on the first of the month, she would release the king. The money was paid, but Germany refuses to let him go. I have written only a little, but there is much for you to think of."
>
> From a Sikh Garrison Gunner in China to a relative now serving in France. (Original in Gurmukhi, dated 3/12/14).
>
> Censor report said that this letter is linked to wild rumours.

*****

"Your witless younger brother, a child in wisdom, and very witless, indescribably witless, writes to you. * He writes to his poor brother, a wise man and shrewd, his dearly beloved, a portion of his heart, the very hair of his body, ** his hearts delight, his body's dear heart, his very breath, his clever elder brother. I am very anxious about you, for if the regiment is sent to war it will be a very bad business. You know nothing about it. For those regiments which have stayed in India know nothing. They do not know how grievously the English are oppressing them. A man finds out as soon as he arrives in Calcutta. The Punjab is more oppressed than other country. For they (the English?) are the Rajas of the Punjab. There is no Punjabi Raja. We are oppressed, but the others do know how heavily. Their plight is worse than that of any other people. The truth is that the German Badshah is a very great hero (bahut bahadur). I cannot tell you how many men he has killed. He had sunk many ships and done much damage. I have heard that many men of the 15th are dead. Only a few are left. All are dead. Every regiment that goes (to battle) he destroys. He is a great man (bahut bahadur). We get news from the papers. We get many newspapers and learn all the news. I have heard, and it is also in the papers, that seventy thousand (in words) 70,000 (in figures) men have perished. We hear that the German Badshah will win. The German Badshah said 'I will not fight with the people of the Punjab. I shall fight with the 'Topi-walas.' *** Doubtless this was true, but when the Punjabis came to fight what could the unfortunate man do, but kill all the regiments? He has done great damage. And, my brother, what do they give you? Eleven rupees all told. It is a shame. The white soldiers get 100 or 80 or 70 rupees. After years of labour some of our officers manage to get 100 rupees. Death would be better than this. Where there is work to do, there they send us, the pay is small. But, my brother, what do you others know about it? Does anyone tell you anything? The Sahibs know, but who tells his men? But we know what our people are suffering. All the Punjabis who are returning from America, in ships, 100 or 50 or 40 at a time, and all the Punjabis who are in America have taken an oath not to remain in America. So none remains in America and all are coming away. No fresh migrants are going there. No one goes to any island (sic) ---- neither to China, nor to America, nor to Africa, nor to any other place. From every island they are coming back. Since the war began no new Punjabis have come, but from every island they are returning slowly and steadily. My brother, the Raja against whom is the fighting is the country of the Germans (sic). **** He is the German Emperor. He is very good. He has said 'You go to your country and look after it. I have nothing to say to you.' What else can I write? (Now) you know. The duty which I have to do here is very hard. Not a pice comes in. I have only a few pice. Tell --- to cut his name and run home. There is no advantage (in staying on). China is no good. Now I send my 'fateh' to you and to my section, Nos. ----. Reply soon. The date of writing is 27 the year 1914 (sic). Forgive mistakes. God is true.

Your younger brother writes to his elder brother."

* The writing is in a formed but uneducated hand. The spelling and grammar are bad. I am inclined to think that the writer believes what he writes to be true and is honestly warning his brother. Doubtless his 'news' is from German sources.

** Orthodox Sikhs do not cut their hair. All this fulsome address is exceptional in a Sikh letter.

*** Topiwalas = people who wear hats – i.e. Europeans, and, in the Punjab, Englishmen.
**** Likely refers to the operations at Tsingtao (27th August – 7th November 1914).
'Fateh' = victory. Used as a word of greeting.

From a Sikh in Hong Kong, to his eldest brother, sent with reinforcements to France. (Original in Gurmukhi, dated the 27th December 1914).

*****

Tsingtao

"I am glad to hear that you have been promoted to Naik. Second, I am glad that you have been left in the depot. The regiments that have gone to the war have suffered very severely. What more can I say? Every regiment in the French war has lost 500 men killed. You are very lucky to escape the war. Now I will write about myself. 450 of our men went to a fort in an island. The fort belonged to the Germans. Japan was fighting them. One British regiment & 450 men of the 36th Sikhs. I also went. I came through that war safe. The Japanese lost 6000 men ___1700 wounded & the British regiment also lost heavily. Of us two men were killed. Three officers were wounded & twelve sepoys. Now we are ready to fight again. Do not be anxious. I am very glad that you have remained in the depot. Had I been killed, there would still have been you to look after the women. I am very pleased about this. Do not be vexed at that which I have written. It is quite true about the regiments in the war. I myself have seen them. We are very fortunate. When we attacked by night, we had no hope of return. Now we are in Hong Kong. I am very pleased that you are at the depot. You must not write anything about the war to me. Nor must you write about the war to the village. For they get frightened."

From a Sikh in the 36th Sikhs at Hong Kong to his brother in the 14th Sikhs. The writer is under the impression that his brother is at the depot in India, but as a matter of fact he is with a reinforcement in France. (Gurmukhi, dated 22/1/15).

*****

Photograph of 2nd Battalion The South Wales Borderers, along with a detachment of the 36th Sikhs, formed the bulk of the British troops sent to assist the Japanese in capturing Germany's naval base at Tsingtao (Qingdao) in China. (Courtesy of the Council of the National Army Museum, London)

*****

Canada

Have Courage

Arise (ye) brave lions! Why are you lying asleep stretched at full length? Those who were behind you have gone ahead and have reached the sky.
Arise ye brave lions! Take daggers in your hands. Carry your drowning community to the other bank (of the river).
We are lagging behind the rest of the world and are repeatedly knocked down. It is now time to realise (that) this (lit. the) state will pass away.
We are not allowed to go to foreign countries and (all the) islands have been shut (to us). Understand, ye Indians! That an inauspicious moon has risen.
The world is scoffing (at us) and we have fallen into the pit of the lower regions. And yet we do not feel ashamed. Indeed, the messenger of Death has left nothing.
Our leaders are enjoying every comfort (but) the poor people have lost everything and their future is dark.

Harnam Singh, Victoria, Canada, *The Khalsa Sewak* (Amritsar), 18th February 1914.

*****

"I am in great anxiety about you because no letter has come from you and many of our people have gone to Europe and have perished there. There is much else besides, but I cannot write it to you. Perhaps if I did, my letter would not reach you. Here in Vancouver there is no work to be had on account of the war and there is much distress among our people. They are in difficulties for food and can get no work. All work is stopped on account of the war. I would come (to India) but on the way the Germans sink the ships. The Germans have written that any ships that come into their hands, they will sink them all. And if any of us were to reach our own country, they (the government) would catch us in our homes and arrest us. I do not know what fault the men who come from abroad have committed, but they are caught and put in jail for nothing. Here there is no work to be had, and if we go to our own country we are put in prison. Why, no one knows. At present we cannot come. Here we are unemployed. Tell me who of our fellow-villagers are with you and where are you and all about it. You ought to stay at home and defend your COUNTRY, and not go to anywhere else. One of our regiments was at Singapore. They were going to send it to Europe, but it refused and is now occupying the fort. The men said, 'We refuse to go to Europe, but will stay in Asia and fight in our own country, if anyone comes to take possession of it (or is in occupation of it).'"

From Partab Singh, Agassiz, British Columbia, Canada, to Jit Singh, 31st Lancers, attached 29th Lancers, serving in France. (Gurmukhi, 30/7/15).

(The letter has been forwarded from India).

*****

United States

"You write about returning home by Christmas time. Think well about what I say to you. I say do not return home yet – not for six months – There is great disturbance at sea and the route is not clear … I strongly advise you not to go home at present. Listen to what I say. One can go home now only at the risk of one's life."

From Asa Singh, (Censor No.637, 38th C.I.H.) France, to Makhan Singh, California. (Gurmukhi, dated 26/9/15).

*****

"Do not fancy your family so much, my brother, and use your brains! ………….. As regards your advice not to return home before the end of the war, I do not intend to return until the war is over. I know all there is to know and get the news of the war from day to day. Perhaps I know more about it than you do! Eat well, eat as much as you can, do not save money. Since I came to America I have not wanted for money. I earn in a day what you earn in a month. Eat (i.e. spend) without stint – that is my advice. I have taken to farming. I have seven ghumaos under millet and twelve under cotton. The day I pick the first cotton crop I shall send 300 rupees."

From Bishen Singh, A 58 Star Route, Elecentro, California, to Kishen Singh, 4th Cavalry, France. (Gurmukhi, October 1915).

*****

Argentina

"They do not speak English here but Spanish, but I know both. We work in the office in Spanish. We have about 250 Sikhs in the country now not more, and they work mostly on sugarcane. I have been in the Railway service ever since I came here. I get about Rs. 90 a month including allowances, but everything is fearfully dear now owing to the war. I hope to return to India next year. Owing to the war there is not much to be made but I shall get 3 or 4 dollars a day after the war."

From Santa Singh, La Plata in Argentine to Harman Singh, 9th Hodson's Horse, France. (Urdu dated the 7th July 1917).

*****

Abyssinia

"The Army Newspaper comes to me. The Minister Sahib sends for it and gives it to me. I get the war news from it. The Minister Sahib has also given me a war map which I have put up in my verandah. No one now shows me the war telegrams. The reason is that the present Minister cannot speak Hindi. The former Councillor (?) was Colonel Doughty Wylie. He knew Hindi and used to explain to me the telegrams as they came. It is the Guru's will that Colonel Doughty Wylie went to the war and was killed in the fighting at the Dar-Danial (Dardanelles). He received two bullets one in each side of his breast. On the 6th July a new Councillor came in his place. His name is Mr Keppel Sahib, Councillor. He does not understand Hindustani or Habshi (Abyssinian). He knows French and Italian."

From Dfdr. Gurcharan Singh, Addis Addeba, Abyssinia, to Wardi Major Channan Singh, 3rd Skinner's Horse, serving in France. (Gurmukhi, 8/7/15).

*****

East Africa

"My dear brother S. Hari Singh,

Fateh to you – I am alright here, and I wish your welfare always from the Almighty. I received your letter and noticed its contents. It has infused a new life to my dead mind. Your letter gave me so much pleasure that all the shocks and sorrows were removed from my mind. My dear brother, undoubtedly you would have been extremely sorry to hear of the death of Kartar Singh; as the proverb goes, that he who suffers from the pain feels it. I cannot express the state of my mind at this time. The world is all dark to me just as everything becomes dark by the solar eclipse. It is difficult to remove the shocks of my mind. But there is no other remedy except sorrow (patience). It is true that man has to die one day, but even death may come at some suitable time. The shock affects the man's mind in the same way as the worm (weevil) does to a tree and the "Rishis" too say the same thing. (The writer of the letter then repeats some Punjabi verses of one Waris-Shah poet in support of the above fact).

Dear brother, you can just think of the state of my mind. Kartar Singh has left an everlasting shock on my mind which would never be healed up. It is out of my power to express in words the sorrow and grief with which I am overwhelmed. Brother, the family life seems pleasant, but it is full of trouble and sorrow. (The writer here gives some story of Rama in the support of his views to the above effect). When the idea of Kartar Singh strikes my mind, it becomes hardened with grief and I am at a loss what to do.

Dear Brother, the battle is going on in this country at its hottest. From Mowasa to Qibo there is a jungle extending over 500 miles and every kind of animal is found therein. It is so thick and dense that even in the daytime it appears to be dark like a night. Anyhow the place has been inhabited by these people to the extent of 2 or 3 miles along the Railway line and also the place called Victoria Nianza Lake. These are the German possessions and the English carry on their trade therein to a certain extent. The cotton is produced in abundance. The chief articles of trade here are, the skin of the wild animals such as goat, cow buffalo, seed of sesamun (Til) peppers, ivory etc. These people (The English?) have got three workshops viz., at Mowasa, Niraubi and Qibo. The Viceroy of this country imposed a tax of Rs. 15/- on each individual, but it was not paid at Niraubi, and it was paid twice by the people of Mowasa and Qibo. Now these people (the emigrants) stopped all work there. No work was done at Niraubi, Mowasa and Qibo for about a week. This information reached the German (Emperor) so he invaded the country and said to the Viceroy "You are not a king, if you really are a king, come and fight with me". The emperor called the English as effeminates as they are receiving the money from the subjects by oppression which is not an act of royalty. Then the German (Emperor) sent his son and his consort to Australia for a visit. They were both killed by these people. The German Emperor said to them "I was making necessary arrangements for you for the last 33 years, and I was looking for an opportunity which I have got now. Either you will remain (rule) here or I. Six warships were sent from this place and the news of 6th November says that they were destroyed by the Germans, and a place called [Kasi?] was looted and set on fire by the Germans. There is a very big German fort at Moanza, and all the ships pass below that fort. When these ships pass by, they are destroyed and sunk by cannon fire (by the Germans). It is near us.

But the second battle is raging fiercely at Makati Line near Niraubi and the third place is Boti which is near Mowasa. The Germans are defeating Italy, Australia, France, Belgium and other petty dominions, have reached near England. Fourthly the German is lying ready at Zanzibar and Darul-Islam (Dar-es-Salam) which are the seaports here. They have spread sea mines (bombs) there – whenever any British cruiser comes from or goes to Bombay and it comes in contact with the wire, which gets fire suddenly and the bomb explodes and reduces the ship to pieces. This wire is not visible, it remains under water 5 feet deep from the surface and the ship goes 10 feet deep in the water.

Again there is a large Indian army here. The armies of Nabha, Patiala and Jammu States are all collected here. But the Rajas who accompanied them have been kept under custody (Nazarband). Because the English told them, that "you are Sikhs you should go to the front and fight in the battle". Upon which they replied, "you should do so first and when you are killed there, then our turn will come", and thus arose a dispute, and now these Rajas say that they will help the Germans.

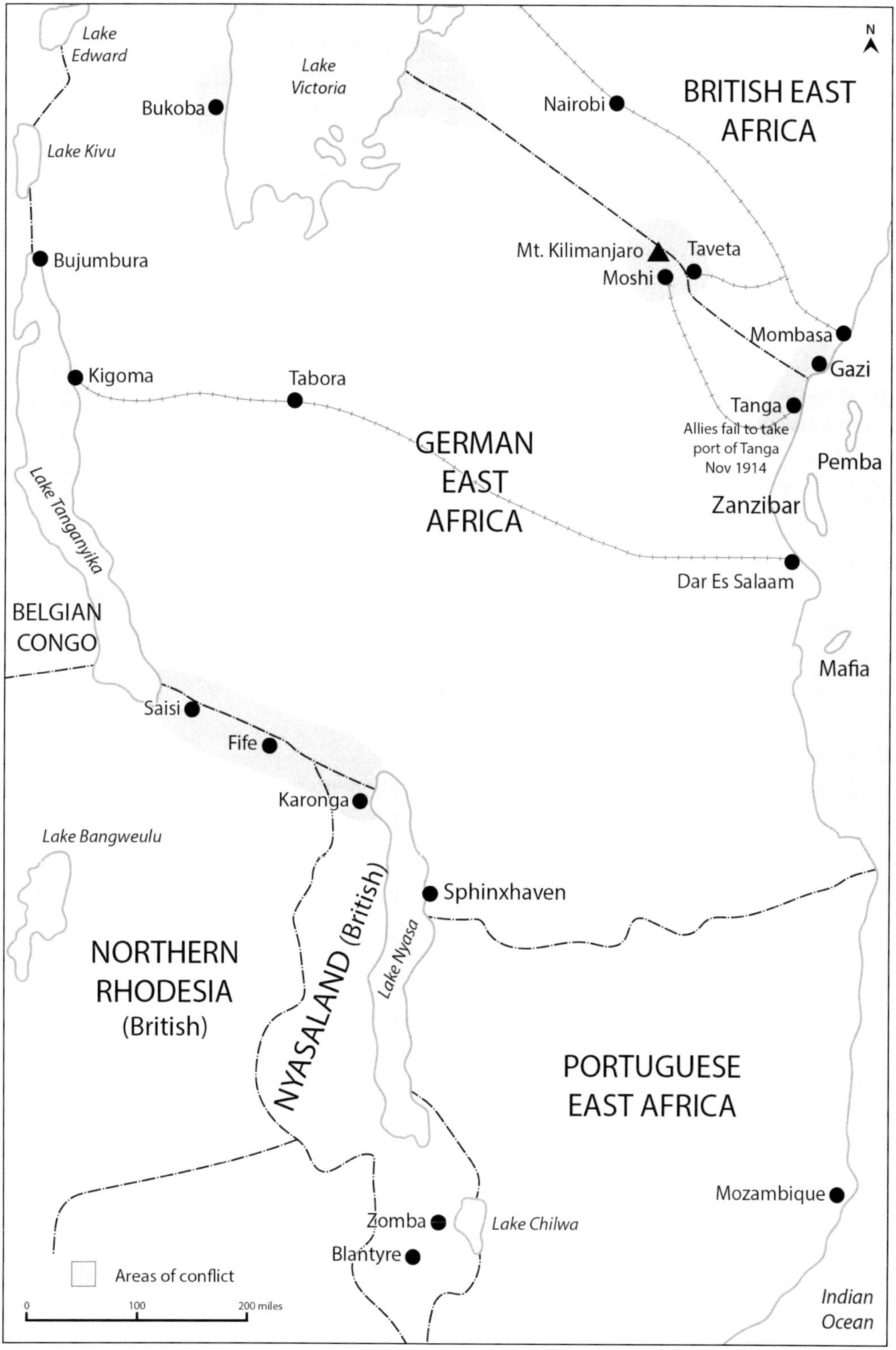

Map 4: East Africa, 1914-18.

Again many persons who were working here in the workshops, have been expelled from this country at their own expense, and it has also been announced to us that if we want to go to India, we can do so at our own expense, but we have to pay Rs. 150/- to the Government. But we the Indians replied that we should be sent back in the same way in which we were brought here, and we should also be given some guarantee entitled to us.

The condition of the country is such that sometimes we hear that the enemy has come to such and such place today, at another we hear that they will be at another place tomorrow. Brother it is a question of life and death for us. I will see you if I would return safe otherwise there is no hope. You would kindly send a letter to the house so that it may give some satisfaction to them. I have written to you a full account and I am not certain whether you will again get my letter or not. I have received the dak after the after a couple of months and inform Rattan Singh fully about Karan Singh and his whereabouts. A letter from Karan Singh was received along with yours but therein he wrote he was going out and he will inform his future whereabouts, but he did not do so.

Dear Brother, I do not want to write a letter, my ambition is to reach my country, but everything depends on fate. P.S. I send you a newspaper. Read it yourself or tell your other friends.

Yours obediently,

Sd. Uttam Singh."

Note: The letter contained a copy of the "Ghadr" newspaper.

Rough translation of a letter sent by one Uttam Singh from Africa, Uganda Railway (Sarban Chhap?) dated the 6th November 1914.

*****

Photograph of officers of the Kapurthala Force, *The Times of India Illustrated Weekly*, Sept. 30, 1914, prior to their deployment to East Africa. (Avtar Singh Bahra collection)

*****

German Atrocities

"It was on the afternoon of the 13th January 1915, at Jasin in German East Africa, that all the other members of my party were killed and I myself fell wounded (in three places, in the knee, one in my side below the ribs and in the back). None of the enemy came near me till 8 a.m. of the next day. Then an African Lance-Naik and a sepoy (called Askari) came in sight. The Lance-Naik began to take off the clothes of a sepoy of my regiment who lay dead at some distance from me and the sepoy aimed his rifle at me to kill me. When, however, I raised my hand the Askari saw my wrist watch which tempted him. He took the watch, Rs. 8 in cash and a knife from my pocket and walked away. The Lance-Naik then approached me and asked, as he looked at the mark of the watch at my wrist where the watch was and, pointing to the stars on my shoulder straps (meaning that I was an officer) further asked about my binoculars; but I replied by a gesture that everything had been taken away. I may state that I had previously thrown all my accoutrements, ammunition and my pocket book in to the sea, so that the enemy might not avail himself of their use, and the tide had carried them all away. Then other German Askaris came to the scene and relentlessly stripped me of all my clothes, leaving a Kachhera (a small Sikh drawer) only on me, and they several times kicked me with their boots while I lay wounded and helpless. I lay thus in the same spot for 32 hours although I was seen by a German Officer and by Askari parties and known to be alive. The tide rose in the inlet and I escaped drowning only by dragging myself to one side with great difficulty and getting my head on to higher ground. After all these long and most painful hours, I was picked up by the Germans and conveyed to the depot of a German Regiment three miles off from the scene of the fight; but even then my wounds were not dressed, nor was any food given to me. After fifty five hours I received a handful of rice given to me by another prisoner of War (a Lance-Naik) who saw that I was quite exhausted with hunger. I was made to lie exposed in the open for another twenty-four hours and only then was I put in a thatched cell with another wounded sepoy, who soon after died. In this cell I was left to lie on the ground without even straw for bedding or a blanket to cover myself; after three days I was given a grass mattress. None cared for me there; meals which consisted of rice and dal were very irregular and there was no arrangement for attending the sick and dressing the wounded. Lots of them died from lack of attention. I got fever on account of my wounds and my temperature rose very high from the 18th of January to the 2nd of February, but no medicine was given to me, nor even a sheet to cover my body. A German doctor came to the patients, but he entirely neglected his duties, as he simply looked at them and walked away, without giving any medicine or examining them. On the very first day of my arrival at the depot of the Regiment, a German Officer came to me but, as he could not understand me, he brought with him the next day an Indian doctor to act as interpreter and I was questioned as follows:

(1) What are the functions of the officers, non-commissioned officers, buglers and scouts in the Indian army?

(2) What is the strength of the force at Mombasa?

(3) What is the strength of whole force in British East Africa?
(4) What are the different positions of the camps of the troops in British East Africa?
(5) What Regiment do you belong to?

I gave brief answers to these questions; for instance, I said that there was a very large army at Mombasa and in the whole of British East Africa, and that steamers after steamers loaded with troops were coming from India. I said I could not tell the position of the camps of the troops as whole of British East Africa was full with the troops. The duty of the officers is to command and of the buglers to sound the bugle and I said that I did not know more than that. I told him that I belong to His Royal Highness the Maharaja of Jind's Regiment. Other Maharaja's in India were also helping the British Government. On my answering that every one of them was helping with all his resources and had, provided a very large number of troops in every theatre of the war, the German officer looked very vexed and annoyed, and stamping his foot on the ground said something in his own language. He seemed disappointed and enquired why the Maharajas helped the cause of the British Government. I said for the simple reason that we were all very happy under the British Rule, as the British Government was very just and kind & was the best Raj that India ever had; on which he seemed still more annoyed but did not question me anymore. In the depot I also met sepoy Salabat Khan of our Regiment who had been wounded and taken prisoner some four or five days later.

On the 2nd of February I was brought to Tanga, where my wounds were dressed for the first time after 18 days, and I was then sent to Krugwi on the 4th. During this journey I was not given either food or water. On the 7th of February my leg was amputated, and another operation was performed on the 17th March. Even in this condition of acute suffering, due to the severe pain of my wounds and operations, no one attended me or cared for me in the slightest. At Krugwi I was given a linen sheet, one long shirt, one blanket, and two pillows, but these clothes were all very dirty. Up to this I had been kept almost naked for twenty three days and dragged from place to place with high fever and in a wounded condition. For four whole months I was never able to remove the mud from my body. A proposal was made to me to cut my long hair (which we Sikhs keep so sacred); but I boldly asserted that I preferred to have my head removed rather than my hair cut. At this place (Krugwi) one day a non-commissioned officer (a German) came to me and asked me why the Indians were fighting for the British when they had no Raj of their own. On my replying that we Indians were true to their salt and would ever remain so and were moreover extremely happy under the British Raj which was just and generous, the non-commissioned office angrily said alright and pointed to my leg, saying in Swahili that it too would be cut off. I replied that I did not care a bit, whether my head and hands were amputated, I should always remain loyal and faithful to my King-Emperor and the Maharaja. A Jemadar of the 101st Grenadiers who knew English used to act as interpreter in the hospital, etc. One day at Krugwi a surgeon photographed me with my hair all dishevelled.

I was kept at Krugwi till the 28th of June 1915 and was then sent to Tabora, which I reached on the 15th of July. During this journey very little food or water was given to me and I was put to great inconvenience. At Tabora also the meals were very irregular. Sometimes we received rice, at other times dal only and this continued up to December. Then I received some clothing, which were kindly sent by His Highness the Maharaja Sahib Bahadur, and I began to receive a little more consideration. But still no change was made in the quantity and quality of the food. In January and February 1916 only once in a week was I given rice and one day atta of jawar or bajra and for the remaining days only grain which I boiled myself; and for this even enough water and fuel were not provided. From July to September 1916 I suffered from dysentery, but no medicine was given to me. In July even salt was stopped. They were starving the prisoners by giving very meagre and unwholesome food and with such poor food the prisoners were forced to labour for twelve hours without a break, carrying stone or lime for nine miles, loading and unloading, cutting grass and wood and fetching water. The prisoners of war were chained by the neck for the first month and were always kicked. They were even made to do scavenger's work.

I may state that one Indian in particular whose name I suppress had become notorious in troubling the prisoners of war – his own countrymen. This fellow is said to have originally plied hackney carriages for hire at Mombasa and subsequently to have been employed in Mombasa Police, but to have run away to the Germans, in order to escape punishment for some offence which he had committed in Mombasa. He was kept in prison for some time by the Germans as an enemy subject but was afterwards employed as an interpreter and later he was give the management of the distribution of rations. In this last capacity as the supervisor of labour he showed inhumanity and disregard of all moral obligations and had become a brute himself, utterly unmoved by any sense of sympathy. He used to beat and abuse the prisoners of war and never distributed the full quantity of rations allowed but sold it and took the proceeds. In this he was helped by a German soldier. In most cases he did not give the prisoners the clothing supplied by their own regiments or received for them from India as presents, and thus made much profit for himself. For instance, he sold a pair of socks for Rs.

4. If this man ever comes back to India severe notice should be taken of his disloyalty and misbehaviour.

In contrast to the cruelties of the Germans and this worthless black guard I am glad to say that my own countrymen, and two English nurses helped me very much, and I gratefully mention their kindness. First of all, was doctor Muhammad Din of the ......Rifles (also a prisoner of war) who gave all medical relief and dressed our wounds and took every possible care of us. Doctor Muhammad Din was kind and patriotic and was always anxious to mitigate the pains of the wounded by affording them every assistance in his power, as he felt for the prisoners very much. He also used to arrange to secure presents for them. Always quite willing and cheerful at his self-imposed task of helping the wounded, he it was who recused many lives from the clutches of death. His very sympathetic treatment and great anxiety for our welfare have put us under a deep debt of obligation which it is impossible to repay. The English nurses also felt even the slightest pain which the wounded suffered and were greatly touched by the heart rending sufferings of the prisoners. These noble souls were very kind and paid all attention to the wounded and sick amongst the prisoners and also used to give pieces of bread to us secretly, so that the Germans would not detect it.

This was necessary as they would not tolerate any kindness, however small, to be done to the prisoners. A Sikh named Hukam Singh, of Chak Sarwan Nath, of Ludhiana District, who was formerly in railway service in German East Africa and now plies a hackney carriage at Tabora, did great kindness to me by giving me presents worth Rs. 80 from time to time. His charity based on patriotism was a heaven-gifted blessing to me amidst my cruel enemies. There was another kind hearted man named Chhaju, who secretly sent presents for prisoners.

Among the prisoners the Germans used to spread false rumours –

> that the Amir of Kabul had allied himself with Turkey and had invaded India, capturing Lahore;
> that there had been a great rising in Bombay and the Hindus and Muhammadans had joined hands against the British Government;
> that Nairobi and Mombasa had been taken by the Germans and so on and so forth.

They appealed to the Muhammadans to help Turkey instead of the British Government and they also haughtily stated that one German sepoy could stand against 8 British soldiers.

As regards the spirit of German Force I think that they are very much depressed and are growing hopeless. The German army of Askaris have no regular arrangement for transport, which is carried by their women when proceeding on guard duty. I may note here that some of the sword-bayonets of the Germans for the Askaris are made of ordinary iron and not of steel and were used even for clearing the jungle. The treatment by the Germans of their African Army is cruel. The Askaris are not given any pensions for wound or injury and when admitted to the hospitals their pay is cut. The wives of those who are killed in action receive pay for four months only; then they are told to re-marry.

On 19th September 1916, when the Belgians captured Tabora, the Germans carried away with them the able-bodied prisoners of war, and left behind the cripples only like myself. With the capture of Tabora by the Belgians, we were put in pucca barracks and the rations began to be regularly issued and my troubles through the grace of God ended.

As far as I know there were 85 companies of Africans and 1,400 German troops at Tabora.

The Indian shop-keepers in German East Africa were forced to make over all their property, excepting 200 rupees each and one bag of rice, to the German Government."

Statement of Subedar Harnam Singh of the Jind Imperial Service Regiment. *The Khalsa Advocate*, Saturday, March 10, 1917.

*****

Anand Marriage in British East Africa

"Sir – It was the first occasion that any marriage ceremony was solemnised according to Gurmat rites. It was therefore a novelty for the neighbouring communities and a pleasure for the Sikhs who though sitting at such a distance have none the less Sikh hearts within them. The marriage of Bhai Thakar Singh, brother of B. Ishar Singh, was celebrated under the auspices of the local Singh Sabha. On the morning of the 25th of April a Kirtan of Asa-di-War was recited. Then the marriage party proceeded for the Railway Station. In the procession Sri Guru Granth Sahib was installed on a nicely decorated carriage driven by two horses. On arrival at the station, a special train was waiting which carried the party to Apiland. A hearty reception was given by B. Ishar Singh, the bride's father.

Next morning after the Kirtan and lectures, the ceremony of the marriage was solemnised according to strict Gurmat rites as contained in the "Gurmat Parkash", published by the Chief Khalsa Diwan. Among the visitors on this occasion were several European ladies and gentlemen who watched the ceremony very keenly, throughout, and seemed greatly impressed. Both the parties gave donations for charitable and Panthic purposes and this happy function came to a close. Though such an account might not be interesting in the Punjab where it has become a very common thing, in Africa, where it was the first occasion of its kind, it produced a great interest and educative influence."

Dasaundha Singh, Assistant Secretary, Sri Guru Singh Sabha, Nairobi, 27-4-1918.

The Khalsa Advocate, Saturday, 8th June 1918.

*****

Indar Singh, son of Bhag Singh Jat, of Dina Tahsil Mogha, District Ferozepore, 22 (Indian), of 27th M.B. No.1169, sepoy states:

"I do not know the dates of my arrival and departure from East Africa. My battery went to East Africa in 1914. About 1 1/2 years later I was taken prisoner on a Trolley line near "Nargomba" [sic]. I was kept prisoner for 6 1/2 months and was released about 18 months ago. I was in hospital at the time, the hospital was attacked and captured by the Belgians and so I was released.

While I was prisoner, I was forced to work as a transport cooly, I was stripped absolutely naked save for a "langotah" [loin cloth]. Every stich of clothes was taken from me. Only two heads of Indian corn was given to me to eat daily, if I refused to carry the burden given to me I was beaten with a hide whip "Kaboko".

That is all that I have to say. I saw no one worse used than this in my time as prisoner."

Rawalpindi, 14th January 1919. (SI) J. Wilson Johnston, District Magistrate.
Note: Indar Singh's manner was straight-forward and seemed intelligent.

*****

Mesopotamia

"Jewan Singh, Utam Singh, Bhagwan Singh, and many other people have died at Baryana. But now the plague has entirely ceased. For the rest all is well. Kartar Singh went back to India in April. All the rest of us are well. Do not be in any way anxious. The state of affairs here is as follows: The name of the place where the fighting is going on is Nasiria and the enemy have a very strong entrenched position there. There is a great river and our troops advance by the river and come out. Afterwards they cannot find the enemy's position, while the enemy can fire at them very easily and they have destroyed many of our machine guns and caused very severe loss to our men. The fighting at Nasiria began on the 4th of July and has been going on every day. The enemy has his foot very firmly, but perhaps with great difficulty his foot will be broken. Here there come many wounded every day to the Field Hospital. The land there is very swampy, but we are sitting here at Basra. There is nothing for cavalry to do there."

From Karam Singh, 16th Cavalry, serving in Mesopotamia, to Mohan Singh of the same regiment (attached 6th Cavalry) serving in France. (Urdu, 1/8/15).

*****

"I was pleased to hear of your welfare, but much concerned to hear that the Colonel was displeased with you. You pay very little attention to what I say to you repeatedly. Remember that the work you do now will gain for you a good name or a bad name which will last you the rest of your life. For this reason you must always bear in mind your own honour and the honour of your family. There is nothing in life better than honour. See, my Colonel has praised my work and again at the victory of Kut-el-Amara he gave great praise. You on your side say your Colonel is displeased with you. I have heard that three native officers have been sent back from France. Here also two native officers have been punished. Be careful, do your work honestly and well and bear in mind the honour of your family."

From Riss. Hoshyar Singh, 16th Cavalry, Expeditionary Force D, to Jemadar Harbans Singh, 9th Hodson's Horse, France. (Urdu, 10/11/15).

*****

"We have got a fine opportunity of fighting. No doubt you are right in thinking that you too are fighting but you are having a very different time from us for you have everything you can want while the country here is absolutely uninhabited and desolate. Never mind, when we are winning, we are equally indifferent to comfort and inconvenience."

From Jemadar Risaldar Hoshyar Singh, 16th Cavalry, D. Force, Mesopotamia, to Jemadar Harbans Singh, 9th Hodson's Horse, France. (Urdu, 30/1/16).

*****

Photograph of Indian soldiers inspecting a crater left by a bomb, Mesopotamia 1916. (Courtesy of the Council of the National Army Museum, London)

*****

"The reason for delay in writing is that orders forbid us to write in envelopes (i.e. closed letters). We were allowed to send cards, but I could not get any. The fighting here is very severe. It is much more severe than against the Germans."

From Kirtar Singh, 33rd Cavalry, Force D, Mesopotamia, to Teja Singh, 9th Hodson's Horse, France. (Urdu, 5/2/16).

*****

"We left France on 8th November, and since the 4th January we have been engaged in the fight against the Turks. Here the work is very heavy and there is not even time to write letters. Moreover, they do not give us postcards to write. In France there was no lack of anything. It has remained for us to encounter the greatest of difficulties in this place. There is no sign of milk or sugar, and for drink we have nothing but the water of the Djlah (Euphrates)."

From L.D. Dalip Singh, 4th Cavalry, D.Force, Mesopotamia, to L.D. Chattar Singh, 2nd Lancers, France. (Urdu, 7/2/16).

*****

"We have joined the Army in the vicinity of Baghdad. On the 17/12/15 we embarked (from Marseilles?) and we reached our destination on 8/2/16. Up to the present time our force has not been engaged in any fighting, but we are prepared to commence fighting. The fighting here is very severe, and the country dry. I will let you know later what happens."

From Mulla Singh, "D" Force, Mesopotamia, to Sawar Chanda Singh, 2nd Lancers, France. (Gurmukhi, 9/2/16).

*****

"The news of the regiment is good. There is great activity as regards recruits and horses and many drafts go to the front. In Basra we have suffered many losses. All the Indian regiments (from other countries) have returned and gone towards Basra. The Cavalry too have suffered heavily. All the mules that were in Cavalry regiments are here, have been requisitioned for the front. There are no mules left in the regiments. All the mules are gathered together at Sialkot and from there they are dispatched to the front. Many camels too go to the front. Everywhere there is much activity. The Turks are in force."

From Dfdr. Dial Singh, Jabalpur, C.P., India, to Dfdr. Tara Singh, 32nd Lancers attached 30th Lancers. (Urdu, 12/2/16).

*****

"Fighting is very heavy in Basra. Many wounded are arriving. The losses are heavy there because there are no trenches. Moreover, the water is bad and there is much sickness."

From Dyal Singh, Depot 32nd Lancers, Jhabalpur, India, to Dafadar Tara Singh, 32nd Lancers attached 30th Lancers, France. (Urdu, 19/2/16).

*****

Indian troops lined up to receive inoculations, Mesopotamia 1916. (Courtesy of the Council of the National Army Museum, London)

*****

"I am very anxious because I have received no letter from you. Rumour is rampant that your regiment had been surrounded (besieged). Owing to no letter having been received from you, I am afraid the rumour is true. Therefore, as soon as you receive this letter, send a reply."

From Mool Singh, 6th Cavalry Bde., France, to L.N. Lal Singh, 20th Punjabis, Mesopotamia. (Urdu, 6/3/16).

*****

"You ask where we are. We are on the Tigris in Arabia in a place one month's march from Basra and before that we had a month at sea. We are marching every day and have the greatest difficulty about water. There are no trees to be seen anywhere. The misery which we are enduring here is as great as the comfort we enjoyed in France. But we are fit and well and must be thankful for this."

From Mala Singh, Jemadar, Mesopotamia, to Sowar Bhagta Singh, 9th Hodson's Horse, France. (Urdu, 11/3/16).

*****

"The 7th Brigade is surrounded in Mesopotamia. Attempts have been made to rescue them but without success. There was a fight on 6th March and heavy losses to us in the attempt to relieve them. Some men of ours are in the besieged force, 20 in number. They have eaten their horses and mules. They have a quarter of a pound of flour each per diem. We are hopeful of being sent to join the relieving force."

From Gunga Singh, Depot 16th Cavalry, Lucknow, to Dafadar Jaswant Singh, attached 6th Cavalry, France. (Gurmukhi, 21/4/16).

*****

"I have heard nothing about the fighting in Mesopotamia except from the newspapers. They say General Townshend has been surrounded for four months by the Turks and that large forces are being sent by the English to relieve him. Last Sunday there was very stiff fighting and our troops took several Turkish trenches, but, owing to the floods from the Tigris, could not maintain their positions."

From Balwant Singh, Rouen, to Gardur Jai Singh, Sahib, Sialkot, India. (Urdu, 24/4/16).

*****

"I was for 5 months amongst the besieged in Kut. When we were starved out we had to put up a white flag. All the fit men were taken away as prisoners towards Bagdad while the sick and wounded were sent direct to India. The trials which we underwent are beyond description. You are a wise man and know everything and you will understand. I am now on three month's sick leave."

(Postscript in English to above letter written by one Harnam Singh retired postmaster is as follows):

He together with ten thousand men were obliged to eat horses and mules' meat through hunger. Only 5 tolas wheat was given to each man for 13 days. On the 29th April there was nothing to eat, hence General Townshend was obliged to disarm his army and to accept war imprisonment with all his men."

From Ram Singh, 16th Cavalry, Ludhiana Dt., Punjab, to Balwant Singh, Signal Troop, 1st Indian Cavalry Division, France. (Urdu, no date given).

*****

"It is a matter of great regret that our brother Chet Singh has been taken prisoner at Kut-al-Amara. Other men from Dhudial who were with him, have also been captured. Well, we should not grieve, nothing is to be gained by grieving. At the end of the war, they will return home alive. All those brave fellows did their duty faithfully to the very end. They deserve the highest praise. This event (i.e. their being made prisoners) was written in their fate, and no one could have prevented it."

From Karm Singh, Machine Gun Section, Sialkot Cavalry Brigade, France, to Kalyan Singh, Jhelum Dt., Punjab. (Urdu, 8/6/16).

*****

"I have come back from the Basra Hospital. The two Sikh Squadrons of the 12th were left in Basra and the Dogra and Musalman squadrons were for two months in the firing line at Nasiringeh. Sowar Bokul Singh was killed, and some men were wounded, and some were taken prisoner. Wardi Major Ullam Singh and Colonel Wintle, and Major Tahourdi and Ram Singh and others were killed, and the regiment is very distressed. There is nothing here but date trees. It is a deserted place. These Arabs are a bad lot."

From Dafadar Narain Singh, Head Salutri, 12th Cavalry, Bombay, to L.Daf. Fateh Din Khan, 28th Lancers, France. (Urdu, 29/6/16).

*****

"We are having a rest here. A good many of us are suffering from fever and stomach troubles but the bulk of the Force is in excellent condition and ready for fighting. There has been no serious fighting yet here but now that the cold season has come we expect some. Major ____ commands us. There are very few of the old officers left."

From Subedar Mit Singh, 47th Sikhs, Mesopotamia Field Force to Jemadar Arjan Singh, Rouen, France. (Urdu dated the 11th October 1916).

*****

Indian soldiers, horse wrestling, Mesopotamia. (Courtesy of the Council of the National Army Museum, London)

*****

"Listen to the tale of Ressaidar Ajaib Singh. He accompanied Genl. Townsend in the retreat and became besieged in Kut-al-Amara. This valiant force made 1½ months rations last for 5 months and during the whole time resisted a greatly superior force of the enemy. A ship that was going to their assistance with provisions was caught in a storm and went aground in the river. When the rations were completely consumed, the force delivered themselves up to the enemy, who were greatly impressed by the brave resistance of the General and his troops and treated them with much honour. The greater part of the force is now in Konia, in Turkey. I began to receive letters from Ajaib Singh about 1½ months ago. He says that all the Sikh Sirdars are quartered in one large building. They suffer no inconveniences and have no work to do. It is like being at home and except for separation from their friends that have nothing to complain of. They get £7 per month for their expenses in which they are able to live exceedingly well. Everything necessary is obtainable. They expect to return soon. Our Sircar has made great arrangements for their welfare. Assistance reaches them even from London."

From Sunder Singh, Professor, Sandiman High School, Quetta, India, to Bela Singh, Jemadar, 7th Hariana Lancers, Remount Depot, Rouen, France. (English dated the 12th October 1916).

*****

"In reply to the appeal issued by the Deputy Commissioner, Sialkot, asking the assistance of all patriotic persons in the District to help in the recruiting for different services in Mesopotamia, I gave up the idea of joining the Medical College and volunteered my services to the supply and transport department. I was appointed as a Tally Clerk on Rs. 126 p.m., and, was ordered to proceed to Basra on 19th October 1916. I started from Rawalpindi on 20th October, reaching Karachi on 22nd whence I sailed for Basra on 23rd October, 1916. Here is a diary of my travel from Karachi to Basra.

"S.S. Umballa"
23rd October 1916
The railway journey from Lahore right up to Karachi was troublesome as the sand and the burning heat were very oppressive. We got our food in the Dining Car. We alighted at the Karachi Cantt. Station and were taken to the Rest Camp whence on the 23rd evening the train took us right up to the mouth of the harbour.

We were at first given seats on the Deck but a representation being made to the Captain that we were officers, he gave us two cabins I got a first class berth equipped with beds and all other comforts. We got our food cooked in the 2nd class and got meals four times a day. Tea, biscuits and butter in the morning; Fish, Mutton, Bread, Arraroot, Jam, Butter and Eggs at breakfast; Rice, Curry and Chatni at noon; Chicken, Rice sweet, bread and fruit in the evening. In fact, we were right royally fed.

There are many men on this ship going to Basra from Lahore and Quetta Divisions also. Many of them belong to Sialkot. In fact, we are jolly company and I have therefore felt not even for a moment that I am going thousands of miles far off from my mother land. I have had absolutely no trouble up to 24th October. The sea is calm, and the season is neither warm nor cold. It is very refreshing.

My mother, wife and sisters must have felt my separation very much as I did not see them at the time of my departure. But my going to Basra was inevitable and nobody could have stopped it. I was determined to respond to duty's call and serve the benign government in this time of need. I am sorry, however, that I did not see them at the time of my departure, but I did so purposely lest they should stand in my way. Besides, my departure was so sudden that I could not help avoiding it. I sincerely hope that the Almighty Father will bring me back safe to see you all happy and prosperous.

24th October. I wish I could post this letter today, but I see nothing else but water and water on all sides. "Oh waves of the ocean! Take this message of mine back to Karachi and thence entrust it to the winds to my own sweet home."

25th October. After finishing our morning meal we saw to our great joy our ship sailing along the shore, we were hardly ten miles off from the Persian Coast near Bandar Abbas. We hope to pass near Bushire tomorrow. How pleasing it was to see the signs of habitation after the monotony of the sea. It was my desire to have my life insured and I would have done it at Karachi, but I did not do so as I had not consulted you about it. If you permit I may do so now.

27th October. I had fever yesterday on account of constipation. I was treated in the ship hospital and I am alright now. Our ship is now sailing through a narrow strait

– Persia to our right and Arabia to our left. So close are we to the Persian coast that we can see trees and horses all along the coast. We hope to reach Basra tomorrow evening.

S.S. Umballa River Tigris.
28th October 9 p.m. Our ship is now anchoring in the River. It reached Basra late in the evening and so we could not disembark, but we will do so tomorrow. The ship is anchoring at Basra port but a little off from the jetty. The speed of the ship was very slow as the water in the river is not very deep. On both sides of the river we saw nothing but sand and date trees. Climate here is just like that of the Punjab. I will send you a wire tomorrow intimating my safe arrival here.

Morgil (Basra).
1st November: We are resting here in the rest camp but cannot say where I shall be posted. I will let you know as soon as I am settled.

Makine (Basra).
7th November 1916. I was transferred to this place on the 3rd instant. It is about 4 miles from Basra. The work is not very hard except that we have to go every now and then to Ry: Station to hand over stock. I am just coming back from a Rail-head 100 miles off from Basra. Of course I cannot expect to get the ease and comfort I used to enjoy at Sialkot, but one does not feel any trouble when he has to do his work.

Let me hope you have shifted the family from Sialkot to Lahore and my dear mother, wife and sisters are all now with you in Lahore. I will try to send you, if possible, a parcel of fresh dates of Basra as my humble present in connection with the birthday anniversary of Guru Nanak Ji, our lord and saviour which falls day after tomorrow. I have a servant who cooks my food. 'Makina' is just close to Basra and there is no trouble about board and lodging and I feel quite at home."

Extracts from the diary of S. Indar Singh. *The Khalsa Advocate,* Saturday, 16th December 1916.

*****

"As to the letter from that person of whom I spoke, do not send it in the ordinary envelope because it has to be franked by the Sahib. What you should do is to get a green envelope and send the letter in that or better still get two or three green envelopes and give them to that person to send her replies in. We are in great discomfort for it is bitterly cold and the mud is deep. We cannot get on without long boots but even they do not stand the water long and the men's feet have begun to get bad already. Give my salaams to the "bit of my heart" and tell her how I am suffering and give her this letter in French (enclosed a letter for a French girl)."

From Jemadar Ghulla Singh, Mesopotamia, to Jemadar Bachittar Singh, 6th Cavalry, France. (Urdu dated the 19th December 1916).

*****

Photograph of Indian and Arab personnel loading a cart with post for soldiers of the 3rd (Lahore) Division, Mesopotamia 1916. (Courtesy of the Council of the National Army Museum, London)

*****

"I am continually praying that God may give you the victory. The fall of Baghdad and Kut-el-Amara has caused the greatest joy here, and the enemy is also retreating in France. It is evident that the faces of the Germans will shortly be blackened, and that God will give our Government the victory."

From -----, Jammu, Kashmir, to -----, 9th Hodson's Horse, France. (Urdu, 15th March 1917).

*****

"We went into action and the Major Sahib ordered us to put our horses into a ____ and to bring our machine guns into action. A bullet hit me in the thigh. The Major Sahib at once cut my breeches open with his penknife and bandaged me and sent for the stretcher bearers. But I said I would not go in a dooli but on my horse so I got on my horse but by the time I got to the dressing station I was very sorry I had not taken the dooli as I could not dismount. The Doctor Sahib helped me off and at once took out the bullet and then took down my name. On the 25th a crowd of motor ambulances came up and I was put into one. We went half speed as far as the railway and there I was put into a hospital train which travelled slowly. Just think of the wonderful bandobast of the Sirkar to have everything ready before we arrived!"

From Daffadar Amar Singh, Mesopotamia to Jemadar Kesar Singh, 2nd Lancers, France. (Urdu dated the 27th March 1917).

*****

"I have not had time to write before. We are 38 miles beyond Baghdad. You have no doubt seen in the papers the large number of Turks we have taken prisoners and the quantity of machine guns."

From Indar Singh, Havildar, Signal Section, 7th Division, Mesopotamia to Sowar Hakum Singh, 9th Hodson's Horse, France. (Urdu dated the 22nd April 1917).

*****

"I am very happy and comfortable and have gone far beyond Baghdad. You have seen in the papers all about Baghdad and Kut-al-Amara. If the Guru wills it, all will be for the best. We have joined hands with the Russians. The Turkish forces are thoroughly broken up and will soon make peace."

From Jemadar Baldev Singh, 86th Punjabis, Mesopotamia to Bahadur Singh, 36th Jacob's Horse, France. (Urdu dated the 29th April 1917).

*****

"Sikhs residing in Ammara [sic] are glad to hear that a gurdwara is about to be built in Basra and adding that it will be still more useful if another gurdwara is built in Ammara. Ammara is a sanatorium in Mesopotamia, in conquering which the Sikhs have shown great devotion and bravery. Government and the people are aware that Sabi Arabs reside in Ammara, who call themselves Arab Sikhs and naturally love other Sikhs. As by the kindness of our benign Government, this town is about to become a great city, it is desirable that a gurdwara should be built here."

Natha Singh, Sub Assistant Surgeon, General Hospital, Amara, Mesopotamia, *The Loyal Gazette* (Lahore), 29th April 1917.

*****

"We (all Indian ranks) have the honour to make the following petition:

Our first Guru Nanak Dev Sahib Ji having come from Mecca, visited Baghdad, which is well known in Sikh History as "Wali Hind" in order to perform various religious rites there.

Now, when our regiment arrived there and visited the place, it was very anxious to build a gurudwara in the memory of our first Guru Nanak Dev Ji and the gallant Sikh soldiers who have died in Mesopotamia during this war.

The funds for this purpose, will be collected by this regiment, other Sikh regiments and Sikh Chiefs of the Punjab.

We now beg to request that you will kindly obtain the sanction of higher authority to build a gurudwara in the place referred to, which is quite close to the Baghdad Railway Station and on sanction being obtained the necessary arrangements for collecting funds will be made."

10th August 1917: Translation of vernacular petition from the Sikh Officers of the 14th (King George's Own) Sikhs, to the Officer Commanding, 14th (King George's Own Sikhs).

*****

I, NATHA SINGH, Sepoy No. 579, 48th Pioneers (Sikh),
SAY AS FOLLOWS:
"I was captured at Kut and sent to Baghdad, then to Mossul, and then to Ras El Ain. I was sent to Constantinople for 26 days only and then back to Afionkara hissar. It was there that my hair and beard and moustache were forcibly cut off. It was said to be an order of superior authority. I objected strongly that it was against my religion, but they paid no attention. There were about 100 Sikhs who were treated in the same manner. They also compelled us to wear small caps. Our hair was cut by machinery."
14.3.18

*****

I, ATMA SINGH, bugler, 67th Punjabis, 2054, (Sikh),
SAY AS FOLLOWS:
"I was captured at Kut on 29/4/16. I was taken to Ras El Ain and employed on the construction of railways with other Hindus for six months, then transferred to Constantinople after one year and four months. The Turks were very oppressive and sometimes prisoners remained two days without rations. An improvement was affected when this was put in the hands of the "German Railway Company" this was about March 1917.

My hair and beard were forcibly cut on 25th December 1916 in a quarantine camp, the name of which I do not know. The only explanation given by the Turks was that they do not approve of our custom and that we were "Kafirs". They also took off our "safas" and made us wear caps. My "safa" was removed and the cap put on by a Turkish officer. We were also made to eat beef."
14.3.18

*****

I, HAKIM SINGH, Lce-Naik, 22nd Punjabis, 588, (Sikh),
DO SAY AS FOLLOWS:
"I was captured December 1st 1915 during the retirement from Suliman, taken to Baghdad, Mossul and Aleppo and then to the camp at Ras El Ain. Without halting there we were taken to Afionkarahissar. We stayed about 1½ years there.

Both in Baghdad and Afionkarahissar my beard and hair were cut in spite of our protests on religious grounds.

The Turks at least made some difference in their treatment of Hindus and Mahommadans. In Afionkarahissar there were about 200 Mahommadan prisoners and about 180 Hindus. The Hindus were worked much harder than the Mohammedans. The O.C. of the camp at Afionkarahissar made a considerable profit in the following way: when a parcel was received soon after a former one, he would impound the clothes etc. received with the first and sell them in the town.

I know that the Indian Mohammadans resident in Constantinople used to print a newspaper in Urdu – I do not know its name – and send it to the Indian Mohammadan prisoners. I have never seen the paper."
14.3.18

*****

Guru Nanak's Visit to Baghdad

"Guru Nanak travelled far and wide to preach his gospel to the world. There is no doubt that he visited Mesopotamia and made a stay in Baghdad, as apart from Janamsakhis, Bhai Gurdas mentions it in his work. For the Sikhs a great point of interest after the fall of the historic city of Baghdad, was to visit the exact place sanctified by the stay of Guru Nanak there. Many attempts were made to find it out by all the Sikhs that could afford the time, and many a tramp proved fruitless, but at last it was found to be settled that a place near the Railway Station, south-west of the town, was the place. The place was a building containing the tomb of Bahalol Dana and another tomb, one in each room. The room containing the tomb of Bahalol is the bigger of the two, and one corner of it is devoted to Guru Nanak. In the wall is a stone with the following inscription in Turkish:

'You sleep in this tomb in the direct protection of God. You came alone from your parental home, and you have entered this new place alone. I invoked divines for inspiration about the date which came in this world (meaning that) Sayid the disciple obtained the well-deserved reward – 927.'

When the above translation was done I pointed out that it had no reference to Guru Nanak – a thing I looked for in it. The translator then gave the following translation:

'You sleep in this tomb under the direct protection of God. Baba Nanak Fakir, you have entered this new place alone, I invoke, etc.'

One can see at a glance that the second rendering is a misfit. The words (Baba Nanak) in the context mean father and mother respectively in the Turkish language. There appears to be very little doubt from the context that the inscription refers to some deceased person and is like those commonly found on tombstones. There appears to be some doubt as to this place being the exact spot where Guru Nanak made his stay.

It is for the purpose of settling this point beyond any doubt that these lines are written. It is therefore requested that those who can throw any light on the question may do so in the interest of the whole community.

The following further points are submitted, which are likely to throw some light on the question:

1. Early in April 1917 the stone was not in the wall where it is at present; indeed the Arab caretaker then professed to have no knowledge of any other stone except the unimportant ones referring to the tombs. He said the place was the tomb of Bahlol Dana and he had no knowledge of Baba Nanak or any "Pir" from India.
2. Bhai Karm Singh the Sikh historian, who visited Baghdad before the war, has fixed a place just outside Sheikh Abdul Qadir Jailani's gate, to the north-east of the town, as the abode of Guru Nanak sojourn here. It stands to reason as that is the place one would naturally expect the Guru to go to reach those in quest of Truth, Ghulam Qadir Jailani's tomb being visited by all pilgrims. The Bahlol's place is on the other side of the river and presents no feature inviting to a man of Guru Nanak's mission.
3. While explaining the cause of the stone being absent for so long the caretaker said that only his elder brother, who was in Basra during the early part of the occupation of the town, knew of its existence, and when he returned to Baghdad sometime after its fall he dug the stone out of the ground.

4. The elder brother, asked about the thing, made the following remarks: The Stone was inscribed just after Guru Nanak left this place and was put in the wall by one of his disciples. About 15 years ago the building which contained the two tombs fell to the ground and when collecting the debris many old tombstones were found, as the building was in the centre of a cemetery. They collected all the stones and put some in the wall (there were three there which looked very much older and worn out than Guru Nanak's stone and had no reference to the tombs in the building), but the one in question was not put in the wall for scarcity of "joo" (cement); which when pressed further for some better excuse he said that he considered this stone in particular too valuable to be put in the wall as there were thieves about. He, therefore, wanted to remove it to the house for safety's sake. However they did not take it to the house and for 15 years it was lying in the building on the ground, he was careful to explain, it was exactly underneath its present place in the wall. It was fixed in the wall after the occupation of Baghdad last year.
5. The elder brother remembers a poem which Guru Nanak composed and sang while he was here. The poem is not written down anywhere, but it has been handed down, generation to generation. Following is the poem:

Translation:

I have been called a "fakir" in all countries and I have travelled over all distant parts.

I arrived in Baghdad Sharif to see Bahlol Dana who has been pointed out to me.

I have brought myself close to him out of love for him because he is a "fakir" known in distant countries.

People of India, this is Mecca, the place of safety and the place for the "fakirs".

It is the same as Medina. When I saw its Light my heart began to soar high with happiness.

Could this be the work of Guru Nanak?

1220 Hijra is given as the date of the death of Bahlol Dana on the stone inscription in the building; this was 927 as given in Guru Nanak's inscription.

1. Sayid, says the caretaker, mentioned in the inscription on the stone was his ancestor, who was Guru Nanak's contemporary and between them both existed a harmony of thought.
2. When at first the Sikhs came to this building, the caretaker professed to have no knowledge of their Guru as the Baba Nanak he knew was a thorough Mohammadan. Later on, when the Sikhs persisted in coming there and offering money he had to yield to their wishes.
3. A photograph of the stone was taken in October 1917, and the inscription showed the year 927 underneath. Another photograph was taken in February 1918, when the inscription showed the year 917. In the latter instance, the stone was white washed and the letters gone over with black paint. In October, the caretaker, at the request of the writer, copied Guru Nanak's inscription in the note book, which shows 927, and yet the stone shows 917 now.

There could not have been any mistake in understanding what the caretakers said in Arabic as the writer had two very good interpreters with him, in addition to himself knowing enough to check the translation.

Would the Sikh public publish what they know on this question in the interest of the whole community? Those who visited this place early and settled it as the place should be able to throw strong light on the matter, and it is, hoped that they would do so and soon."

Fateh Singh, Sub Major, (Asst. Censor), Baghdad, 9th May 1918.
The Khalsa Advocate, Saturday, June 29, 1918.

*****

Malay States

"We are glad to learn that the riot at Singapore has been suppressed by the efforts of the 36th Sikh Infantry, which we hear is now in search of the missing rioters. It is the same 36th troop of the Sikhs whose 21 brave fighters stood against thousands of the enemies at the battle of Saragarhi and in whose commemoration two memorials, one at Amritsar and the other at Ferozepore, were built."

Article, *The Khalsa Advocate* (Amritsar), 20th March 1915.

*****

"About 3 P.M. on the 15th February 1915, I was asleep in the Malay State Guides' lines and was awakened by a shot. As I was getting up I heard another shot fired.

I sent 1799 Gunner Santa Singh to tell Captain Maclean that there was firing in the 5th Lines.

He came back with orders to take cover and save our lives.

I gave orders to all the men to get behind cover.

About 3-4 hours afterwards Captain Maclean came down. I saw him coming and I heard some shouting and saw a lot of men coming from the opposite direction; there was a lot of firing and I saw Captain Maclean fall and I said to the men, "Fall back, get under cover and make your way to Singapore."

Amongst those coming from the opposite direction I saw none of our men; there was a lot of firing and there may have been some of our men, but I don't know.

The Captain was very good and kind to us and I don't think there was any man who had a grudge against him or would do a thing like that after giving these orders to the men; we went down through the jungle to the road.

I ordered Atta Singh (driver) and Kala Singh (gunner) to remove the breech and blocks of the two guns, which they did and hid them close by in the jungle.

Then we began to make for Singapore through the jungle and met two Sepoys of the 5th Light Infantry. Two of our drivers, Harnam Singh and Partab Singh (both here) came up and our party now consisted of six.

We forcibly took away the rifles of the two Sepoys of the 5th Light Infantry and made them give up their ammunition.

One of the rifles we gave to Nand Singh and the other to Lachman Singh.

Three of us had rifles from before.

We tried to bring along the two Sepoys of the 5th Light Infantry as prisoners but seeing about one hundred men of the 5th Light Infantry coming up we let the two men go and hid ourselves.

On the road which goes from Pasir Panjang to Singapore we met two ladies. I was the first to come out of cover followed by the others.

Seeing us the ladies became afraid and I sent Chanda Singh, who speaks English, to tell them not to fear, we had come to help them.

We escorted the ladies to their motor about 200 yards away.

I told Chanda Singh to ask the ladies to permit us to ride in their motor also.

They allowed two of us. The others also wanted to get in.

The Mem Sahib said, "It will break the car," but Chanda Singh said, "It is only a little way; let us get in."

We saw some sailors on the road who presented their arms at us and we held up our hands and so did the ladies.

The motor stopped and we delivered up our arms; Chanda Singh explained to the Officer in charge, as did the ladies, what had happened, and we went on with the ladies walking and a little way farther the ladies got into another car and went off.

We went along about two hundred yards where we met a party of sailors; Chanda Singh explained the position again and they let us through.

By the Monopoly we met a Gunner Officer who took us to Headquarters at the P. and O. Wharf.

The lady who was here just now (Mrs. Robinson) was one of the two ladies.

My party consisted of myself, 1184 Corporal Chanda Singh, 2069 Gunner Nand Singh, Gunner 2554 Lachman Singh, 2616 Gunner Partab Singh and 2614 Gunner Harnam Singh.

The two men of the 5th Light Infantry who we disarmed had no beards. They were young soldiers. They wore Khaki shirts, dhotis and khaki turbans.

I have been in Singapore about seven months.

I heard the men of the Malay State Guides saying that the Mahommedan Officers of the Malay State Guides had put the men up to say that their agreement did not apply to foreign service.

I have been only two months in Alexandra Barracks and cannot say about their reasons for mutiny.

If we had all been asked in the way that Captain Maclean asked us more than half the regiment would have gone.

When the firing first broke out I heard the Sepoys of the 5th Light Infantry shouting out, "Come to Tanglin.""

Havildar Sohan Singh, Mountain Battery, Malay State Guides. Evidence to Court of Enquiry, Mutiny of the 5th Light Infantry, Singapore 1915.

*****

"About 3.15 P.M. on the 15th February 1915, I was in my tent. A shot was fired from the direction of the 5th Light Infantry quarter-guard. Immediately afterwards the alarm bugle sounded. We received orders to get into uniform. I went to the tent and saw Havildar Sohan Singh, who was the senior Non-Commissioned Office of the camp. Bicycle orderly Santa Singh came shortly afterwards to this place and told us the Sahib's orders were that we were not to fall in but to take cover, Surayan Singh ordered me to go to the quarter-guard to reinforce the guard. Surayan Singh was on guard. I ordered Surayan Singh to go to the drivers. At this time there was a double guard, Roshin Deen and Sultan Ahmad. I ordered them to take cover close to the mule lines near to some broken ground. Both sentries had rifles. I took a rifle. A certain number of the rifles – the balance of the rifles were still in the quarter-guard tent. Some of them had been taken by their owners, I presume. In my corps the men who were over near the guns on these occasions did not take rifles; rifles are only taken by ground scouts, range finders and others. Surayan Singh had told me that a certain number of men had taken rifles but did not say who. There were about three or four rifles left. These rifles remained in the tent. I did not see them again. I asked him why he abandoned these rifles and he said a tremendous attack was made on them from the direction of the 5th Light Infantry barracks. The men of the 5th Light Infantry attacked them. There must have been anything from one hundred and fifty to two hundred of the 5th Light Infantry who attacked us in the direction of the mule troughs. Their men were shouting "Sahib Subadar: Sahib Subadar." But I could not say if he was an officer. There was a man there in white clothes. They brought some boxes of ammunition and this individual whom I took to be an officer, said "Shoot the Malay State Guides. These men are going to help the Government." If they had had time to get out their ammunition we should all have been shot, but we escaped into the jungle. When we got the order to retire, the guard also disappeared. They escaped into the jungle. I moved off shortly afterwards into the jungle and we had got about half a mile from my lines when I met two men of the Malay State Guides: 1963 acting Bombardier Lal Singh, and 2645 Driver Ram Singh. They had no arms. A great deal of firing was going on behind us and we crept through the jungle. Whichever way we went there was a sound of firing and we didn't know where to go. It was about 8 o'clock at night. We three sat in the jungle the whole night. Next morning the firing was still going on and we did not know where to go. We left the flag staff hill on our right, and arrived at the Central Police Station where there were the General and some other officers, and some of my corps. We were interned together. We never met anybody in the jungle from the time we started till the time we got out. I left my rifle in the quarter. I cannot say what became of the ammunition. There was no time to get either a rifle or ammunition, as we had to save our lives."

1952 Bombardier Pal Singh, Jat Sikh of Amritsar District. Evidence to Court of Enquiry, Mutiny of the 5th Light Infantry, Singapore 1915.

*****

"On Monday 15th February at about 3 P.M. in the direction of the 5th Light Infantry quaterguard there were shots. I was in my tent. I put on my uniform and went to my mules. The bicycle orderly who had been sent up to Captain Maclean came back and told us not to fall in. About ten minutes later, Captain Maclean's orderly came down and told us to save ourselves. Just then a Subadar with about one hundred and fifty men of the 5th Light Infantry came along. I know he was a Subadar because other people said so and he gave orders. I would recognize him if I were to see him. He was wearing earrings and was fat. He wore white clothes. He had a short beard and moustache. (Witness here goes out and identifies Subadar Dunde Khan from amongst seven prisoners as the Subadar of whom he speaks). The Subadar said "Those people who will help me I will let go. I will shoot the others. I will not let you people go as you want to give help to the Government." Then I took a rifle from one of the 5th Light Infantry who told me to. Some seventeen or eighteen of us had been surrounded near the mule troughs and they also were given rifles and four or five packets of ammunition; then I ran into the jungle with the 5th and gradually shook them off and got away by myself. There was firing going on from the high ground above the camp at the Malay State Guides. I gave myself up to the police at the Central Station the same night about 9 P.M. with my rifle and ammunition."

2438 Driver Bishan Singh, Malay State Guide's Battery. Evidence to Court of Enquiry, Mutiny of the 5th Light Infantry, Singapore 1915.

*****

"I recollect about 3 or 3.30 P.M. I was in the office with the engineer Tuan Haiskew and Tuan de Vries. A large number of sepoys came to the factory. They had rifles. One man said to me "Who are these Tuans?" I said that they were Blanda (Dutch). Both my Tuans went to their house but returned in about a quarter of an hour's time. Shortly after this man (identifies Subadar Wahad Ali) came with others who were armed. He asked, "Who lives here?" I said "Dutchmen". He said, "I wish to speak to them." He then came upstairs with me. He said through me that he wished to telephone to his Tuan. My Tuan telephoned but there was no reply. He then said, "I am not a bad man, I am a good man; and I am afraid of our men. If I return there I may be shot. My Tuan said, "Where do you want to go? If you like you can stay here." He said he didn't want to go into the rubber store. My Tuan then said, "You can go to my coolie lines." He went there with his men and slept in the coolie place (tempat coolie). Next morning – my Tuans had left the previous evening about 6 P.M. – this man (Wahad Ali) said he wished to telephone but he could not get any answer to his ringing. He and his party remained in the factory for three days. They had no food.

I told this man that if he would put all the rifles and ammunition into a room I would lock them up safely for him. He said "Baik," I did this and got into communication with the police at Keppel Harbour who telephoned to the Central Police station. A motor car came and took away all the rifles (thirty five or thirty six I think) and ammunition and all the sepoys holding up a white flag, who met the car. They went off with the motor car and two police (Malays)."

Sunder Singh, Watchman at Pasir Panjang Rubber Works. Evidence to Court of Enquiry, Mutiny of the 5th Light Infantry, Singapore 1915.

*****

"We came from the Fatehgarh Depot. I had 54 men effectives and 6 men in hospital: of the 54 men, 15 had obtained leave from Captain Maclean, who was looking after the detachment, to go to town. There were actually 39 men present in the barracks, including myself. It would be somewhere about 4 o'clock on the afternoon of the 15th February when the detachment – some inside the barracks, some outside and some cooking, heard the sound of firing. The firing took place in the direction of the cookhouse to the south-west of our barrack. When I heard the firing I came out of my quarters on to the verandah on the south side, and saw about 50 men. We saw them coming towards us in scattered formation. They were dressed in all sorts of kit. Many were dressed in khaki turbans and mufti. We took our rifles from the kote and I gave each man a packet of 20 rounds of ammunition. I posted the men around the barrack room on each of the entrances, of which there are several. While I was issuing ammunition, I saw some men of this party return in a westerly direction across the lower ground. I saw the barracks on the other side of me were deserted. We were left alone in our quarters, which is "Q" block. About 10 minutes afterwards while I was distributing ammunition, the party returned. I never heard anymore. They seemed to go in the direction of the recreation ground and there was firing in that direction, but I was too busy issuing ammunition and seeing after my own men to say exactly what had occurred. We stood in our barrack room the whole night. I saw one man who might have been a Malay who had been killed. I saw something had gone wrong with the other regiment and I collected all my party in the barracks and we never stirred out of them. We thought we should probably get orders from Captain Maclean. I never heard any more firing until 4 A.M. the next day, when I allowed my men to go out to the latrine. I heard the sound of firing from about the same direction as I heard it before. The firing came from the west, but I could not see as it was dark. We had no food that night. About 5-30 A.M. I collected all my men together, took the spare rifles, of which there were 21, and marched out of the barracks down the road towards where the road joins the canteen. When we got near the crossroads there was a firing line of white troops formed up lying in the road and ready to shoot at us. I had a white cloth, which I waved at them. The party of British troops split up into two portions, one getting to the north of us and the other going along the road to the east. Nobody could understand a word we said, and I asked an officer to get someone who did. We met an officer who signed his name in my book as Major Thompson. I handed over to him my 21 spare rifles, and Major Thompson formed us into fours and marched us into town and brought us to the police station near Tanglin, which is in Orchard road. At the police station Major Thompson was with us and put us into a motor car and brought us to the Central Police Station. We had no rations that day because there was no place for us to cook them in. The next day my detachment were sent out to the Race Course."

Lance Havildar Nand Singh, 2187, of the 36th Sikhs. Evidence to Court of Enquiry, Mutiny of the 5th Light Infantry, Singapore 1915.

*****

"We, the Sikhs here assembled, do desire to tender expression of our feelings of loyalty to the British Crown.

The Sikhs are a comparatively small nation, but their services to Britain have been of the highest character. They have fought shoulder to shoulder with British troops on many occasions in the past – in Afghanistan, Burma, Egypt, China and Persia, while the part they played in the suppression of the Indian Mutiny will never be forgotten during the whole course of British History. In all these campaigns the Sikhs have shed their blood unsparingly and without complaint.

With reference to more recent events, we are proud in the knowledge that all recognise how nobly our soldiers have acquitted themselves during this world war – in France, Gallipoli, Egypt, Mesopotamia and Africa.

Some time ago, when the numbers of men recruiting in British India were issued by the Lieutenant Governor of the Punjab, it was discovered that no less than one-fifth of these men were Sikhs, whereas the Sikh population is estimated at no more than one-hundredth of the total of 300,000,000 and over, of the Indian people, thus demonstrating most clearly that our sacrifices have been overwhelmingly out of proportion to our numbers.

We are a military people, and as such, we regard loyalty as a religious principle: the ancient precepts of our Gurus, the Great Teachers, may be summed up in this exhortation: - "When serving thy master, face the foe bravely, and leave the question of life and death in the hands of God." It is our religion that has made us what we are today – the Sikh people; and wherever we may be, we will be ready to serve in the interests of the Crown.

In Conclusion, Sir, may we request you to convey these our sentiments to the King-Emperor, giving him full assurance that, be the Sikhs in their homeland of India or abroad, they will always be prompt and eager to do his bidding, and fulfil his commands."

The Sikhs in Perak.
IPOH, 25th June 1916.

*****

"Gurdit Singh has written from home to the effect that Bachan Singh should not be sent home (Perak) yet, because security is taken from all those who return home from foreign countries and they are not allowed to leave their houses."

From Bishen Singh, Perak, Malay State, to Havildar Jaimal Singh, 57th Rifles, A Force (wrongly addressed to France). (No language, No date).

*****

Persia and Baluchistan

"And the news of this place is as follows: - At first the battle raged with the Turks in Arabia with great violence, but the Turks were defeated everywhere. We are still fighting with them, but my Squadron (A) is separated from the regiment and has come into Persia and taken possession of Bushire. Formerly the English were the friends of Persia, but they have now occupied their country, and the whole of the country is prepared to fight. The enemy have collected in great numbers, and there will be much fighting, concerning which I will write to you hereafter. Five or six men of my regiment have been killed, and others have been wounded and sent back somewhere."

From Tirath Singh, of some Cavalry Corps (Rank and Corps not stated) Bushire, to Sowar, Sawan Singh, 16th Cavalry, attached 29th Lancers, at the front. (Urdu, 14/8/15).

*****

"We had a fight on the 9th September. The enemy numbered between 400 and 500 men, and my regiment drove them from their trenches. After this, my squadron, in which there were 75 men, made a frontal attack on the enemy. The enemy suffered greatly from this attack, and two of our British officers, two Indian officers and eleven non-commissioned officers were killed in the fight, and ten were wounded. The enemy was on foot and all were armed with rifles. Thank God we escaped on that day. Wait and see what happens in the future. Your luck is good that you have never seen such an enemy and remain in comfort. No one can have experienced so great hardships as Force 'D' suffered. Well, it is a question of fate."

From Riss. Lahna Singh, 16th Cavalry, Bushire, to Acting Lce. Dfdr Lal Chand, 2nd Lancers, France. (Urdu, 3/10/15).

*****

"The climate of this place is very bad. If we stay another year here we shall first lose all the hair of our heads; it will all fall off. Secondly all our teeth will go bad. I expect we shall be transferred to the Pindi division; that is what people say. It never rains in this country and is exceedingly hot … And that three rupees' increase of pay, is it only for France or for active service elsewhere? Be sure to let me know. We are in Ahwaz City; it belongs to King Karoon. * There are very many palm trees here."
* A mythical potentate of enormous wealth.

From Ganda Singh, apparently at Ahwaz, Persian Gulf, (censored by an officer of the 12th Cavalry) to Sohan Singh, 38th Cavalry, France. (Gurmukhi, Oct.1915).

*****

"You write asking what we are doing. We are doing just what you are. Do you imagine that we are strolling round the village collecting fuel (lit: cow dung)? You catch a sight of the enemy every now and then, we man the trenches every day, dismounted. Do not be anxious. There is no danger. The battle does not move back and forwards – it is trench fighting. Our army is pushing back the enemy but does not allow the Germans to advance. We fight in great spirits. This is not Persia, stay where you are – out of it! You say we do not see the enemy – we see him more than you do!"

From Naranjan Singh, in France, Sowar 20th or 34th Horse, F.P.O.19, to Daf. Piara Singh, 7th Lancers, Persia. (Gurmukhi, 18/10/15).

*****

"Do not be anxious about us; we are quite all right. We live in the town in a large house. We have beds to sleep on. Cows' milk is obtainable, and wine too is easily obtained. We have no difficulty in supplying our wants. But I am anxious about Lal Singh. We have received very little information from his direction. I expect they are having a hard time. I am constantly anxious about you too. I learn from your second letter that you have come out of the trenches which I was very glad to hear. We three brothers are engaged in the war. It is a matter for congratulation. The pity is that we are all separated."

From Jem. Hera Singh, 16th Cavalry, Bushir, Persia, to Dfdr. Gurmukh Singh, 36th Jacob's Horse, France. (Urdu, 19/12/15).

*****

"You say I did not post any letter to you. That is quite true. The reason is that I went ahead with 50 men. There it was not possible to obtain postcards or envelopes and, moreover, there was no post. Now, having arrived back at the first place, I write to you after two months. We, that is the British Officer, myself and 50 men, had a severe engagement with the enemy. All day long, firing continued, but by the grace of the Guru we sustained no losses. We made one German prisoner. For the rest, all is well."

From Harnam Singh, Risaldar, 28th Light Cavalry, Nushki Column, Robat, Baluchistan, to Sawar Bhagat Singh, 2nd Lancers, France. (Gurmukhi, 19/2/16).

*****

"L.D. Batna has been sentenced to two years imprisonment. His fault was that he was sent to a certain picket but did not go there. He remained behind. He did not go to the place he was told to go. The place where he was told to go was the place from which the enemy obtained water – there was no water anywhere else. The enemy obtained their water supply and retired. What more am I to write? Brownlow Sahib, himself, went and caught the Lance Dafadar."

From a Sawar, 28th Light Cavalry, Nushki Column, Fort Robat, to Baghail Singh, 28th L.C. attached 2nd Lancers, France. (Gurmukhi, 24/2/16).

*****

"Our Government's star is now on the ascendant for they have just scored a notable success in Africa. In the Persian Gulf, they have conquered 300 miles of Asia, and have got so far as to surround Baghdad. Russia has conquered Erzeroum and the two Governments will between them knock out the Turks. The Turks are now at their last gasp. When Turkey itself is subdued, then you may say that our Government has won. Keep your spirits up and you will hear sometime in this year 1916, that all the Government's enemies are conquered, and that peace has arrived."

From Mehr Singh, Quetta, to Jemadar Kartar Singh, 18th Lancers, France. (Urdu, 13/3/16).

*****

"Our Hospital travelling from Peshawar via Karachi reached Bushire on 20th March. This place is 100 miles south of Basra in the east of Persia. We are included in Force D. Our hospital is installed in a large double storied house, with an extensive compound. The climate of the place is good. Up to this date it is cold. The water is brackish, but for drinking purposes pure water is brought in from a distance on mules. The rations are good and meat plentiful. Vegetables are scarce, but obtainable. The flies are very troublesome. On account of them one gets no rest anywhere."

From Narinder Singh, 51 Indian Stationary Hospital, Force D, Bushire, Persia, to Raffi-ud-Din Khan, Sialkot Cavalry Field Ambulance, France. (Urdu, 24/4/16).

*****

Sikh soldier at rest, Bushire, Persian Gulf 1916. (Courtesy of the Council of the National Army Museum, London)

*****

"I was very pleased to hear from you. Your country is truly a fine one. I will tell you something about this country in which we are. It is a horrible place and we can get nothing at all. The dust storms are such that you cannot move about. You cannot get any milk and as for gur you pay a rupee for half a pound. Cloth is very dear and in short in this hilly and jungly country you can get nothing. There is no water and you often have to go seven miles to get any. As for rations we do not get the liberal supply that you do for we have no railways for supply and no ships. Everything has to come by road on camels. It takes sometimes 1½ months for rations to arrive from Quetta and thousands of camels die on the way. The people are a wretched half-starved lot of the lowest type. We are not allowed to write any more."

From Dfdr. Mathu Ram, 28th Light Cavalry, Seistan, to Dfdr. Harnam Singh, 28th L.C. attached 2nd Lancers, France. (Urdu, 10/9/16).

*****

"Here we can get nothing, and the hardships are greater owing to one Cavalry regiment only being here. There is no information about our return. We are in Persia and are in contact with the Russians."

From Indar Singh, 28th Light Cavalry, Birjand, Nuskhi, Siestan to Joga Singh, 28th Light Cavalry attached 2nd Lancers, France. (Gurmukhi dated the 22nd October 1916).

*****

North-West Frontier

"Now the fighting on the frontier has completely ceased, but we have not left this place, because there is still danger from the enemy."

From Hoshiar Singh, of the Guides Cavalry, posted at Swabi on the Buner Border (Peshawar Dt.) to Jem. Jagan Singh, 29th Lancers, serving in France. (Urdu, 16/9/15, after an account of the fighting at Rustam and Shabqadr).

*****

"And, brother, we came to Subalkad (Shabqadr) on the 29th, and on the 5th a great battle was fought. The enemy lost 1000 men, killed and wounded. In the whole regiment only one was killed and one subedar and seven sepoys were wounded. In the 36th regiment, three men were killed and ten or twelve wounded. The Colonel of the British cavalry and five troopers were killed, and ten wounded. There were no other casualties."

From Dalip Singh, 21st Punjabis, F.P.O. No.63, N.W.F. to Sepoy Ujagar Singh, No.3203, 93rd Punjabis. (Gurmukhi, Septr.1915).

*****

"My dear brother Dhanna, I beseech you – Fate apportioned us a long sojourn in this place – others were not meant to come here. I am very well but it is a weary time of woe for me, the while the people at home snatch all the pleasures of life. A heavy burden of trouble is upon me. No doubt this is the work that Sikhs should do – were it only for our faith – but these people look on us as worse than dogs. What have we profited by it all?"

From Nika Singh, Signaller, 21st Punjabis, A Coy. Peshawar. F.P.O.63, to Sepoy Dhanna Singh, 3839, 35th Sikhs, attached 47th Sikhs, France. (Gurmukhi, 29/9/15).

*****

"We are in a place about 25 miles from Peshawar and the enemy is gathering again for another fight. The enemy is about three miles off. I shall write on the 2nd or 3rd of October what has happened. All of your regiment have come. There are four brigades here. There is also trouble brewing in the place you went from, Bannu. My belief is that the world is on the point of being destroyed. It looks as if the end of the world must come, perhaps in one year, perhaps in two."

From Nika Singh, 21st Punjabis, Peshawar, to Dhanna Singh, 35th Sikhs, France. (Gurmukhi, 30/9/15).

*****

"No one takes any interest in the wounded. They have no honour......There is fighting going on in Mohmand country. The Mohmands have inflicted severe losses on the Guides and other regiments. Our regiment has not yet got orders to move."

From a Sepoy in Kohat (55th Rilfes?) to Nand Singh, 55th Rifles, attached 57th Rifles, France. (Gurmukhi, 12/11/15).

*****

"Here there is no rain and the price of corn is high. Many men are enlisting voluntarily. They are quite ready to do the Sircars work, because the Sircar fights for right...... The airships have arrived here and do patrol work. The Pathans have become very apprehensive. It is not probable that they will be able to gather together again, for should they do so, one bomb dropped from an airship would disperse then and inflict great loss on them. For this reason it is impossible for them to assemble again."

From Rai Singh, Schoolmaster, 13th Lancers, Risalpur, N.W.F.P, to A.D.L. Gurdit Singh in France, 13th attached 19th Lancers. (Urdu, 11/2/16).

*****

"My regiment is out on the frontier posts where numerous dacoities take place. The upper Mahsuds often make raids and capture wealthy Hindus and take them off and worry them. They ask for high ransoms 5000/ or 10,000/, and if they get them they let the Hindus go, but if not, they murder them.........This tribe is all of this kind and this comes of their want of education. It is drink that has ruined them. To begin with they are ignorant and uneducated, and the liquor robs them of their reason. Our men are to blame for never warning and instructing them. The Sikhs ought to do it, and if you do not do this you are responsible also."

From Subr. Indar Singh, 25th Punjabis, Bannu, India, to Jemadar Bishan Singh, 19th Lancers, France. (Urdu, 25/4/16).

*****

"We went forward from Peshawar to Shabkaddar about 30 miles on the 25th September. The Hill tribes have commenced to give trouble again. In France we used to get straw to sleep on, but here on active service we have to get through the night rubbing our bodies on the bare stones."

From Sadhu Singh, 30th Lancers, Shankargark, Peshawar, to Nand Singh, 20th Deccan Horse, France. (Gurmukhi, 1/10/16).

*****

"Peshawar is just like a cantonment. There is always some commotion going on. Moreover the cold is intense and there is much dust. No doubt the people in France are saying that the 30th Lancers are having an easy time; but as a matter of fact the Regiment is having much harder times than it had in France."

From Kapur Singh, Jemadar, 30th Lancers, Peshawar, N.W.F.P., India to Amar Singh, Jemadar, Machine Gun Squadron, Ambala Cavalry Brigade, France. (Urdu dated the 6th November 1916).

*****

"It was our fate to leave the fine climate of France and to go to a horrible country where climate and weather were most deadly foes. It was afterwards our fate to lose 15 of our comrades in this country, buried in Rawal Pindi. The first week of our arrival plague broke out and we lost 15 men in 3 squadrons but now by the favour of the Guru all is well. You may think us lucky on having got back to our country, but I can assure you that every one of our regiment thinks field service a hundred times better than this."

From Risaldar Chanan Singh, Rawal Pindi, India to Wardi Major Katar Singh, 18 K.G.O., France. (Urdu dated the 30th December 1916).

*****

"Here everything is frightfully high in price. The armies have gone up in the direction of Cabul and huge forces have assembled towards Jalalabad. I hope that the Amir Sahib has opened a way for the forces of our King. If so it was very good of him."

From Gulab Singh, Gujar Khan, Rawal Pindi to Kartar Singh, 6th Cavalry, France. (Urdu dated the 15th January 1917).

*****

"The state of affairs is that at Peshawar the Government have made excellent arrangements. Barbed wire entanglements have been placed from Abazai to Mechni, a distance of 35 miles and posts have been established at intervals of 800 yards. In front, there is a live electric wire and if any one comes in contact with it he is unable to get away."

From Ram Singh, Rurki, U.P., India to Radha Singh, Dafadar, Indian General Base Depot, France. (Gurmukhi dated the 15th March 1917).

*****

"On the 29th March a party of raiders came of whom 7 were killed and 10 captured. We lost one Sowar killed and five or six men of the infantry were wounded. We have got aircraft here and armoured motor cars. We have an immense amount of work compared with what we had in France and not a moment to spare."

From Akhtar Singh, 31st Lancers, Bannu, India to Kabul Singh, 29th Lancers, France. (Urdu dated the 7th April 1917).

*****

"The Masuds are giving the Sircar much trouble on the frontier. For this reason the Sircar has collected a considerable force here, in order to make war on Waziristan and punish the Masuds heavily."

From Bachan Singh, Jemadar, 11th Lancers, Dehra Ismail Khan, N.W.F.P., India to Chet Singh, Daffadar, 11th Lancers, Remount Base Depot, France. (Gurmukhi dated 23rd May 17).

*****

Gallipoli

"Waryam Singh sacrificed his life in battle on the 4th prox. Well, brother, you probably get some newspapers about the war – the whole story of his regiment has been written there. The 14th Sikhs have given full proof of their loyalty and their name will once more be inscribed in Sikh history."

From Gurmukh Singh, 66th Punjabis, I.E.F. "D", to Nk. Dasaunda Singh, Bombay Bodyguard, attached 3rd Skinner's Horse, France. (Gurmukhi, 1/10/15).

*****

Photograph of Sikh troops cutting down a tree used by Turks as an aiming mark, Gallipoli Peninsula 1915. (Courtesy of the Council of the National Army Museum, London)

*****

This brave son of the Kalgiwala was present in the bold charge made by the immortal 14th Sikhs in Gallipoli on the 4th of June, for which their names will remain writ large on the roll of immortality. He had received 6 bullet wounds and had therefore come back to India. A lean tall young man he, his appearance made the stranger wonder if he was really the Subedar of such a gallant regiment as set as naught the effect of the machine guns and all other infernal devices of the enemy and won the day. But those that knew how the spirit of Guru Gobind Singh emboldened a single man to fight a hundred thousand and a sparrow to hunt down hawks, at once convinced them of the fact that bravery and Sikhs are the only terms co-existent with and co-genial to each other. As the valiant Sardar Narain Singh stood up to the pulpit, a thrill of admiration passed in the audience so that all greeted him with shouts of Sat Sri Akaal reading welkin. Then it was in his simple soldier-like tone that he addressed the audience as follows:

"Khalsa brothers, I cannot sufficiently thank you for the honour that you have extended to a humble person like me. It is all due to the grace of Wahiguru and the kindness of the benign Government that we can attain to such a noble end of our lives as is coveted by rishis and bhagats. I am a Subedar of a gallant regiment, the 14th Sikhs, which fought in s. I regret words at my command fail me to make an adequate demonstration of what was the state of our minds when we knew that we had to encounter the enemy. Even a minute left to fixed time was for us a long year, we moved our feet and ground our teeth in extreme impatience and prayed most earnestly that the fixed time might come soon. And how gratified we all were when the moment of march came, was testified to by the awe inspiring loud shouts of Sat Sri Akal. Did we remember our dear and near or thought in the least about our own lives? Oh No, certainly not. Nothing but the thought of Sat Guru's Amrit and duty to our beloved Government reigned supreme in our minds, and we vied with one another in its demonstration. And believe me Khalsa ji it is bare truth that when the bugle sounded 'march', and we brandished our bayonets, the very photo of Guru Gobind Singh was the only thing we saw to our right, left and front. And what a spirit this holy sight infused in us, I cannot explain in words. It emboldened us to march on, piercing through the abdomen of the enemy, unmindful of the havoc being wrought by the horrid machine gun. We shouted Sat Sri Akal and chanted the Shabads of Halla (attack) as ours was a nuptial procession. Those among us who fell wounded or dead, we minded never, as the only thought before us devotion to the Guru, who was so omni-present in the march and adherence to the Government. I received 6 many bullet wounds, but by the same Guru's kindness, I am hale and hearty quite willing to go to the front again. Khalsa Ji, I am grateful that I have proved true to him whose salt I have eaten and wish that all my brothers should do the same."

The gallant Subedar Sardar Narain Singh of the 14th Sikhs, article, *The Khalsa Advocate*, Saturday, October 23, 1915.

*****

Egypt

"Our ship began its march on the 22nd at 3 o'clock in the day-time. The beds are good. The arrangements for food are rather bad. Bedding is not searched. There are two Darbar Sahibs (Granth or Sikh scriptures) on board. We pray and sing hymns continually. There are ships without number passing hither and thither, and there is no fear of any kind. The Sikhs, Dogras, and Musalmans all subscribed towards scarfs to cover the Darbar Sahibs. We collected two pounds nineteen shillings and two franks. The Darbar is exhibited even on board ship. We are very fortunate. We stay four days in Egypt and shall buy the scarfs for the Darbar Sahibs."

From Santa Singh, on board ship off Malta, to Bishen Singh, in hospital at Brighton. (Gurmukhi, 29/7/15).

*****

"We left France on the 17th August and embarked on the 21st. On the 26th of the same month we reached Ismailia. There we stayed till the 20/11/15. Then we spent a week at Lakhjatar (? Alexandria). This place is called Mathru. It is 24 hours' journey by sea. All the country belongs to the Arabs. On the 12/12/15 we had a fight with the Turks. Four men were killed and seventeen wounded. There has been no fighting since. The enemy is seven miles off. Our regiment came first and the others came after (sentence erased)."

From Ram Singh, 15th Sikhs, Mathru, Egypt, to Batn Singh, No.5 Mountain Battery, France. (Gurmukhi, 24/12/15).

*****

"We have left Ismailia and are at Mathru. This is a place on the boundary between Egypt and Africa, and the Bedouins here are in revolt. On the 12/12/15 there was a great fight. Of the Australian Horse twelve men were killed and 16 wounded. In the British regiment there were 40 killed and 30 wounded. The 15th Sikhs had four killed and 22 wounded. In the end we retired 16 miles. But the (enemy) had terrific losses. We do not know for certain (the amount). This country is not like France, but the billets are very large. All the officers (on the other side) are Germans, and they have German machine guns etc........My foot is still bad. When I have marched twelve miles, it begins to hurt. But I am none the less in no way grudging life or strength in the service of the government, because Captain Macrae of the 45th is here. He is a Double Company Commander. The British and Indian officers of the 15th Sikhs do not like men of other regiments being promoted. So far as they can, they keep the promotions to their own regiment, but there are not more than 100 men of the 15th here. The rest belong to other regiments."

From Surveyor Ganga Singh, attached 15th Sikhs, F.P.O. No. 310, Mathru, Egypt, to Jem. Hazara Singh, 30th Lancers, France. (Urdu, 25/12/15).

*****

"One hundred and fifty wounded men of the 15th Sikhs have been distributed over the Air-Craft Factory. But they are separate from the regiment and have no right to promotion, or the like. So I have been sent from the base to join the regiment. Every man strives to do his duty with heart and soul in the hope of advancement. If this hope be removed, (he thinks that) to undertake all this toil is useless. If I live I hope for advancement. For the Guru sees. Here too there is fighting but not so severe. The regiments are sniped at every night. The Bedouins put to death every man they catch. They took a British soldier and cut his throat. On the 12th there was a big fight. There is fighting everywhere. In the Punjab in the Ludhiana District, forty men have been hanged and two hundred put in prison, because the Zaildars, headmen and Patwaris of the village had been dismissed for preaching revolt against the government."

From Surveyor Ganga Singh, attached 15th Sikhs, F.P.O. No. 310, Mathru, Egypt, to Jem. Sahib Singh, 30th Lancers, France. (Urdu, 25/12/15).

*****

"We are engaged in fighting. (Our enemy) is the Arabs, and the people of the country who are fighting against us. There is a city called Mathru beyond Alexandria which we have taken. Our camp is there, but the depot is on the Ismailia Canal. In the first fight, of our people four were killed and sixteen wounded. (Details of the other losses given)......We killed a lot of Turks with the bayonet. That is the way of it. Tell us your news. If you can, please send an electric torch. I am now in the Sudan (a part) of Africa."

From Basant Singh, 15th Sikhs, Mathru, (F.P.O.No.310), Egypt, to Sowar Sarain Singh, 35th attached 47th Sikhs, I.E.F. 'A'. (Gurmukhi, 28/12/15).

*****

"I congratulate you on being made a Lance-Naik. After eight months in the Dardanelles I have come to Egypt. The 14th Sikhs all desire to be remembered to you and are very pleased about your promotion. Shyam Singh and Umr Singh have become Havaldars. All the others have either been wounded or have offered up their lives for the British government."

From S.A.S. Daulat Singh, 21 Mountain Battery, Egypt, to Lance-Nk. Arjan Singh, 3rd Skinner's Horse, France. (Urdu, 29/12/15).

*****

Since the day that we were born, we have known many sorrows,
Since we took birth from that day we have had no rest.
When Sikhs see the field of battle, they charge.
Our couch is upon the ground and our cushion is of bricks,
Those who see us weep and beat their hands.
Our senses do not remain, when the shells are fired;
They do not even leave a trench when they explode.
Three lines are drawn and the foot soldiers fight,

The big guns fire from behind and make great havoc,
The projectile weighs one hundred and five pounds.
When it explodes it devastates the enemy.
The Mountain Batteries which you know
Go right into the firing line and smite the foe.
The machine guns rattle so that the senses are reft,
Their fire is so frequent that none can bear it.

From Kehr Singh, No.21 Mountain Battery, Egypt, to Signaller Bhaga Singh, 18th Lancers, France. (Gurmukhi (verse), 30/1/16).

*****

Sikh soldiers wrestling in desert, Suez 1915. (Courtesy of the Council of the National Army Museum, London)

*****

"You complain of delay on my part in answering your letters. I do not say "I cannot write", by the favour of God and your good self, I have sufficient knowledge to be able to read and write. But the trouble is that the green envelopes which used to pass under our own signature in France, are not issued to us here. Only one letter per man per week is countersigned here. If the countersigning officer did the work of countersigning quickly there would be no difficulty (in countersigning a greater number of letters) ... The news of this place is that except for heaps of sand there is nothing to see. Beyond the town there is no sign of vegetation. When we get leave of absence we go to Suez and refresh our eyes with the sight of the verdure. There is no need for us to chew our bread. In our bread and pulse and vegetable food sugar (he speaks ironically and means "sand") is deposited by God. You have done well to sit in that heaven like country, France, while we have been placed in this hell. Since I came here I have had fever three times. I used to be in splendid health in France."

From Bant Singh, Gharwal Infantry Brigade, Egypt, to L.N. Bahadur Singh, 9th Hodson's Horse, France. (Urdu, 18/4/16).

*****

"Our ship left Marseilles on the 14th August and on the 17th we reached Malta. There we embarked a number of European troops, and on the 18th we went some 50 miles to "Old Malta", on the 21st we left Old Malta. The voyage is so dangerous that I am unable to describe it. There must have been some very lucky person on board, through whose good fortune we escaped injury, because after leaving Malta three torpedoes were fired at us."

From Chain Singh, Alexandria, Egypt, to Nihal Singh, Kot Dafadar, Remount Depot, Marseilles, France. (Urdu, 24/8/16).

*****

Aden

"In the 12th regiment, 13 men have been sent to Jail – 3 havaldars, the rest Sepoys – and three Indian Officers have been dismissed. The havaldars and Sepoys have got one year's imprisonment."

From Pala Singh stationed at Aden to Lance Naik Thakur Singh, Driver, 7th British Mountain Battery. (Gurmukhi, dated 31/3/15).

*****

"Tulsa Singh was wounded and is now prisoner with the Germans. He is quite well. Have no anxiety about him. In the assault of the 25th September of last year our double company lost 17 Sikhs killed, missing, and prisoners 7, and there were 58 wounded. Many of the wounded are now quite fit again and have re-joined the regiment. The Saini Sabha of Marara Gurdaspur, sent a donation of Rs. 100/- for our wounded Sikhs. Out of this I have given Rs. 15/- for the reading of the Grunth for the souls of the dead, and I have arranged for the distribution of the balance amongst those Sikhs who were wounded in France, as to be unfit for further service. And thanks have been sent to the Saini Sabha through the Deputy Commissioner Gurdaspur."

From Jagaindar Singh, Aden, L.D. Pritam Singh, 32nd attached 30th Lancers, France. (Gurmukhi, 29/2/16).

*****

Sinai and Palestine

"The attack began on 19th September. We captured Damascus on the 1st October, which means that we took from 200 to 250 miles of territory from the enemy. The enemy never got the slightest chance to make a stand. 60,000 prisoners were captured.

The prisoners were in a very bad state, weak with hunger – kit and clothes in bad ways. All the equipment, arms, artillery etc. were made in Germany.

This part of the country which is the part near Damascus is very beautiful. There are quantities of grapes and pomegranates and all kinds of fruit. At the present season pomegranates and grapes are most plentiful. We are existing now and eating our food of maize cobs. Rations will soon be arriving. We whet our appetites with grapes.

We shall advance further. The Cavalry have done great and valiant deeds. The Sharif of Makkah will be made Sultan of the Arabs under the suzerainty of the English.

In this battle, the Arabs have taken a great share on the right flank. The Arabs hate the Turks. Whenever they catch them singly they kill them and rob them of their clothes.

Show this letter to all the Indian Officers. Our losses were extremely slight and in particular our regiment and the 6th Cavalry came off well. The End."

From a Sikh Risaldar. Dated 5.10.18. – (Port Said).

*****

Sikh mountain battery, Palestine 1918. (Avtar Singh Bahra collection)

*****

"I took part in an attack and in that attack we broke the line. I am in the country of Egypt. There is now no war anywhere here. The English have smashed the Turks, and in the attack that I took part in, they captured all the Turks. They captured 50 to 60 thousand prisoners. Now we are sitting in perfect ease and comfort. The Sikhs had heavy losses. I and Man Singh were both in the attack. God protected us. There was no hope of surviving. The fire of the artillery and the machine guns was very heavy. Our ears could hear nothing and in that place, brother could not recognise brother. It was like the roll of thunder clouds in the month of Sawan. As the lightning flashes on uncles and nephews so the shells of the artillery flashed over us. * As the proverb says, "There is a great difference between seeing and hearing." Thy honoured father, we fought hand to hand. The very earth was forced to quake…………………"
* Refers to the belief that if uncles and nephews sit together during a thunderstorm one of them is sure to be struck by lightning.

Extract from a letter from a Sikh to his father. (Original in Urdu). Dated 28th Oct 1918. – (Port Said).

*****

Australia

The only Indian in the Australian army

Private Gurbachan Singh claims the distinction of being the only Indian whom the Commonwealth Government has sent from Australia to fight for the King and Empire in Europe. He took the trouble, the other day, to come from the camp where his battalion is in training in England, to see me and told me how he struggled to obtain the opportunity to serve his Emperor on the field of battle and how he has fared since then.

When I saw Gurbachan Singh entering the gate, I could scarcely believe he was an Indian. He wore the soft, "slouch" hat, with its brim turned up against the Crown on one side and fastened with the Australian emblem – A copper rising sun, with the British Crown in its centre, held in place by a leather strap under the chin that the Australian soldiers wear. His form was muffled up in a khaki raincoat that hung from his shoulders to his ankles like a long cape. He had on heavy brown boots, and he carried a walking stick. That is the way an Australian soldier looks when you see him walking about on the street when it is raining, as it was when Gurbachan Singh came to see me. I have seen many Australians with darker complexions than his and had I passed him casually without knowing that he was an Indian, it would never have entered my mind that he was one of my own countrymen. I would have taken him for a pleasant looking, well set up weather beaten Australian farmer.

Gurbachan Singh crossed the threshold with the Sikh Salutation, Shri Wah I Guru Ji Ka Khalsa, Shri Wah I Guru Ji Ki Fateh, on his lips.

"I hope." I said, "that you did not have much difficulty in entering the Australian Field Force."

A Wave of Enthusiasm

"I cannot say that I did not", he replied, like a man who says what he thinks without mincing words. "The outbreak of the hostilities", he continued, "inspired Indians in Australia with a martial enthusiasm unlike any that they had experienced ever before. Many of them were officers and men who had retired from the Indian army after fighting for the King Emperor in many campaigns, and who treasured the medals that had been given them as rewards for bravery. I, myself, had been through the Chitral and Tirah campaigns on the North West Frontier, and had served in South Africa with the Supply and Transport Corps during the Boer War, and went through the siege of Ladysmith." He did not need to relate these details about himself, for the long ribbon that he wore on his left breast told its own tale. "Although many of us", he went on, "had held commissions in the Indian Army – he spoke of Jemadarships, Subedarships, and so on – 'we were willing to serve as mere privates in the Expeditionary Force that Australia was organising. There was one Musalman among us who owned a large number of camels in Western Australia, who was eager to raise a Camel Corps. There was a Sikh farmer with a large acreage who wanted to make himself responsible for raising two hundred recruits. There were thousands of Indians in Australia, and we hoped that a regiment might be recruited from amongst us and sent to Europe for service." There he stopped, and I ask him what happened then.

"This is what happened" he replied, "We did not get the chance. We were told that only "substantial Europeans" were being recruited, and since we were not "substantial Europeans" we could not be enlisted in the Australian Field Force. We were, however, given to understand that we could go and join the contingent that India is raising for foreign service."

"But how did you get in?" I enquired.

Punjab Pertinacity

"It was this way", he answered. "I received a notice from the Government urging men of military age to enlist for the duration of the war – the sort of notice that other Australians received. I presented myself for enlistment at the recruiting station nearest my place. I told the officers who examined me that I had fought for the King Emperor in three campaigns. They seemed to think I was too old to fight now, but I satisfied them that my age at the time was only forty two years six months, and that I was quite fit. My earnestness finally overcame all opposition and I was taken in. My happiness would have been complete had I been passed for service at the front, but I was classed CI. I was, however, glad to be enlisted at all and felt sure that sooner or later I would have my chance to fight in Europe."

"Was that the end of your difficulties?" I questioned him.

"Not exactly," he rejoined. "Attempts were made later to shut me off. But in my enthusiasm I had made a considerable sacrifice in leaving off my business, and I asked them to take my sacrifice into consideration, and let me stay in. I won my point."

That was, indeed, the true Punjabi pertinacity, of which Gurbachan Singh appears to have more than his share, for he not only succeeded in staying in the Australian

Army, but later persuaded the military authorities to send him to England as a unit of a draft that they were dispatching. He very proudly drew out of his pocket his pay book and showed me that he was now classed as AI – fit for any army work. He drew my attention to the letter "S" that meant he would have the desire of his heart, and fight on the Continent.

"Why are you so eager to fight?" I asked.

"Well, you see", he said, "I am a Sikh – and fighting is in my blood. Besides, the Germans (Turks?) killed one of my people – Subadar-Major Sardar Balwant Singh Bahadur. Last and most important of all, this is a time of emergency."

A Democratic Army

"The papers are full of it", he said. "You can hardly pick up a newspaper without seeing words like "need for men" staring at you. Besides, the soldiers are constantly talking about it. I must tell you that our battalion is full of educated men – Men who have sacrificed a great deal to come over here to fight for the Empire. One of my fellow privates is a bank manager – the head of a prosperous financial institution. Any number of my comrades are owners of farms and business firms. They are all fond of reading and are interested in every subject under the sun. I could not remain long among them without knowing that the present is a time of great crisis for all the Allied Nations."

This intelligent answer led me to say to the Sikh private: "I am going to take a countryman's privilege and ask you quite plainly if you were educated when you left India, thirteen years ago."

"Not educated in the English sense", he answered straightforwardly. "I hardly knew six words of English when I landed in New South Wales. But I was not exactly ignorant. I had been taught Punjabi at home by my father, who was a local grandee. Afterwards I went to the village school and learnt Persian. As I told you already, I was in the Indian Army for many years, and got to see something of India, not to speak of South Africa."

"It was enterprising of you." I remarked encouragingly, "to go Australia when you did not know any English to speak of. I see by the way you talk that you do not have any difficulty now in expressing yourself fluently in English."

"I have been talking in Punjabi with you most of the time I have been here", he re-joined, "because I was hungry to talk my own mother-tongue with someone from my Motherland. But I have not the least difficulty in making myself understood in English."

After a pause he added apologetically: "Perhaps I ought to know more English than I do, for I have spent thirteen years in Australia. There was, however, no one to teach me, and I had to pick up words here and there, a few at a time. Our own people in Australia (the Indian settlers), among whom I lived, speak roughly, as, indeed so my comrades in camp."

"I hope that your comrades treat you well", I observed.

"They consider me as one of them. They make no difference at all. They find it difficult to call me Gurbachan – or Gurbachan Singh. I am known as "Singh" among them. They have no idea that there are lots of Singhs, and that they do not belong to one family. They seem to think whenever they read your articles in the papers that I must be your cousin or some other relative of yours. There is, however, an officer among us who has been in India, and who knows about things Indian. He can speak Hindustani – which he does whenever he sees me. His wife is now in Australia, but she was born out in India and she, her husband, and their children all want to go back to India. The Major Sahib treats me with great kindness. I wish you could meet him."

"You are quite happy and comfortable and do not wish that you had not enlisted in the Australian Army?" I asked.

Australian Camaraderie

"Yes, I am", he responded, "I will never regret that I entered the Australian Field Force. I am well treated. The pay is also good – six shillings a day, though you do not get it all, the Government having thought it best to treat one shilling as differed pay, and to ear-mark another two shillings for deposit in the bank so that when a man goes back to civil life he will have something to fall back upon. It is a good arrangement. But the question is, of course, will a man go back. It is War, and you cannot tell what will happen. But we soldiers never worry about the future, and death has no terror for us. Soon the desire of my heart will be fulfilled when I cross the channel and confront the Germans."

I parted with the only Sikh private in the Australian Army with a heavy heart and felt sorry that other Indian settlers in Australia had not been given the chance to fight. The Commonwealth Government does not, however, stand by itself in this matter. So far as I know, only three or four of our settlers in Canada have been allowed to join the Canadian Contingent. The other day a friend of mine saw one of these Indians dressed up in the Canadian uniform, who was ready to go to the front, and told me that Indians in the Dominion are all eager to fight. Now that the Canadian authorities are planning to introduce compulsory service, it is to be hoped, that our countrymen settled in Canada will be given the coveted chance.

St. Nihal Singh. *The Khalsa Advocate*, Saturday, 18th August 1917.

*****

7

Voices from the East

A dust storm is blowing in our country. It is dark, and we cannot see.

Those acquainted with the facts know that the Chief Khalsa Diwan has done little good to the Sikhs.

The price of sugar is three sers the rupee and of ghi one ser. Everything is dear – including what one buys in the bazaar.

It is now two years since you went away. Many people return on leave so why do you not come?

The censored letters archive held at the British Library contains letters sent to Sikh soldiers from all over the world, including India. This chapter includes many of these letters and other Sikh voices from India. Indian soldiers far away from home would rely heavily on these letters for news from home. The Censor would also be interested as he felt that the Indian public may be more politically motivated than the average Indian soldier.

The letters from India covered a plethora of subjects and included questions to the Sikh soldiers about their location and potential movements. Some wanted updates on possible leave from the army and updates on previous letters where, for example, a soldier had been injured. Numerous letters from India tried to give soldiers an indication of the current situation in the Punjab. Many told of high prices. “There has been no rain. For this reason the price of grain has become very dear”, lamented a Sikh soldier from the 89th Punjabis. Famine was a constant concern for many Punjabis and in 1915 the Punjab was also affected by a serious outbreak of plague. The Censor states in his report in July 1915, “Deaths from plague in the Punjab have in the late been at a rate of well over 2000 a day, although the disease does not appear to prevail in all parts of the Province. It is not surprising, therefore, that the men whose homes are in the infected districts should find their letters gloomy reading.”

Letters also gave news of events and unrest in the villages, pleas from loved ones for long gone sons to return home as soon as they could; advice on how to fight, retain religious and tribal pride and gain *izzat* (honour). Letters also sent soldiers updates of how the war was progressing from an Indian perspective. Some of this news would not be available to the soldier on the Western Front and these letters were vital for them.

Much of the information shared by people from the Punjab would be garnered from what many would read (or be told by literate people) from newspapers and journals. At the time of the Great War there were scores of newspapers circulating in the Punjab. These newspapers were examined by the British authorities to ensure that nothing objectionable was written; penalties were severe, including the seizing of printing presses. The proprietors tended to be relatively well off people and generally the Sikh newspapers were organs of Sikh organisations. For example *The Khalsa Advocate* was pro–Chief Khalsa Diwan and *The Khalsa Akhbar* was not. Due to the harshness of the Press Act, Sikh newspapers were keen not to antagonise the Government and were loyal to the British during the Great War years. They were strong advocates for recruitment and also used blatant propaganda when required. They shared news on the war but reversals such as the Gallipoli campaign would feature many months after the actual events.

Although tightly controlled, the newspapers did give an insight into many areas of Sikh life in the Punjab. Sikh newspapers were able to comment on religious, political and social events of the time. Throughout the Great War, Sikh newspapers discussed the control and condition of Sikh holy shrines. The Rakabganj Gurdwara affair and the *Ghadar* 'conspiracy' also featured heavily, along with the trial of the 'conspirators'.

Articles were also written on the *Komagata Maru* and *Budge-Budge* episodes, '*halal/jhatka*' meat controversies, *dacoities*, recruitment, attacks and rebuttals of Arya Samajists, lack of Sikh representation on Boards and Councils in the Punjab and many other issues affecting them. Articles also covered letters sent by Sikhs who had moved abroad and their experiences. Sikhs had moved to faraway places at this time such as Argentina and Australia. Racism experienced abroad was also a common theme in places such as South Africa and the United States.

Many newspaper articles yearned for the spiritual and political upliftment of the Sikh people. They asked Sikhs to remember their heritage, forget caste prejudice (which was exploited during British rule), fight for the right to speak Punjabi and write in *Gurmukhi*, and to preserve the distinct Sikh identity which was under attack from many places.

A fascinating story in the 1915 Sikh newspapers was the proposal that territory conquered by the British in Africa from the Germans, known as German East Africa (most of modern day Tanzania), could be utilised as a colony for Sikhs and Punjabis. This may have been a reaction to the emigration of Sikhs to the white dominions such as Canada. The Sikh newspapers certainly thought it was a good idea for it may prove a further incentive for Sikhs to fight in the war. Another interesting story was the proposal to build Gurdwaras in Mesopotamia, in places conquered by the British, and the reactions in India to these proposals, both for and against.

On examination of the different stories carried in the Sikh newspapers, it becomes apparent that they were first used as a tool by the British for propaganda, as loyalty to the British was key. It also becomes clear from social and political stories that Sikhs did not or were not allowed to get involved in significant political decisions, nor have any real say in the control and management of their important religious shrines. The British seemed to have controls in place to determine and manipulate Sikh thinking, through the control of the major Sikh shrines, manipulation of the Sikh press, aristocracy and educational establishments.

Sikh reformers and intellectuals tried to revive Sikh history and Sikh thinking during this period. Sikh educational conferences included long speeches on how the Gurus teachings were still relevant. Tract societies produced cheap pamphlets on a large scale, covering many subjects, with Sikh revival being the main aim, and included stories of Sikh heroes and warriors of yesteryear such as Hari Singh Nalwa and Akali Phula Singh.

Although the editors of Sikh newspapers tended on the whole to be loyal to the British, there was one area of the newspapers, via letters from readers, which gave a glimpse into the world of the readers themselves. These covered a variety of topics and included poetry of very high quality and covered a myriad of subjects. Poems were submitted regarding the war and the involvement of Sikh soldiers. Special editions and supplements were printed on religious occasions such as the birth anniversaries of the Gurus. Poems espousing the greatness of the Sikh message were common. Poems would also preach the value of loyalty and covered many aspects of religious thought.

*****

"One more item has been added to the already long list of forfeitures under the Press Act. This time it is a Sikh paper, named the Khalsa Akhbar. The result is a natural consequence of the agitation about the Gurdwara Rakab Ganj wall. We most sincerely wish that our fears might prove wrong; but from what we have heard, it is clear that there will be no end to this agitation unless some more popular decision is arrived at by the Sikhs themselves and the Government. We have read the article considered criminal by the Provincial Government. We do not think that it deserved such a harsh treatment. At the same time, we would like to request our brothers at Lyallpur that they should rather thank the members of their own community about the Gurdwara affair than criticise the action of the Government. We cannot help praising them for their enthusiasm and the spirit of self-sacrifice they are displaying in the support of their convictions; but it would be better if they were to convert the more influential section of the community to their own views."

Article, *The Sikh Review* (Delhi), for August and September 1914.

*****

"In a subsequent issue of our paper in commenting upon the speech of His Honour the Lieutenant-Governor of the Punjab, at the Khalsa College, we ventured to draw the attention of the Government towards our soldiers in the Indian Army. We pointed out the fact with gratitude how interestedly the English Military officers had tried to keep the spirit of Sikhism living among the Sikh in the Army and how magnanimously they promoted our soldiers to ranks yet opened to Indian soldiers.

The Civil officers, however, did not do much in this respect for Sikhism. They have indirectly the management of the Sikh Gurdwaras in their hand, they have also the option of restoring the Sikh sadhus to their respective Sikh gaddis which carry a great amount of jagirs, and at the same time, they have the patronage of allotting them in the Government by appointment in various Civil departments as well as the honorary posts in Municipalities, District Boards, Legislative Council, etc., etc. The Gurdwaras are being managed for the conversion of Sikhism into Hinduism. In the recognition of the Sikh Sadhu Mahants to hold jagirs no discretion is even made to find out whether they are really Sikhs. In the same way when any appointment in the Government service is given to the Sikhs no trouble is taken to see if our incumbent is a bona fide one. In consequence of this indiscretion, Sikhism of the old type is degenerating in villages as well as in towns. This can be seen from the recruiting officers, and the Military Commanding officers, how much trouble they have to take in reviving Sikhism among the recruits they take into the Army. Had this not been the case, and had bona fide Sikhs received the proper share in the Civil administration, the Government would have been in a position to know the real grievances of the bona fide Sikhs.

Hindus, and more specially Muhammadans, have many privileges over us. In nearly every department of the Government offices, some of the vacancies have a fixed number generally reserved for the Muhammadan candidates. For the Sikhs, the Government has indeed, frequently given assurances, but we are sorry nothing substantial has yet come out in an appreciative form."

Article, *The Punjab Darpan* (Amritsar), 14th November 1914.

*****

A FLIGHT OF IMAGINATION

O! What this bright day hath brought
What a perfect morn hath nature wrought
The green grass is wet with dew
Which seems but ready to bid adieu.

The birds are singing melodies sweet
The stream is giving harmonious beat
The nightingale hath mourned at night
But now seem full of delight.

The cock with its lively din
Scatters the rear of darkness thin
From the side of some hoar hill
Through the high wood echoing shrill
Cheerily rouse the slumbering mourn'
And looks upon the world in scorn.

I hear the lark begin his flight
And singing startle the dull night
From his watch tower in the skies
Till the dappled dawn doth rise.

The dale, the mountain atmosphere
All around far and near
There is pleasure everywhere.

Right against the eastern gate
The great sun begins his state
Robed in flames and amber light
The clouds in thousand liveries delight.

Straight mine eye hath caught new pleasures
While the landscape round it measures
Russet lawns and fallows grey
Where the nibbling flocks do stray.

Mountains on whose barren breast
The labouring clouds do often rest
Meadows trim with daisies pied
Shallow brooks and rivers wide.

A second sun it soon espies
Suspended in the vault of skies
The sun is giving enormous light
Light bright and snowy white.
He sends His cooling rays all around
And cools the hot heads on the ground
As soon His rays have reached the earth
Everything has doubled its mirth.

The flowers have opened to His touch
The cats on seeing have left their search
The roaring lion has stopped to see
And has left the poor lamb free.

The howling wolf no longer chases
And the sheep fearlessly grazes
The swooping hawk has left its prey
When it has caught His bright ray.

The rays of sun have travelled far
And have sanctified all
Have driven away the clouds of sin
And spiritual showers now do fall.
The earth freed from the burden of wrongs
It seems as if it is singing a song.

The tyrant Mughals, who slaughtered Hindus
And did treat them as their slaves
Have been killed by spiritual swords
And been sent to the dreadful graves.
The king of graves and grave for kings
For them the knell of death doth ring.

His rays have sweetened 'Rethai' bitter
And have made swans from crows
And have made the blind pools glitter
And gladdened the sad drooping brows.

The wind doth blow from pole to pole
Telling the world of a powerful soul
Guru Nanak is the second sun
A sun's son not God's son.

He was sent in this world by God
To show people the right path
To free the fallen from tyrannous hands
And to curb our pride and wrath.

He preached humility and self-control
To win the world first win your mind
Love God and seek him in your soul
Then only shall you mukhti find.

O'Nanak I cannot praise thy worth
More is thy due than more than all can pay
Thou hast given me every pleasure and mirth
Thy very thought has made me gay.

O give me power that I may
Always to God my prayers say
Strengthen my soul that I may rise
Above the world and care not worldly prize
Splendour dazzle me in vain
And I regard no worldly fame.

And this shall ever my prayer be
O Holy Nanak to live with thee
In unreproved pleasure from
And may my heart a compass be
That may always point to thee.

Harbhajan Singh, Second year, Khalsa College, Amritsar.
The Khalsa Advocate, Saturday, 21st November 1914.

*****

"I cannot write any news to you. You will understand."
Note: This is a regular expression in letters from the front, where letters are censored. What it means here I do not know. It will certainly give rise to wild rumours in the 34th.

From a Sikh in the 12th Pioneers Nowshera to a Sepoy of the same regiment with 34th Pioneers in France. (Undated and no language given).

*****

"It is generally observed that whenever any Sikh gentleman is taken in some superior department or is given a high title, voices directly or indirectly arise from some quarters against him. The Sikh press being too weak, no resistance is offered from it, and that is the reason why in the case of getting higher posts, as compared with the people of other nationalities, the Sikhs always dwindle in comparison.

We have several times been pointing out in the columns of our paper about the existing paucity of the Sikh youths in nearly all the departments. There is not a single Sikh in the Indian Civil Service, there are very few Sikh Munsiffs and Extra Assistant Commissioners. There is a paucity of the Sikhs in the superior Traffic Branch, and in the superior Police Department their number is very meagre. In short, as compared with the people of other religions, the number of Sikhs is always insignificant. In our opinion, all this is the result of the weakness of the Sikh press which cannot meet the demand of raising an adequate voice in favour of the drawbacks which the Sikhs have to encounter with."

Leader, *The Khalsa Advocate* (Amritsar), 6th March 1915.

*****

"A dust storm is blowing in our country. It is dark, and we cannot see."
(Note: "darkness" – injustice or ignorance).

To a Sepoy in the 107th Sikh Pioneers from his wife in Gujrat. (Gurmukhi, dated 10/3/15).

*****

"Although the services which the Sikhs have so far rendered have been rendered, not in the hope of compensation, but simply to discharge the duty which loyalty imposes on them, still, in view of the way in which the Pioneer has presented the subject and also the fact that the Sikhs and the Punjabis do stand in great need of a colony where they may settle without let or hindrance, there is no reason why we should not fully support the proposal. For if the Sikhs are told that they will be allowed to settle in a certain colony after it has been conquered, they will fight all the more enthusiastically and complete the work of months in weeks."

Article, *Sher-i-Punjab* (Lahore), discussing the Pioneer article on reserving German East Africa for Indian emigrants, 11th March 1915.

*****

"*Father.* – Officials have become Satan-like. They snatch away daughters and daughters-in-law from the houses of the Hindus and are forcibly converting them to Islam.

Lawlessness is prevailing in India. Oppressions are being practised on helpless and religious persons. The kings have lost the quality of mercy.

Son. – When hundreds of sins are committed in the world, it is necessary for the true devotees of God to sacrifice their lives. In this way alone can religion and mercy come in to existence and the oppressions of the tyrants be exterminated. Saints and Mahatmas should give their lives. It is necessary today to make sacrifices."

Article, *The Panth Sewak* (Lahore), 26th March 1915, publishes a dialogue between Guru Tegh Bahadur and his son.

*****

Ram Singh in the Trenches

This new-fangled manner of fighting,
Goes sorely against my grain;
I loathe being down in these trenches,
Like a bandicoot-rat in a drain.

Not thus were the ways of my fathers,
When they fought for their country with Gough;
It was "Charge!"and a thousand brave fellows,
With a scream of defiance, were off.
I hate all this peeping and peering,
For a shot now and then at a head;
For me the fierce fight to a finish,
With thousands of wounded and dead.

The shells are screaming above me,
Like demons at odds for my soul;
I'm made for a rush at the gunners,
But I'm buried alive in this hole.

Yet amid all the roar and confusion,
The moon shines as sweetly on high;
As it shone that last evening in Jhelum,
When Mothi bade me good-bye.

Mothi, my beautiful Mothi!
I remember her pitiful face,
With the glistening tears in the moonlight,
As she held me in loving embrace.

I shrank from the journey before me,
I was held to the spot by her charms;
The Bugle! I summoned my courage,
And tore myself out of her arms.

A letter has reached me from Jhelum,
And the light has gone out of my life;
My Mothi's dark hour was luckless,
And now I've nor babe nor wife.
I see her out there in the moonlight,
Down there by the temple tank –
What is this in my hand? It's a rifle!
Where am I? My mind seems a blank.

What's that? It's a shell? I've been dreaming,
Another Lall Singh lies dumb!
But Mothi's out there in the moonlight,
She's calling me! Mothi, I come.

I leap with a scream from the trenches;
Like a fiend through the bullets I go.
Mothi!!! They think I am a devil,
As I leap in the midst of the foe.

Ah, this is real war – to be stabbing,
And screaming, and panting for breath;
The seventh! My Mothi, I'm coming!
Ah, this is real fighting; it's ... (death).
Truth

The Khalsa Advocate, Saturday, May 8, 1915.

*****

"It was you who enlisted Harnam Singh – that is put him in the way of earning a livelihood. But nobody then knew that a war like this was coming. It was not your fault. And so many folk put their kinsmen, brothers and nephews into service. (Many people did this), therefore, you have no cause to be distressed. God knows the way of God. Your remorse is of no advantage to us. May the Almighty keep you happy and bring you home in safety."

From Malik Singh in India to Punjab Singh in the 57th Rifles, serving in France. (Urdu, 23rd May 1915).

*****

"And the talk of the regiment is that it is going to Chitral (beyond Malakand) that is to say 400 men will go, and 200 of the 36th; and those of the 35th are altogether young recruits."

From Gulzara Singh, 35th Sikhs, Rawal Pindi, to Naik Chattar Singh, 35th Sikhs, with 47th Sikhs at the front. (Written in Gurmukhi [cypher]).

*****

"It is quite true that on the 16th of April a robbery, or rather a burglary, took place in the village of Khurd. Owing to the unrest in the Punjab there have been a large number of burglaries, and the same story comes from all sides. The same state of affairs continues without change. I suppose it was only my turn. The loss amounted to about three hundred rupees in cash and jewels and a large quantity of clothing. Nihal Singh was at the bottom of it. I will pay him back some day if I get the chance. For the present we must lie low. The people of the village brought pressure to bear on me, and induced me to forgive him, but the fellow is a scoundrel. Well, well, if he does it again he will meet with his bane (agar karega to bharega). ----------- Kot Dfdr. Hardit Singh has not yet gone on pension but it is rumoured that he will go shortly. For the present he has been kept at the Depot. He has taken a lot of trouble to keep himself from being discharged. Abdul Ghafar helped him, otherwise he certainly would have been discharged. The Major did not intend to keep him. It is expected that he will shortly go again on recruiting duty. He did not want to do so but he was called a Dam Fool and told he must. The Major told me that I too must go to get recruits. I replied "that I was a native of Sialkot district, and the recruits which I brought before had not been accepted, so what use of sending me again". The Major replied that he would certainly take Sikhs from Sialkot district. I said that if I could be reimbursed what I had spent on the former recruits I should be glad to go. Otherwise I should prefer to be excused. So far the matter remains undecided, but it is quite impossible to get recruits in our parts."

From [?] Singh, Depot, 4th Cavalry, Bareilly, to Jemadar Kartar Singh, 4th Cavalry, serving in France. (Urdu, 1/7/15).

*****

"I got an envelope containing an unstamped card, just the same as you did. When I think of Dulip Singh's arrangements, tears come into my eyes. Well, may God keep him ever in health. I cannot say anything to you, because I am a child before you, but I tell you that the position is very difficult and critical. Whatever you are told to do, do not refuse and never argue about anything. For I have heard that at Marseilles men of rank of Havaldar have been flogged, over quite trifling matters. You must reflect that we have nowhere to go and cannot cut our names, nor do anything else."

From Didar Singh, to Pay-Sowar Karam Singh, 9th Hodson's Horse. (Urdu, 22/7/15).

*****

"I returned from Cantonments on the 1st of June. My knees are a little better, but I cannot use them freely yet, nor straighten them out. The doctor did not extract two small bullets from the bone, as he feared that this would do more harm than good. This year there is no rain and the harvest is spoilt. No one can get his pension papers and we do not know when they will be distributed. They also keep back two months' pay."

From Santa Singh, Pensioner, Post Office, Sham Chaurasi, Hoshiarpur to Benta Singh, 2992, 57th Rifles, France. (Urdu, 31/8/15).

*****

"The dog Jack is dead. It is very sad. So wise a dog would be hard to find. He was more than a dog, and in many ways better than a man. No man could be so obedient as Jack was. No praise is too high for him. Well it is the Guru's will. Fate has cut short his sojourn in our house, and all our sorrow cannot bring him back."

From a Sikh lady in India to her husband an I.O. in France. (Urdu, 1/9/15).

*****

"There is no plague anywhere xxxx There has been no rain at all in Lyallpur. It has rained in Jullundur and Hoshiarpur. The maize is good. The sugarcane planted in the Kikriwali is not first class but average. As there is no rain a single man hardly suffices to water the crop, and in our village only Sohan Singh and Devi Chand have planted cane. Owing to the famine we are not using the well (this passage is not clear – apparently the writer means that the Persian well would not repay expenses). The maize will be good. Gur is four sers the rupee. Wheat is dear – four rupees six annas the maund. Please send at once any money you have to spare, so that I can pay it out in a lump sum. The money you sent before has not reached me yet."

From Ram Singh, Orderly, District Court, Lyallpur, Punjab, to Kabul Singh, 47th Sikhs, France. (Gurmukhi, 1/9/15).

*****

"There has been no rain in our village and there is famine. The harvest is ruined and the people are very hard up for fodder. Grain is very dear. Wheat is four rupees the maund, Gram three rupees. Gur is five sers the rupee. The price of sugar is three sers the rupee and of ghi one ser. Everything is dear – including what one buys in the bazaar. There is no plague. In Fattehgarh there has been good rain. It rains every day and the harvest is good. But produce is very dear even here. A great many of the men returning from the war have been granted pensions and everyone gets two or three months leave. Of our lot two men have taken pensions, Bir Singh and Banta Singh – they get 8 rupees – that is to say at the second class rate. They have gone home. The others have been given leave. We have not yet got our decision, Hukam Singh, Hem Singh, Buta Singh, we three reservists are still here. All the others have gone before the board and left. We shall go before the next board, and shall let you know the result."

From Hem Singh, Fattehgarh to Sundar Singh, 47th Sikhs, France. (Gurmukhi, 2/9/15).

*****

"The court has sentenced sepoys Wasakh Singh, and Narain Singh, to be shot, but the Commander-in-Chief reduced their sentence to ten and five years' imprisonment with hard labour, respectively. Today they are being sent to jail. No.2886 Sepoy Bhan Singh was caught by the 18th Cavalry, and the Commanding Officer has given him two months' imprisonment … And now from the depot and that of the 92nd, as many recruits as possible are to be here by the 15th of October. I have sent a wire for 48, and the 92nd have telegraphed for 72 … In this place one day all the brigade was exercising, when Captain Hallowes saw that a German padre was writing down all about the parade. He had him arrested as being a spy. He will now be sent to Ahmednagar."

From Harnam Singh, Jubbulpore, to Jemadar Mul Singh, 93rd Burma Infantry. (Urdu, Septr.1915).

*****

"I am coming on service too, but I have got no definite orders yet. So when I get them I will write. And brother be you faithful to the salt of the Sirkar. Do your work with the greatest pleasure. This is the way to please your superiors and the great Guru too. This war will not last for ever, so you must make the name of your father's house. The jagir that was given to you by government was given to your ancestors on just such an occasion as this."

From Mehr Singh, to Kali Singh, 47th Sikhs. (Gurmukhi, 1915).

*****

The Goddess of Learning

An ode to the Sikh Educational Conference

Learning! Those who feel thy power
And with patience worship thee
World's might upon them dost thou shower
And from poverty set free
Noble goddess! fame, wealth and rank
Loiter at thy lover's feet.
As we pebbles find on sea bank
His majestic waters greet.
To learn all this noble teaching
How disciples knew of thine –
I mean the Sikhs – are beseeching
To attend thy sacred shrine!
How with eager open eyes we, wait
Thy eighth holy longed for day!
Crowded will be Ferozpur's gate,
And shrine full o'beards dark and grey.
Living martyr's such a figure
As hath sacrifice his life
We shall thee see full of vigour
With his learned, zealous wife.
There we shall see his love for thee
Stuffed up in all the bricks
Of a grand shrine from self-love free
Which built poor wealth of the Sikhs.
We in fable's gods believe not,
But, believe alone in two –
Sword: thy sister goddess who taught
To defy foe fierce; and you
For peace, truth, and justice wrought she
In unrivalled mighty hand;

Peace, truth and justice brought she;
Outdrove savage away from land.
But it's thy turn now to drive and
Darkness from this glory land;
Though much more severe task, no doubt,
Yet, we hope thou wilt withstand.
At thy bloodless altar we will give
Sacrifice of gold's vain pride;
"Die ye or for noble deeds live"
So taught us unrivalled guide
By thee, we are too poor in gold;
Do thy blessing 'pon us show
That in mental field we may hold,
Firm feet to fully show our power
Many poor youths but for money
With their mental wealth decay:
As the flowers full of honey
In a desert fade away.
Blessed are the pilgrims who had been
To your Learning's holy shrine;
But blessed who will me call we've seen
Not once even temple fine?
My unseen love! I have praised thee
Other masses as have done;
Art thou go fair as they tell me
Truly go dearest everyone?
Though I could not see thy garden
Nor sweet-scented flowers bloom,
Yet, naught could their scents' heart harden
That could reach me in my room.

Mr Mohindar Singh of Jammu. *The Khalsa Advocate*, Saturday, 11th September 1915.

*****

"A letter has come from our village which I enclose. There has been no rain. For this reason the price of grain has become very dear. Wheat is 19 sers, grain 25 sers, ghi 1 ¾ sers, maize (for sowing) 7 sers local weight. Two rupees purchase one bundle of straw. Prices are very high. If you get a letter from home, send it to me. What I told you has come to pass. (This seems to refer to the recent attack). You must understand this. Give me the latest news of the regiment and tell me who are the new Indian Officers, havaldars, naiks and lance-naiks who have been appointed." (This would amount to a statement of the casualties in these ranks.)

From Lewa Singh, 89th Punjabis, (apparently away from the regiment) to Naranjan Singh, 89th Punjabis, at the front. (Urdu, 30/9/15).

*****

"Let a Signaller read this carefully. It is very earnestly requested that if anyone reads this letter on the way, he will let it pass and not detain it."

(Gurmukhi, written in Morse code) "If you write with the juice of the ak plant and black (? Carbon) paper we shall dry and read (the letter). For (the writing) will become black. Or write with onion juice the news about the war."

From a Sowar, 5th Cavalry, Shabqadr, India, to Bhan Singh, Guide's Infantry, attached 57th Rifles, France. (Gurmukhi, 4/10/15).
Separate sheet of paper with letter.

*****

"I have not had a letter from you for a long time, but I get news of you from your letters that come to your mother and brothers. I think you have now spent enough time in Europe, and you might now come back to Kapurthala. The weather here is delightful just now. It is quite cold. We are all very anxious about your health. If you were here, we could all look after you, and you could get excellent treatment. I think that, if you had not gone to Europe, by now you would have been all right again, and there would have been no need of taking further leave. So now I think you had better come back to India. If you do not care about living in Kapurthala, you can live elsewhere, for example, in Lahore where there are very good doctors. All is well at home."

From Sundar Singh, Kapurthala, Punjab, India, to Sirdar Arjan Singh Sahib, C/o Messrs Thos. Cook & Sons, Marseilles, France. (Urdu, 19/11/15).

*****

The Advent of Sri Guru Nanak Dev

The Great Guru Nanak blessed the earth
From Heaven coming, taking birth,
To bring to truth and Virtue's way
The mortals who had gone astray.
The Sun of Righteousness when shone;
'Twas light all around and gloom was gone;
The clouds of Doubt did disappear;
And firmament of Faith did clear.
Bewildered by so many a creed
Humanity felt True Guru's need.
Then came the Guru us to lead;
How noble mission His indeed!
True name of God, He taught to all;
Distinguish not He great from small.
A Hindu or a Musalman,
Well versed in Ved or Alkoran,
Who all external rights observes

But from the Path or virtue swerves –
Who goes to temple, mosque or shrine;
But has in him has no Love Divine –
Doth not Eternal Bliss attain;
His formal piety is in vain.
The Brahmans and the Mullahs fight;
In finding fault they take delight;
But Truth by them is seldom sought
Their wrangling leads to gaining nought.
Then why this narrow minded strife
To waste the precious Human life?
"True name of God" says Nanak,
"Saves sinners in the iron age."
All Guru's Sikhs, today rejoice
And here Sat Guru Nanak's voice.
Say Wah Guru all with one accord
And glorify the name of Lord.

Bhai Bishan Das Puri, M.A. *The Khalsa Advocate*, Saturday, November 20, 1915.

*****

The Nativity of Guru Nanak

Guru Nanak! how sweet thy name and thy thought
"Be sweet and all thine" early who us taught?
Vermillion lips did lispingly this sing
Oh platform o'love the hostile world to bring.
Thou taught this lesson all of us as one.
None but the wise did listen and all fools shun.
Oh! who can but jeweller's I discern
A diamond and the value it can earn?
As welcome is't impatient nightingale,
The cheerful summer over lovely dale;
As water-drought a blessing at the last breath,
To parched throat in agonies of death;
So were thy sweet words sure heart-healing balm,
To the troubled Hindu souls and true Islam.
In temple Dorn'd Ram, in mosque did Rahim.
And all souls thou taught part of His Realm.
As countless sparks of fire to all sides fly,
And taking several turns in same fire die;
As all the rivers, maybe be great and small,
Are fed by ocean and in ocean fall;
So taught us thee; our souls proceed from Him,
In Him their goal; but our sight being dim

We cannot full discern that 'tis the case,
So stumble at each step in the worldly-race
When bitter chill severely bites the face
And thick mist all around spreads over the place,
With vapour dense sights blunt all around
And everywhere all are shivering found
How welcome are to all the sweet sun's rays,
And how we foresee coming happy days?
So truth and justice were extremely pleased
To find themselves from jealous faith released.
Or have you ever seen a ship catching fire
A main amidst the flames each while rising higher
Consuming thousand lives all great or small
To pray for dear lives who on their knees fall;
With woeful tears in eyes cries raise to heaven
But fire and water both to their ruin given;
How all impatient hearts throb and wait
Approaching death – the horrid end of fate?
But if in such a state God grant their prayer
And send a ship t'safe all them bear
Image what their joy would be to feel
Their prayer granted, and how once more they'll kneel,
So bears across the endless sea of life,
The soul, (away from tempting worldly strifes)
His all-beloved message heaven sent
And leaves behind the body which was bent.
To burn with pride and longing's rising fire
And t'hoard up wealth was highest whose desire.

Bhai Mohindra Singh, Student, B.A., Class, Jammu. The Khalsa Advocate, Saturday, 20th November 1915.

*****

Sat Guru Nanak Plunge and his Recovery

"Who treads but me these tangled paths of wood?"
These were the words that on a sudden shot
Out of my lips, while in the grove I stood –
The grove of bushes, trees and wandering thought.
There beauteous work of Lady Frost did lie
Yet safe from heedless hand of sun's first ray.
How bright the trees and grass, nay even the sky!
The snow white garb and hair quite grey
Of you old man, that with the heaviest tread
Came creeping on, made charming harmony

With fog and mist that choked the breeze and spread
On sleepy Bosom of the stony Leh, -
Like size that interweave a painful breath.
The old man came. His prepossessing form
Was lank and feeble made by fear of death
But yet it bore of many a spent up storm
A trait or two with here and there a touch
Of well spent days, the days of youth and cheer.
He was a Lyrist – I must call him such,
Through lyre, his instrument had no such year –
A wandering son of song " I trace my birth
- A Sikh you seem – from faithful Mardana."
He paused and cast his thoughtful eyes on earth,
Then up, - "My home is far off Nankana"
The name was quite a thrill to soul and brain!
The man had sacred blood, which Nanak Dev
Had with his song engrained. The news he gave
Stirred up my heart to prayer. And hark a strain!
'tis Lyre that breathes soft in murmurs sweet
Down motionless he sits as in an agony
Except his hand that travels in full heat
Among various strings to find a symphony
Or make the hearts throb deep by cadence wild.
The voices, the magic voices, in the Lyre,
That latent lay, have stirred to fire
The drowsy heart that like a sleepy child
Lay on the downy breast of careless ease.-
A voice! Yes, old musician's lips do move
All movements in my mind the moment cease
A calm like season as of raptured love
Has crept on gently over my soul profound.
The voices! My sweet God! I am spell-bound.

Professor Teja Singh, B.A., Gordon College, Rawal Pindi, *The Khalsa Advocate*, Saturday, November 20, 1915. (Extract).

*****

"When you write, be kind enough to send me an interesting paragraph setting forth clearly the justice of the British Government and its wisdom and foresight and its appreciation and recognition of the services of our Indian troops. I will get this article printed in the "Fauji Akhbar" in our joint names, for such an article will be very useful to the public, just as you have seen in other papers."

From Jawahir Singh, State Photographer, Bhopal, India, to B. Chattar Singh, 38th C.I.H., France. (Urdu, 26/11/15).

*****

"God save the King. I really hope that God may help our King."

From a Sikh boy in India to his father in the 6th Cavalry, France. (English across the top of a Gurmukhi letter, 15/12/15).

*****

"We hear that the Indian Cavalry is returning from France to Egypt. You write that you are able to obtain your desires in France forthwith. I doubt whether you will be able to do so without marriage; but marriage is possible only on the condition that the French lady adopts our religion and custom and dress of the Sikhs.........do you go into the trenches in the winter? Tell me how many times you have been in the trenches. Remember that all who distinguish themselves in this war, will certainly obtain a grant of land from the Government. I have myself read it in the Lyallpur Gazette, and it is commonly spoken of."

From Darbard Singh, Chachrauli, Punjab, India, to Har Narindar Singh, 3rd Skinners's Horse, France. (Urdu, 19/12/15).

*****

"My daily prayer is that our government may gain a real and decisive victory over the Germans. With my prayers for you are mingled prayers for the whole army. Do not think about your native place. The duty of the brave is to fight, and gain victory over the foe and win fame in the world. For this cause the brave were sent into this world, and do you fulfil your mission."

From Lalji Mal, Ferozpur, India, to Rissaldar Mokand Singh, 3rd Skinner's Horse, France. (Urdu, 7/1/16).

*****

"You asked in your last letter whether I have had the ceremony of the "Sabdchauki" (reading of the Granth Sahib) done. I have not, for this reason that Sikhs are forbidden to assemble together. If they meet together, they are promptly arrested."

From Phuman Singh, Ludhiana, India, to Jemadar Bir Singh, 30th Lancers, France. (Urdu, 8/1/16).

*****

"On the 30/12/15 I was sent on detachment to the Pezu Pass, where I expect to remain for three months. For here there is great danger from the enemy. I think that, under your shadow, I too will volunteer for the front. May the True King bring you home safe and sound from the war. May our king have the victory over that king. Night and day I am ever praying to Guru Nanak Dev to bring my uncle home safe from the field of battle."

From Dhian Singh, 52nd Sikhs, Pezu Darra, N.W.F.P., India, to Jem. Dalip Singh, 11th Lancers attached 19th, France. (Urdu, 10/1/16).

*****

"Stresses the necessity of the Panth remaining united and on preserving the Bungas, over which the flag of the Sikh gurus proudly floats. Let it be sufficient to hint here that any carelessness and laziness will result in the Sikhs becoming silently and slowly absorbed by the neighbouring communities just as the Buddhists and the Jews have been absorbed. Those days are gone by when the Sikh heroes, on hearing that an insult had been offered to their Bungas, came from Bikanir to Amritsar and put the arrogant men who insulted the Harmandir to the sword. Those days are gone by when the brave Sikhs conquered Delhi but abandoned it on an assurance that the gurdwaras in or about Delhi, which were nearly in a state of extinction, would be rebuilt; when by the strength of their arms they obtained the grant of jagirs for the maintenance of the gurdwaras from that very Moghul emperor who willingly or unwillingly had offered an insult to the gurdwaras of Delhi. "Bear in mind that the Sikhs abandoned the throne and government of Delhi, merely on the stipulation that their gurdwaras would be maintained and their Bungas and their flag preserved. Are the Sikhs still actuated by the same holy feeling?"

Sardar Harchand Singh, Rais of Lyallpur and proprietor of the Khalsa Akhbar. *The Khalsa Akhbar* (Lahore), 11th January 1916 (a special issue devoted to the celebration of Guru Gobind Singh's birthday).

*****

"Babu Bhagwan Singh's father has been killed in a fight. A fight took place in the village against the Musalmans. And two of his cousins were wounded."

From Sher Singh, Sialkot, Punjab, India, to Dfdr. Harnam Singh, 6th Cavalry, France. (Gurmukhi, 18/1/16).

*****

Guru Gobind Singh's Benevolence

He sat in lap of Father,
And spoke in gentle tone,
What is the matter Pa with you
Why you feel unpleasant rather.
You look aggrieved, who are these men,
By you, with folded hands,
Absorbed in thoughts. I wonder,
Say, what you are thinking then.
Your long silence make uneasy to me,
Pray let me know the cause
You had never been such ere this
In which flight now placed are ye.

Nay! Son don't meddle in such affairs,
You are child, and possess no power,
To understand,
What charity they had to bear.
Reverend Father, cannot refrain self
Asking this question from you.
As they look men of dignity, in sorrow
Holding lot of wealth and pelf.
Father Speak, I implore thee to speak,
Goodness's sake! I am perplexed,
Your silence is unbearable
Your kindest word I seek.
Your words oblige me then hear now the tale,
They come from the Valley of Kashmir,
To state their grievances,
All that they now bewail.
One sacred head is needed to save them all away
From cold clutches of calamity,
Which always awaits them;
Under Heaven's sway.
They are troubled all round all find none to save
They wish to be sheltered somewhere;
Under a powerful flag,
From the prejudice a hands of knave.
That is all Father! That on your breast rest,
To save these poor people and India
No better head can be found.
Than yours in test.
A joyous shriek was heard amongst all,
Sat Guru Tegh Bahadur embraced him
Who spoke so bravely in Durbar
Saying loudly, "There is no Fall."
Can ever such heroes be found under heaven,
Who spared life for Benevolence,
He did the philanthropic deed,
And sacrificed lives Seven.*
Come and enjoy the day of his birth,
Who came to show us path
Through the tiresome and weary life
With greatest joy and mirth.

* (1) Father (2) Self (3) Four sons (4) Mother.

Mr. N.T. Singh of Shahdara. *The Khalsa Advocate*, 22nd January 1916.

*****

"Regarding what you say about the money. I have not received anything up to date. I sent four petitions to the C.O. but received no answer. Then I sent a petition to the General and another to the Commander-in-chief at Delhi. Neither replied. I went personally to the office of the 6th Cavalry but got nothing. Kindly send the money quickly, because the well at Raiya has fallen in, and Wasawa Singh will not let me draw water from his well. Without a well, no one will undertake to cultivate the land. I am in doubt whether the money is due from the 6th Cavalry or from the 5th. Without fail send Rs.500 /- at once, otherwise the land will lie fallow."

From Ganda Singh, Sialkot Dt., Punjab, to Dafadar Makhan Singh, 6th Cavalry, France. (Urdu, 3/2/16).

*****

"You said you were wounded in the leg, since then I have heard nothing. I am very concerned. I hear that the war is increasing in violence, and my heart is depressed. Get a month's leave of absence and come and see me. I am very anxious to see you....... Except for you I have no one, you are my god. Get the leave of absence. If you can't get it, send for me to come to you."

From his mother, resident at Santpura, Gujrat, Punjab, to Shiv Ram Singh, Dafadar 2nd Cavalry Brigade. (Urdu, 4/2/16).

*****

"Yesterday, 27th February, the 15th Sikhs returned to Peshawar from France. A circumstance which caused much happiness. When they started from the Railway Station, two English regimental bands and two Indian regimental bands went in front, then came the sacred Grunth carried on horseback, and the entire 15th Sikhs regiment followed. It was a fine sight. Without fail let me know when you will return."

From Wazir Singh, Clerk, P.O. Peshawar, N.W.F.P., India, to Karm Singh, Sialkot Cavalry Brigade, France. (Urdu, 28/2/16).

*****

"I understand that you are in France, and not in Egypt or Mesopotamia. Germany has been preparing (for this war) for 40 years, whereas we have been preparing for only 1¼ years. Now certainly our side of the balance will become heavier and heavier while the German side will become lighter and lighter. May God speedily give the fruit of your efforts and sacrifice. Our eyes are fixed on you. May God bring the end of this war quickly."

From Kishan Singh, Ajmer, Rajputana, India, to Bachitar Singh, 30th Lancers, France. (Urdu, 17/3/16).

*****

"Get nice clothes made for Jrishan Singh (the writer's son) and tell Golab Kor (writer's wife) to look after his upbringing as much as possible, because in this country children of his age by reason of the care taken in their upbringing, speak as well as wise men."

To Risaldar Ganda Singh, (Pensioner) Ludhiana, Punjab, from his nephew (no name given) Meerut Cavalry Brigade. (Urdu, 27/3/16).

*****

"I am serving in the regiment. They made me a Kot Dafadar, now they are pressing me to accept promotion permanently to Jemadar. I have refused three times, but they still keep pressing me. I will not accept. If I am ordered to go (as Jemadar) I must go, but I will not do so willingly ... The news about Pertab Singh is that I received a letter from him d/20/11/15, since which date no letter has been received, either in his village or by the Regiment. He is with the besieged brigade of D. Force in Kut-al-Amara. No news has yet been received as to whether they have been relieved or not. Whatever God wills, will happen. We are anxious for him day and night. His family is in a helpless condition. When they see Pertab Singh again they will be relieved. Pertab Singh allotted Rs. 10/ per mensem for his family. One month's allotment was paid. No further payment is forthcoming. What is the reason? No one knows."

From Chur Singh, 66th Punjabis, Jhelum, Punjab, to Atar Singh, 6th Cavalry, France. (Gurmukhi, 30/3/16).

*****

"That was an excellent letter of yours and I had it translated and showed it to my bara sahib. If everyone wrote to his family in this way it would have an excellent effect. By the Guru's grace the villainous enemy will soon be rooted up. May He bring you all back safe and victorious and those days are near I believe. In this part of the country (and indeed everywhere) no one has the slightest doubt of victory. It is merely a question of when we shall finish the war, but be it near, or far off, victory is ours."

From Sant Singh, Simla, to Risaldar Major Sirdar Hira Singh, 30th Lancers, France. (Urdu, 28/4/16).

*****

Great Thoughts (The Sikh Religion)

My soul, seek shelter in God's holy name;
Pondering on this should'st thou all thought employ.
No more thou'lt grieve, hemmed in by mortal fame,
But gain in God Nirvana's final joy. Pain is arsenic, the name of God is the antidote.
O ignorant man, take such medicine as shall cure thy sins.
If thou desire to play at love with me,
Come my way with thy head on the palm of thy hand;
Put thy feet on this road;

Give thy head and regard not human opinion.
Blest the paper, blest the pen, blest the ink,
Blest the writer, Nanak, who writeth the True Name.
He who batheth in the immortal water of divine knowledge taketh with him sixty-eight places of pilgrimage.
The egg of superstition has burst;
The mind has illumined;
The Guru has cut the fetters of the past –
And freed the captive.

Kishen Singh, III year class. *The Khalsa Advocate*, Saturday, April 29, 1916.

*****

"This is a consolation to us that in the end victory will certainly be gained by our King, but we had no idea that that noxious creature (i.e. Germany) would be able to fight for so long. This too is certain, that if the Government had made peace with it; it would sooner or later have striven to raise its neck again. But we believe that now it will not be able to raise its head again till the Day of Judgement. The general public are now calm. Formerly they were somewhat disturbed, but now no one is disturbed. The post comes regularly and with it come letters from the warriors at the front, which are read out for the edification of all. Now there is no longer any feeling of doubt or apprehension. This alone remains, namely, the longing for the return of loved ones."

From Sahib Singh, Sub-Inspector, Police, Nabha State, Punjab, to Jemadar Kartar Singh, 18th Lancers, France. (Urdu, 16/5/16).

*****

"My father, it is said here that the Canadian and Australian troops have told the Government that they are quite prepared to undertake the duties of the Indian troops, who might then be sent back to their homes. Is this correct? If it is, then let me know when you are likely to return."

From Basant Singh, Patiala State, Punjab, to his father, Bakhshish Singh, Risaldar, 19th Lancers, France. (Urdu, 19/5/16).

*****

"We hear from all sides that the fighting is now very intense, but you have told us nothing about it, nor have you said where you are. Other people write and describe their circumstances. We have also heard that all the (Indian) forces have arrived in Basrah. I don't know whether you are in Basrah or in France.........there is one thing in particular that I wish you to do. Write a letter direct to your mother as that will give her comfort. Tell her that you will return very quickly – because day after day she declines her food and the children seeing her grief, fret. I have tried to comfort her but without effect."

From Mathra Singh, Rawal Pindi District, Punjab, India, to his son Gurmukh Singh, 6th Cavalry, France. (Urdu, 6/6/16).

*****

Oh archer, speed your winged dart
A message send to India's heart
Awake from sleep, the time is near
Your quarrels cease, the warning hear!
The eddies whirl your ship of state
Be up and doing, ere too late!
The warring nations drain their blood!
Oh men of India stem the flood!

From Hazara Singh, 30th Lancers, Ambala, Punjab, India, to Pertab Singh, Risaldar, H.d.Qrs., 2nd Indian Cavalry Dn. France. (Urdu, 23rd June 1916).

*****

"I am very unfortunate in that I am unable to join you in this war. I applied to my officers to be allowed to volunteer for Military service, but they answered that if the Police Force went to the war, who would look after law and order in the country? And they added that it was not the work of the police to fight in battle."

From Narain Singh, Sub: Inspector of Police, Nagpur, India, to Suraj Singh, Risaldar, 2nd Lancers, France. (Urdu, 23/8/16).

*****

The Use of Kirpan

"Sir, I beg to draw the attention of your esteemed readers of the fact that the Frontier Law does not allow the Sikhs to keep a Kirpan in their possession. Of course, it does allow us to keep even a sword in our houses, but at the same time it forbids us to take either Kirpan or sword outside the four walls of the house. The religion says that every Sikh should wear Keshas, keep a Kara (iron bracelet), Kachhehra (short breeches), Kangha (comb) and Kirpan always on his person. It is really regrettable to notice that we are debarred from the privilege, which our brothers in the Punjab enjoy. I request the Chief Khalsa Diwan to memorialise H.E. the Viceroy to the effect that the Sikhs in the Frontier may be allowed to keep a Kirpan in their possession."

Jaswant Singh Mongia, Misgran Bazar, D.I.Khan writes (extract): *The Khalsa Advocate*, Saturday, August 26, 1916.

*****

"It is now two years since you went away. Many people return on leave so why do you not come? We have also heard that our kind Sircar has made arrangements to exchange all the regiments who have been at the front for two years. Your regiment will therefore come back sooner or later. May God give victory to our King George the Fifth, so that the world may be at rest again, after the Germans, who have had so many mothers' sons murdered, have been ground into the dust."

From Kartar Kor, Gojra, Lyalpur, Punjab, India, to her brother Tara Singh, 6th Cavalry, France. (Gurmukhi, 28/8/16).

*****

"Give us some information about the country you are in. You need not say anything about the war if you are forbidden to do so, but surely the censor would not object to your writing about the country. One cannot say when it will please God to bring this terrible war to a conclusion. Now Rumania has also joined our side, and we are therefore confident that our Sircar will win the victory. Where are you now? Have you seen Paris yet or not? We hear that it is the most beautiful city in all the world. You will surely have seen it by now."

From Mehtab Singh, Raisina (Delhi) Punjab, India, to Kalyan Singh, Dafadar, 6th Cavalry, France. (Gurmukhi, 5/9/16).

*****

"From your letters and the newspapers we feel sure that the Germans are near the end of their tether. It is true that the tyrants' neck has now been bent. It will be a glorious day when you come back victorious with a medal for bravery. You will see my chest swollen with pride! When you come back with your breast covered with medals with what pride will I show you to my friends. I am delighted to hear of the comfort in which you are. In such a great war our King has not allowed a single sowar to suffer any discomfort and I am comforted by the thought that the Guru will soon bring round the day of joy. We only wait now to hear the actual words of your success. The enemy is now uselessly spilling blood. Why does he not submit? What is the use of his trying to go on breathing? When he has got to die what can he gain by struggling to live?"

From Sahib Singh, Nabha, India, to Jemr. Katar Singh, 18th Lancers, France. (Urdu, 21/9/16).

*****

"Now we believe that you will soon return to your native land in good health and crowned with victory, because the enemy seems now to have become weak, and God has given fresh help in the shape of Rumania."

From Rai Singh, 13th Lancers, Amballa, Punjab, to Gurdit Singh, Lance Dafadar, 13th Lancers, attached 19th Lancers, France. (Urdu, 21/9/16).

*****

"In my judgement, after this winter, Egypt, Turkey, Bulgaria, and Austria, will be in our possession, and Germany alone will be facing the Allies. The Germans too, know very well, that they have only a few days left. I expect, therefore, that you will soon return, having secured victory."

From "General" Bakshish Singh, Patiala State, Punjab, to Bakshish Singh, Risaldar, 19th Lancers, France. (Urdu, 24/9/16).

*****

"Whoever returns from France gets a present of Rs. 25/- and is allowed three months leave. If anyone returns "unfit" he is pensioned. Everyone wounded in the chest or head is sent straight to India as "unfit". When one leaves Bombay for home one gets: a white turban, a white sheet, two knickers, a pair of shoes, a white shirt, a white coat and a pair of white trousers. Also two handkerchiefs, a cake of soap and a bottle of hair oil."

From Rattan Singh, "Wounded reservist" 30th Punjabis, Delhi, to Wariam Singh, 36th Jacob's Horse, France. (Urdu, 25/9/16).

*****

"Write and tell me all about the place where you are. In which country is the war being fought? Which King's troops hold the trenches? How many Kings are on our side and how many on the enemy's side?"

From Indar Singh, Shamkot, Punjab, to Chattar Singh, 6th Cavalry, France. (Gurmukhi, 25/9/16).

*****

"Do not write any word to your mother other than your welfare because she becomes distraught if she hears the slightest word of danger. What you said in your letter about enemy aircraft circling over you and your escape there from caused her much distress."

From Ludhiana District, Punjab, India, on behalf of his mother to Hazara Singh, Dafadar, 36th Jacob's Horse, France. (Urdu dated 3rd November 1916).

*****

"The proposal undoubtedly is an interesting one. So far it has not struck the Sikh public. After hearing from Major Goodfellow some of his men might now spread the idea but so far it was unknown amongst the people. I have heard some of the ruling Chiefs, whose forces are now fighting in East Africa, discussing such schemes. Any trace of it that might be found in the Punjab is in a kind of hope to immigrate to Mesopotamia which perhaps was due more to one of Lord Hardinge's speeches. This hope never developed into a demand nor was it ever discussed by the public.

At one time in 1913, when the question of immigration was keenly felt in the Province and most of the immigrants were expected to be returning to India, majority of whom were Sikhs. Looking to what sort of ideas they had, some of us thought the desirability for finding some place for them to settle outside of India; so that agricultural or other population might not be affected by their ideas. The Budge Budge riots, and other seditious activities of the Bengalis followed by the War changed the situation. Some of the worst men had entered the country and subsequently had to be interned. The question of dealing with them after the War is one to be considered by itself.

The scheme as proposed by Major Goodfellow is, as I understand, for the benefit of Sikh soldiers who served in the War. If there ever arises a chance of considering it I am very doubtful as to the advisability of taking Sikhs alone into account. Nearly all the Punjabi soldiers, Musalmans, Hindoos or Sikhs, who form the overwhelmingly majority of the Indian Army, come from agricultural classes and will all expect similar reward. And besides Punjabis other Indians who may not be agriculturalists will also expect something in its place though in different kind. Therefore, the question of reward is one to be considered by taking into account the whole of the Indian Army. Any scheme which though meant for all but in practice affecting particularly any one community is likely to create jealously and discontent.

This proposal at all events might form a part of the whole scheme of reward. I should, however, hesitate to say if it would be popular. For Punjabis generally emigrate not for agriculture but for high wages which they get in the Colonies. After settling there, they might think of acquiring some land but it is purely the high wages and living as cheap as at home that attracts them.

There is another aspect of the question, i.e. to try such a colony as an experiment for finding an outlet for intending emigrants. I should recommend, if possible, to try the experiment though I should not at all be certain for reasons in the last paragraph if we would ever be able to persuade them to go to such a place on agricultural speculation alone. This, however, should depend on prospects and other facilities. We cannot expect Punjab agriculturalists to go anywhere for lesser prospects when Punjab itself is fairly high if not higher than in most of the Provinces, and particularly agricultural labour. And the population also has not much increased as to make it compulsory for the inhabitants to emigrate.

If the matter is at all to be referred to India I am strongly of the opinion that it should be treated secret. I believe, as I see from the papers, that Major Goodfellow will not give any publicity to his proposal."

Note by Sirdar Daljit Singh, d/- 6th November 1916.

*****

"A letter was received from Jamal Singh on the 5th November in which simply this was said "there is no news of Jit Singh, he is missing and it was added that "when Jit Singh was dying he begged me not to tell his father and mother that he was dead, as they would grieve greatly." In another part of the letter he said that "he is well and happy." This in short is what Jamal Singh said, and I am enclosing the letter. Do take it your Commanding Officer and ascertain why Jamal Singh wrote thus. We have ceased to eat and drink through anxiety and will only be reassured when we get a letter from you. We sent a telegram of enquiry to the Depot at Ambala about this on the 7th November."

From Ralla Singh, Shahpur District, Punjab, India to Jit Singh, 36th Jacob's Horse, France. (Urdu dated the 7th November 1916).

*****

"According to Reuter, the commission which was appointed by the Government for the purchase of wheat has obtained permission to export 11 crore and 20 lakh maunds of wheat to Great Britain, France and Italy. This appears to be the reason why the prices of wheat and flour are running so high. Government should fix a uniform rate at which rate should be sold in the country, so that under the pretext that Government is purchasing it wheat merchants may not raise the price of wheat so high as to make it difficult for people to fill their stomachs."

Article, *The Punjab Darpan* (Amritsar), 22nd November 1916.

*****

"I want you to tell me in what country you are. If you are on the Suez Canal make a mark like this, and if you are in France like this, and if in Mesopotamia like this."

From Gurdit Singh, 51st Sikhs, Julandar, India to Kehar Singh, Signaller, Sialkot Cavalry Brigade, France. (Urdu dated the 19th January 1917).

*****

"The wheat is good, but rain is badly wanted. Clouds abound but there has been no result. The crop will be very short unless we get rain. The train service has much diminished for every three trains only two run now. For a month there have been no goods wagons available and we can send nothing by rail. We are in great trouble over this. Only Government goods are carried. They say it is due to a shortage of coal, but the result is that trade has stopped."

From Prem Singh, Sargodha, Punjab to Pir Hasan Shah, 36th Jacob's Horse, France. (Urdu 23rd January 1917).

*****

"His Highness the Maharaja of Faridkot has agreed to pay all the expenses in connection with the building of a gurdwara at Basra will be received with joy by the Sikhs. Government has thankfully acknowledged the valuable gift and it is hoped that the foundation of the gurdwara will be soon laid in Basra."

Article, *The Loyal Gazette* (Lahore), 28th January 1917.

*****

"Whenever the newspapers come I look at the casualties in the Indian Army. My three nephews are in the 56th Punjabis. They have all been wounded and after having come home for a short while, have returned to the front. For this reason I am very anxious about you, and the eyes of all your relatives are fixed on you, as the eyes of children remain intent on the kites which they fly. At the commencement of the war in 1914, it was rumoured that the weight of the German Army would be thrown in our direction (i.e. India). Now we hear that in treading Rumania under foot, the Germans have opened the Kabul road to the Turks. Movement of troops are taking place on our frontier and people are apprehensive lest a strike be made in our direction. But there is no cause for alarm for the Guru will help our Sircar. It is intended to get the Sialkot Brigade ready for the front. Moreover, the Germans are now striving hard for peace, and it is expected that the war will soon be over. Making peace is the work of the Kings. We have suffered great loss by the blowing up of a munitions factory in England, but there is no cause for anxiety."

From Uttam Singh, Kot Dafadar (retired) Lyallpur, Punjab, India to Didan Singh, Jamadar, 19th Lancers, France. (Gurmukhi dated the 31st January 1917).

*****

"Many persons appear to be under the impression that as the so called leaders hold charge of national banks, schools, orphanages and other institutions, it is impossible to put an end to their ruinous tactics. But it should not be impossible for the Sikhs to set right a handful of their leaders. Those acquainted with the facts know that the Chief Khalsa Diwan has done little good to the Sikhs. It has failed to safeguard their political rights and has even trampled upon their national feelings. Acting simply on personal grounds, the Diwan has forcibly prohibited many a noble Sikh from serving his community. Our simple minded leaders tremble at the mention of politics and consider it an act of sedition to demand rights from the Government. They do not bring the troubles of the Sikhs to the notice of the authorities for fear of incurring the latter's displeasure. The non-official members of the Viceregal Council, who are admittedly loyal and command full confidence of the Government, submitted a reforms petition to the Viceroy. But the leaders of our community smelt sedition even in that petition and openly refused to append their signatures to it. In view of all this, it is necessary for the Sikhs to re-organise the Chief Khalsa Diwan."

Article, *The Khalsa Akhbar* (Lahore), 2nd February 1917.

*****

"We deplore the attitude of bigoted and narrow-minded Maulvies who are protesting against the proposal to build a gurdwara at Basra. Maulvi Adbulbari, who has become notorious for his bigotry, has urged other Maulvies to oppose the proposal. But he should bear in mind that Basra is no longer ruled by the Turks or bigoted Maulvies but is under the suzerainty of the British Government. The Sikhs have, therefore, a right to build gurdwaras there. It is hoped that Government will take full notice of the

Maulvi's conduct, so that bigoted Mullahs may not have the courage to create disunion among the people."

Article, *The Loyal Gazette* (Lahore), 4th March 1917.

*****

"Is the Chief Khalsa Diwan a representative body of Sikhs. If so, why is not the whole Sikh community permitted to elect its members. If it is not a representative body, it should declare it represents only a special class. If this is done, there will be nothing to object to. But it appears from the Diwan Committee that members are taken from its sub-committees and not from the Sikh public. This brings out the unrepresentative character of the institution."

Article, *The Panth Sewak* (Lahore), 14th March 1917.

*****

"We urge the extreme necessity of Sikhs laying the foundation of a new, constitutional and living organisation, composed of the representatives of every Sikh society and capable of safe guarding their political rights and communal feelings. As the Chief Khalsa Diwan does not command the confidence of the Sikh public, its doors should be shut and the following words inscribed upon them: - "Here is the inauspicious place where resolutions, calculated to dishonour the Gurdwara Rikab Ganj of Delhi, built in honour of Sri Guru Tegh Bahadur, were passed forcibly and deceitfully and the seed of dissension was sown in the Panth. This is the place where our political rights were slaughtered with the sharp sword of personal benefit. This is the house which had for long been the den of traitors to the community and was once known as the 'Chief Khalsa Diwan'."

Article, *The Khalsa Akhbar* (Lahore), 16th March 1917.

*****

"This cantonment of Bolarum is a very bad place. Butter and milk and vegetables are unobtainable. An arrangement has been made by the Regiment to cultivate a small garden to provide vegetables for the Sirdars. The rations of dal and flour are adulterated with dirt and grit. In fact we undergo as much hardship in the matter of food, as is experienced in field service."

From Kahn Singh, Granthi 7th Hariana Lancers, Bolarum, Deccan, India to Teja Singh, Lance Dafadar, 7th Lancers attached 20th Deccan Horse, France. (Gurmukhi dated the 19th March 1917).

*****

"The present days are very bad. There are frequent storms and in some places there has been hail and rain. In my opinion there will be a severe famine; because people have consumed all their stocks of corn, and the spring harvest is not yet ready."

From Bhagat Singh, Amritsar, Punjab, India to Kehar Singh, Lance Dafadar, 2nd Lancers, France. (Gurmukhi dated the 11th April 1917).

*****

"Today I have to draw the attention of my brethren to a most simple and well-known fact that we Sikhs are Wahi Guru Ji Ki Ka Khalsa or "God's own". This simple term conveys the most lofty ideals and is pregnant with real wisdom as distinguished from cunning that acquires everything for self-gratification. Our Hindu brothers believe in 33 crores of Devies and Devatas and innumerable Rishis and Munis along with Parmatma, our Muhammedan brothers professedly take their name from the great Prophet Muhammad of Arabia, our Christian brothers are called after the son of God-Lord Jesus Christ; our Buddhist and Parsee brothers are also named after their respective prophets, Lord Buddha and the great Zoroaster. But we are Wahi Guru Ji Ki Ka Khalsa and cannot afford to do anything or act in any way that may be displeasing to Akal Purkh – our Father in Heaven. I know perfectly well that every religion has got the same similar basic principles to teach, but as we are "God's own", far greater responsibility naturally rests on our shoulders for leading true, pure and ideal lives in whatever position we are placed and stations in life we occupy. We should treat the rest of the world in the same way as our common Father treats it. Can anyone of so many peoples claim that he, his religion, his denomination, his nation, his country, or his continent is the sole recipient as God's blessings? Can anyone further say that God is either Hindu or Muhammedan, either Christian or Buddhist, either Zoroastrian or Bahaist, Arya Samajist or Sanatanist? If not, why do some of our friends try to make out that we are either Hindus or Muhammedans. We cannot but follow God, being His Own, and be as much as one as the other. In fact, we are a universal people, all embracing, all loving and shall try to serve to the utmost of our ability, the whole of humanity without distinction of caste, creed, race, sex or colour. This is one of the fundamental principles that requires to be pressed home to all engaged in the sacred work of Sikh Education. The managing committees of our schools and colleges their staff and the students should always have this lofty ideal of the Sikhs being a universal people and Sikhism being a universal religion in view while imparting secular education for material advancement to those who knock at the doors of the Sikh educational institutions.

Having so far dealt with a true life, I come to the next point of a clean life. Guru Nanak Dev Ji Maharaj says: That is, truth the purest of the pure can only stay in a clean vessel. We have not only to keep our body, clothes and environments clean, neat and tidy, but we have to harbour no impure thoughts as all actions are the result of thought and when thoughts have been purified and controlled, actions get purified and controlled automatically. This cardinal point also deserves to be specially dilated upon in all Sikh seminaries. Their staff and students must not remain satisfied till a firm conviction is brought about that it is most important to purify thought by immediately driving away all bad, impure and selfish thoughts from the mind and by replacing them by good, pure and altruistic ones – by no means a very difficult task.

Having spoken about a truthful and a pure life, I come to the third point, a life with lofty ideals. May I say in all humility that it is hard to conceive of loftier ideals than those preached and lived by our Great Gurus. While the greater bulk of humanity is struggling after worldly possessions and is working hard for enjoyments that are to be obtained in a Swarga, Heaven, Paradise, or Bahisht, and some higher people are hankering after Mukhti, Salvation or najat, the summum bonum for the Gurus and Guru Sikhs is a yearning after atonement with the Infinite or an intense love of God and identification with Him."

Paper read by Shrimati Savitridevi, daughter of Bhai Rup Singh, retired Extra Assistant Commissioner, Lahore, at the tenth session of the Sikh Educational Conference, held at Lahore, on 7th April 1917. (Extract).

*****

"From the newspapers we learn that at the present time the feet of the enemy are slipping. Everyone, both high and low, is pleased to hear that America has joined with the Allies in the war. May God speedily give victory to our Government and their Allies."

From Albeyl Singh, Gujrat District, Punjab, India to Bachittar Singh, 6th Cavalry, France. (Urdu dated the 24th April 1917).

*****

"Regarding your enquiry about leavened (i.e. French baked) bread. You need not hesitate at all to consume it. But you should strictly abstain from eating flesh and drinking wine, which are both forbidden and noxious; and also antagonistic to that state of mind and body which is necessary for the proper contemplation of God. You must also abstain from having any liaison with another man's wife. If you have a book extract from the Guru Granth read a portion whenever you have the time. This will keep your mind pure. Recite your prayers daily. God is everywhere the Protector of those who serve Him."

From Sowar Singh, Shrine of Dehra Baba Jai Mall Singh, Amritsar, Punjab, India to Khushial Singh, 19th Lancers, France. (Urdu dated the 24th April 1917).

*****

"Now I will tell you of an event which I thought to keep from you, but which I now disclose lest some enemy should make you acquainted with it. Your uncle Nanak Singh Colour Havildar, and your brother Amar Singh were killed in the battle at Tonk on the 5th May. Their death has caused me indescribable grief but who can prevail with God? My beloved son, when your turn comes to attack the enemy, take good shelter and fire "rapid" on the enemy, so that you may fulfil your duty towards your King. I cannot do anything about your return, but I have learned from reliable source that the 6th Cavalry and 19th Lancers have for some time been ready to return but owing to the dangers of the sea, their return has been made difficult for a time."

From Arjan Singh, Rawal Pindi District, Punjab, India to Gurmukh Singh, 6th Cavalry, France. (Urdu dated the 27th May 1917).

*****

"We fear that misguided and selfish people are trying to take us back to the depths of party spirit and distinctions. It is a pity that some of the Sikhs are trying to hold themselves aloof from others because some are Jats and others are Khatris. It would be tragical if the Sikhs ever succumbed to such temptations. A Jat Sikh Conference or Khatri Sikh Conference or an Arora Sikh Conference are humbug terms. A Sikh is a Sikh – he is no Khatri, Jat, or Arora. Those mischievous people who persuade us to think like that or talk like that are like the wolf in the sheep's clothing – They are Hindus under the garb of Sikhs sent in to sow dissension and split. They are the 'spies' of non-Sikhs ever ready to throttle us and blow up our super structure which took us centuries to build. We must treat these men as 'cheats', 'mischief-mongers', or 'point-faced spies' and every drastic form of treatment should be accorded to them. We do not find much fault with non-Sikhs if they try to undermine our organisation because mutual rivalries and jealousies are signs of life and growth. We, therefore, do not much object to the Hon'ble Lal Chand's advocacy of the cause of Jats because it pays him to wean away Sikh and other sympathies under the semblance of a Jat. But we have got no toleration for that 'Sikh' who strikes at the root of our existence by sowing the seed of caste and split. Such a one is a treacherous man – a traitor to the cause of our community. He should be an eyesore to us. His existence should be desecrated."

Article, *The Khalsa Advocate* (Amritsar), 16th June 1917.

*****

"We were very sorry to hear of your being wounded. Do not be concerned because to be wounded in this war is an honour. We are all very proud of the work which you have done for the Sircar in this war. May the Guru give you the full reward of your service. We trust that your wound is now healed and that you shall return to India shortly."

From Kartar Singh, Gurdaspur, Punjab, India to Dalip Singh, Dafadar, 36th Jacob's Horse, France. (Urdu dated the 29th June 1917).

*****

"You must know that a mail steamer that carried the English and French mails of the 31st May was sunk near Bombay through a mine. No lives were lost but the mail sank, with the exception of 30 bags which floated to the shore. By good fortune your letter was in one of these bags."

From Atar Singh, Ludhiana District, Punjab, India to Gobind Singh, Lance Dafadar, 31st Lancers attached 20th Deccan Horse, France. (Urdu dated the 5th July 1917).

*****

"How long do people say the war will continue where you are? Here the common belief is that it will last another two years. Now America has joined the Sircar, it is probable that the war will speedily be finished. May the Guru soon give peace!"

From Bhola Singh, Kashipur, Naini Tal, U.P., India to Narain Singh, Sub-Assistant Surgeon, 19th Lancers, France. (Gurmukhi dated the 19th July 1917).

*****

D.P.M., 4th Military District.

The following inset copy of a communication from the wife and legal next-of-kin of the late No. 2255 Private S. Singh, 43rd Battalion, is referred for favour of attention and reply to the enquirer direct. She should also be advised in respect to her claim to consideration under the War Pensions Act, and if eligible, the necessary forms forwarded for application.

"I beg most respectfully to lay before you the most pitiable condition of mine for your most favourable consideration. My husband, named Sarna, No. 2255 was serving in the European Australian Regiment No. 43 in your charge, and was sent in front at France, but he died at his imperative duty as owing his duty towards the Govt. of Australia. Wire shows that Sarna No. 2255 died on the 10th June 1917 at France in front.

Words fail to express my mournful feelings and my miserable condition, and hence, I therefore see no one else except you who may do me any kind of favour for supporting my life as well as saving my virtue (faith) etc. My father-in-law and the real brother of my husband are no more ready to support me for my lifetime, and it would have been much better if I might die before my husband did. Moreover above stated both the relatives of mine are trying that they may have all the money deposited by my husband in the Bank for themselves, but as a rule no one has a prior right than a man's wife has. Further your Excellency may do what is proper. My husband was a young lad of 30 years and now my life is burden upon me in this world. From Australia before he has given his name in your regiment No. 43. He put all his riches in some bank through the Government of Australia or say through your Excellency. I therefore most humbly and respectfully beg the favour of you kindly granting me the pension and at the same time ordering the officer of the bank to send all the money my husband put there in Australia at Malbuman (Melbourne, New South Wales) to better my life. Awaiting a favourable reply at your benevolent hands."

(sgd.) Partap Kor (Singh)
V. Chhokran
Post Office Moron,
Tahsil – Phillour,
District – Jullundur,
Punjab, India.
Major, Officer i/c Base Records.

Copy of letter sent by Partap Kor, wife of Private Sarn Singh No. 2255, to Government of Australia, 14th September 1917.

*****

"When will those happy days come when we shall meet again? Perhaps we shall not meet as I am off to Mesopotamia to fight there. We have been hoping to see you for three years but now we realise that until the cursed Germans and Austrians are subdued it is impossible for us to meet."

From Karam Singh, 10th Lancers, Multan to Hazara Singh, 9th Hodson's Horse, France. (Urdu dated the 14th September 1917).

*****

The Kikar Tree

I grow upward, my march is heavenward
My face is turned to the God of the skies!
Nor village, nor city, nor palace, nor hut I need in this world of thine, O world!
I am he who can pass his days without a roof on his head, in rain, sunshine, hail and storm:
I love to look at the God of the skies,
I need but a small piece of ground for my roots just to stand, to blossom, to fructify and die!
I need no raiment, nor food from thee, O world!
The rain-water is enough for me,
I drink and I grow.
I live on air, I desire naught,
I am all alone in myself, the ascetic of centuries past and the ascetic of the centuries yet to come!
And even for me, O world!
Thou hast but an axe

(Translated from the Punjabi Original)
Puran Singh.

By Bhai Veer Singh, *The Khalsa Advocate*, Saturday, September 15, 1917.

*****

III – Sardar Hari Singh's courage and chivalry.

One fine morning, my friend Sardar Gopal Singh and I started for a visit to Jamrod, an outpost on the Khaibar road. We were informed at the Peshawar Cantonment Station that the train was not to leave that day as the portion of the road washed away by the downpour of a day before had not been fully repaired. We were extremely disappointed and were going to give up the idea of the excursion when we caught sight of the mail tonga leaving for the place. We were offered seats, and of course, we were only too glad to accept them. The Pathan driver before leaving the Cantonment limits added four more men, while near Sardar Hari Singh's Burj, a couple more of the Border Police came to roost there – making a total of nine for one tonga! On the way, we saw the gangs under and overseer repairing the permanent way. The work seemed to proceed in a happy-go-lucky way. I wondered in my heart of hearts as to what was the use of a railway on which traffic could be held up for two days by a single downfall of rain.

After some three hours, we were set down at the gate of Jamrod fort. A soldier of the Border Police was standing at the door of the serai, with a loaded gun, with which he was fumbling all the time, while a soldier of the XXXV Sikhs was guarding the fort gate with only a thick stick.

We met our friend Sardar Harnam Singh of the Postal Department. He was all courtesy and kindliness. He placed at our disposal, all the available information, and the gallant Sardar Hari Singh Nalwa.

An Afridi thus related an anecdote of the great General. One day when he was brushing his teeth with a twig of Phulahi (Acacia Arabica), outside the fort, a Pathan of the Jam village, after which the Jamrod fort takes its name, was returning home with his wife. 'Are you not afraid' remarked he, 'that living in the land of the Pathans, you move about so fearlessly? What would you do, if someone were to kill you here, on the spot?'

'We are', replied the Sardar, 'Sikhs of Guru Gobind Singh and he will help us in dire distress.' 'Come' retorted the other, 'and have a fight. Accompany me to my village, let me leave my wife there and then I will have a trial of your prowess.' 'You will' he added he, 'be my guest there, and none else will touch a hair of your head.'

The Sikh chief agreed and walked with him to his native place. The Pathan handed over to the Sikh Commander a sword and a shield and took the same himself. The whole village turned out to see the sight. The Pathan was challenged to strike the first blow. He inflicted a mighty stroke, which was received on the shield by his opponent. The Sardar then had his turn. The blade cut the shield in twain and entering through the Pathan's left side came out of the right. The life was not yet extinct.

Our hero then took his fallen foe in arms and tearing his upper turban tried to bandage the wounds. The dying Afridi was wonder struck at this novel treatment and turned a questioning look on his gallant opponent.

'When whole' remarked the Sardar, 'you were my foe and we fought, now that you are wounded and helpless, I owe it to you as a Sikh to nurse and comfort.' The words produced a deep impression upon all. The Afridi commanded his men not to injure the Sikh Warrior and to take him in a litter, back to the fort.

The villagers when they came to know subsequently that the man of prowess was Sardar Hari Singh himself, bewailed their folly in allowing him to escape.

Tales from Sikh History. Published by The Khalsa Historical and Literary Society, Rawalpindi, December 1917, pg. 23. (Extract).

*****

The Golden Temple

The roads from all direction run with the swiftness of the winged thoughts,
To the spot where I stand waiting for my Lord,
In the centre of the things;
And every road speaks to me in the breathless accents of its panting hearts:
"Awake! Dream no more!
Behold! Fold thy hands in prayer to heaven

There cometh, thy King riding on His Fairy Purple Steed!
Hark! Thy sound of this ride in our breath of life!"
And before my eyes, rises the Golden Temple in the middle of the Lake of Immortality,
As the sun rises, out of the sea on the dark worlds,
The gleams that its minarets shoot!
The morn that break all
The music that emanates from the hearts of the earth
The waves of the Ocean of Immortality clad in magic smile of the dawn dance with the Morning Song of Praise,
They joy floats on the surface of waters,
From the eyes of the Priestess Divine falls a drop of dew in the opened mouth of a thirsty flower
It is my heart, and my eyes close with an inspired sweetness of slumber,
My soul dies with joy,
And as the roads call me out again,
I had already gone to sleep deep as the depths of the Passion,
And as I lie on the marble floor of the Golden Temple,
A rein of money softly patters down on the sleeping me,
The Bee forgets her flower in the perfume of my death and hovers around my soul humming the name of the beloved.
Alas! When He cometh,
I am asleep in the echoes of His Name, in the echoes of the joy, with which the waves of the deep weep and like the sister hearts leap as many flames of fire to my soul:
Ah! I am sound asleep,
When my king cometh to listen to the Song of His Devotees;
And when he is gone,
I rise with a pain and a pang that I had not known before,
To a still newer and deeper "Naming Him"
And for ever more.

Prof. Puran Singh, F.C.S of Dehra Dun, *The Khalsa Advocate*, Saturday, 29th December 1917.

*****

IV – The Last Fight of Akali Phula Singh

It is the hour of dawn on the 1st day of Chet, 1881 (Bikrami) corresponding to March 14, 1823, A.D. The Khalsa army under the command of Maharaja Ranjit Singh himself is encamped in the open plains of Akora. The spy had brought overnight the disquieting news that the hordes of the "Jehadis" (Moslems engaged in a religious warfare) have swollen to large dimensions and are entrenched in strong positions on the top of Tarki hill, on the other side of the Kabul river, at a distance of some six miles from Nowshera.

According to the old traditions of the Khalsa, the holy volume (Sri Guru Granth Sahib) is opened and the chiefs of all the units take up their seats. After the Asa-di-war (morning hymns), a unanimous Gurmata (resolution) is adopted that delay would only augment the enemy forces and embolden him in his arrogance, besides affording an opportunity for Muhammed Azim Khan to join the tribes with his Afghan troops.

The Maharaja accordingly began to dispose of his army for the coming fight. Fifteen-hundred of the troops are placed under Akali Phula Singh to deliver the attack from the east, three thousand men are entrusted to Sardar Desa Singh, Majithia, and Sardar Fateh Singh, Ahluwalia, to charge from the west. Generals Allard, Hari Singh and Rattan Singh and Prince Kharak Singh are given command of 5,000 soldiers including six hundred Gurkhas to meet the frontal attack of the Ghazis. The rest of the forces are kept in reserve under the guidance of the Maharaja himself to reinforce as the situation demands.

All the forces begin slowly to march past their beloved sovereign riding his charger standing on a prominence. The contingent of Sardar Desa Singh is passing under review when a hasty spy drops in, bringing the news that the brothers of Muhammed Azim Khan have already joined the host at Tarki, while he himself with 10,000 Afghans and 40 big guns is collecting boats to cross the river to combine all the forces. The Maharaja is cast down at this intelligence, and desires to alter the Gurmata arrived at in the presence of Sri Guru Granth Sahib, postponing the offensive until the arrival of the heavy artillery, which is following under General Ventura.

When Akali Phula Singh hears that the Maharaja is cowed down and is anxious to act otherwise than in accordance with the unanimous Gurmata of the Panth in the presence of the Sri Guru Granth Sahib, he is put out beyond measure, and seeks him at once 'yes', broke in the Akali, 'Today the enemy is very strong indeed, but it is against the tradition of the Khalsa to ignore a Gurmata when once passed.'

The Maharaja urged in reply the argument favouring his point of view.

'But' re-joined the Akali, 'we cannot and must not go against a Gurmata, even if the number of the opposing forces be redoubled. The Kalgiwala is at the back of our resolution. He is with us at all times.'

The Maharaja, however, reiterated that it was futile to move without heavy guns.

The Akali at this burst out saying 'you are a prince, in the pride of power and pelf, you may do what you please. We are, however, not held by the trammels of the world and are, therefore, ready even to die to further our Gurmata. What better felicity for the Khalsa than martyrdom in defence of the honour of the Panth?'

With these words of farewell, the Akali turned his horse towards the Ghazi camp. He stood up and offered a prayer which in its intense fervour thrilled from the heart, of the man and quivering through the hearts' breasts of his companions rose on the wings of sincere devotion to the throne of Him, who receives and grants the yearning of fervent human-souls. Remembering in the well-known Khalsa style, the ten Gurus and the Holy volume, he continued in the words:

'Seest Thou, O Kalghidhar Father, the Muhammadan army is in myriads. Thy Khalsa is going to launch against them with the sole desire of preserving the sanctity of Thy Gurmata. O Bajanwale (Lord of the Hawk) Satguru we are ready to lay down our lives in the cause. Our lives were consecrated to Thee on the day that we took Thy "Amrita". It does not matter much, therefore, whether we keep or lose our bodies. Do Thou but this day save the honour of the Khalsa and grant victory to Thy August Panth.'

The prayer pierced through the heart of every listener and steeled his men for prodigies of valour. Some pushed their horses into the river and others crossed on boats and gave the battle at once.

Thirty thousand Pathans were furious on seeing the dash of a handful of Akalis and sent a storm of bullets and balls through them. The Akalis were advancing with their characteristic impetuosity and dauntless courage but difficulties of ground and numbers seemed for a time, almost insuperable.

Their gallantry and the odds against which they were fighting so heroically, touched the heart of the Sikh Chief and he too decided to cast his lot with his brothers. He ordered the Sardars to back the Akalis according to the plan concerted in the Gurmata, while the Maharaja himself pushed forward. The battle now developed into a bloody struggle, and all the units strained all their nerves to wrest entrenchments of the hill tops. The stone covers and rugged heights proved too much for even the indomitable valour of the Maharaja's troops. The Maharaja at this juncture, proceeded in person to second the efforts and directed General Allard to sweep the hill with his cavaliers. Still the objective was not achieved.

The hour of noon has come but still the Ghazis have not been dislodged. The "Lion of the Punjab" seems at this moment, to wear the looks of despondency. But in a moment, the figure of the Akali leading his men on to the heights appears to turn the scales at once. The Chief gathers fresh strength, spurs his men to persevere and in an instant the Akalis burst upon the fortifications of their enemies. Just at this moment, a bullet breaks the knee-pan of the "mighty man of valour" and passing through lays the horse dead. The Akali jumps up and beckoning an elephant to be brought up, takes his seat in the Howdah and begins to direct his men.

The struggle now develops into a hand-to-hand combat. The whole pain resounds with the cries of 'Akal Akal' and 'Allah hu Akbar'. The friend and foe get inextricably mixed up. The Pandemonium is let loose, on the world.

The newsman runs up at this juncture with the information that Muhammad Azim Khan endeavours to push on his army to the other side of the river to succour the Ghazis. General Ventura has fortunately just joined with his train of artillery. He and Sardar Hari Singh are directed to dispute the passage of the Afghan Chief and keep his men pinned to the ford.

The Gurkha regiment is at the same time, directed to charge the hill. The Akalis have in the mean while routed he tribes, 'You have', shouted their leader, 'won the day but see that not a Ghazi escapes with life'. With a detour, therefore, the flying enemy is enveloped and cut down in thousands. A bullet from an Afghan carbine in this melee, pierces through the shoulder blade of the Akali commander, but it is not fatal, and he continues to ply right and left. The Khalsa forces are giving hot pursuit when another shot is lodged in the forehead; the hero reclines in the Howdah. A soldier takes the elephant aside, seats it down and feels the beloved Akali but life is extinct.

Sardar Hari Singh and General Ventura returning with the news of the flight of Muhammad Azim Khan completed the work of victory. This defeat of the Jehadis sealed the fate of the Frontier but alas! the Akali was no more.

The Maharaja cremated the body with full military honours, his war-torn features were relaxed and in the funeral ovation the veterans of a thousand fights were standing bathed in tears.

A monument was raised to the memory of the hero with vast lands of the village Pir Salak for its upkeep. But alas the present manager is frittering away the estate at his own sweet will.

Tales from Sikh History. Published by The Khalsa Historical and Literary Society, Rawalpindi, December 1917, pg. 27. (Extract).

*****

O Punjab of Guru Gobind Singh, Realise Thy Self

O Stones of the Punjab
Rise and sing His praise who made ye all souls
Fleshless men moved about as figures of Light,
Blessing all creation with their swords of the subtle flame,
They who passed Death's door freely and returned again,
Till Freedom was won for ye all.
When Guru Gobind Singh founded the Punjab as the heart of the world
A new heart made of God's own flesh,
Guru Gobind Singh Himself in every man
Future of the world's life starts from this beat of God's Heart.
The Kingdom of Righteousness the Khalsa triumphs
And nothing shall oppose the ideal
The Punjab spiritual as brought forth by Guru Gobind Singh
Like a seed would grow as all Humanity to come,
Guru Gobind Singh seated in every home of man,
The father of the child-man,
The playmate of the adult
And the son Himself
Claiming the soul as Khalsa
O Punjab of Guru Gobind Singh Realise thyself.

Brother Puran Singh, F.C.S. of Dehra Dun, *The Khalsa Advocate*, Saturday, January 19, 1918.

*****

"We have learnt with great concern and surprise that the local municipal committee, which is practically devoid of Sikh representation on it, has under contemplation the earthening up of Santokhsar. Santokhsar, as our readers know, is one of the four tanks that surround the Pool of Immortality – the Amritsar. It is a historic shrine sacred to the memory of Sri Guru Arjan Dev, and the biggest of the rest. Its state, no doubt, for some time back has been quite neglected and deplorable. But that affords no reason why it should be done away with at all. There are a hundred and one ways to mend it only if one cares to. The committee has so far been quite unsympathetic towards it and we seriously doubt if the apathy was not voluntary."

Article, *The Khalsa Advocate* (Amritsar), 9th March 1918.

*****

"Now take the relation of man with God, as preached by Guru Nanak. Man and woman are equal before one another and before God – a truth higher than ever preached before in India – nay, even in the whole world except in Arabia. Woman becomes more sacred, her dignity even higher than man's so much so that our Guru could not adore God but in her disguise. Christ could not think of a better relation between God and man than that of a father and son. With Guru Nanak, however, a wife's constancy to her husband represented more befittingly the relation between a faithful man and God. A son may not be the constant companion of his father after his marriage; but the wife is always wife, always constant always seeking support of her Lord and Love. During the foreign tyranny the effect of oppression was greatest on the Indian females. What was sadder still, they had lost respect even in the eyes of their own kinsmen. But, with the advent of Sikhism, where man became more precious in the sight of man woman too gained a dignity and respect, which though not amounting to that exaggerated worship so conspicuous in the west, was yet an unprecedented improvement on the relation existing between the sexes in India. The result was a kind of chivalry unlike anything that had appeared in Europe or Rajasthan. The Sikh became a knight, who had no personal motive, no passion of worldly love, to inspire him in the performance of his duty. The sight of wronged innocents or oppressed weakness was sufficient to move him to action. The Arthurian legends may be likened to King Rama's adventures, the Carolingian romances to Raja Rasalu's and the Armadis romances to the tales of Rajasthan. But for Sikh chivalry, we can find no parallel. The knights of all other chivalries belong to the court of gallant Indra, but the Sikh knights belong to the court of – whom else but Guru Nanak.

Woman has also gained the religious rights. Hinduism, like Judaism, had denied her practically all share in immortality. She had no personal religion, no spiritual responsibility, no claim, no part in the law of God. She was denied all access to holy scriptures. She was to remain content with the mere performance of domestic, social, and individual duties, never to vivify or heighten them by the rays of God's eternal love. Poor, Indian woman! Even in her happiest lot there is always felt a void in her heart, which ever - acting piety alone can fill; and she whose portion is to suffer, whose lot is lonely, O what misery must be hers, unless she can lean upon her God, and draw from His word the blessed conviction that she is not forgotten, that His love, His tenderness, are hers, far beyond the feeble conception of earth. Guru Nanak felt for the suffering woman-kind and gave them their full share in the goodness of God. Religious congregations were thrown open to them. They were to partake freely in all the religious and secular observances, and no social custom was to hinder them in doing so. Sikh women to this day seen attending all occasions of public worship, all conferences, along with the members of the other sex, and their conjoint as well as alternate singing, in which they often lead the chorus, must move the heart of every man, who wants to see what Guru Nanak did for woman kind.

Man who was told before that the body, being the source of sin, was to be condemned, that his continuing to live in the world was a crime, now was taught by Guru Nanak to believe that his body was the temple of the Supreme Being, and that, as such, instead of being mortified, it deserved to be cherished as a precious gift of God.

Guru Nanak's conception of God was also higher than the world had known it before. The God of the Mohammedans had too much of the fire of Hell and the chains and the rod of his wrath about him. The Hindus never had one God, or if they knew one, it was only at the head of a legion of god lings, a little God –

In his floating rest and snaky shade,
Who slumbers on beside the nectar urn.

With them their impersonal (*Nirgun*) God was too far above the world or indistinguishable from His own creation. As a (*Sargun*) personal God, He came in contact with them only in a supernatural way or through Avataras, which gave occasion to the rankest superstition. In Hinduism man does not walk with God as in Sikhism. Therefore we do not find prayer much used in Hinduism. Guru Nanak, on the other hand, lived in God as a fish in the water, and with God like a wife with her husband. He is in constant communion with Him through prayer.

Guru Nanak's moral laws are written on the tablets of eternity. They are not made up of human ideas and notions about things, which the mere increase of knowledge makes incredible. They are not mixed up with absurd miracles, revelations and mis-calculations about the creation of the world. The world may change its theories of life; it may overhaul the whole relations of science, history and what is received as religion, but Sikhism will not have to undergo any least change in its creed. Sikhs can only change by going out of Sikhism."

Guru Nanak and his mission, Part 1. By Teja Singh, Professor of English and History, Gordon Mission College, Rawalpindi. Published by The Sikh Tract Society, Mahilpore, March 1918. Doaba Educational Press, Lahore. (Extract).

*****

Sikhs and the Reforms

"We are glad to know that the draughtsmen of the scheme have been prudent enough, unlike Lords Morley and Minto, to recognise the claims of the important and loyal Sikh community to a separate electorate. It has been always recognised that the Sikhs are by far of the greatest political importance. Their gallant deeds of valour in the defence of the Empire now and ever since their connection with the British, have won for them an immortal place in the pages of history. While they form less than one per cent of the entire Indian population their honourable contribution of 20 per cent of the whole Indian Army, is a fair index of their war like spirit and loyal attitude.

At a time when the chivalrous deeds of the Sikh regiments (47th, 14th and numerous others) are quite fresh in the public mind and are inspiring the deeds of the British Army, the refusal of the Sikh demands would have been the greatest blunder.

But be it said to the credit of those at the helm of affairs that they have done what was exactly expected of them. We quote below the exact words in which separate representation for the Sikhs is proposed to be ceded to them:

We have been pressed to extend the concession (of communal representation) to other communities. Some have based their claims on their backward and others on their advanced condition. Thus the Sikhs in the Punjab, non-Brahmans in Madras, the Indian Christians, the Anglo Indians, and the Europeans have all asked for communal representations. The large land owning classes also generally desire representation in an electorate of their own. Now our decision to maintain special electorates for Mohammedans makes it difficult for us to resist these other claims. But as we have said, in the case of Mohammedans we have felt ourselves bound by promises given and renewed by Secretaries of State and Viceroys and in their respect at all events our recommendation involves no new departure. Any general extension of the communal system, however, would only encourage still further demands and would in our deliberate opinion be fatal to the development of representation on a national basis in which alone a system of responsible Government can be rooted.

At the same time we feel that there is one community from whom it is inexpedient to withhold this concession. The Sikhs in the Punjab are a distinct and important people. They supply a gallant and valuable element to the Indian Army, but they are everywhere in a minority and experience has shown us that they go virtually unrepresented. To the Sikhs therefore and to them alone we propose to extend the system already adopted in the case of Mohammedans.

The felicitous terms in which the concession is ceded to the Sikhs is really worthy of the enviable deeds of the great Sikh community. We feel grateful to Mr. Montagu and Lord Chelmsford for the recognition of the Sikh importance and demands."

Leader article, *The Khalsa Advocate*, Saturday, 13th July 1918.

*****

"Sikhism does not mean any particular set of mystical doctrines or speculative opinions. It is not the hysterical pietism of our so called saints, who confound extravagance with earnestness. Neither is it the mental jugglery of the modern or ancient philosopher who could in a moment prove you to be the veritable God or show you up to be a miserable vermin struggling hopelessly in the meshes of Maya, or against sin which was originally introduced into the world for the ultimate glorification of God. But it is a positive rule of conduct to be followed everywhere in life.

Divinity can reside as comfortably in the kindly heart of a weaver as in the crumpled brain of a philosopher. There are no higher or lower tasks in life. All tasks are noble, even the shoemakers. Guru Nanak was a shopkeeper, a Government servant, and, towards the end of his life, an agriculturist. The greatest charge that Dr. Trump and the Rev. Mr. Guilford have been able to bring against Guru Arjan is that he was engaged in trade. The charge is the creation of these gentlemen's own mind. But, even if true, is trading incompatible with religious life? The greatest glory of the Sikh scriptures is that they give an honourable place to the contributions of Ramdas a shoemaker, Sain a barber, Kabir a weaver, and Nam Dev a calico-printer! The thing is, in Sikhism all honest work is sacred. The qualities of head and heart required for the promotion of different occupations may not always be the same, but opportunities of service and energy to be spent in it are everywhere the same.

In ignorance of this truth, which is amply illustrated in the Sikh history, we begin to erect special programmes for our lives and consider ourselves not called for service so long as no extraordinary opportunities are offered to us. We wait for some heroic chance, when we may be able to justify our zeal for religion by offering to be burnt alive or suffer martyrdom in some approved out of the way fashion. In the meanwhile, as potential heroes, we go on merrily in a kind of moral twilight, singing hymns and blessing mankind, while exhorting others to do what we ourselves are unable even to attempt with all our saintliness and silent virtue. The whole life seems to be dedicated to making others good by – advice; as if being good or making good was as easy as a song: as if goodness did not require the whole experience, active as well spiritual, of a man's character. The practice of virtue is not a simple thing as the mere repetition of a text, or the singing of a sacred song. It has to be hammered out with the constant blows of active suffering and sacrifice. Our Guru himself has a very beautiful text for the preparation of a perfect character:

Thus is coined the ideal at the true Mint:
Patience the Smith works in Chastity's forge.
He melts the immortal nature in the melting pot of Love,
With the blast of Suffering and the bellows of God's tear,
And on the anvil of common sense he hammers it out with the hammer of Divine Word.*

* Japji, 38.

So far we have spoken of the individual experience. But that is not all. Human life is many sided. We may be placed as independent workers in ordinary affairs of life. There the rule of conduct to be followed is not necessarily the same as when we stand at the head of affairs when more than one individual is concerned. When duty is of a complex nature it may happen that one line of action is not reasonable, which in other cases might be quite justifiable.

The tender virtues like Humility, Mercy, Courtesy, etc., may in certain cases be inoperative and may not secure the moral end so well as the stern virtues of Courage, Justice, Honesty, etc. The inability of most other religions to realise this complexity and practical difficulty of religious duty has sorely tried their effectiveness before the modern world of increasing complexities. Their followers, unable to stretch their doctrines to cover the many sided activities of modern life, have relegated Faith to particular sets of opinions. Inquire of them, what a king should do? Or what a politician should do? They would say, "don't know! Ask a statesman". Sikhism is quite fit to meet the many sided questions of modern life."

The Sword and Religion by Teja Singh, Professor of English and History, Gordon Mission College, Rawalpindi. Published by The Sikh Tract Society, Lahore, September 1918, Doaba Educational Press, Lahore. (Extract).

*****

8

Tell my loved ones

I never cease thinking of the time when I parted from you at Lahore.

Many sons of mothers lie dead. It is God's will that this is so, and what is written is true.

Mother, think of me always as though I were sitting near by, just as I imagine you always as being beside me.

We are in a snare. We cannot escape.

Letters to family and loved ones were common in the censorships. This chapter brings some of these letters together, the majority from the Western Front but also some very interesting ones sent late in 1918 from Port Said in the Middle East. Letters flowed home across all of the Punjab, to mothers, fathers, brothers and sisters. It is interesting to note that numerous letters to and from Sikhs were from undivided Punjab and now many of these places would be found in modern day Pakistan. Little did the Sikh soldiers know that within 30 years the Punjab that they knew, farmed, fought over for centuries, would never be the same again.

Letters to family included news of loved ones and their possible return. Some early letters home from the war told family and relatives not to join up, "It is very sad. As soon as a man arrives here, he is killed", described a Sikh soldier. Many soldiers became weary of the war and sent despondent letters home. Letters home to mothers were quite emotional, usually discussing the probability of a return home, and missing home comforts and food.

Numerous Sikh soldiers implored their families to be strong, as strong as the French people they had seen during the war. The Sikh soldiers were very impressed with French women and bemoaned how Indian women were somewhat inferior. They felt embarrassed when French women asked why Indian women could not write letters. The Sikhs learnt many things from their long stay in France.

Near the end of the war in 1918, letters to family from Port Said in Egypt were sent to the Punjab from Sikhs fighting the Turks in the Middle East. These gave updates to family about their location and also the fact that the war was nearing its end.

*****

"My sister, I write with sorrow that Harnam Singh is a prisoner in the enemy's country. News of this will have reached you beforehand. We have heard that six men of our regiment are prisoners in Germany. They are quite well and happy, because the Germans deal very lovingly with the men of India & treat them very well. Now he is in no danger of his life. Have no anxiety on his behalf."

From Makhan Singh a clerk in the 47th Sikhs serving in France to his sister in India. (Urdu, dated 14/3/15).

*****

"The General has announced that in a week or two a large force is coming from England and then the Lahore & Meerut Divisions will be sent back to India. So I can expect to be certain to see you in May or June next, granted that I am spared. We shall ask to be sent to Jullundur. Perhaps we shall be sent there perhaps not; but we shall try our best."

From a sepoy in the 47th Sikhs in France to a friend at Jullundur in the Punjab. (Urdu, dated 14/3/15).

*****

"When are you coming to dig trenches? Let me know and we shall come to see you. We have time for this. Do the Sirkar's work quietly. This will be to your advantage. I have seen the state of the men in the third (Cavalry); it is very bad. (Follow some illegible letters). Such a state of affairs ought never to be. When you go to fetch milk, wait for it outside. Do not enter anyone's house. Do the Sirkar's work and get into bed. Be ready to do at once any work that comes to you. Never be absent. This is my earnest advice."

From Dula Singh (No.2069?) unit not stated, (P.O.13), to Lance Naik Buga Singh, 3rd Skinner's Horse. (Urdu, 6/7/15).

*****

"There is a lull in the trench fighting, but the fighting at sea is very fierce. So all the ships have been stopped. There is only one way open and by that way the journey to Bombay takes six months. In England the nights are very short. They only last for five hours. It rains every day. The men do not do so much work as the dogs. The dogs churn most of the butter. Railway trains run seven storeys up off the ground. There is a track on each storey. If one who has left goods in pawn takes them away, there is no cause for lamentation."

From Santa Singh, now in hospital at Barton, to his mother in India. (Gurmukhi, 20/7/15).

*****

"I will tell you about the war, though you must not tell those at home. Do not come to the war, even though they give you a Jemadari. Dry bread at home is better than that."

From Naik Narayan Singh in hospital in England, to his brother in India. (Gurmukhi, 21/7/15).

*****

"I have often written this to you before, but you have perhaps forgotten. Do not mix with bad men who steal and commit such crimes. Do all you can to help the government. Men who are on the side of order in this crisis are in a strong position while those who are against it, stealing and robbing, are (so it seems from what we read in our daily letters) being put in jail right and left for their crimes. Be wise, attend to your own business, and you will live in peace."

From Kishen Singh, 4th Cavalry, France, to a friend in India. (Urdu, 16/8/15).

*****

"I did not see Thakur Singh. It is very sad. As soon as a man arrives here, he is killed."

From Labh Singh, 59th Rifles, France, to a friend in India. (Gurmukhi, 16/8/15).

*****

"As tired bullocks and bull buffaloes lie down in the month of Bhadon* so lies the weary world. Our hearts are breaking, for a year has passed while we stood to arms without a rest. x x x x Germany fights the world with ghastly might, harder to crush than well soaked grain in the mill. For even wetted grain can be ground in time. x x x We have bound ourselves by oath under the flag and we must give our bodies."

*August-September. When the tanks are full of water, from which it is often difficult to dislodge tired and hot cattle.

From Santa Singh, hospital, Brighton, to his uncle in India. (Gurmukhi, 18/8/15).

*****

"My father is dead. Our house is destroyed. Ganda Singh has been imprisoned for seven years and we shall die here. There is no way of escape. Only the lucky man returns and the man who loses an arm or a leg."

From a Sikh in hospital, Brighton, to Mangal Singh, 10th Lancers, India. (No language stated).

*****

"WE perish in the desert, YOU wash yourself and lie in bed. We are trapped in a net of woe, while you go free. Our life is a living death. For what great sin are we being punished? Kill us, Oh God, but free us from our pain! We move in agony, but never rest. We are slaves of masters who can show no mercy. The bullets fall on us like rain, but dry are our bodies. So we have spent a full year. We cannot write a word. Lice feed upon our flesh, we cannot wait to pick them out. For days we have not washed our faces. We do not change our clothes. Many sons of mothers lie dead. It is God's will that this is so, and what is written is true. God The Omnipotent plays a game, and men die. Death here is dreadful, but of life, there is not the briefest hope."

Poem by Santa Singh in a letter to his wife – (Gurmukhi, 18/9/15).

*****

"It is beginning to be cold again here. The place is good enough. Anyone who came here could study and learn a lot, but he would need much money. The education of Europe is exceedingly good. I think every one who came here and took pains (would profit by so doing). Well it is not a question of our powers, but of money."

From Nanak Singh, Rishi, at Rouen, to Gurmukh Singh, his son, Rawal Pindi, India. (Urdu, 27/9/15).

*****

"I never cease thinking of the time when I parted from you at Lahore. It will be the great kindness of the Guru if we meet again. Write and tell me all your news and do not do any sort of villainy. If my conduct had been good, why should I have come to this place? Mind your own business at home and stay there and attempt no evil with any man. Do that which is sukh (pleasant) and not that which is dukh (disagreeable) ....You write that you have bought a she-buffalo. That is very good news. You also write that both calves have been ill. Write and let me know how they fare. I am very anxious. Treat them with great kindness. And on the day on which you begin to drink the (juice of the) sugar-cane, on that day give them your gur and moth (lentil) as fodder."

From Sepoy Ishwar Singh, 57th Rifles, France, to his brother Sundar Singh, Jullundur Dt., Punjab, India. (Urdu, 28/10/15).

*****

"When I read your letter my heart was more happy than I can describe. My body swelled with joy till my clothes could not retain it. I was as pleased as the husbandman when he sees the rain falling, as the babiha when the rain drops fall on his head. I longed for your letter as the calf longs for its mother's milk."

From Mukand Singh, Jullundur Brigade, France, to Man Singh, Nabha. (Gurmukhi, no date stated).

*****

"I am very well. Do not be anxious. Uncle Hira Singh is very well. Do not be anxious. It is very cold here, but we get plenty of warm clothes........................Has Ujagar Singh not yet entered the service? Let me know the date on which he does so. We are all well here. Have no anxiety on our account."

From Indar Singh, 9th Hodson's Horse, France, to his father, Ferozpur Dt. Punjab, India. (Urdu, 28/11/15).

*****

"Chur Singh has suffered martyrdom in the war. The 47th Sikhs were charging, --- Sahib said 'Chur Singh, you are not a Sikh of Guru Govind Singh, who sit in fear inside the trench!' Chur Singh was very angry. Chur Singh gave the order to his company to charge. He drew his sword and went forward. A bullet came from the enemy and hit him in the mouth. So did our brother Chur Singh become a martyr. No other man was like Jemadar Chur Singh."

From a sepoy of the 47th Sikhs in hospital, Brighton, to a friend in India. (Gurmukhi, 14/12/15).

*****

"Never write again such things in your letters as before. If you have any need of anything, money or the like, write and say so. For our letters are read before they reach us, and if such things are written in a man's letters, it is not well for him."

From ? F.P.O.No.15 (29th Lancers or 36th Jacob's Horse), France, to his wife at home. (Gurmukhi, 22/12/15).

*****

"I have had no letter from Jhanda Singh since he embarked. If one has come to you, let me know. I am very anxious, because of late many ships have been sunk. We have a great deal of work, and it is very cold. It is always raining. We have been dismounted and have to do duty as infantry."

From Bhagat Singh, F.P.O.No.39 (38th C.I.Horse or 2nd Lancers), France, to his home in India. (Gurmukhi, 24/12/15).

*****

"I spoke about our departure in my former letter. That is all wrong. We are still in France. The former order has been cancelled. If there should come any other, I will let you know. No date has yet been fixed for our departure."

From Bhawgan Singh, H.Q.? Cavalry Brigade, France, to his mother, Rai Bareilly, India. (Urdu, 10/1/16).

*****

"My dear brother, your letter reached me and gave me great pleasure, and I understood all that was in it. But it gave me even more pain than pleasure, more than I can say. It was my fate (to serve as a soldier). What can I do? But you acted with great folly and stupidity. Well, you ought not to have done this. If you had to enlist, you should have written to me and I should have given you an answer after due consideration. But you know nothing of all this. The wise have said "Dry bread at home is good as a feast abroad." I am older than you. You should have consulted me &c &c." (all against enlistment).

From Jit Singh, F.P.O. No.18, France, to Sepoy Asa Singh, 15th Sikhs Depot, Multan, India. (Urdu, 11/1/16).

*****

"Now we meet by letter, we cannot meet otherwise. Kali Das has said:
The mother seeks the embraces of her son,
Putting the fear of her husband from her heart,
One says, 'My sisters, what need is there of sight,
When the blind have pointed out the way?'
The deaf have received the message of the telegraph
And the dumb have chanted a hymn,
Eunuchs have made marriage, and she-asses are fed on cream,
Cripples go hunting and the hare pursues the lion
The gnat devours the tiger and the time comes that roses stink.
Folk inhale filth and silk is so hard that no hand can touch it,
Stones become softer than wax, the sea is drained,
And the man without hands grips the lance,
Cows and she-buffaloes give milk no more
And the bull-buffaloes fills the pail with milk.
Palaces are built of sand and the 'air' supplies the beams,
The owl grows mournful in the forest and quits the desolate place,
The charitable draws back his hand and the miser scatters largesse.
The king begs for alms and the needy gives to all comers,
The sparrow strikes the hawk and the elephant fights with ants.
The mango and pomegranate are torn up by the roots,
And the thorn is planted in their stead.
The sweeper turns capitalist and lends to the Khattri, who begs for luck-pennies,
Croesus is beggared and asks for an obol by the roadside,
The pimp is seated on the committee and the Todar Mal serves as an orderly.
The infidel repeats the five prayers and the Qazi omits his morning ablution,
The sheep bathes in the Ganges, and women ascend the pulpit.
The Raja leaves his pleasure and becomes an ascetic, and the washerman tries to bleach black garments,
The grasshopper grows breasts and comes into milk, and the rat kills cats.
No one cares for the parrot or the mynah, but cages and teaches the crow,
The swan flees away and the 'bagla' feeds on pearls,
The devil says to God "Why hast Thou made false warfare to be regarded as true?"
My brother, these words that I have written to you, why have I written them? If they are all true, then I can meet you again. But if Kali Das wrote them falsely, then shall we never meet again."

From Bhan Singh, 6th Cavalry (?), France, to Hira Singh, Jullundur Dt., India. (Gurmukhi, 30/1/16).

*****

"Mulkhi was at first at school in Sham Chaurasi. Then he went to Khalsa High School at Jullundur, and was initiated into Sikhism. Anyhow he was quite devoted to his studies, when some boy stole all his clothes and other things from the boarding-house. His grandfather fitted him out completely afresh. But the boy who had stolen his clothes was never found. A few days afterwards Mulkhi took another boy's clothes and some cash. But he was found out. He was ashamed to go back to the school. He went straight off, and without asking anyone enlisted in the 21st Punjabis at Quetta. I had made all arrangements by letter for his betrothal to the daughter of a dafadar of my regiment. When the dafadar went to see Mulkhi (Mulkha Singh), this was the account of him that he got from the school. He went straight back to Sialkot. The whole story was in a letter which I had from home and I meant to put that letter in an envelope and send it to you. But I dropped it somewhere. So now I am sending you this brief account of Mulkhi........There has been no rain in our country and there is a great dearth of fodder.........Live in unity all together and call ever on the name of the Guru. Keep yourselves from the society of strangers."

From Bishen Singh, 19th Lancers, France, to Daulati, Box 6 Marysville, California, U.S.A. (Urdu & Gurmukhi, 9/2/16).

*****

"This (France) is a very fine country. The father and mother invite a visitor to kiss them. If he declines, they are offended. Then all the family, men and women, indulge in indecent talk, and are very much amused. In the presence of the father, one will say to two others "Go and sleep together", and they will all laugh. It is indeed a very free and easy country. Nothing is prohibited, whatever maybe done. In the presence of the father and brothers, one (a man) will catch another (a girl) by the arm and lead her outside. They (the father and brother) will say nothing. They are quite at ease."

Note: The above was excised from the letter as being calculated to convey a wrong impression and discredit our Allies in India.

From Lance-Dafadar Chanda Singh, to his wife Pertab Kor, Lahore, Punjab, India. (Gurmukhi, 15/2/16).

*****

"I have understood what you wrote. What you have heard as to our being made Musalmans, is quite untrue. There are no Musalmans in this country, and all that you say is untrue. There is only one caste (i.e. religion) in this country...........No one says anything to us here (i.e. interferes with our religion).

And those of our brethren who have gone there (i.e. those who have gone to Germany as prisoners) are made much of there. Be quite clear on this point. We have not entered the trenches this year. We stay in villages behind (the fighting line). We have no privations. We get milk. We make tea three times a day. We don't know at all where the war is (i.e. we are so comfortable that one would not think there was any war). We have nice houses to live in and chairs to sit on at all times. We don't know in which country the war is, so do not have any anxiety on my account. I am not like a cowardly rat that stays in its hole. I am at the front. And what people say that those who go to the war are dead men. That is false. True I might die sometime. Today, or tomorrow. Then why are you anxious. Don't you like the idea of death in the field of battle? We consider it very meritorious. Many fine fellows amongst our brethren have died on the field of battle and who are we (that we should shrink from the sharing the same fate?). And those of our brethren who have died on the field live for ever (i.e. their names are always honoured)."

From Maha Singh, Sialkot Cavalry Brigade, France, to his wife Jewan Kor, Patiala, Punjab. (Gurmukhi, 25/2/16).

*****

"I desire that Makhan Singh (writer's son) should not be made to wear jewellery. He should instead be well clothed..........In this country no articles of jewellery are placed on young children. Still the children are more beautiful than I can describe. I hope you will abstain from getting jewellery (for the children)."

From Bir Singh, Ambala Cavalry Brigade, France, to Prem Singh, Nakodar, Jallandar, Punjab. (Urdu, 31/3/16).

*****

"I learn from your letter that Basant Singh, Kehar Singh, and Mohan Singh have gone to the war. Tell me whether their regiment has gone, or whether they have gone in reinforcement to some other regiment, so that I also may write to them. Do not grieve because they have gone to the war; have faith in the Guru. If a man is destined to live, a single hair of his head will not be disarranged (by the war)."

From Bhagat Singh, 38th C.I. Horse, France, to Santa Singh, Amritsar. (No language, no date).

*****

"I must let you know that I have no intention whatever of trying to get back to India before the close of the war. If I live I hope to return in about two years because there is no hope of peace until the enemy is thoroughly beaten and I can't come home before then unless I should be severely wounded. This is as God shall decree. Ordinary sickness or an ordinary wound will not bring me back. You must therefore arrange marriages and do all that is necessary for the house. This is the time for me to serve the Government and also to get some distinction for myself."

From Dafadar Tara Singh, Sialkot Cavalry Brigade, France, to Gujar Singh, Ludhiana, India. (Urdu, 10/4/16).

*****

"I received your letter in which you complain that you have not heard from me for a whole month. I am very much ashamed about this as I write every week. It is no doubt true that you have not heard, since the Germans have sunk many ships, among them occasionally the Mail ship."

From Hazura Singh, Sialkot Cavalry Brigade, France, to his mother, Ludhiana District, Punjab, India. (Urdu, 29/4/16).

*****

"I have received your letter and understood its contents. I, with my own eyes, saw you fall wounded by a bullet and for this reason it is not necessary for me to write more than is sufficient. If Government does not invalid and pension you on the one hand, or keep you as sick in a hospital on the other, take your discharge. Do not put yourself to trouble. God will provide something, more or less, for you at home. The wages of the soldier are for the fit. For the rest you are able to judge for yourself. Tell the Doctor sahib frankly that if the Sirkar considers you fit, you desire to be discharged, as you are not a malingerer. Health means everything. You know the saying 'If a man has health, he has the whole world.'"

From Attar Singh, Sialkot Cavalry Brigade, France, to his son Chanan Singh, 2nd Lancers, Saugor, India. (Gurmukhi, 17/5/16).

*****

"I have received and understood your letter. You say that I intentionally do not return on leave, since my fellows have all returned. You speak truly. No doubt I had privation at home, whereas here I am very comfortable. For when I was at home, I slept in a string cot, now in the battlefield I get a real spring bed with a mattress and quiet spot to place it in. As home I used to get coarse bread, whereas here I get cakes of wheaten flour. When I get so many fine things here to eat and wear what shall I get by going home! This is what is passing in your mind. Now listen and I will tell you the reality of my situation. First answer me this question – on the battlefield is there comfort or trouble? Ask those who have been invalided from here and pensioned. You sit at home and invent ideas. My soul knows and God knows the true state of affairs. You, sitting in the bosom of your family and conversing with your friends, what do you know? The trials which we have to undergo are beyond description, and we are not permitted to write about them. To sleep on the bare ground at all times, to have insufficient food with no certainty as to when you will get it. To be well for ten days and ill for five. To be constantly anxious about those at home. To be concerned about my own life. Yet you say "he has forgotten his home as he does not come"! Why don't you say at once, "he has gone on a visit to his wife's relatives, or he is enjoying a stroll in the bazaar at Anarkali (Lahore), and that is why he does not come"! And you look, great generals and Colonels whose salary ranges from Rs. 2500 to Rs. 3500 per mensem, and whose homes are only 4 hours distant, are not allowed, even one day's leave, to go and see their families, and what are we that we should get leave! The journey going and returning occupies three months. You, at home, and all our friends, no doubt, have made up your minds that none of us who have come to the war, will return alive. We expect the same. Now, what have you to say. You be wise, and should act prudently. About the marriage if Narain Singh offers marriage accept it. What more do you want? Harnam (his wife) is no doubt very unlucky. I know this well. She thinks that I have run away and deserted her. I am very lucky on the other hand, since, (she says) I sleep in houses on real beds. As a fact, I have neither comfort by day nor sleep at night. Let Harnam Kor know that pleasure and pain are a portion of our lot on earth. Do not write such things in your letter again. Before, I was resigned and settled in mind, but since reading your letter I am plunged in grief."

From Rurh Singh, 38th C.I. Horse, France, to Kehar Singh, Lyalpur Dt., Punjab. (Gurmukhi, 23/5/16).

*****

"You tell me to take leave and come home for the marriage. You are a sensible man, and you have intercourse with those who know the state of affairs, and yet you write and tell me to take leave and return! Is this the time to ask for leave and can anybody give leave? If they (the bride's people) insist on my returning and say it is possible for me to get leave, well, two of their family are here viz: Surain Singh and Chattar Singh, let them send for them to return and see what happens. If they return, I will return too. If they (the bride's people) wish to marry her elsewhere, let them do so; it is of no consequence. Don't you realise how far away I am? It is not possible to come away from here until the war is over. If they (the bride's people) are now so persistent, where were they when I was in Cantonments in India? At that time I could have got as much leave as I desired. The present is not the time to get leave. Do not write petitions to my Commanding Officer. People will ridicule me. Do you think of what is proper or not? Alas!"

From Natha Singh, 38th C.I. Horse, France, to Harnam Singh, Amritsar, Punjab. (Urdu, 23/5/16).

*****

"Nowadays the fighting is very violent everywhere. There has been a great naval battle, in which 14 British and 15 German ships were sunk. Amongst the German losses were two very big ships. The fighting took place in the sea between Germany and Norway. One or two German ships in addition to the above are missing. One ship costs a crore of rupees to build. In size it is equal to a village. The loss of life will be known later. In this naval battle the Germans have suffered very heavy loss. Nowadays, the Germans are making very violent attacks in the direction of Verdun. In two days they have expended as much ammunition, as had been consumed previously in the entire war. Notwithstanding this intense bombardment, and all other efforts made by them, the Germans were entirely unsuccessful. It seems likely that the war will end this year."

From Bishan Singh, Sialkot Cavalry Brigade, France, to Arjan Singh, Jullundur, Dt., Punjab. (Urdu, 6/6/16).

*****

"I hope some day that I shall again be the light of your eyes because, so far as I can see, there is no fear of my being extinguished. About the future, no one cares. When I write in this way to my wife, perhaps you, and the others who hear the letter read, think it a matter to be ashamed of. If you do, it is due to ignorance on your part, which makes you misconstrue my meaning. Experience in Europe makes one realize that we (in India) are like stones. For this reason I wish, and in fact earnestly desire, to consider as shameful things only thieving, lying and evil deeds."

From Ralla Singh, Dafadar, Sialkot Cavalry Brigade, France, to his father Harnam Singh, Ludhiana Dt., Punjab. (Urdu, 7/6/16).

*****

"Mother, the news is that once only in five months I have not received a letter from you. My thoughts are always with you. Mother, put your ear down and listen to me, do not fret and I will soon be with you again. Put your trust in God, and imagine that I have merely gone to Lyallpur, think that I have been delayed there by the Sirdar or that I am not yet ready to return home. Mother, think of me always as though I were sitting near by, just as I imagine you always as being beside me. Be of good cheer mother, because there is nothing that I have done which is hidden from you. I tell you truly Mother, I will salute you again. Do not grieve, for I tell you confidently, that I shall bow before you again in salutation. I will come in the dead of night and knock at your door, and I will call loudly so that you may wake and come and open the door to me. With great delight you will open the door and hold me to your breast in a loving embrace. I will then sit beside you and narrate all that has happened to me of good and evil. Then, having rested the night in comfort, I will go out after daylight has come. Those brethren of the Khalsa whom I meet, I will salute. Returning home, I will eat my bread with pleasure and happiness. You, mother, will say to me "Shall I give you some ghi?" I will shake my head in refusal and say "Mother, I do not want any." You will press me to have some, and I will gently push my plate towards you. You will fill the plate with ghi, and I shall eat it with much delight. Believe, Mother, that this homecoming will take place, just as I have described it. I see you constantly before me. It seems to me as if it were but yesterday that I bent to your feet in salutation, while you placed your hand lovingly on my head. I am indeed a very fortunate man to see you again so, in imagination."

From Thakur Singh, 38th C.I. Horse, France, to his mother, Amritsar Dt., Punjab, India. (Gurmukhi, 7/6/16).

*****

"Tell your mother that the marriage cannot take place before my return. If it is performed in my absence, there will be trouble for all of you. I wrote and told you before that if Sohan Lal is in a hurry let him do as he pleases, but it would be well to wait for my return – otherwise it would not be a matter for congratulation. At the end of the war, a marriage could be arranged elsewhere. I do not think it proper that the marriage should be performed while I am away. Think over this matter well and explain it to your mother. There is only a little time left and so there is need to hurry. Sunt Singh is now doing very good work, and I do not wish that he should take his discharge solely on account of this marriage. He would incur disgrace for generations before the Sircar. This is not the way with Indian Officers. It is the duty of a soldier at the present crisis to do his work well and faithfully and not to show any weakness. Sundar Singh, cook, has reached Ambala. He was afraid of the work. Here all the cooks and other servants are well, and have no trouble of any kind. What he says about the troubles and difficulties of this place is all lies. He speaks so because he is ashamed and does not wish people to know that he was afraid......Everyone will return home in a short time."

From Pertab Singh, Resaldar, 30th Lancers, Marseilles, France, to Hazura Singh, Ambala, Punjab, India. (Urdu, 26/6/16).

*****

"I have received dear Nand Kor's letter full of love. On reading it my heart is troubled. I know very well that he who loves truly, ardently returns love; but we, nowadays are absorbed in such a work that we have lost all capacity for love. Alas that we should have become so stony-hearted!"

From Rala Singh, Jemadar, Sialkot Cavalry Brigade, France, to Indar Singh, Jagraon, Ludhiana District, Punjab. (Urdu, 22/7/16).

*****

"As far as possible keep your conduct blameless, because a man can derive much benefit through good conduct. Conduct has a great effect on one's life. One should not hesitate even to sacrifice one's life of one's family, one's country or for one's King. Whenever any opportunity offers itself to show bravery one should immediately grasp it. One should never lose confidence in the power of the Guru Maharaj. When your time comes to reap advantage, you will certainly do so. There is plenty of time yet. Keep on doing the Sircar's work faithfully, and the Sircar will assuredly reward you. When victory has been obtained the Sircar will surely reward you with honours and with land."

From Kartar Singh, Risaldar, 35th Sindh Horse, Jabalpur, India, to Dalip Singh, 35th Sindh Horse, attached 36th Jacob's Horse, France. (Urdu, 3/8/16).

*****

"There is no information up to the present time about Sukha Singh. A letter has been received by Man Singh from his son Harbachan Singh who is a prisoner of war in Turkey. He says he is quite well and happy. I expect we shall also hear from Sukha Singh some day."

From Hazara Singh, 36th Jacob's Horse, France, to his mother, Ludhiana Dt. (Gurmukhi, 25/10/16).

*****

"I have every hope that we shall soon meet. Either I shall come on leave or the regiment will be relieved. The names and numbers of all the men who have been here since 1914 have been sent into the office, and something will come of it. Either we shall be granted leave or we shall be relieved, that is quite certain."

From Mian Singh, 6th Cavalry, France, to his wife, Patiala State, India. (Gurmukhi, 30/10/16).

*****

"Tell my mother that I am very comfortable, indeed more comfortable than I would be at home and she should not worry. It is only that I am always dying for a sight of my dear ones and I lack nothing else. Tell the women to be brave like men. I am astonished to see the women of France, beautiful as they are, they brace themselves up and show greater pluck even than men. They are even ready to arm themselves and take part in the fighting. My mother and wives ought to show courage like them."

From Chada Singh, Field Post Office No.18 to Indar Singh, Ludhiana, India. (Urdu dated the 6th November, 1916).

*****

"The regiment is not returning at all, and what Risaldar Narain Singh said about the matter is entirely false. Leave will probably be given to a very few men, those who have urgent affairs at home. I am not likely to get leave, nor do I wish to go, even if I could succeed in obtaining permission, till the war is finished. Because if I were to go on leave, it would be very hard to return. When I used to go on leave before, I used to be very disciplined to return to the Cantonment, how much more disciplined then would I be to return to the war! When I return I will tell you all about the war. It is impossible to write about it. The war will not be finished for a very long time. It will certainly not be finished before 1918. My regiment will certainly not return. The Guru Maharaj has kept me alive for 2½ years, is it likely then that he will not keep me alive for another 2 years? I have pledged myself not to return (on leave or ill) until I return with the entire Regiment."

From Hazur Singh, 6th Cavalry, France to his mother, Ludhiana District, Punjab, India. (Urdu dated the 30th November, 1916).

*****

"The work for which we came to Europe is still unfinished and therefore I have little time to write letters. You write to me to get leave and come home somehow or other as the household affairs are going to rack and ruin. Whatever happens until we conquer the German b_____s nothing can be done, whatever happens at home. When we have got the Germans down we shall come home with great joy. I long to see the old people again but I don't see how I can get back to India."

From Tara Singh, F.P.O. D.6 to Gopal Singh, Rawal Pindi. (Urdu, dated the 18th December, 1916).

*****

"The treatment which we have received here at the hands of our king is such, that no son or daughter could have received from hands of a father. You must of course be anxious about me, because I am so far removed from your eyes; but know well, that all the days of our sojourn in this country are days passed in a living paradise. Other people see paradise after death, and then only if their fate is good; but we through the favour of God have seen paradise with our living eyes. What is spoken of as the Millennium of Truth, is already in this country. These people (the French) always speak the truth. There is neither treachery, nor theft, nor deceit, nor backbiting, nor slander amongst them. In short we have never seen, man, woman or child at strife with each other, nor have we seen anyone weeping. In fact, I have neither got the words nor the pen adequately to praise these people."

From Santa Singh, 21st Calvary attached 20th Deccan Horse, France to Indar Singh, Ludhiana District, Punjab, India. (Gurmukhi dated the 22nd of December, 1916).

*****

"Do not be disturbed. The Sircar has sanctioned leave to 5 per cent. The names have been sent in and accepted. Orders have been issued for us to be ready to leave. We will leave as soon as permission is given. Owing to dangers en route, leave has been postponed for a little while. As soon as the route has been cleared of dangers, leave will commence. My Sahib (superior British Officer) will write when I leave, and say that as I have done such good work here, I should be retained in India. Therefore, if God wills, we will leave in about a month."

From Hira Singh, Sub-Assistant Surgeon, Lucknow Field Ambulance, France to his brother Gurbachan Singh, Bhera, Shahpur, Punjab, India. (Gurmukhi dated the 26th December, 1916).

*****

"I hear that Sirdar Chattarpal Singh wants very much to join. You must try and get him into some good regiment. You must try and remove any doubts he may have just as you did with Teja Singh. As regards the latter, you must go and see his Sahibs and see what you can do about his promotion. Do not think at all of the fact that if Chatterpal joins you will have three sons serving. If it is the Guru's will we shall escape even from blazing fire. If we help the Government on such an occasion as this we shall reap our rewards. Take him to the Deputy Commissioner and make him join and don't listen to what people say."

From Hazura Singh, 38th Central India Horse, France to his father Risaldar Indar Singh, Pensioner, Lahore. (Urdu dated the 8th January, 1917).

*****

"The news of the death of Munsha Singh was a great shock to me and I grieved greatly; but resignation to the will of God is our only recourse. No one can estimate the losses which this terrible war has occasioned. Many noble families have been completely wiped out by death and not a single person has escaped to mourn their death. Grief for such losses is unseemly, as they occurred in the Field of Honour, and so we also should not grieve for our loss. This world is the abode of trouble and trials, and if one desires to get any happiness in it, it is necessary to be resigned."

From Gurbakhs Singh, 19th Lancers, France to Punjab Singh, Zemindar, Hoshiarpur, Punjab, India. (Urdu dated the 22nd January, 1917).

*****

"Be cautious in spending money on jewellery (for the marriage). Money put into jewellery is lost. If jewellery must be provided, let it be small in quantity and of gold. In no other country but ours do women wear jewellery. We should certainly imitate them. Moreover, they do not marry till they are more than 20 years of age."

From Indar Singh, 29th Lancers, France to Gopal Singh, Amritsar, Punjab, India. (Urdu dated the 22nd January, 1917).

*****

"In this country every man and woman is literate. When they ask us here why our women are illiterate, we cannot give them an answer. They say "who writes your letters at home?" These things cause us to be ashamed. Learning is an excellent thing, make arrangements for my daughters to be taught."

From Chattar Singh, 38th Central India Horse (?), France to Sirdar Hira Singh, Jullundur District, Punjab. (Gurmukhi dated the 31st January, 1917).

*****

"I have sent you thrice before pictures of his Majesty. As you framed those and put them up on the wall opposite the door, so do the same with this portrait after framing it. Worship it every morning when you get up. This is an act of religious merit and the portrait will be a memorial. Every morning pray to the Guru that He will give victory to the King. Do not be anxious about me. I am quite happy."

From Jemadar Khizan Singh, 36th Jacob's Horse to his wife, Nabha, India. (Gurmukhi dated the 6th February, 1917). (Enclosure, New Year's Card for Indian troops).

*****

"It is very wrong of you to work yourself up into a state of illness through anxiety for me. Just look at the people here. The women have their husbands killed and yet they go on working just as hard as ever. It does one's heart good to see them. May God teach our women to behave like them! You must let these words sink into your heart and must be brave as a man."

From Jivan Singh, Wardi Major, 2nd Lancers to his wife, Gurdaspur, Punjab. (Urdu dated the 7th February, 1917).

*****

"We are serving the Sircar well and have no anxiety about the war. Lakhs of other mothers' sons are also present at the war. We are not tobacco consumers. We are Sikhs, and the duty of the Sikhs is to exalt in battle and show their prowess. When we were in India, except for God, we feared no one, and enlisted of our own free will. Now people say we enlisted from fear of the police; but we have no regard for Lumbardars or Police or anyone else. If we had had anything to fear from the police, we should have soon settled accounts with them. Our object (in enlisting) was to obtain some benefit from the Sircar and now people say we enlisted from fear of the police! Let it be well known that if anyone oppresses our families or injures our crops, we will, if our lives are spared, return and deal out to them just what they have dealt out to us."

From Jewan Singh, 19th Lancers, France to Nur Din, Chokidar, Sialkot District, Punjab, India. (Urdu dated the 4th March, 1917).

*****

"Leave is closed. When you write to me in future or to any other officer, do not say anything either about leave or marriage. It is very improper to write about these matters and all the officers get annoyed when they are mentioned in letters. For this reason, never write anything concerning these matters. Leave cannot be granted so do not ever send in a petition regarding leave (for me). I have no difficulties or inconvenience of any kind."

From Naubat Singh, 6th Cavalry, France to Mathra Singh, Rawal Pindi District, Punjab, India. (Urdu dated the 6th March, 1917).

*****

"I have received your letter, and note your wishes; but unfortunately French watchmakers will not mend a watch which was made in Germany. I don't know why."

From Sewa Singh, 6th Cavalry, France to Chattar Singh, Jullundur District, Punjab, India. (Urdu dated the 25th March, 1917).

*****

"The reason why I have not written recently is that for the last month the entire Cavalry has been in the front line. At the present time the Germans are growing weak and, leaving a front of 19 miles, have gone back. We have been brought to the trenches for the work of patrolling this conquered country. When an opportunity offers, we will also join in the attack. Our Army is continually on the move and the enemy is in retreat, many German prisoners are being taken."

From Sant Singh, 19th Lancers, France to his mother, Rae Bareilly, U.P., India. (Urdu dated the 22nd April, 1917).

*****

"Do not suppose that there is a disgrace in losing one's eyes. You can always get a glass eye put in. In Europe in this war numbers of men have lost limbs and eyes. This is an act of God and it is of no consequence. It is not a thing to be ashamed of in my opinion. As for what you say about my return, if my life is spared I hope to be back in October."

From Jemadar Ghalla Singh, No. 17 F.P.O. to his wife, Ludhiana, India. (Urdu dated the 10th May, 1917).

*****

"I had a dream on the night of the 6th and saw Gulzar Singh who looked very well indeed and was well dressed but there was nothing on his head. I was very pleased to see him and then my eyes opened and I was terribly disappointed to find it was a dream. Although residence in Europe has modified our ideas a good deal, still I cannot think this was a good dream. May the Guru Sahib keep Gulzar Singh and all of you from all harm."

From Nand Singh, 6th Cavalry, France to his father, Rawal Pindi, India. (Urdu dated the 13th May, 1917).

*****

"Look, my mother, do not allow anxiety to enter your mind. I am quite well. You must have heard all about my condition from Ishar Singh and Jeswant Singh. My condition is quite satisfactory. Have no concern about me, mother. I shall return soon. I am not one that will die here. The war is about to end, and I shall be at home before the next winter begins."

From Kartar Singh, 6th Cavalry, France to his mother, Jullundur District, Punjab, India. (Urdu dated the 11th June, 1917).

*****

"This long separation has unsettled my mind. God knows when this calamity (of war) will be removed from us, and a new spirit enter our half dead bodies. Why has our Government ceased to think of us who have been exiled from our native country for three years, while at the same time diverse calamities are devastating our homes? Why cannot something be done to release us from this servitude? There must be hundreds of fresh men in India who are only too ready to come in our place."

From Jagat Singh, 19th Lancers, France to Jai Singh, Kot Dafadar, 19th Lancers, Sialkot, Punjab, India. (Urdu dated the 18th July, 1917).

*****

"We have expectations that the Sircar will make some arrangement for us this year. I have been saying "I will come today. I will come tomorrow", simply to encourage you but no one really knows what is going to happen. Hundreds and thousands of men of various nationalities are collected together."

From Kartar Singh, Kot Dafadar, 19th Lancers, France to his wife, Rawal Pindi, Punjab, India. (Gurmukhi dated the 28th July, 1917).

*****

"You say that you are about to write a petition for my return. Do nothing of the kind. If you do it, I will not return, and I will cease to write to you. See to it, that you do not disgrace me in this way. I am engaged in the war, and have no desire for matrimony. I am very much better off than I would be if I were to marry in this way."

From Ujagar Singh, 38th Central India Horse, France to Gurdit Singh, Amritsar District, Punjab, India. (Urdu dated the 31st July, 1917).

*****

"The pensioners left on the 26th July for India and when they arrive you can talk to them. The rain here is very heavy and the fighting is going on just at it used to do. It will take a long time to finish the war. We can get no leave. Do not expect me to be back for two years more."

From Hazura Singh, 6th Cavalry, France to his mother, Ludhiana. (Urdu dated the 3rd August, 1917).

*****

"As to what you wrote about leave no one has got leave from here and it is very difficult to open leave from a country at such as distance. Still I am hopeful that Government will make some arrangements this year because all the men have been away from their houses for such a long time, and in consequence, household affairs have got into a muddle and it is absolutely necessary for every one to go home."

From Jagat Singh, Sialkot Brigade, France to his wife, Amritsar. (Urdu dated the 22nd August, 1917).

*****

"'British' rank has now been sanctioned for Indians. It is a matter for much congratulation that our Government has conceded this right to us."

From Jeswant Singh, Dafadar, 19th Lancers, France to Dr. Prem Singh, Rawal Pindi, Punjab, India. (Urdu dated the 14th September, 1917).

*****

"My heart is always yearning to meet you again; but I cannot come as duty requires me to be here. If I were to feign sickness and return, it would be a great disgrace for a young man like me. It would be better to drown myself. This is the time when the Sircar needs men, and it is our duty to help the Sircar with all our hearts, even to death. Our Guru has said that must be faithful to authority set over us and that if we fail to be so, we shall meet with his condemnation when we die. There is no doubt that during my absence, you suffer much; but in my opinion you should not repine. My desire is to return only after our King has secured victory. It is against my wish to return leaving our work here half finished."

From Mohan Singh, 34th Poona Horse, France to his mother, Amritsar District, Punjab, India. (Urdu dated the 25th September, 1917).

*****

"I am always thinking of you; but what I am to do? There is no remedy. It is a difficult matter to go to you. There is no end to the war. Yes, if you were to make a complaint by means of a petition then all will be achieved. If you were to write and say "He is my only son" then perhaps they would give me leave; but not otherwise. My heart is very heavy. Neither will they give me leave to go and visit Prem Singh and reassure myself as to his condition. It is difficult to understand what is in the mind of the Government."

From Pertap Singh, 6th Cavalry, France to Natha Singh, Pensioner, Rawal Pindi, Punjab. (Urdu dated the 10th October, 1917).

*****

"In this world a brother is a great blessing. I have been here now for 3 years and when I think of my father and mother and sisters and brothers, I say in my heart "O God what sin have I committed that I am thus exiled from my native land", and I pray to Him to let me meet them once again."

From Sahib Singh, 6th Cavalry, France to Jeswant Singh, Rawal Pindi District, Punjab, India. (Urdu dated the 15th October, 1917).

*****

"My old mother writes that she is at her last breath and that I must come back and set the house in order. My heart is utterly broken at hearing this. But I am helpless. There is no leave to be had and the war is not over. My thoughts are always on my home. I cannot sleep at nights and when I work in the daytime my thoughts are always wandering. Our only hope is on the Guru's aid."

From Bhagwan Singh, 18th Lancers, France to Sirdar Tauna Singh, Kangra. (Urdu dated the 29th October, 1917).

*****

"You suggested my retiring on pension but it would be a bad thing for me and I cannot do it; and there is no reason whatever for my return to India as I am strong and healthy and do not approve of making any excuse to get back. The Guru's orders are to be true to one's salt and not to deceive the master in any way. In accordance with the Guru's orders, I am doing my duty. No leave to India is being given."

From Harman Singh, 19th Lancers, 6th Cavalry, France to Kalimud Singh, Ludhiana. (Urdu dated the 12th November, 1917).

*****

"God will reward you for all that you are enduring for my sake. I know what you have to put up with; but I am helpless. We are prisoners here. I asked to be allowed to retire on a Sowar's pension in lieu of a Dafadar's; but my fate does not allow me to return. There is no reliable information about our movements. Nobody knows what may happen; but there is little hope of our going away. The fourth year has commenced. Rely on God, Who is the Master of the entire world. Call on His name. Peradventure, He may look with favour on the people."

From Kaka Singh, Dafadar, 2nd Lancers (or 38th C.I.Horse) France to his wife, Ludhiana, Punjab, India. (Gurmukhi dated the 13th November, 1917).

*****

"This is the fourth Diwali festival since I left India. The state of things in India and in France is very different. The chief difference is that in India tonight everyone will assemble in his house with his wife and children and father and mother and other relatives and will have an excellent meal and be full of rejoicings. Here we see the very opposite. Everyone is separated from his kith and kin and is thousands of miles away in a foreign country. Yet thanks to God I am fit and well and have everything I want and there is only one worry – separation from you."

From Jemadar Man Singh, 6th Cavalry to Sirdar Jeinal Singh, Director of Agriculture, Jhalawar State. (Urdu dated the 17th November, 1917).

*****

"If you desire to come here, there is no reason why you should not do so. What you have to do is to write a petition to the Viceroy, saying that your husband has been in France for four years, and that you desire to be enlisted in some hospital corps and sent to your husband in France. Add whatever else you please. You will get a proper hearing."

From Tara Singh, 6th Cavalry, France to his wife, Lyallpur District, Punjab, India. (Gurmukhi dated the 7th December, 1917).

*****

"Be it known to my sister, that our meeting is a very difficult matter. Perhaps it will take place in the world to come."

From Pertab Singh, 6th Cavalry, France to Sher Singh, Rawal Pindi District, Punjab, India. (Urdu dated the 7th December, 1917).

*****

"You accuse me of having forgotten my home because I do not come on leave, as others have done. Well those who have gone on leave have from Busrah as no one goes from here. Consider, a hunter having trapped a bird, places it in a fine cage, and tends it carefully, still the bird thinks longingly of its country and notwithstanding the fact that in its own country it did not get any of the dainties it receives in captivity, it is always pining to be free so as to go home. If that is the case with a bird, do you doubt, that I, a man, longs for his own home!"

From Naringen Singh, Q. Battery, R.H.A., France to Sujan Singh, Jullunder, Punjab, India. (Urdu dated the 17th December, 1917).

*****

"Do not be surprised if you do not hear from me often, as I have much work to do. More in fact than I can describe. If God wills it I will see you again but if not, well no matter, as there are hundreds of sons of mothers who will never see their families again. Think it a very fortunate matter indeed that you receive letters of my welfare. More than this I cannot say, as there are stringent orders which forbid me to do so."

From Rur Singh, 6th Cavalry, France to Bahadur Singh, Sialkot District, Punjab, India. (Urdu dated the 18th December, 1917).

*****

"Those who have long service and those who have urgent private affairs are now going on leave from here, viz. those who can bring some interest to bear in their case in India. Some little time ago I saw in the newspapers that if a man had only one son, that son would be required to serve in the army. I know that affairs at home can only be managed under great difficulties as you are now very old, and such affairs cannot be managed by women. If you were to use your best endeavours, I could come. Send a petition to the Deputy Commissioner, and if he sends it here with a recommendation I could come without any difficulty, and I could help the Sircar in the Depot. This you can say in the petition. This is the only way in which I could come to you."

From Shiv Ram Singh, 6th Cavalry, France to Saran Singh, Ressaidar, Gujerat District, Punjab, India. (Urdu dated the 13th January, 1918).

*****

"To my child give milk and ghi. Now is his chance to feed. Don't make him work at ploughing. It is hard work. If he can do it let him cut up the "chari". For ploughing, keep a servant for three months. You have got three buffaloes giving milk. Keep the milk of one of them and give it to the children, fresh. Don't buy and sow too big an area of wheat, but get a big area with fodder crops for the buffaloes. Arrange according to the Rauris (?). Then there will be no difficulty."

From a Sikh Jemadar to his brother, dated 10th Sep 1918. – (Port Said).

*****

"I have been wounded in the left thigh, but do not be disturbed. It is an ordinary wound; the bone is uninjured. I am well. I left Indra Singh very well. I am under treatment in hospital. I hope to be quite well very soon then re-join the Regiment.

Tell all the family not to worry. Collect them together, and let this letter be read out to them, so that their anxiety may be removed.........women's hearts are easily disturbed. Give my love to my children. The wound is slight. Do not worry."

Extract from a Gurmukhi letter from a Sikh Subedar to his brother. Dated 25th Sept. 1918. – (Port Said).

*****

Sikh visiting his young family. (Courtesy of the Council of the National Army Museum, London)

*****

"My Mother, I am very well. Keep sending news of your welfare. I am always thinking consciously about you. When I get letters from you my heart is happy. The letter which you sent to Ram Singh and myself we received on the 18th. In it you write that Mawani's father has died of cholera at Basra, but the new does not make me feel certain about it. Her brother has not had this news. Please send full information. You write that you have sent me a parcel of pencils, combs, books and thread. I have not received it. On the day when your letter arrived, I sent you two letters; since then I have not written, I have had no leisure. The other reason is that there have been no posts.

I will tell you of the day of the Bakr-Id, the story of the battle. You should all assemble together and hear it. What I shall write will be the truth. The war is going on on two fronts. In front of the English are the Turks whose country is in Baghdad and Egypt. In France the war is with Germany. The battle that is going on is going on on all fronts from Baghdad to France.

My story is of the attack that took place on the morning of the Bakr-Id. There were 800 guns firing on a three mile front and they went on firing from 3 o'clock till 8 o'clock. Then the last trench was broken. These trenches had been the line for one year. The English suffered no losses here. I am referring to the Turkish trenches. The English captured 60,000 prisoners and 100 guns, three trains and railway carriages. They captured all the stuff in the railway stations, it was beyond counting. I cannot describe it.

On our front no trace remains of the enemy. The Cavalry are moving over an area of 100 miles and find no trace of the enemy. The enemy is making peace. The English say they will kill all their enemies and then make peace.

Now I am going to tell about the Germans. On the day of Bakr-Id in France, the English captured 36,000 Germans and 350 guns. The Germans are up for a compromise. The Turks and Germans are in a very bad state. The war will be ended this year.

Ram Singh and I have sat down together and written this newspaper. The English are in a very good state. They will get victory this year. Then the world will have rest. By God's power we shall meet soon. Do not be anxious about me. I am well. What I have written is true. There is no falsehood in it. I will write again in eight days. Dear Mother, I will keep writing to you. Please keep writing frequently to me. The enemy is nowhere to be found. The Cavalry ranged across sixty 'kos' and find no enemy. I will write again in eight days."

From a Sikh Sepoy to his mother. Original in Gurmukhi. Dated 12.10.18. – (Port Said).

*****

"We are fighting with heart. It is expected that our "Shahinshah" will have a great victory. It is a matter of days only. We have been driving the Turks as a Tiger drives Jackals. Believe this and the "Khalsa" is very courageous; and as the tyrant Aurangzeb treated the Sikhs we treat the Turks, and it is with the real Turks we are fighting. You don't ask how I am getting on and when I shall return. You are spending money. Had you not spent money and so got into debt over there, I would have saved money here and brought it home and lent it out on interest. I have spent my money. You tell mother that I have never sent any money. Alas, I have come to know that all the world are friends to money. Without the idea of getting money they don't give one bread even. It is like parents to a child. They rear him with care, and when the child grows up, he begins to abuse and push about his parents. All serve him who have money, and take no notice of anyone else. If I send you money you'll think highly of me; if I don't send you money you don't even ask after me, no matter whither I go. Do as seems good to you. I know nothing of you, and your dwelling and your expenses and your

income. I have given up; act as you like. Whenever I come home on leave, you will say: "I have no money and I have nothing", and look mournful and lugubrious, and you will all squabble and wrangle amongst yourselves to a degree that I can't express. Well do as you like.
Obedience to my Mother."

From a Sikh to his elder brother. (Original in Gurmukhi). Dated 19.10.18. – (Port Said).

*****

"Greetings, we haven't heard from you for a long time. What is the reason? Do you dislike writing or are you too busy? I have several times thought that you must have been thinking that I am dead, but we are living. As long as there is life there is hope.

Now listen to my troubles. I will state them. I have suffered before, but never as I am suffering now. What is the use of writing a lot? I will write a little............

We got bread after 14 days and in 36 hours marched 58 miles. After that at 6. P.M each man got 2 chapatties. There was great scarcity of water.

The regiment is made into three squadrons, now of only 3 troops each. Perhaps it is intended to make one regiment from the whole Brigade. Don't be anxious about me. My skeleton remains, nothing else. You know that life depends on food."

Extracts from a letter from a Sikh Sowar to his mother, (original in Gurmukhi), dated Oct: 25th 1918. – (Port Said).

*****

"You write that the Indian army has driven back the Germans, and I am telling you the story of it. Where the Indian army goes, the enemy retires. The Indian army is very valiant. When you hear the news about Turkey, let me know, and then I will send you the true story of it. The whole regiment captured about 1500 Turks. The final point is this, that when I get home, I will tell you the whole story."

From a Sikh Sowar to his father, (original in Gurmukhi), dated about Oct: 25th 1918. – (Port Said).

*****

"My brother, you wrote that Pumma was not listening to your advice, but was living at her parents' house. My brother, according to your advice I sent a letter to Mirpur, and I got a reply saying that she would now come to you at Fateh Rikan. I have great hope that she will have reached you. If she has not come, please let me know.

I sent Rs. 60/- to my Father but no one has informed me whether he received it or not. I sent you many letters, but dear brother, I am very sorry that you have quite stopped writing to me. Now please do be looking out for us, we will be coming back very shortly. I will send you information before I go on the steamer.

We have received the peace-letter from Turkey, showing her need of peace. Now there is nothing to be feared; you may rest assured – there is no fighting now, nor even the sign of it. The Turks have lost their 'Raj'; like bad days passing away. The Turkish organisation was very poor compared with that of the English. They used to pay the soldiers only Rs. 30/-. They were not given any rations. The soldiers threw away their guns, and stood still on account of hunger. The Government in which there is oppression cannot stand for long. The Turks were led on by the Germans. German officers were the commanders of the Turkish army. The Germans used to bring the most beautiful girls of good Turkish families, and keep them in the trenches for immoral purposes. This was a bad act of the Germans. The houses of the Turks, are vey splendid and well built, but they are very dirty, and there is a bad smell about them.

The soldiers in the trenches had made tunnels underneath the hills as long as the side of a "square" in a canal colony. They used to live in these tunnels like rats who make their holes in the pond. The country is altogether hilly, and is worth seeing. It is beyond me to praise it. *"In the name of India, the trenches were conquered". I cannot estimate the reward which the Emperor will give his valiant soldiers for this.

Have no anxiety about me."

*"INDIA KE NAM MORCHE PER FATTEH HAI"

Extract from a Sikh Sepoy's letter to his brother. (Original in Gurmukhi). Dated 3.11.18. – (Port Said).

*****

"I am well and ever pray to God for your welfare. I have sent several letters and received no answer. I do not know if you have failed to receive them, or if for some reason you are displeased. In every letter, I have enclosed an envelope for a reply. I have heard that there has been a fight with the Gol-Klahan people, resulting in grievous hurt to Sant Singh and Jiwan Singh. Please tell me the cause of the fighting and give me particulars about the injuries. Who is this Jiwan Singh? I heard that the Jats only allowed 20 bighas* of land to be cultivated. Who opposed this? Send me their names and parentage. Was mutation of names affected in the names of all or not? Let me know about this too. One year has passed. Do you advise my bringing a suit? Ask the Patwari and the Girdowar Sahib and let me know their opinion quickly. If you require any help from me in fighting the matters, I am ready. I will put in an application to the effect that I had given my land to 50-r-20 for ploughing, and that 50-r-20 have prevented them ploughing and assaulted them. I hear that Gandha Singh has written a letter to his home saying that I have been troubling him. If we reach home in safety, I will ask him in presence of you all what trouble I have given him.

Please pay my respects to the Patwari and the Girdowar Sahib, and let me have a speedy reply."

*Bigha, roughly 5/8 of an acre.

From a Sikh Subahdar to his brother in the Punjab. (Original in Gurmukhi). Date 5.11.18. – (Port Said).

*****

"The position is that my father and brother are living near you, and you must keep an eye on them, since you are the Lambardar. Their fields too are near yours. I am sending you a sheet of paper on which I have written some of the facts of the war. In this direction everything has been settled with Turkey on the 21.10.18. They have accepted all the conditions.

With the Germans it was settled on the 15th day of KHATIK, and all the prisoners, both ours and theirs have been released. There is no news yet as to when we shall reach our country.

The Germans are accepting all the terms which I have written below. 2,000 aeroplanes he will hand over. The expenses of the damage which he did to the great cities of France, and the two ships full of sovereigns, which he captured he will return. He will hand over 500 of the boats which went under the sea and sank ships. He will pay compensation for the 50,000 soldiers which he sank in the ships. When these conditions are finally accepted, the peace will be complete. If they are not accepted, there will not be peace. If the thing is not settled by the beginning of MAGR, the war will start again.

The Germans will have to accept the whole terms.

It will be gladness for the whole world.

The paper as I have written it shows the terms that have been sent to Germany.

She is also ready to pay the expenses. The King of America is the greatest of all.

(AMRIKA WALA BADSHAH SAB SE BARA HAIN).

He has said: "You must all accept the committee that I shall make; if anyone does not accept it – I will again start war on him." I have invented a story to make you laugh:- The guns of the King of America take a day to fire, and each shell kills off a whole district with fright*. You can imagine that such a King has some power to make peace.

AP KHIYAL ZIYAD WHO BADSHAH
ZOR SE SULAH KARA SAKTE HAIN.

No one has the strength to fight against him. There are big forces on their way back, and we hope to be back in India in the month of PHAGON. If the war starts again we shall go to France. The German intends to make peace. To pay such heavy damages is difficult for him.

He has to pay the bill for both sides."

* This is Sikh humour.

From a Sikh Sepoy to the LAMBARDAR of his village. (Original in Gurmukhi). Date Nov 15th 1918. – (Port Said).

*****

"After greetings, let it be known to you that by the Grace of God I am well and flourishing. Even praying to God for my health and well being. I pray to God that your dutiful servant may soon get sight of you and obtain the privilege of kissing your feet. I am a traveller, and am in a strange country, and have scant leisure; they are the reason for me not writing before. Hence you must continue to inform me of your welfare without waiting for a letter from me. Two or three days ago the Indian mail arrived but there was no letter in it from Uncle – nor from you. I did get one from my mother's brother Diyal Singh, which said that my maternal grandmother had taken up her abode in Heaven. I grieve from her loss. Such is God's work. Strange are the ways of Providence. What dangers and vicissitudes are written in my Fate. At one time, the sufferings of heat; at another the pains of cold. At one moment I perish from thirst; at another I have a surfeit of water. At times, I roost on a rock, at times I relax on soft sand. At one time not a morsel of food; at another an abundance of grapes and melons. In short mysterious are the ways of the Immortal God. From passing through innumerable changes of life and surroundings, the very structure of my body has undergone change. At one time from being in a cold climate my complexion was as fair as a British soldiers; at another, from exposure to heat and sun, it was as black as a negro's. As to hairs of my head and beard, what can I say of them? They, too, poor things have seen all sorts of changes; at one time brown, at another white, at another black. At times flowing with perfumed oils; at times be filled with dust and dirt.

Now listen to the description of my present surroundings. We are camped on the sea-shore, the breeze is cool. Near my tent, that is about a hundred-and-fifty yards from the sea, a net is erected from it to within fifty yards of me; this net is decreed as a death-by-the-stake for poor helpless tired out quails.

When the cold sets in, the quails migrate from cold countries where they live and fly to a barren climate. After a long journey over the "Greek Sea" (A Lake)* they arrive weary and worn, hungry and thirsty. When not at sea and high up in the air they view the distant land and drop joyfully to alight on it. There they are snared in the miles of nets, erected by tormentors and become suspended, heads up legs down. If by any chance any bird escapes the nets, the poor things lies on the ground helpless from exhaustion. They are gathered by hand by the fowlers, to become delicate morsels for rich and poor.

I pray to Almighty God to guard in safety all my relatives, intimates and friends, and to hasten the day of my return to them."

Note – The writer is probably with a Cavalry Regiment on the coast of north of Jaffa.

From a Sikh in Palestine to his Uncle, a Sikh Officer. (No Date). – (Port Said).

*****

9

Recruitment, Pay and War Loans

There is a tremendous rush in recruiting. Parades are going on all day.

At one time we had great difficulty in getting recruits, so the authorities are now giving a bonus of Rs. 50 per head.

I have heard that they are taking subscriptions (for the war loan). If anyone asks you for money do not give it.

Dr Annie Beasant, touring the Punjab in 1918, "The most atrocious, tyrannical, barbaric and inhuman methods were employed by Sir Michael O'Dwyer and his agents to obtain recruits."

Recruitment, pay and other financial considerations were regularly mentioned in letters to and from Sikh soldiers during the war. Sikh recruitment grew year on year during the Great War period, 12,293 recruits enlisted by the year ending 31st July 1915. 14,973 by the year ending 31st July 1916; 16,234 by the year ending 31st July 1917; 31,265 by the year ending 31st July 1918 and another 14,160 by 30th November 1918. This came to a total of 88,925 Sikh recruits over the duration of the Great War.[1] The subject of recruitment seems a strange contradiction; soldiers returning from the fronts injured or otherwise must have discussed the ferocity of the war, but year on year the number of Sikh recruits increased. There may have been many reasons for this and this chapter discusses the many underlying factors for this as revealed from the letters.

Some letters post their introduction to the war, naturally advised friends and relatives not to enlist. "It is a great mistake to enter this fire", states a Sikh soldier on finding that his brother had enlisted. Others ask for relatives to keep an eye on people to ensure that they do not fall foul to the "wiles of recruiters and get enlisted."

Rumours about recruitment tactics flowed in Sikh letters. Some Sikh soldiers at the front mentioned forced recruitment tactics being used and their unhappiness about this. Letters from India in 1915 mention wholesale recruiting on a large scale, "The country is being recruited without regard to youth or age. Every man who is found is recruited." Letters suggest that there were tremendous efforts put into recruiting by Indian and British Officers.

1 De Witt C. Ellinwood and S.D. Pradhan (Ed), *India and World War I* (New Delhi: Manohar, 1978), p. 216.

Letters from the front from Indian officers also encouraged recruitment, "It is a duty to complete recruiting", states a Sikh Rissaldar Major. Other Sikh soldiers felt it incumbent to support the *Sircar* in their time of need and many were proud of their soldiering traditions and wanted to ensure that they continued: "Seven grandsons of one grandfather are now in the service. You must now try to get the eighth brother to enlist", encouraged a Sikh at the front.

Colour photolithographic recruiting poster, aimed at Commonwealth countries, 1915. (Courtesy of the Council of the National Army Museum, London)

In early 1916, the letters start to discuss a slowdown in the number of recruits available. A Sikh says in his letter that: "Recruits are very scarce, and we are put to much trouble as a consequence." Rumours abounded about recruitment targets for soldiers and officers who went on leave, such as incentives being available for soldiers bringing back a certain number of recruits. Conversely, other rumours stated that there were punishments in store for those who failed to bring back recruits.

Letters continue to ask whether pressure is being applied to recruit and a Sikh at the front mentions that "intimidation is often used". A Sikh from India writes to an Indian Officer at the front that "When we do get them they are treated harshly and run away and then when they are caught they are sent to prison." He then states that people are wary of coming forward because of this. Even the official Punjab war chronicler admitted that coercive methods were used to recruit in the Punjab:

"There were a few districts in which the news that a Government Officer was coming sufficed to empty the villages within a five-mile radius! In these, there was an undeniable estrangement."[2]

In June 1917, an enlistment bonus of Rs. 50 was introduced for new recruits, the volume of Sikhs entering the service increased. There was a huge push from this period onwards with regards to recruiting, multiple tactics were utilised, not all by any means ethical. The Lieutenant-Governor of the Punjab, Michael O'Dwyer, admitted to being aware of the nefarious tactics employed by his officials when he deposed before the Hunter Committee inquiry into the Punjab disorders in January 1920:

> Q. You held a durbar at Gujranwala in August 1917?
> A. I think I did.
> Q. At that time Mr. Hamilton was the Deputy Commissioner of Gujranwala, and after that Colonel O'Brien was appointed by you?
> A. Yes.
> Q. In that durbar you rebuked the people of Gujranwala for their not joining the ranks?
> A. Yes, I think so.
> Q. Now there was another Durbar in August 1918?
> A. Yes.
> Q. According to the figures for 1917-18, one man in every 150 of the population on average had joined the colours?
> A. Yes.
> Q. And then after some time you said that the average was one man in every 14 in military age?
> A. Yes; I am very glad to know that the result was so good. Of course in some districts, it went up to one man in 3.
> Q. This result has been obtained through the successful and zealous efforts of your energetic Deputy Commissioner, Colonel O'Brien?
> A. Yes.
> Q. You will also know that the village quota system was introduced for this purpose?
> A. In certain districts. The military situation at that time was very critical. The Premier appealed for men. The military authorities and the Government of India, I think, agreed that India should raise 500,000 men during the next year. We in the Punjab were asked by the military authorities and the Government of India to provide 200,000 men. We agreed to provide that number. We said that we would endeavour to provide 180,000 combatants and 20,000 non-combatants. In the public meeting held at Lahore, we, in order to do that, just as the Government of India had apportioned the 500,000 men among the various provinces of India, started apportioning the 200,000 among the various districts of the Punjab and the recruiting organisation had to decide what measures should be taken?
> Q. Under this quota system it was brought to your knowledge that every village was to give so many people, and if the village was not prepared to give so many people, the

2 M.S. Leigh, *The Punjab and the War* (Lahore: Superintendent of Government Printing, 1922), p. 28.

> village panchayat would go and sit *dharna*, and that until these recruits were brought they would not leave the village?
> A. That was done entirely as a local arrangement; it was not done as a Government measure at all. A good deal of the recruiting details were left to the local recruiting boards.
> Q. My point is this, this fact was brought to your knowledge, was anything done to dis-associate the Government from it?
> A. What particular act?
> Q. This sitting in *dharna*. What happened is this. Certain persons connected with recruiting went to a large village and said, "you ought to supply so many recruits." They said it would be very difficult, and the recruiters said, "We will not leave unless you can." The village had to pay the expenses of their living and food.
> A. I do not think so, anyhow it was a matter of local arrangement. You must not take these matters very seriously. I do not think that was very great pressure at a time of great need.
> Q. That is not my point, my point is this, all these facts having been brought to your notice, can you refer this committee to any public announcement where you said these things were wrongly done. I will show you that you everywhere praised them. So far as my knowledge goes, during the three or four years of the war, all these various matters were brought to your knowledge and there is not a single public announcement saying you did not approve of them.
> A. I think over and over again in various places I deprecated any coercion being resorted to and any improper methods being used…[3]

Other tactics included giving recruiting targets for local officials such as *Tehsildars*, *Lumberdars* and *Zaildars* directly from the Deputy Commissioner of a District. One *Zaildar* mentions that: "If I did not supply the men in that time I should be dismissed from both my Zaildarship and lumberdarship." Thus, a mixed picture emerges from the Sikh letters with regards to recruitment – some agree and whole heartedly endorse recruitment. However, letters from the front itself show knowledge of forced recruitment. Letters from India highlight pressure being applied to many different types of officials to achieve recruitment targets. Outside the letters, rumours circulated about intimidatory tactics being used to recruit to the army. Monthly meetings were held where results for local recruiting were published, with officials thus either being publicly honoured or admonished for not achieving their targets.

Local officials would be left alone to reach their targets, which ensured that coercion and harassment could be used. Pressure would also be applied on the women of a village to ensure that male relatives would be harried into joining up. Villagers in some districts rose up in defiance of these tactics and there is evidence of local officials being murdered due to the abominable recruiting tactics they employed.[4] Moreover, the recruitment had created a reign of terror in the

3 V.N. Datta, *New light on the Punjab disturbances in 1919, Vols. VI and VII of Disorders Inquiry Committee evidence. Vol 1* (Simla: Indian Institute of Advanced Study, 1975), pp. 187-188.
4 Ibid., p. 188.

Punjab villages. As a result of forced recruitment, it became common to hear villagers speaking of sons or brothers who had disappeared or were expected to disappear.[5]

From a social perspective, Sikhs believed traditionally in soldiering, with many generations of the same family being soldiers. The Sikh newspapers were nearly all pro recruitment but for differing reasons. Recruitment fairs would take place where Sikh 'leaders' would recommend joining up, generally in areas with high illiteracy. The average Sikh could not find employment in the civil services easily. Their foremost religious shrines were under the control of Hindu *mahants* (mainly), whereas the army seemed to encourage Sikh religious 'orthodoxy'. Add to this the fact that plague and high prices were rife during the war period, enlistment to the army may have been their only remaining option. The government also wanted to keep the Sikhs busy so that they would not join any revolutionary activities. While a combination of factors may have driven many to enlist, the military and civil administration worked together in concert to create and exploit all means to boost recruitment figures.

Huge *durbars* were held during the war period with speeches given from the Lieutenant-Governor Michael O'Dwyer. The majority of these occurred during 1917-18 as the need for manpower increased. Russia had withdrawn from the war and Germany now had more men to pit against the British who, in turn, increasingly looked upon India to fill the gap. O'Dwyer would use these speeches to encourage enlistment detailing deeds of heroism and by comparing the different 'martial' groups in the Punjab and their valorous efforts in the war. He also seemed to split the Sikh contribution by caste by exhorting *Jat* Sikhs (more divide and rule). He hoped that this would stimulate rivalry between districts, communities and castes. An example of this can be seen in a speech given by O'Dwyer at the Ferozepore *durbar* on 4 August 1917:

> I must confess that while Hoshiarpur is making a splendid effort, which for the time being has placed it first in the Division, the figures are disappointing as regards Jullundur and particularly so for Ferozepore. They are certainly not what I or anyone who knew the people of Ferozepore had expected. When I spoke to you at the beginning of the war in the durbar of January 1915 I ventured to say that there were few districts in India which had sent so large a proportion of their manhood to the front. At that time I was thinking of the 14th, 15th and 36th Sikhs and other distinguished regiments who have since done so well on the fields of France and elsewhere. I am afraid that the position is very different now, and that Ferozepore instead of being among the first is among the last of the districts of the Province in its rally to the cause of the King-Emperor.[6]

In a speech at the Amritsar *durbar* on 17 of April 1918 O'Dwyer observed:

> I appeal to the great martial clans of the Manjha, the Sindhus, the Gils, the Dhillons, the Chahils, the Randhawas and Sidhus, who formed the backbone of the Armies of the Khalsa – to show the martial ardour and enthusiasm which distinguished them in the past. If regard be had to available numbers the Mazhbi Sikhs have far surpassed the Jats. All honour to the Mazhbis; but do the Jats view the Cavalry of the Mazhbis

5 Mohinder Singh, *History and culture of Panjab* (New Delhi: Atlantic Publishers and Distributors, 1988), p. 161.
6 Michael O'Dwyer, *War Speeches* (Lahore: Superintendent Government Printing, 1918), p. 50.

> with equanimity? Can they afford to allow themselves to be surpassed in loyalty because under the British Crown they have grown rich and prosperous?[7]

As the war continued into a fourth year the need for manpower increased and by 1918 recruiting methods seem to have gone to extraordinary lengths. New incentives were introduced such as extra pay and special commissions, land grants and special privileges. The Punjab government went into overdrive to influence public opinion and get the required number of recruits. They did this through a well-orchestrated and well-funded publicity campaign which was engineered by the Punjab Publicity Board. This was a five pronged attack, targeting the press, lectures, entertainments, schools and women's organisations, along with Singh Sabhas amenable to their cause.

The Board plastered the province with literature and posters and tracts in *Gurmukhi* and Urdu, propagating recruitment under the British cause. Every conceivable tactic was used, over 145,000 posters adorned buildings in the Punjab. Even jail inmates were offered pardons for agreeing to enlistment; 5,000 prisoners agreeing to join the labour corps in Mesopotamia. Articles in newspapers made appeals to Indian women to urge relations to go to the front. Others such as *The Khalsa Samachar* 'urged Sikhs to provide more recruits than any other community.' Others tried to stimulate recruiting by saying that 'Sikhs needed to defend their homes, wives, children and country!' *The Haq* newspaper, which was endorsed by other Punjabi newspapers was a key propaganda tool and was produced in all the Punjab languages, including *Gurmukhi*. Its circulation was very high, reaching nearly 100,000 copies a week and *The Haq* was used to advertise marches and public holidays attributed to Allied victories in the war.

Thus the question of why Sikhs came forward in large numbers to "volunteer" in comparison to their overall numbers is a complex one. There were many different reasons including tradition, social circumstances, necessity and coercion.

One area which links to recruiting is the financial concerns of letters written to and from the front regarding pay and subscriptions to war loans. The Indian soldiers and relatives were aggrieved when their pay or family allotments did not reach home on time. Especially as pay was as low as Rs. 11 per month at the beginning of the war, rising to Rs. 17 in 1918. Letters home ask relatives to contact depots to ascertain why this was happening. Similarly, some Sikh soldiers discouraged relatives from subscribing to the war loan for reasons such as, "My son is present at the war, why then are you taking money from me?" However, contributions to the war loan were enforced in many cases. A *Sardar* Sant Singh of Lyallpur relates:

> War loan was forcibly levied in this district. Title-hunters exacted war loan from the masses in order to win honour for themselves. Rs. 33 per square were forcibly levied *en masse*. No exception was made. Even an adjudged bankrupt had to pay it. The history of this levy is interesting. It was proposed that every square-holder should be made to give Rs. 33, the value of one acre of land, to the Government. No squareholder was consulted. The proposal came from the title-hunters. It was accepted by the local authorities but was modified by the local government. In place of gift, the local

7 Ibid., p. 116.

government took it as a loan, the interest going to the improvement of the village, and not to the individual contributors.

Lambardars had to furnish recruits on the penalty of forfeiting the Lambardari rights. Several were actually dismissed. Thus the value of a recruit goes to Rs. 500. Police sent up people to be bound down for keeping peace. Magistrates refused bail and sent them to the lock-up, till they agreed to furnish recruits. Criminal prosecution was withdrawn on the accused after agreeing to offer himself as a recruit.[8]

*****

"Here it is said that men are being forced to enlist in India, and they also say that plague is very rife. Write me news of our country xxx. So long as the war goes on no sound man can return to India – only those who have lost a limb can return. In my heart I feel that I shall have to go back to the war."

From Gurdit Singh, Sepoy in Hospital, Brighton, to his father in Amritsar, Punjab. (Gurmukhi of 6/4/15).

*****

"Tell me how the war has affected India. Here they say that men are being compelled to enlist, and that the Government has realised the land revenue for three years in advance. There are other various rumours too. Are they true or not?"

From Gurdit Singh, now in hospital in England, to a friend in India. (Gurmukhi, 20/4/15).

*****

"The money that I send home, how does it arrive? If they give notes from the Post Office, do not take them. If they give you rupees or pounds, take them, but if they do not give these, do not take notes. Send them back and say that you will not take them and write me a letter. I will arrange about it."

From Prem Singh, 15th Sikhs, serving in France, to his home in India. (Gurmukhi, 27/4/15).

*****

"What sort of troop are you enlisting – raise a Malwa one, because in the regiment this troop is broken up. If you do raise one you will become renowned in that you have reformed a worn out troop, so mind you do it xxx or food we get rations which are good, but we are much thinner than we were in India."

From Mohan Singh, to Jemadar Mohan Singh, 38th K.G.O., C.I. Horse, Agar Malwa, India. (No language stated).

8 *Collected Works of Mahatma Gandhi, Vol. 20*, p. 24 <http://www.gandhiashramsevagram.org/gandhi-literature/collected-works-of-mahatma-gandhi-volume-1-to-98.php>

*****

"I have received a letter from my father saying you have enlisted without consulting anyone. You have acted very foolishly, because it is a great mistake to enter the service at this time, because everything is on fire. It is a great mistake to enter this fire.

None of the old army is left alive. Out of the regiment there only remains 50 or 60. The Germans have settled the affairs of all the others. Now recently joined recruits of two months standing are being brought to the trenches."

From Lance Naik Rawel Singh, No.3 Ammunition Column, R.F.A., to his brother Shankar Dass, 66th Punjabis, dated 15th May 1915. (No language stated).

*****

"No complete unit has gone from Quetta (to the war) – only two companies from here and four companies from there. That is how it is being done. They are raising the whole country. There is no end to it – from one (place) they send two companies, from another four. The country is being recruited without regard to youth or age. Every man who is found is recruited. No limit is placed in a regiment, nor is it stated how many men are required. Even if the regiment amounts to 1600 or 1800 men, recruiting goes on."

From a Sikh in Quetta to Sant Singh, 12th Pioneers, with 34th Pioneers in France. (Gurmukhi, 12/8/15).

*****

"Teja Singh has written that you have enlisted. You have done well, but you made a very great mistake in not asking permission from your parents first. And if you wanted to enlist, you should have gone to Teja Singh. And my brother, you had great trouble with your studies, now take great ease and contentment. Do your work zealously and well, and whenever we meet, we will talk about it."

From Narayan Singh, 25th Cavalry, Marseilles Base, to Jalmeja Singh, Recruit, 28th Punjabis, Lahore, Punjab. (Urdu, 28/8/15).

*****

"I hear that Pala Singh has enlisted, and Bela Singh too. I am very pleased about it. If we were not to come to our government's aid at such a time, we should be a useless lot. We must honour the hand that feeds us. I know that Fatteh Singh has done great service. Already there are five brothers doing our government's work in Europe, and we have done well to add another two to the number. I am delighted. We and our brother Sikhs will gain more credit than ever. Seven grandsons of one grandfather are now in the service. You must now try to get the eighth brother to enlist. I am sure that this would be published in the newspapers. If this happened throughout India we should have done more than we have. You must make further efforts and Fatteh Singh must push on with his service and get Besakha Singh to join. That would please me much. Get the eighth to enlist and let me know when it is done."

From Sarwan Singh, F.P.O.11 to Fatteh Singh, 47th Sikhs, Fattehgarh. (Gurmukhi, 5/9/15).

*****

"Bahal Singh has returned to the war (Europe). He has done harm to many by volunteering a second time. For many (of those that did not volunteer) have had to go without pensions or had their names struck off the regiment, others have been packed off again to the front, or given a gratuity by the board."

From Asa Singh, F.P.O.64 near Shabqadr, Peshawar, to Gandhara Singh, 84th Punjabis attached 57th Rifles, France. (Gurmukhi, 19/9/15).

*****

"If you can do anything, you should certainly try and get recruits so far as it lies in your power and put your heart and soul into the performance of your duty. Besides you are intelligent enough to see that your interest points that way."

From Riss. Rur Singh, 30th Lancers, to Dfdr. Nanak Singh, Ludhiana, Punjab. (dated 26th September 1915). (No language stated).

*****

"Indar Singh asks me to tell you not to let Channan Singh enlist. Here they worry us up and down."

From a Sowar in the 4th Cavalry, France, Marseilles, to a friend in the 33rd Lancers, Saugor. (Gurmukhi, 23/10/15).

*****

"Write and tell me if my younger brother has gone into service. I have heard that people of our village have been forcibly enlisted in the army. Tell him I am very anxious for him not to enlist anywhere. Tell him also not to bother about me. I am well and happy..............We have also heard that some men have been arrested of the Singh Sabha who were preaching to the people."

From Sarwant Singh, Brighton, to Bakhtawar Singh, Ludhiana. (Gurmukhi, 28/10/15).

*****

"Here on the 1/1/16 I got a letter from Karam Chand in which he stated that Balwant Singh had left home. This gave me great distress (distress described at length). He also said that the search had been made in several places, but no trace had been found. I am in great anxiety &c &c. I am afraid especially about one thing. Men are much wanted in the Army now. They do not regard size, but take any man, and many men have come from regiments to get recruits. He may have fallen a victim to their wiles and been enlisted........The parcel which I sent you on the 15th December from here will not reach. The ship, so I hear, sank on the way. The parcel contained (details given) ....a serious loss. Very evil days have come."

From Ward Orderly Pal Singh, K.I.H., Brighton, to Kaka Singh, Amritsar Dt., India. (Urdu, 1/1/16).

*****

"Many men here are complaining about their pay, that it is not being sent to their homes. I do not know the reason. I myself got a letter from home written on the 5th Jan. (sic), and had heard several times before this, that only a payment of Rs.15/- has reached them on the 15th October, and seven payments of Rs.10/- each had been made. Eight payments in all had been received. Since the 1st August I have raised my allotment to Rs.15/-, but the increase seems to have been made with effect from September instead of August. Since then no payment at all has been made ... It is true that we are here to be killed, but here we are wandering about, here and there, and we get no money, neither is it sent to our homes. This is very unfair on us. Please let me know the reason why my pay has been stopped."

From Hira Singh, F.P.O. No.18 (? Cavalry), France, to Dfdr. Tara Singh, Depot 6th Cavalry, Sialkot. (Urdu, 9/1/16).

*****

"I am sure that by the time this reaches you will have got your commission (as Jemadar). Every one in the village says so. In our village we have done well in recruiting. But in this neighbourhood they are all Musulman savages and will have nothing to do with service in the army. We pray to the Guru, all the time, especially the Sikhs, that our government may have a speedy victory."

From Sikandar Singh, Gujranwala Dt., Punjab, India, to Dfdr. Tara Singh, 6th Cavalry, France. (Urdu, 9/1/16).

*****

"There is a tremendous rush in recruiting. Parades are going on all day. We do not get off duty before 8 p.m."

From Dafadar Dya Singh, 32nd Lancers, Jubbulpore, India, to Lance Dafadar, Tara Singh, 32nd Lancers attached 30th Lancers, France. (Urdu, 14/1/16).

*****

"For the past six months I have been on recruiting duty. At the present time many recruits are being enlisted. They come forward eagerly."

From Ajit Singh, Delhi, India, to Rissaldar Major Hira Singh, 30th Lancers, France. (Urdu, 17/1/16).

*****

"I am longing to see you. On the 23rd January, twenty five men including myself and Jemadar Gurbachan Singh are coming to join the 33rd Cavalry in Field Force "D". Amr Singh has gone off on recruiting duty. He has not been made a dafadar yet, though there are many vacancies in the squadron. There is recruiting going on in only one troop and there is little chance of that being brought up to strength. There are vacancies in it at present and no one is bringing any recruits."

From Lachman Singh, 22nd Cavalry, Bolarum, India, to Jemadar Kesar Singh, 22nd Cavalry, attached 2nd Lancers, France. (Urdu, 18/1/16).

*****

"If you can possibly manage it get your name struck off the rolls and come away. By any means in your power, good or bad, you should save your life. In the end, do as you please. I have written to you frequently about this matter, and I am very concerned about you … Write as soon as you receive this letter (lit: before eating your food) and tell me everything about the war … No snow whatever has fallen here this year … It has been ordered in England, we hear, that all European (English) adults are to be compulsorily recruited. Here many of our men have enlisted. More cannot be found (to enlist). Men are very scarce."

From Amir Singh, Forest Dept. Muree, Punjab, to Sawar Kanh Singh, 34th Poona Horse, France. (Gurmukhi, 2/2/16).

*****

"Why do you not get an order from your officers to raise recruits. In the Punjab there are so many men out of work, that they could not be counted. There is no village in the Punjab where 100 men could not be recruited. If all these men were immediately enlisted, then the work would be brought to a termination forthwith. This indeed is the very best way of conquering the enemy. Do something or other to get the order for general recruitment issued."

From Man Singh, Pensioned Rissaldar, Hoshiarpur, Punjab, to Jai Singh, Jemadar, 6th Cavalry, France. (Gurmukhi, 3/2/16).

*****

"You say that you have heard that the Cavalry is to return. This is wrong. The Cavalry will not return before the end of the war. A letter has come from the Colonel of our regiment to our Captain to say that discrepancies have been detected in the accounts, and that the Pay-Dafadar has been found guilty of embezzlement. So he is under arrest. When the matter is settled, I hope that the whole of my pay will reach you. I have spoken to the Captain about it again today … Sirdar Shioder Singh and fifty men have gone to the front to dig trenches. They will be back in ten days. We are having excellent football here. So far we have beaten all the other regiments and are shortly to meet the 9th, and if we defeat them, by the Guru's grace, we shall be the victors among all the regiments."

From Hazura Singh, F.P.O. No.39, France, to Indar Singh, Lahore Dt. India. (Urdu, 6/2/16).

*****

"I have heard that since I left home only one instalment of Rs. 10/- has gone to my home. No more has been sent. Why not? Please explain. Ask Arjan Singh. It is only my pay that has not been sent, or are all in the same plight?"

From Santa Singh, 21st Cavalry attached 34th Poona Horse, France to Lance-Dafadar Harnam Singh, 21st Cavalry, Lahore Cant., India. (Gurmukhi, 9/2/16).

*****

"The following men (here the names are mentioned) have gone on recruiting duty. Recruits are not to be had in the Punjab; it is quite empty (i.e. no men suitable for recruits are left)."

From Hardit Singh, Deolali, Bombay, to Gurdit Singh, 39th C.I. Horse attached 18th Lancers, France. (Gurmukhi, 11/2/16).

*****

"Balwant Singh is on recruiting duty but has only got three recruits up to date. They are very difficult to get, especially Sikhs. I am doing my best and I hope we shall get what we used to."

From Risaldar Major Suraj Singh, Depot Delhi, 11th Lancers, to Jemadar Dhalip Singh attached 19th Lancers. (Urdu, 11/2/16).

*****

"My son, since you left not a pice of your pay has reached me and I don't know where to turn. You must make some arrangements. Speak to your commanding officer about it."

From Kirpa Singh, Patiala, India, to Sowar Gurdit Singh, 9th Hodson's Horse. (Gurmukhi, 12/2/16).

*****

"Recruits are very scarce, and we are put to much trouble as a consequence. British officers go on recruiting duty."

From Dyal Singh, Depot 32nd Lancers, Jhabalpur, India, to Dafadar Tara Singh, 32nd Lancers attached 30th Lancers, France. (Urdu, 19/2/16).

*****

"Why is it that not a pice has reached my home? Money is very much needed there. Ganda Singh has written about the money. Without fail, send the money to my house.

Whatever you order is done. In the case of the men of the 6th Cavalry Rs.30/- a piece is regularly paid monthly to their families (and why are we not dealt with in the same way [?] … Rissaldar Hakim Singh and Surain Singh send drafts (of men) right enough; they might send money to their homes as well. All our men receive letters (from their homes) to the effect that not a pice is paid to them."

From Makhan Singh, Dafadar 25th Cavalry attached 6th Cavalry, France, to Jemadar Narain Singh, 25th Cavalry, Bannu, India. (Urdu, 25/2/16).

*****

"It is four months now since I made an allotment of Rs.20/- a month for my family, but not a pice has reached my home. Speak to the Rissaldar Sahib and make an effort to have the money sent. The allowance of men of other regiments are paid regularly (to their homes) then why not ours?"

From Harnam Singh, 25th Cavalry attached 6th Cavalry, to Natha Singh, 25th Cavalry, Bannu. (Urdu, 25/2/16).

*****

"I regret very much to hear of trouble about recruiting. It is not proper. Make every effort quickly and do the work. It is a duty to complete recruiting and no delay whatever should be allowed to occur. I hope that when I receive your next letter I shall find that there is no longer any anxiety about recruiting."

From Rissaldar Major Amar Singh, 38th C.I. Horse, to L.D. Hazara Singh same regiment, Agar-Malwa, C.I. India. (Urdu, 7/3/16).

*****

"Give as much assistance as you can to the Government in the matter of recruiting. Whether the men are Hindu, Mahomedans or Sikhs. There is much credit in this."

From Jemadar Ganda Singh, 6th Cavalry France, to Gobind Sahib, Gujar Khan, Punjab, India. (Urdu, 7/3/16).

*****

"Why have you stopped my pay? I hear from home that they have received pay for 7 months only. Why don't you send my pay home? My uncle writes to say that when he was absent at Rawalpindi the postman brought some money for him, but as he was not there to receive it, the postman returned it. Be so kind as to send to my home all the pay that is due."

From the same to Dafadar Tara Singh, 6th Cavalry, Sialkot. (No date, No Language given).

*****

"I hear that very few Sikh recruits are being enlisted into the regiment. You and Sirdar Bava Singh are both present there. You should strive to get recruits with all your ability and energy. This is no time for slackness. Consider the way in which the whole country is exerting itself and doing its duty."

From Peshawra Singh, 19th Lancers, France, to Sirdar Mahindar Singh, 19th Lancers, Sialkot, Punjab. (Urdu, 9/3/16).

*****

"We get few recruits nowadays. We make great endeavours, but we cannot get them. I go to the village in a few days."

From Bhagat Singh, Recruiting Agent, Rawalpindi, India, to Ishar Singh, 30th Lancers, France. (Urdu, 10/3/16).

*****

"My friend, do you not feel ashamed? You must be trying for promotion to Naik since you try and induce Saudagar Singh to enlist. I am very displeased with you. It is desirable that you should not enlist him. If you do enlist him, I shall be very displeased with you."

From Surain Singh, 9th Hodson's Horse, France, to Ishar Singh, 11th Lancers, Delhi, India. (Gurmukhi, 13/3/16).

*****

"Regarding what you say that you have enlisted in our regiment, I am very pleased to hear it. I hear though that you have gone to get recruits. Make an effort to get recruits. If you fail to get recruits the people (of the regiment) will make a jest of you. Enlist the following (names of six men and the villages in which they reside). When you return from recruiting duty, volunteer to come (here) with the next draft. If you really wish to come, they will certainly send you: that is the custom. As to what you say about your advancement, the matter is in the hands of God. Whatever is written in your fate that you will certainly receive. A man has to work honestly and well, then God takes note of him."

From Risaldar Major Fateh Singh, 6th Cavalry, France, to Sawan Singh, Ludhiana, Punjab. (Gurmukhi, 21/3/16).

*****

"Write and tell me how things are with you. Then men who return to India from here, how are they treated? What do they get in the way of pension and the Chanda fund? The amount of pension, which is awarded to them, is it reduced or increased subsequently? When pension is awarded to them, are they treated well in addition? Write and tell me precisely and truly what is done. How are the people of the country treated? Are they treated harshly or otherwise? And what about recruiting, how is it conducted? If the recruiting is bad, is any pressure put on the people? What help do the Sirdars (Indian Officers) give in the matter of recruiting? Write and tell me fully how the country is being dealt with."

From Basant Singh, 6th Cavalry, France, to Ganda Singh, Dafadar, 6th Cavalry, Sialkot, Punjab. (No language, No date).

*****

"I am going to ask you to do me a favour. Now's the time for everyone to do what he can, and I am here. Recruiting is not what it might be and I want you to help in it. If you can get hold of any recruits, send them to Dafadar Chubar Singh. It will be a great kindness and I feel sure you will do your best."

From Sowar Amr Singh, 38th C.I. Horse, or 2nd Lancers, France, to Sirdar Chandra Singh, Amritsar, India. (Gurmukhi, 17/4/16).

*****

"There are heaps of recruits to be got without trouble. Jat Sikhs are not easily got. All the other castes are enlisting freely particularly Mahomedans, from whom we get 7 or 8 applications every day. Other castes are not so easily got but we are working hard. We can get lots of hukka smoking Brahmins in Jalandar and Hoshiarpur but not Brahmin Sikhs. In Sialkot we have begun to get Labhana recruits and also plenty of Mahomedans there. There is no need to go about seeking them. They come in of their own accord. Now, by the favour of the Guru we have got a dozen or so Jat Sikhs and I hope we shall be able to send you some for your B Squadron."

From Ganda Singh, 6th Cavalry, Sialkot, to Lance Dafadar Basant Singh, 6th Cavalry, France. (Urdu, 26/5/16).

*****

"The confusion and chaos which Atar Singh used to declare was always to be found in the "riding school" but have now established one in our regiment itself. In our squadron, there are sections of new men who are addicted to the use of tobacco. If one remonstrates with them, they declare that without tobacco they would die. Some come from the Hissar district, others from the Ambala and Simla districts. It is difficult to tell where these barbarians (jangli) have come from, I have never even heard of the names of the villages from which our recruits now come. Truly confusion and chaos have entered the regiment. Nothing is safe. Whoever finds an opportunity, immediately makes away with things. One never seems to have one's proper turn in the kitchen. If two of them sit down to food, the remainder of the party have to content themselves with playing tunes on their plates (that is to say they devour everything and leave nothing for the rest of the party). The recruits fight for and grab the food. I cannot describe the state of affairs properly. Both men and horses are new! No one pays any regard to what he is told – he does whatever he pleases."

From Amar Singh, L.D., 10th Lancers, Loralai, Baluchistan Agency, India, to Harnam Singh, L.D., 10th Lancers attached 9th Hodson's Horse, France. (Urdu, 30/5/16).

*****

"I have received your letter and understood its contents. I have heard with much satisfaction of the fact that you and Mansa Singh have made a number of recruits. At the present time it is a very laudable act to help the Sircar by getting recruits."

From Rurh Singh, Ressaidar, 30th Lancers, France, to Chet Singh, Ludhiana Dt., Punjab. (Gurmukhi, 4/6/16).

*****

"There are 60 recruits at present and the Resaldar is out collecting more. They keep coming in, fine stout young fellows. When the Risala was at its full strength, we had no such stalwart young fellows, wrestlers and good at tug of war. Most of them are 5'9 and 5'10 but none are under 5'6. There is not a single weak recruit among them and none of them have got beards. It is quite true to say that there is not one among them who is not good looking. It is known here that the 7th will come back from field service and its place be taken by the 22nd."

From Faqir Singh, Poona, India, to Sowar Gujar Singh attached 18th Lancers, France. (Urdu dated 9th October 1916).

*****

"Agricultural operations are going on all right. Cotton is at 5 seers the rupee. Men are being impressed and sent forcibly to the Expeditionary Force."

From Ganda Singh, Nabha, India, to Fazal Singh, 19th Lancers, France. (Urdu dated the 27th October 1916).

*****

"The cavalry lines here have all been dismantled and a battery has taken its place. There is a new battery made up of pensioners. Batteries of this kind have been recruited also at Meerut and Lucknow."

From Jemadar Surain Singh, Cawnpur, India to Jemadar Bhaspur Singh, 2nd Lancers, France. (Urdu dated the 31st October 1916).

*****

"Do your best to get well soon and rejoin the regiment because this is your opportunity to serve. Consider, after how long an interval of time we have now found an opportunity to serve, therefore it is incumbent on us to keep well and to make the most of this opportunity to discharge our obligation. Till you are fit to return here, you should without fail do all you can to push recruiting. In short, it is incumbent on you to do your duty in any way in which it comes before you. It is very important that you should exert yourself in recruiting, because owing to the despatch of reinforcements to France, there must be many vacancies in the Depot, and everything possible should be done to fill them. It is with the most profound regret that I have to announce to you the death in London of Major Barr Sahib. His death is a great calamity for the regiment."

From Amar Singh, Risaldar Major, 38th Central India Horse, France, to Mehal Singh, Ressaidar, 38th Central India Horse, Depot Agar Malwa, C.I. (Urdu dated 7th November 1916).

*****

"The Deputy Commissioner is a very stern man. I don't know where he has come from. I cannot get to see him. He demands recruits and it is very difficult to find any. I am trying hard to get recruits and hope to get some shortly. Then we will see what can be done."

From Mathra Singh, Lumberdar, Rawal Pindi District, Punjab, India to Naubat Singh, Lance Dafadar, Signal Troop, Sialkot Cavalry Brigade, France. (Urdu dated the 10th November 1916).

*****

"Our Regiment reached Bolarum on the 2nd November and on the 7th all the men from the field were given leave. The recruitment of Sikhs for No. 5 Troop has been stopped. They have filled up 1/2 a Troop with Jats. The 6th Troop was filled up with Sikhs by Risaldar Bishan Singh with much trouble. At the commencement of the war he enlisted 79 men for this purpose. The Jats taking counsel with Kalandar Khan, Risaldar Major, decided to make up another troop of Jats. Carrying Major Grattan Sahib with them, they obliged Bishan Singh to go on pension. Now there is great difficulty about recruitment. The 'izzat' of Sikhs in the regiment is not equal to even that of a syce. Major Carnegy Sahib Bahadur, becoming angry, has gone to make recruits. All this misinformation is due to the dissension amongst the Sirdars."

From Kahn Singh, 7th Hariana Lancers, Bolarum, Deccan, India to Hazura Singh, Risaldar, 7th Lancers attached 20th Deccan Horse, France. (Gurmukhi dated the 14th November 1916).

*****

"Now the Sahib has issued this order that any man going on leave will forfeit his travelling expenses unless he returns with two recruits. For this reason I am not now going on leave."

From Lal Singh, 2nd Lancers, Allahabad, U.P., India to Pala Singh, 2nd Lancers, France. (Urdu dated the 20th December 1916).

*****

"Men who are sent on leave just now are supposed to go recruiting when they are on leave. If they do not bring in any recruits they are punished and have to pay their fares both ways."

From Gandar Singh, Lance Dafadar, Saugor, India to Niranjan Singh, 2nd Lancers, France. (Urdu dated 31st December 1916).

*****

"Write often and in each letter tell me about recruitment – how many vacancies there are for Sikhs. I have written to you for this reason that Colvin Sahib has written to the Colonel Sahib saying there are 26 vacancies for recruits and that the only men offering are either too short or too weak. He also wrote to the Colonel Sahib about the recruitment of 'Malwa' Sikhs, and the Colonel Sahib together with the other Sahibs were of the opinion that 'Malwa' Sikhs should be recruited. At the present time Risaidar Basant Singh commands "right B". He is a 'Malwa' Sikh and is pressing for the recruitment of 'Malwa' Sikhs. I and the other Sirdars took counsel together and sent the Risaldar major to the Colonel Sahib urging him not to sanction the recruitment of 'Malwa' Sikh, and telling him that if he did so, it would be a great disgrace for us. The Colonel Sahib said, he would not do so if we forthwith filled up the vacancies. Therefore I write and beg of you to provide men for the vacancies as rapidly as possible, also give all the assistance you can to 'right B'. If you fail in this, it will be a great disgrace. No doubt you too are very concerned about the matter and doubtless recruits are difficult to obtain; but tell all our people to exert themselves and fill the vacancies within two months. All the other 'Majha' Sikh Sirdars have also written to their people and their friends about the matter. If the vacancies are not filled quickly then No. 3 Troop will be lost to us ('Majha' Sikhs). You need not tell people about this but exert yourself to the full, so that I may be able to give a satisfactory reply to the Colonel Sahib. If each of the men under you were to bring one recruit that matter would be satisfactorily arranged. Both pay and pension have now been increased and rations are provided free by the Sirdar, and it is probable that you will have no further difficulty in getting recruits."

From Natha Singh, Risaldar, 38th Central India Horse, France to Mal Singh, Jemadar, 38th Central India Horse, Agar Malwa, Rajputana, India. (Urdu dated the 9th January 1917).

*****

"At the present time it is the duty of us all to give whatever assistance we can to our Sircar, and the very best way of assisting is to obtain recruits. For this reason I write to tell you that my regiment is short of men and to ask you to get recruits and have them accepted."

From Amar Singh, Risaldar Major, 38th Central India Horse, France to Santa Singh, Batala, Amritsar District, Punjab, India. (Gurmukhi dated the 9th January 1917).

*****

"The Sahibs have stopped all leave. A man who goes on 14 days leave has to bring back 2 recruits and for ten days, one. If this order is not complied with, the man is fined and punished. This is the state of things in the depot."

From Ganda Singh, 2nd Lancers, Allahabad to Jemadar Bharpur Singh, 2nd Lancers, France. (Urdu dated the 17th January 1917).

*****

"The news from here is that it is a very good thing to serve in the Army, because now pension has been increased and pay also. It is very beneficial, for those who serve (in the Army) and all who eat the Government salt, should now aid the Government."

From Ujagar Singh, Dafadar, 38th Central India Horse, France to Sangat Singh, Amritsar District, Punjab, India. (Gurmukhi dated the 28th January 1917).

*****

"The advice you gave me was sound when you said, I should not retire on Rs. 4 pension. Now, pension has been raised to Rs. 5 after 15 years' service, and to Rs. 6 after 18 years' service. The Sircar has dealt very kindly with us."

From Sawan Singh, 18th Lancers, France to Magar Singh, 37th attached 18th Lancers, Marseilles, France. (Gurmukhi dated the 13th February 1917).

*****

"80 Sikhs and 20 Jats from our Regiment are going to France, all drafts to France are composed firstly of volunteers, secondly of men formerly invalided from Busrah and lastly of recruits. None of our men were invalided from Busrah but men from other regiments have been invalided. No one who has not been home on leave is taken into a draft for France. They say to him, first go home on leave and when you return from leave, you may volunteer."

From Chachal Singh, Dafadar, 16th Lancers, Loralai, Baluchistan Agency, India to Bishan Singh, Dafadar, Marseilles Remount Depot, France. (Urdu dated the 23rd February 1917).

*****

"Take my advice and do not let Thakur Singh enlist. Military service is very hard, and a man's heart becomes full of regret with longings for his home. Moreover, the Sircar takes an oath from each person recruited, and if any acts contrary to his oath he is very severely punished. This is quite true, there is nothing false in it. Even if Thakur Singh does not do any work, do not let him enlist, otherwise he will regret it."

From Gian Singh, Driver R.H.A. attached 2nd Lancers, France to Wazira, Hoshiarpur District, Punjab, India. (Gurmukhi dated the 3rd May 1917).

*****

"I don't quite remember what I wrote to you about, but I think you must be referring to what I said about recruiting. You write and make us somewhat ashamed on the subject of recruiting by asking why we do not do more. My answer to this is that it is difficult to get any recruits. When we do get them they are treated harshly and run away and then when they are caught they are sent to prison. When a man goes on recruiting duty people abuse him and say, 'The last lot of recruits you sent to prison, and now probably you will get this lot hanged.' Do not be anxious. We here are doing everything we can to promote recruiting."

From Nihal Singh, Depot, 38th Central India Horse, Agar Malwa, India to Risaldar Major Amir Singh, 38th Central India Horse, France. (Urdu dated the 4th May 1917).

*****

"Teji Singh is well and happy and is desirous of enlisting. They now give a bonus of Rs. 50 to each recruit. Further, if a man brings 30 recruits, he is made a Naik. If one brings 50 recruits he is made a Havildar, and if one brings 100 recruits he is made a Jemadar."

From Amrit Singh, Guide's Cavalry, Hoti Mardan, N.W.F. Provinces, India to Gurmukh Singh, 6th Cavalry, France. (Urdu dated the 13th June 1917).

*****

"We are pressing the enemy hard and hope therefore for victory. We have already taken a large extent of his territory. All our pensions [?] have been raised and every day the kindness of Government towards the army increases; rations are free, and pay has been raised, and various other benefits have been conferred."

From Risaldar Bishan Singh, 6th Cavalry, France to Dafadar Ishar Singh, Sialkot, Punjab. (Urdu dated the 16th June 1917).

*****

"At one time we had great difficulty in getting recruits, so the authorities are now giving a bonus of Rs. 50 per head and now the supply is again satisfactory."

From Nur Singh, Lance Dafadar, 3rd Lancers, Rawal Pindi to Risaldar Surat Singh, 2nd Lancers, France. (Urdu dated the 20th July 1917).

*****

"I hear that the Sircar is asking Rs. 10 from each house. If anyone should ask you for this money, do not give it on any account. Write and tell me about the matter and I will arrange. Don't give anything."

From Narain Singh, 38th Central India Horse, France to Surain Singh, Lyallpur, Punjab, India. (Gurmukhi dated the 5th August 1917).

*****

"The Colonel today wrote to Sialkot about your being enlisted. So go at once to the Major Sahib and when you are accepted write to me. I have thought the whole thing out and it is for your profit. Mind you, enlist and do nothing else. Do not follow any other counsel. I shall be very angry, with anyone who advises you to the contrary. Once you are enlisted eat well and dress well and in your leisure movements, play football. You will be 17 in September, so you must enlist."

From Arjan Singh, 6th Cavalry, France to Bachittar Singh, Khalsa School, Sialkot. (Urdu dated the 16th August 1917).

*****

"I am delighted at your success in recruiting. I am confident that you will go on giving this subject your consideration that the Captain Sahib may have no trouble at all with recruits. Do not have any doubt in your mind. This is the time to serve the King with devotion and loyalty. Through the Guru's aid all difficulties will be overcome. Trust in Him."

From Risaldar Major Sirdar Asur Singh, 38th Central India Horse, France to Kot Dafadar Chur Singh, 38th Central India Horse, Agar Malwa. (Urdu dated the 21st August 1917).

*****

"It is now some time since I received your letter, in which you ask me to use my influence to prevent Rajah Singh from being forcibly enlisted. No one can enlist him forcibly although intimidation is often used. You should appeal to the Tehsildar saying that 4 men of the family are already in the Army and are fighting for the Sircar in the war, and that this one (Rajah Singh) is the only one left to till our fields. This is the rascality of the Zaildar. Do not allow yourself to be intimidated by him. He cannot eat you."

From Amar Singh, 2nd Lancers, France to Karm Singh, Ludhiana District, Punjab, India. (Gurmukhi dated the 18th September 1917).

*****

"If the Sircar begins to collect money from house to house, you should not give anything. You should say 'In my house there are two men only and both are helping the Sircar on the firing line.' What greater help can they give? If you want money send to them for it. Don't you give anything."

From Gian Singh, 38th Central India Horse, France to his mother, Ferozepore District, Punjab, India. (Gurmukhi dated the 25th September 1917).

*****

"I hear that all the Zaildars have received the strictest orders that each of them is to furnish 20 recruits on pain of dismissal. This news is worrying me considerably."

From Bishan Singh, Risaldar, 19th Lancers, France to Kot Dafadar, Sunder Singh, Depot, 19th Lancers, Sialkot. (Urdu dated the 1st October 1917).

*****

"If any Government official asks you for money, do not give it."

From Nagina Singh, 33rd Cavalry attached 29th Lancers, France to Badan Singh, Ambala, India. (Gurmukhi dated the 3rd October 1917).

*****

"With what you write about your joining the volunteers, I am quite in agreement. I think you should do your best to join the movement. By the time you are a doctor you will be an experienced volunteer and it is right and proper to help the Government at such a time. There is no possible harm in becoming a volunteer. It can do nothing but good."

From Tilak Singh, 36th Jacob's Horse, France to Piram Singh, Medical College, Agra. (Urdu dated the 9th October 1917).

*****

"I hear that Gujar Singh has enlisted in the 2nd Patiala Cavalry. I am very glad to hear it. Military service is a very profitable occupation. Tell him to put his heart into his work."

From Arjan Singh, 29th Lancers, France to Nand Lal, Ludhiana District, Punjab, India. (Urdu dated the 16th October 1917).

*****

"I have heard that they are taking subscriptions (for the war loan). If anyone asks you for money do not give it. If anyone forces you to give it, demand a receipt, and send it to me."

From Sher Singh, Dafadar, 2nd Lancers [?] France to Milkha Singh, Jhelum, Punjab. (Gurmukhi dated the 16th October 1917).

*****

"If the Sircar summons Santa Singh to enlist, you should let him go with the greatest of pleasure, and you should have no anxiety regarding him."

From Magan Singh, 38th Central India Horse, France to Sant Singh, Ferozepore District, Punjab, India. (Gurmukhi dated the 8th November 1917).

*****

"May God grant a speedy victory to King George that the anxiety of our hearts may be removed! I am in great trouble. My child of 8 months is dead, and your sister-in-law is dead and thirdly I am threatened with dismissal from my position both of Zaildar and lumberdar. If my life would depart that would be the best solution of the difficulty! On the 29th November, the Deputy Commissioner sent for me and gave me a month to finish my recruiting saying that if I did not supply the men in that time I should be dismissed from both my Zaildarship and lumberdarship."

From Jawala Singh, Zaildar, Lyallpur, Punjab to Dafadar Kartar Singh, 9th Hodson's Horse, France. (Urdu dated the 11th December 1917).

*****

"As regards recruiting it is our duty to help the Sircar. But I do not wish to hustle you in the matter, because of our family 40 persons are engaged in the war, and 100 men have enlisted from our village and are now fighting in Arabia. If therefore no one remains in the family, who is suitable for service, where are recruits to be got from? Moreover for four years now there have been no births in our family. If you do succeed in getting any recruits enlist them in our Regiment for we too are in need of men."

From Kartar Singh, 38th Central India Horse, France to his father Chanda Singh, Sargodha, Punjab, India. (Urdu dated the 24th January 1918).

*****

"Try your best to get recruits. Enlist Uttam, Santa Singh's brother, and any other likely lad you may know."

From Ralla Singh, 36th Jacob's Horse, France to Uttam Singh (Granthi), 36th Jacob's Horse, Amballa, Punjab, India. (Gurmukhi dated the 25th January 1918).

*****

"If anyone takes money from you, write and tell me about it and state the amount taken. You should say to them "My son is present at the war, why then are you taking money from me?"

From Sant Singh, 2nd Lancers, France to Sher Singh, Ludhiana District, Punjab, India. (Gurmukhi dated the 29th January 1918).

*****

"You have never written to me whether you are contributing to the Government War Loan or not. If anyone asks you to pay, decline to do so. If any Lumberdar or other official attempts to force you, write and tell me his name and I will arrange. It is the order that no subscription is to be taken from the family which has sent a member to the war."

From Uttam Singh, 38th Central India Horse, France to Bhola Singh, Patiala State, India. (Gurmukhi dated the 28th February 1918).

*****

"From Sham Singh to his honoured father. As to what you have written about the subscription that it is being collected a second time, it is forbidden to collect subscription from the house of the man who is in the English army. When the subscription actually is imposed, and your share is put at 100, deduct my share before you pay it. If the magistrate says, 'Pay the share also of the man in service', say 'Get his share from him', and say 'He is actually on field service.' If any kind of paper or government letter comes in my name, I can answer it myself. We are three brothers and the subscription falls on us as well. Do not pay my share. If Rs 300 be asked of you, give Rs 200. In the matters of the subscription, I ask you to note what I have said carefully. Do not pay any subscription on my behalf. If anyone worries you about it – I can make arrangements from here. Do not have any concern on my account."

Extract from a letter from a Sikh to his father. (Original in Urdu). Dated 28th Oct 1918. – (Port Said).

*****

10

Sedition, Conspiracies, Komagata Maru and Ghadar

Kartar Singh Sarabha, on the eve of his execution, "If I had more lives than one, I would sacrifice each of them for my country's sake."

Why does not the spirit of Guru Gobind Singh and Hari Singh Nalwa exist in these days?

We have travelled over the sea thousands of miles and have suffered four months imprisonment on the ship, but the tyrants have shown us no mercy.

Thus was the Punjab lost, why do you not understand their (the Englishmen's) deceitful ways?

During the Great War, sedition, particularly amongst Sikhs who made up a large proportion of the Indian army, was a constant fear for the British. Early in the war period, the growth of the *Ghadar* movement and the potential threat to India at a time of war was especially worrying. The French Censorship at Marseilles "has made two seizures of packets containing copies of the notorious 'Ghadar'", reported the Censor in February 1916. This chapter describes some of the Sikh movements that existed during the Great War years.

Letters posted to Sikh soldiers were constantly monitored by the Censors and outright seditious letters would be intercepted. An example of such a letter which was intercepted at Bombay on 13 February 1914, from a Sikh in California to a soldier of the 82nd Punjabis in Nowshera illustrates the concern of the authorities:

> At first there were about ten thousand of our countrymen here but now only about six thousand remain. The English no longer require us and have stopped our migration here. These *badmashes* have plundered us and we shall not escape disgrace unless we get out of their hands. The English are treating us – all of us brother Indians – in the same manner as the Emperor Aurangzeb treated Hindus when he desired to convert them to Islam by force. The condition of our Bharat is worse than that of any country, as we cannot open our mouths to talk. All become terror stricken even at seeing one white man. All Indians living in America and Canada are prepared to kill and die. No one wishes to see these evil Englishmen. The Sikh community has fallen and can do nothing, for the community whose sacred places are taken from it is worthless. The greatest Sikh temple of worship is at Amritsar and has been taken over by the English. Before this, the Khalsa College, at which the sons of all Sikhs were reading, was taken

> away. It is written that it is far better for the community which loses its sacred places to die …The only remedy against these tyrants is that the troops should mutiny …
>
> In addition to expenditure on the English in India, fifty crores are drained away to England. The plague which breaks out is also the fault of the English, for the people have been reduced to such a state of poverty that they cannot afford good clothing and food. Plague never breaks out in any other country except India.
>
> All these facts which I have written have been copied from a paper called Ghadr, which is printed in America. I intended to send you the paper in original, but as its entry into India is prohibited I have written these few things in this letter…..You should write to me what is going on in India at the present time. Also write whether anything is talked about the Government in the regiments or not, and whether men are still giving their heads for eleven rupees as of old. The Englishmen's dogs are better off than our men for they get food by begging. The English take no notice of our begging; we shall have to bite…Do not let the white men know what I have written. Remember, lest you get into trouble; but understand and inform your friends…[1]

In late 1914, passengers of the *Komagata Maru* returned from their abortive trip to Vancouver, arriving back in Calcutta on 27 September. The passengers had had a horrendous return journey, taking over two months, and suffered immensely. When the ship arrived, it docked at *Budge Budge* harbour. The British viewed the passengers and Gurdit Singh as law breakers. A violent altercation took place and nineteen passengers were killed. Many passengers were arrested and some fled, including Gurdit Singh. The remaining passengers were effectively put under house arrest for the remainder of the war. The official report into the *Budge Budge* incident blamed the passengers for the "riot". The Golden Temple manager also condemned the *Budge Budge* "rioters", displaying his allegiance to the British. In May 2016, the Canadian Prime Minister Justin Trudeau offered a full apology for the treatment meted out to the *Komagata Maru* passengers.

In the United States, the *Ghadar* movement had started to take shape by the outbreak of war in 1914. Several members of the *Ghadar* party were Sikhs. Leaflets showing the "true colours" of the British and pleading with co-religionists to awaken from their slumber were printed and sent all over the world. "Oh brave Singhs, the time is not for sleeping. Why don't you look at the world around you?", stated an early *Ghadar* production. Leaflets were printed in many languages, including *Gurmukhi*. One of the leading lights of the *Ghadar* movement in the USA was Kartar Singh Sarabha, a young man who had experienced first-hand the hard ships of labour in the USA. During his period of revolutionary activity, he sang the following song:

Most difficult is the service of the country
Though it is very easy to talk
Those who choose to serve the country
Had to face millions of problems
Those love service of the country

1 F.C. Isemonger and J. Slattery, *An account of the Ghadr Conspiracy: 1913-1915* (Lahore: Superintendent, Govt. Print., 1919), p. 21.

Abandoned all the comforts of home and hearth and become 'faqirs'
Many had faced the gallows smilingly
And many had been sent to the Andeman jail
We cannot bow out
We have become lovers of freedom
We must free our country
May our bodies be cut to pieces.[2]

The British did not want the movement to gain ground in India, it was also worried that the *Ghadarites* may start to work with Bengali "anarchists". Once the war broke out, the *Ghadarites* spurred on by the racism they had encountered decided an armed insurrection was required in India. Thousands of would-be revolutionaries started to return to India. Plans were made to seduce Indian troops (especially Sikh troops) by showing them how the British were stripping their country of its wealth and how they were effectively slaves. Their plans included making bombs and collecting money for revolutionary activities. The Lieutenant-Governor described the situation in the Punjab when the *Ghadarite* activities were at their height:

> In fact, from October 1914 to September 1915, there was a constant series of explosions. All over Central Punjab, the police were murdered; loyal citizens, especially Sikhs known to be assisting the authorities, were shot down or killed by bombs; gang robberies, sometimes with the murder, of wealthy Hindus were carried out to raise funds for the cause; several attempts to derail trains or blow up bridges; factories for the preparation of bombs were established in various places; bombs and materials for bombs were received from the revolutionary depots; caches of revolvers and guns were made in British districts and Native States; an attack was made on the Indian military piquet guarding a railway bridge on the main line close to Amritsar; the guard was murdered and their rifles taken; plans for seizing the arsenal at Ferozepore and the magazines at Lahore and other cantonments were formed; and persistent attempts were made, not in all cases without success, to tamper with the Indian troops in at least a dozen stations in the Punjab and the United Provinces.[3]

According to the Lieutenant-Governor, the *Ghadarites* did not find much success in persuading rural Sikhs and Punjabis to rally to their cause, but they pursued their agenda anyway. A letter from a Sikh at the front to a relative in the USA highlights the fact that the British knew what was happening. "I have got a letter from the village which says that men arriving from America are arrested as they leave the ship, put into the lock-up and thrown into prison." Emigrants from Shanghai, Hong Kong, Penang and Rangoon still tried to return to India, and some tried to enter via Burma. Would-be revolutionaries on board a ship called the *Tosa Maru* were arrested immediately once they reached India. One hundred, of the 173 passengers were sent to jails in Montgomery and Multan. Here they met the Lieutenant-Governor O'Dwyer who sneeringly asked them, "So you claim the Punjab to be yours?" Prompt came the reply, "Yes, and not only

2 Gurcharan Singh Muhay, *A zeal for martyrdom: Kartar Singh Sarabha* (Ludhiana: Lahore Book Shop, 2005), pp. 3-4.
3 Michael O'Dwyer, *India as I knew it 1885-1925* (London: Constable & Co., 1925), p. 197.

the Punjab but the whole of India and we shall rule over the land one day."[4] The British also severely punished anyone found in possession of seditious literature and sent them to prison as a warning to others.

The date for the planned revolt was set for 21 February 1915. However, the revolutionaries were betrayed from within their ranks, and were all arrested. The Lahore conspiracy cases were quickly convened (via "Special Tribunal") and many of the *Ghadarites* were hanged and hundreds transported to the Andaman Islands (See Appendix IV). Nineteen-year-old Kartar Singh Sarabha was one of the men hanged. Many of the accused had put up stout defences, but the number of approvers made demonstrating their innocence difficult. Randhir Singh, a prominent Sikh and alleged main protagonist, was sent to jail and went through terrible suffering. His *jatha* was alleged to have put up the following poster on the gates of the Khalsa High School in Ludhiana:

The Feringhis have looted the country and laid it waste
The people are harassed greatly, O people;
They have taken all riches of India,
And have sent them to England, O people;
These dacoits are looting us day and night
The poor cultivators are starving, O people;
Good pay is paid to the Whiteman
To eat, drink and be merry, O people.
All the rest, soldiers, Sikhs, or Muslims
Have only grams to eat, O people.
The white man shrank back on the battlefield,
Standing at safe distance they issue Orders, O people;
To fight and get killed we are pushed to the front,
In Egypt, Africa, Persia, O people;
The English are not a great power,
Fight and defeat them, O people;
When will ye, Khalsa draw the sword?
And slay the Whiteman, O people;
Make preparation for mutiny soon
To destroy the rule of the tyrants, O people.[5]

He detailed his subsequent jail experiences in his autobiography '*Jail Chitian* (Letters)'. The Lahore Conspiracy trials would continue for quite a few months with more and more Sikhs being sent to jail, or worse. The British hoped that the sentences handed down to the 'conspirators' would serve as sufficient deterrent to anyone hoping to follow in the *Ghadarite* footsteps; they got their wish…

4 Randhir Singh, The Ghadar Heroes: *Forgotten story of the Punjab revolutionaries of 1914-15* (Bombay: People's Pub. House, 1945), p. 14.

5 Randhir Singh, *Jail Chitian, Autobiography of Bhai Sahib Randhir Singh* (London: Bhai Sahib Randhir Singh Trust UK, 2012), p. 25.

By March 1915, the Lieutenant-Governor still concerned about the situation convened a meeting of "leading" Sikhs and Commissioners in Lahore. The outcome of this meeting was that "loyal" Sikhs agreed to set up committees to investigate the political sensibilities of returning emigrants and report their findings to the Commissioners. These committees proved invaluable to the Government and were first rate in warning the Government of potential trouble. Although problems persisted, by 1916, the *Ghadarites* had been defeated. The Lieutenant-Governor, constantly worried about the threat posed by revolutionaries, was one of the most ardent supporters of the Defence of India Act 1915, which when passed, allowed speedy trials for sedition or revolutionary activities. The British needed more control ...

*****

""If you wish to play the game of love
Lay your head upon your hand & come into the street where I dwell."

I pray to all my brothers, Hindu & Mussulman, to join together & break the English lock. There is no withstanding Germany. Germany burns up all who come (against her). Let no army come from India. Soon there will be Mutiny in India. Let all men join & put an end to the English. Germany marches forward dealing death. She has put Belgium to death & half of France. Very soon she will be the death of England too. The bombardment of England began on the 2nd of November. The first German gun carries 18 eighteen miles, the second 25 twenty-five miles, the third 30 thirty miles, & the remainder 40 forty miles. The gun which carries 30 miles where its ball falls kills men all around for a distance of four miles. Very soon the whole world will come under the German sway. India will come next year. On one side you have Germany, Austria, China, & Holland, these five. Germany is a giant in strength & in religion. On the other side are England, France, Russia, Japan, Servia, Belgium, these six. But the giant Germany is utterly destroying the whole six. She has captured & imprisoned four lakhs of their men. She has sunk eighty 80 British men-of-war & has taken seventy 70. Countless soldiers perished in the ships that were sunk. The name of Germany is breathed throughout the world like the name of Harankash (a demon), ___hail Germany hail. Tear off the veil & listen. Verily my words are true. BANDE MATARAM."

Translation of an anonymous letter posted at Vancouver in British Columbia on 4th November 1914 to the address of Subedar Naurang Singh, B Company, 15th Sikhs, Cantt Loralai, Balochistan, India. The original is in Gurmukhi, written in an educated hand, & the language is eastern Punjabi.

*****

"Here in the Punjab dacoities have become very common. The people in their sin do not remember that the Government which protects us is fighting an enemy. They are getting up a mutiny (ghadr), & what trouble is brought upon the Government. We pity their ignorance. The Lord will give them sense. In one week, there have been 15 dacoities. When will God give peace? The Government has made many arrests &

in the investigation it was discovered that the dacoits were men who had been turned back from America."

From a Khatri Sikh in India to a friend in a regiment serving in France. (Gurmukhi, dated 30/1/15).

*****

A Bomb from Bengal
A gun made in France
The Khalsa from India*
Make Germany dance

*Khalsa = The Sikhs. The tribute to Bengali anarchists and the omission of any reference to Britain's share in the war are interesting. The verse is typical of the Sikh in every way.
Couplet in Sikh letter from the front to India. (Gurmukhi of 8/4/15).

*****

"When you return do not bring any arms with you. Anyone who is found armed is not given a trial but is put in jail for seven years."

Scrap of letter (apparently sent from India to California) enclosed in a letter from Bishen Singh, Silsbee, California to Kishan Singh, 4th Cavalry, France. (Gurmukhi, 24/4/15).

*****

"In the letter I wrote to you at Goona, I mentioned the condition of our country (India): the state of affairs I described is now beginning to take form. Think carefully over this. We may expect our country to become a --- (illegible) like America."

From Makhan Singh, Box 840, P.O. Upland, California, to No.3011 L.Assa Singh, 38th C.I.H. (Gurmukhi, 20/8/15).

*****

"Q. – What have you to say?
A. – Twelve days after the Diwali festival, Lal Singh, son of Maya Singh, Jat, of Bhure, Tahsil Tarn Taran, Gujjar Singh, father's name not known, Jat, residence unknown, and another lean and thin Sikh having fair complexion, middle stature, aged 30 or 32 years, came to the Jhar Sahib.
Q. – What was the time then and how long ago did the last Diwali festival came off?
A. – It was the last Diwali and the time was chhakwela in the morning.
Q. – What else have you to say?
A. – Lal Singh said "well Mahant you might have heard something." I replied that I had heard nothing and asked him to tell me what the thing was. He said that the English had demolished the Rakab Gunj gurdwara to build a road there, and that they

might be requested not to demolish it. He also urged me to join the movement, other Sikhs too having joined in it. I replied that I would do the best I could. He added that the Darbar Sahib of Amritsar was now supplied with pipe water instead of river water, that the water of the tank had thus been rendered impure and that this should also be protested against. Moreover he said that the Government had arrested the Sikhs that had gone to Canada in the ship provided by Gurdit Singh, that this action of the Government was not also good and that the Government should be requested by means of an application not to arrest them. Saying this, Lal Singh and his two companions went away. A few days after Lal Singh of Bhure, Natha Singh, father's name not known, a Sadh, resident of Sur Singh, District Lahore, and Budha Singh, father's name not known, resident of Sur Singh, came there.
Q. – Did they come after Diwali; if so, how many days after?
A. – They came four days after Lal Singh's first visit.
Q. – What was the time then?
A. – It was noon time.
Q. – What else have you to say?
A. – All three of them said "you have done nothing in connection with the matter we told you on the previous occasion. The Sikhs have arranged to meet together and hold a consultation and then to act according to the opinion that may be arrived at. A few days later a meeting will be held at the Jhar Sahib."

Five days thereafter, Lal Singh of Bhure, and Balwant Singh, father's name not known, caste Jat, resident of Dudher, tehsil and district not known, came to me. They were accompanied by Kala Singh, son of Gulab Singh, caste Jat, resident of Bhure also. They brought with them a newspaper in Gurmukhi entitled 'the Ghadr' and said that it should be gone through and acted upon. Balwant Singh read out the paper to me. It recited that the English themselves were enjoying ease and comfort and giving us (the Indians) trouble. They also said that the English had arrested and greatly oppressed the crews (the Sikhs) of the ship that had gone to Canada. That paper urged that every Hindu, Sikh, Musalman, who might happen to read it, should act according to it.
Q. – How to act according to it?
A. – They should act according to the decision come to at the meeting. That is to say, if the meeting asked them to fight against the Government, they should fight; and if the meeting asked them to submit an appeal they should do that.
Q. – What else do you have to say?
A. – Saying this Lal Singh made over to me the 'Ghadr' paper. I read it the next day.
Q. – Did you read it to yourself or did you read it out to others?
A. – I read it for myself.
Q. – Have you anything more to say?
A. – Three days later Lal Singh of Bhure came to me alone and took back the 'Ghadr' paper from me. He told me that the Sikhs has resolved to meet together at the Jhar Sahib gurdwara, and that the decision come to should be followed. He said to me also that I should arrange food for 20 or 25 men. I replied that I would do the best I could.

He told me also that some more men would come and that for them he would make arrangements himself. Moreover, he said that the 25th had been fixed for a meeting at the Jhar Sahib.

Q. – The 25th of what month?
A. – The 25th of the English month. It was the month of Maghar.
Q. – What else have you to say?
A. – Saying this Lal Singh went away. Again he came in the afternoon on the 25th alone and said that a meeting would be held that day and that I should prepare food. I cooked food for 20 or 25 men. In the evening the men arrived in two groups......
Q. – How many men were there in the first group and how many in the second?
A. – The first group consisted of 20 or 25 men and the second of 25 or 30 men.
Q. – What else have you to say?
A. – These men came and seated themselves. Soon after Lal Singh of Bhure, Natha Singh, father's name not known, Sadh, of Sur Singh (referred to above), Budha Singh, son of Sawan Singh, Jat, of Bhure, Chuhar Singh, son of Natha Singh, Jat, of Bhure, and Sundar Singh, son of Natha Singh, brother of Chuhar Singh, resident of Bhure, came with loaves of bread.
Q. – How far is Bhure from the Jhar Sahib?
A. – There is a distance of 1 or 1¼ mile between the two.
Q. – How many men assembled there?
A. – Some 50 or 60 men assembled there.
Q. – What took place then?
A. – Khichri was prepared of moth grain and rice and loaves were prepared of wheat. I prepared gram, pulse and bread, which were given to all the people to eat first.
Q. – By whom did you get the food prepared?
A. – It was prepared by the men of the first group and myself. I have three younger brothers, namely Mal Singh, Kartara Singh and Amar Singh. They helped in preparing food. Another brother of mine, viz., Jassa Singh, had gone to the village to do the Path (reciting sacred books).
Q. – To which village had he gone?
A. – The village to which he had gone is called Shekh.
Q. – Did your brothers know what for the meeting was to be held?
A. – They knew nothing. Previously too they used to render help in the preparation of food.
Q. – What else have you to say?
A. – After taking food the people sat on the road inside the dera. Natha Singh of Sursingh said "to have gurdwara Rakab Gunj rebuilt 20 men should be sent first. If the Government arrests them, 20 others should be sent and in the event of the latter being arrested 20 others should be sent. War should be waged against the Government on the fourth occasion?"
The said Natha Singh added that the above was the opinion of Gur Charan Singh of Lyallpur and was correct.
Q. – Do you know what Gur Charan Singh does and where he lives?
A. – I know nothing about him.
Q. – What else have you to say?
A. – The meeting resolved that the work connected with the gurdwara should be done in the above-mentioned way. Then Lal Singh of Bhure said that the 23rd Cavalry of Lahore had sent a man with the word that something should be done towards the

Rakab Gunj gurdwara and that they too would help in the war. Then Kala Singh of Jagatpur said what should be done regarding the pipe water supplied to the Darbar Sahib. In this behalf it was resolved that nothing should yet be done. As regards the interception of the ship of the Sikhs, it was agreed that the Sikhs should be rescued by waging war against the Government.
Q. – Who made this suggestion?
A. – Kala Singh.
Q. – How was war to be waged?
A. – No decision was made as to this.
Q. – What opinion did you give?
A. – My opinion also was that war should be waged against the Government and that measures should be taken in accordance with the opinion of the Sikh brethren.
Q. – What else have you to say?
A. – Then Budha Singh said that the Bengal revolutionaries also urged the waging of war against the Government and showed their readiness to give help. Harnam Singh said that a man had come from Doaba and stated that he and others had no leisure that day and that they would commence war on the 27th when they thought they would have leisure and that therefore the date of commencement of war might be postponed. To this all agreed. Harnam Singh said that the man should be made to accompany the Doaba man and to elicit information about the matter.
Q. – Did the Doaba man come in your presence?
A. – Yes.
Q. – What was his name or description?
A. – I do not know his name. I could not notice his complexion. He was, however, a Sikh of middle stature, neither very lean nor very fat. He had a beard and was aged about 30 or 35 years.
Q. – What else have you to say?
A. – Lal Singh asked Harnam Singh to go and get the required information and paid him Rs. 2. He also told him that he and others agreed to the date of waging war being postponed to the 27th. Thereafter, all went away. Lal Singh addressing me said that the day after next had been fixed for the purpose, and he proclaimed to all present that the next meeting would be held at the theh of Kairon. Then he made over to me a chhavi and said that I would be called if needed. After this all went away.
Q. – Did he give you any chhavi; if so where is that?
A. – Yes he gave over to me one. Four days, thereafter, Parem Singh of Sursingh (aforesaid) took it from me on loan, saying that he required the same.
Q. – What else have you to say?
A. – I did not go to the theh of Kairon, nor was I invited there.
Q. – What else have you to say?
A. – Four days after the meeting at Jhar Sahib, three sowars came there on foot with boot and pattis on in the afternoon.
Q. – What were their names?
A. – One was named Surain Singh, father's name not known, caste Jat, resident of Shahbazpur, Tahsil Tarn Taran, and the names of the others I do not know.
Q. – What else have you to say?

A. – On their arrival the said sowars said "is Lal Singh of Bhure not here?" I asked them why they enquired about him. They replied that they had come from the 23rd Cavalry stationed at Lahore to see Lal Singh, but that they could not find him. I said that he might be at Bhure. They then returned after drinking water. Two hours after their departure two men came from Shahbazpur, and the other was not acquainted with me, nor did I enquire his name. They asked me about Surain Singh and the two sowars. I said that they had gone to Bhure. Two gharis thereafter, Kala Singh, son of Gulab Singh, Jat, of Bhure, came alone and asked me about the three sowars. I told him also that they had gone to Bhure. The two men of Shahbazpur were still there at the Jhar Sahib. They requested me to have Surain Singh and the two sowars sent for. I sent Jora Singh, son of Hakim Singh, Jat, of Kamalpur (who had come there to take bhang) to Bhure. Surain Singh alone came along with him. The men of Shahbazpur asked Surain Singh to accompany them to Shahbazpur where they said a man had come to see him. Surain Singh would not agree to this saying that his companions were at Bhure and that he alone could not go. He then remained with me and the two men of Shahbazpur went away. We took food and went to bed. One or 1¼ pahrs before sunrise two men came. One of them was Jhanda Singh, son of Bhagwan Singh, resident of Shahbazpur, while the other was not known to me. They asked me if Surain Singh was there. I took them to him. Jhanda Singh's companion stated that the men of the Cavalry stationed at Lahore had said that if Surain Singh and the other two fugitives came back they would get them pardoned. At the request of Surain Singh I went to Kala Singh's house at Bhure and brought the two sowars from there. Jhanda Singh and his companions returned while Surain Singh and his companions did not. At day-break, a man, who I did not know came. He was a tall and stalwart man. He said to Surain Singh that he should affect his escape as the Police was coming to arrest him. Thereupon, the three sowars went out. Parem Singh (aforesaid), and Bishen Singh, Jat, of Arpal, District Amritsar (father's name not known) came to Jhar Sahib in quest of Lal Singh. They too fled away to a different direction from that of the sowars. After that the Police arrived and seized the three sowars. Two days later, Lal Singh of Bhure came to me at the Jhar Sahib and said "O Mahant! This is a sword. I want it no longer. Keep it with you." I refused to keep it myself. However, I yielded on his insisting. I received the sword from him and threw the same into a well inside Jhar Sahib.
Q. – How many wells are there in Jhar Sahib?
A. – There are two wells. I threw the sword into the smaller well which is used for drinking purposes.
Q. – Have you to say anything else?
A. – Three days later Prem Singh of Sur Singh (aforesaid) came. He too asked me to keep a sword and said that he did not require it and that he would take it back at the time of need. At first I refused to do so but afterwards I took the sword from him and threw it in the smaller well. Ten or twelve days thereafter Kala Singh of Bhure (aforesaid) came. He gave me a chhura (large knife) with a leather scabbard to keep. I interred them in the mud in the chhappar (pond) in the Jhar Sahib. I produced both the swords and the chhura yesterday. (The Policemen gave two rusty swords and a chhura with a torn leather scabbard, which were shown to the accused).

Q. – Are these swords and chhura and scabbard the same?
A. – Yes, they are the same.
Q. – Have you to say anything else?
A. – I have to say nothing else.
Q. – Had anybody got weapons when the meetings were held at Jhar Sahib?
A. – Many had dangs (clubs), some had chhavis and a few had pistols. I cannot tell what particular person had what.
Q. – Have you to say anything else?
A. – I have to say nothing else."

Signature of – Diwan Som Nath. Magistrate of the 1st Class, District Amritsar. Dated the 18th September 1915.

Translation of a confession made by Bogh Singh, son of Natha Singh, on the 18th day of September 1915, before Diwan Som Nath, Magistrate of the 1st class in the District of Amritsar. Second Lahore Conspiracy Case.

*****

"I have already written strongly advising you not to return home and I hope that my letter prevented your return. I need not repeat myself. I have got a letter from the village which says that men arriving from America are arrested as they leave the ship, put into the lock-up and thrown into prison. So long as the war lasts, do not return to the village."

From Asa Singh, F.P.O.39 to Makhan Singh, Box 840, Upland, California. (Gurmukhi, dated 10/10/15).

*****

"You asked about disturbances our people are raising here. Well, the fact is that we Sikh fools are ignorant. The people who publish the newspapers here are Bengalis, and very bad men. They talk a lot of nonsense and send our men, poor devils, home to India to get hanged and put in jail. They also rob the poor devils who remain, and spend the loot on dacoities etc. But I think that they too are going to suffer for their misdeeds. Now the Sikhs and the Bengalis are divided. Really there is nothing the matter except that the Bengalis are playing the fool."

From Harnam Singh, Box 116, Walnut Grove, Cal. U.S.A., to Kirpal Singh, 1st Sappers & Miners, France. (Gurmukhi, 3/11/15).

*****

"The facts are that I was employed on a ship out here and the ship's company has been paid off and the ship is at anchor here. If any wealthy person charters the ship again, I will go. For the time being I am doing nothing but resting in the Gurudwara. I have been doing nothing since September and it was only a chance that I got your letter. I will write again and tell you all about my plans and how I am."

From Jagjit Singh, Sikh Temple, Hong Kong, China, to Dalip Singh, 3rd Skinner's Horse, France. (Gurmukhi, 27/11/15).

*****

"Q. 1. – Were you once a Tahsildar in British service?
A. – I was a temporary Naib Tahsildar on plague duty as Personal Assistant to Dr. Fisher.
Q. 2. – Is your father Legal Remembrancer of Nabha State?
A. – Yes, when I was arrested he used to be a Judge, High Court.
Q. 3. – Did you meet approver Sundar Singh (A.M.) and approver Ichhar Singh at Bhasaur some years ago, and did you tell Mr. Scott on jail parade that you knew Ichhar Singh?
A. – Don't remember Sundar Singh (A.M.) but remember seeing Ichhar Singh there. I did tell Mr. Scott, that I knew Ichhar Singh.
Q. 4. – Were you at a large meeting at Lobatbadi with some 6 followers when resolutions were passed re the Rakabganj Gurdwara, Darbar Sahib tank, Santokhsar tank, and the excommunication of Sardar Singh, Majithia, and Sardar Bahadur Arur Singh?
A. – I did attend a meeting at Lobatbadi but with no followers, nor have I any followers. I was not invited there but went myself to protest against removal of girls and the teaching staff from Basur which somehow by misrepresentations Ichhar Singh and Sundar Singh had done. They had also falsely circulated that I was to act as patron of the girls' school they intended to establish at Lobatbadi. The Dewan on that occasion was for the school. I was at first refused to speak against their proposal and appeal, but I made myself heard in strong terms repudiating false reports that I was to be a patron: this procedure was disappointing to them as there was no response in terms of funds after my protest. The audience being in my favour, could not be turned out.

Rikabganj matter was brought forward. I pointed out to the audience the utter futility of agitating the matter after a large representative Dewan at Lahore had submitted a memorial to the Government. On this, the assembly there simply confirmed the resolution of the Lahore Dewan assembly.

Re Darbar Sahib and Santokhsar tanks. I pointed out that these matters rest with the Amritsar Municipality. It should be moved first then the Government memorialised.

Re excommunication of Sardar Sundar Singh and Sardar Arur Singh. No names were mentioned but a special committee of Chief Khalsa Dewan was proposed to be excommunicated. I put forward an amendment that the Government should be requested not to treat the opinions of that committee as the voice of the Panth.
Q. 5. – Were similar resolutions passed at P.W. 27 Indar Singh's house at Khanna in Asuj, and did you there say that the British Raj was nearing its end, because it laid its hand on religious things?
A. – No. As far as I can remember one was re "Nath Chaker" proscribed for which Government was to be thanked, the 2nd was to ask Government to proscribe Khalsa Panth ki Hakikat. As to other resolutions, I proposed that this need not be moved as war had begun, we should rather assist Government than hamper it on such an occasion. Some Chamars were taken in the Sikh religion but they again resumed

interdining with their Chamar relations. Ichhar Singh and Sundar Singh (A.M.) kept up intercourse with these men and were put to penalty at Khanna meeting.
Q. 6. – Did you, in Poh, attend a meeting at the Chamkaur Sahib Gurdwara, and tell Sundar Singh (A.M.) and accused Karm Singh of a secret seditious meeting at Ludhiana, and say that arms were expected from Bengal and that suitable men would be found at the annual meeting at Fatehgarh Sahib?
A. – I did go, but never talked of anything of the kind to the men in question. I did not meet these men there. On the contrary, I was busy all the time in the Akhand Path performed for victory of British arms.
Q. 7. – Did you go with Sundar Singh (A.M.) and accused Karm Singh to Fatehgarh?
A. – I did go but did not meet the men in question there.
Q. 8. – Did you and others attend a meeting at Lobatbadi, and decide on the Jhaner dacoity, and fix the 17th Margh for another meeting at Lobatbadi?
A. – No.
Q. 9. – Just prior to the Jhaner dacoity of January 29th, 1915, did you send a message by accused Mastan Singh that you could not attend the meeting?
A. – No, I did not send any message by Mastan Singh. I did send a letter which related to school matters (which was collapsing). I had not my sympathy I evaded going there.
Q. 10. – Did you and your party attend an Akhand path at Narangwal, at which accused 98 Uttam Singh was present?
A. – No, I don't know (98) at all.
Q. 11 – Did you, about 12th Phagan, send P.W. 40 Teja Singh of Samrala with a letter inviting Sundar Singh (A.M.), accused (17) Gandha Singh, Karm Singh, Uttam Singh and other desh bhagats to an Akhand path at the house of Ram Singh, Reservist, at Gujarwal?
A. – There was an Akhand path beginning 6th Magh, lasting three days namely Basant Panchmi day. No Akhand path on 12th Phagan. I did not send any letter to invite any people except Sundar Singh (A.M.), who was made to pay a penalty. I did not know these men.
Q. 12. – Did you hold a secret meeting on the roof, and say that much work had been done in regiments, that two men had been sent to Lucknow and Pindi, and words to the effect that "it was time for men of the Khalsa to move out into the plains"?
A. – No.
Q. 13. – Did you say money was wanted and did Sundar Singh (A.M.) subscribe Rs. 24?
A. – No.
Q. 14. – Did you attend a path held by Gurbachan Singh at Dhundari about February 17th, and after it held a secret seditious meeting there?
A. – No path on 17th February, it began next day after Basant Panchami. Surjan Singh, Lal Singh, Ram Singh, Santa Singh, Mohindar Singh were not there. Santa Singh was written to by me to officiate as Patti. He did not turn up. I complained of his non-attendance by letter from Nabha. I came to know him at the Nankana fair.
Q. 15. – Did Kartar Singh of Sorabha come there on a bicycle, and tell you of a rising at Ferozepore for February 19th, and did you promise to bring your followers? Did Kartar Singh give you flags there?
A. – No, I don't know Kartar Singh at all.

Q. 16. – Did you send P.W. 27 Indar Singh to spread the news in the Bar, and accused (77) Santa Singh of Nandpur Kalour, and P.W. Teja Singh to collect men for the 19th, and say that the regiments at Ferozepore would supply arms?
A. – No.
Q. 17. – Did you entrain with a party of some 20 men dressed in black and having a harmonium and a takwa, at Mullanpur Station, and reach Ferozepore about 9 P.M. on February 19th, 1915?
A. – No, it is not our rule to wear black clothes.
Q. 18. – Were you there detained by British soldiers; but allowed to pass on as a singing party?
A. – No.
Q. 19. – Did you enquire who were armed, and did Kartar Singh of Sorabha and accused (17) Gandha Singh say they had bombs?
A. - No.
Q. 20. – Were you at the reed jungle assembly at Ferozepore?
A. – No.
Q. 21. – Did you and your party, including P.W. Mussammat Nihal Kaur, leave by *Phime ke Kai* Station next morning?
A. – No, never heard of this station.
Q. 22. – After that, did Sundar Singh (A.M.) or accused Karm Singh or accused Kartar Singh visit you at your father's house in Nabha, and did you advise caution?
A. – Except Sundar Singh (A.M.) others in the question never came to me. No advice or caution was given. Sundar Singh (A.M.) came to me probably in the end of Phagan. He wanted my help in money to bribe the police to secure his sons release. I simply said that such a conduct is against Gurus' teaching. I shall not countenance anything of that sort, and that he had go and surrender himself and defend his sons in the ordinary way. If he does not do so I shall report to the police and inform the Panth.
Q. 23. – Did you incite P.W. Bhagat Singh to preach sedition, and did he use to visit you?
A. – No, I don't know him at all.
Q. 24. – Did you know anything about Bhagat Singh's diary (Exh. P.15)? Why are you mentioned in it? Did you give him any money? (vide page 67). Did he show you the diary in Nabha?
A. – I cannot speculate any reason why my name is in his diary.
Q. 25. – Did he visit you on 18th February 1915 to tell you of approver Ichhar Singh's arrest; and did you ask him to join at Mullanpur?
A. – No.
Q. 26. – On the way back from Ferozepore, did you complain to Bhagat Singh that accused Mastan Singh had deceived you by not supplying men and arms?
A. – No.
Q. 27. – On April 24th 1915 did Bhagat Singh visit Nabha, and warn you against the Police?
A. – No.
Q. 28. – Did you meet (P.W. 27) Indar Singh at a Bhog ceremony at Mallawal, and reproach him for not coming to Ferozepore?
A. – Yes, he met me there. He wanted a Path at his own residence. I agreed to do it and dates fixed 22nd, 23rd, 24th Besakh fixed and a Path held where I officiated.

Q. 29. – Was approver Anokh Singh sent to you about February 15th, 1915, by Kartar Singh of Sorabha to get news of accused (98) Uttam Singh?
A. – No.
Q. 30. – Was your house searched in the presence of your mother and maternal uncle on June 22nd, 1915 and was (Exh. P.70) (advertisement of Bharat Mata books) found there? Did your uncle sign the list (Exh. P.69)?
A. – No, I don't know, P.70 does not belong to me. I have never subscribed to Rajput Gazette of which this purports to be a supplement. I have never read such books.
Q. 31. – Does (Exh. P.70) (book supplement to Rajput Gazette, 1909) belong to you?
A. – No.
Q. 32. – Is (Exh. P.172A) your letter to P.W. Ichhar Singh? To what does it refer?
A. – It is in my handwriting; it relates to school matters and not to any meeting. Strong terms exchanged, resulting in greater alienation.
Q. 33. – On May 30th 1914 did you and P.W. Ichhar Singh and Buta Singh (hanged) attend a meeting at Langa Mandi, Lahore, re Rikabganj Gurdwara?
A. – I came on Mela which takes place, Jeth Sudi, 4 every year in memory of Guru Arjan Sahib. Heard that there was a meeting of the Dewan. Large number of Panth. Thousands assembled, went there, never heard Buta Singh, saw Ichhar Singh sitting in the Dewan. It was resolved to memorialize the Government. I stopped the daughter of Ichhar Singh to lecture. He was much annoyed at it.
Q. 34. – Did Ichhar Singh and Buta Singh ask you about youths to go to America to learn bomb making, and did you suggest Sundar Singh (A.M.)? and afterwards speak to Sundar Singh on the subject?
A. – No, I remember a month or so after the Dewan assembly at Longe Mandi meeting a Sundar Singh at Ludhiana, not Sundar Singh (A.M.), he talked of going abroad for education. Since I am always against sending boys abroad I told him my opinion against the idea. He said Ichhar Singh wanted to send him to America.
Q. 35. – Did you send Amli and Hari Singh (L.C.C) to warn accused 98 Uttam Singh about the Police?
A. – No.
Q. 36. – Did you on Magh 8th attend a school meeting at Lobatbadi and next day a meeting at P.W. Ichhar Singh's house, when accused (17) Gandha Singh and accused (98) Uttam Singh displayed pistols, and Ichhar Singh showed 2 daggers?
A. – No.
Q. 37. – The name "Randhir" appears upon a slip of paper (Exh. P.237) said to have been found in a Lahore Ghadr house, can you offer any explanation regarding it?
A. – I cannot imagine why.
Q. 38. – That slip of paper is said to be in handwriting of one Rash Behari Bose, a fat Bengali, do you know anything about him?
A. – No.
Q. 39. – Do you wish to state anything further?
A. - Udham Singh, approver, has enmity with Ichhar Singh and Sundar Singh (A.M.). He was put under penalty, he had shaved and wanted Amrit. I wrote that he should be excommunicated and be apprised of my decision.

Bhagat Singh's father bore me enmity. He was also put under penalty for trying to turn out a Sikh from Dewan audience.

I had heard Anokh Singh with other boys insulted the Sikh Pahal by giving it to a dog. I wrote to his brother Nermal in hard terms and they got annoyed.

Hazara Singh, Zaildar and his brothers bear a grudge against me, Chanan Singh also bears me a grudge.

Kishen Singh also has enmity. I was in his way of getting a testimonial for plague duty. Teja Singh also bears enmity. I will also prove enmity as to other witnesses for prosecution when I will call my witnesses."

Recorded in our presence and hearing and is the full and true statement of the accused. Sheo Narain, Special Commissioner.
Translation read over and admitted correct. 1st February 1916.

69. Randhir Singh, son of Natha Singh, of Narangwal, Police Station Dehlon, District Ludhiana, aged 38:-

Second Lahore Conspiracy Case: 1st February 1916.

*****

"I often remained in the company of Bhai Randhir Singh to learn to read the Granth Sahib from him. I knew him from the time I studied in the Khalsa High School. Occasionally, he came to the Gurdwara to sing bhajans (hymns). I never went anywhere from the Diwan but in company with him. Once I went with him to attend a Singh Sabha at mauza Ballowal. A Chamar Singh who was admitted into the Khalsa panth (community) by being made to drink Amrat, attended the meeting. Nidhan Singh, father of Bhagat Singh, did not allow him to sit in the meeting and get on the well. Thereupon, Bhai Randhir Singh and myself said to the brotherhood that a penalty should be imposed on Nidhan Singh, as he did not permit the above-named Singh to sit in the meeting. Then Nidhan Singh was put to shame in the meeting and was called upon to pay a penalty. Owing to grudge arising from the above fact Bhagat Singh mentioned my name. I am quite innocent. I am parentless and have no relative to look after me. The Police arrested me because of my being an associate of Bhai Randhir Singh. The Police after arresting me took me to a Thanadar who said to me "You are a mere boy of tender age. You should give evidence against Randhir Singh and his Singh companions and thus save yourself. I give you my word that if you do so, you will be let off. If you do not do so you will be hanged. You are yet to enjoy this world. You should certainly stand witness against them." I refused to follow his advice and said that I would not tell a lie, that the court would do me justice and that he could not save me from the gallows. Three days thereafter I was sent to Ludhiana jail. When I was arrested at the Rampura Phul Railway Station I was told that I would be made a witness. But when I refused to give evidence, the Police confined me in the Ludhiana jail. I have been rotting in jail for three months for no fault on my part. I have got no one to look after me. I have no relative. Only the Government will take care of me."

DALIP SINGH
Accused No. 10,
through Dr. M. ALAM, Barrister-at-Law.

Translation of the Supplementary Statement of Dalip Singh, accused No. 10: - Second Lahore Conspiracy Case: the 3rd February 1916.

*****

"Thakur Singh of Risulpur was found in the possession of a seditious pamphlet (lit: "printed copy") against the government, and a sword stick. He has been awarded 7 years imprisonment. And Lal Singh – Puran Singh's uncle deserted when the Regiment was about to leave for the front. He is still missing."

From Bhagwan Singh, Taran Tarn, Punjab, to Lance-Dafadar Pritam Singh, 30th Lancers, France. (Urdu, 3/2/16).

*****

"There has been no rain. The crops are withering. Cotton is very dear. It is all going to Japan and America. The Pathans are creating disturbances. On the 3/3/16, five men of the police were killed and 4 were wounded. Robbery is prevalent, and unprincipled men have spoilt the country. Especially the "American ones" * have done much mischief, and many men are under observation as suspicious characters. There was an engagement near Shabkadar, but after a few days it was finished. We trust that the Pathans will not be able to raise their heads again (i.e. make another attempt).

We (of the 45th) who are serving in the 15th Sikhs are very unpleasantly situated. Since the 15th Sikhs look after their own men and pay no concern to those who are merely attached."

(*Note: The writer appears to refer here to those Indians who some little time back attempted to land in Canada but were sent back by the Canadian Government. It will be remembered that they created trouble in Singapore and Calcutta on the return journey).

From Ganga Singh, 15th Sikhs, Peshawar, India, to Jemadar Sahib Singh, 30th Lancers, France. (Urdu, 6/3/16).

*****

"As to the fighting with the enemy near Peshawar our forces lost slightly but the enemy lost very heavily indeed. I hear now that all is quiet there. What is going on in your direction?..........I must tell you that our brotherhood who came from America have started a sort of mutiny in the country. One man brings a sword and another a pistol, and they get arrested. Then owing to the war with Germany the Government are angry with our people and have given orders that every man of bad character is to be sent up to the Magistrate under 110 Criminal Procedure Code. The Thanadar who is a Brahmin in collusion with my old enemy Rada Ram Brahmin has run in Ganda Singh under this section although for many generations there has been no stain on our family."

From Ganga Ram, Hoshiarpur, India, to Jemadar Sher Singh, 28th Light Cavalry, Robat, Biluchistan. (Urdu, 30/3/16).

*****

"A terrible affair has taken place here. The Supplementary Lahore conspiracy case has been decided in a way that spells disaster to the Sikh people. One hundred of our beloved Sikhs were sentenced to death, and our brother Nand Nir Singh got transportation for life. Now may the Guru help the Sikh people and rescue the drowning ones! It will be a long time before the Sikh people can raise their heads again!"

(The writer apparently means to say that as those who tried to serve the Sikhs have been executed or transported the only protection left is the Guru himself).

From Kalwant Singh, Student, 3rd Year, Agra Chank, to Kot Dafadar Ghamand Singh, 3rd Skinner's Horse. (Urdu, 2/4/16).

*****

"The work for which I came is all right and I want to die under your command at the front. I do not want to be shot by a German-American. I have got the Germans and Hindus connected with the 'Ghadr' sent before the Grand Jury at San Francisco. Those that are left are trying to kill me, so I have put another man on my job; he is a man employed by the Emigration Department. I used to work with the English Inspector because the 'Ghadr' is a paper very much against our soldiery. I went to London in 1907 with a letter that came out in the 'Ghadr' and I gave it to the Commissioner of Lucknow (here follows some unintelligible sentences). When I found that there were many Hindus in California I went there and asked the Deputy Commissioner before going that he would send me there. When I came to England from America, I came at my own expense but was unable to do anything, and I went back again at my own expense. The Hindus, however, got to know that I was there on behalf of the British Government because they knew I had gone to England as I had not gone via China to India. The mistake was not mine but that of the Chicago Consul. As I did not understand English, I went and explained the matter to the English Consul General at Chicago. I told him that the letter which I showed him ought to be sent to the Commander in Chief, Lord Kitchener. He told me to come the next day. I came and saw there a Hindu who was asking the General Consul for help and the Consul General gave him a letter and he began to read it to himself. The letter was by a Bengali and said very evil things about our Army. When I saw this man who was probably a friend of the 'Ghadr' reading my letter I snatched it from him and the Consul General understood what I meant. Then I told the Consul General that I would take the letter to England myself and I did not care whether I lost my life over it as long as the letter got to England as it threatened great danger to the Army. I thought the Germans believed that they could foster a quarrel between the U.S.A. and Mexico and ferment a rebellion among Hindus and Germans. It was I who got Hari Singh seized, the man responsible for the Singapur riot and who had been sent there by the Germans. Hari Singh also advised the Hindus to join the Mexican Army. Bhagwan Singh and Kidar Nath were arrested and many of the leading Hindus tried to get me to join them and promised to make me a Colonel but I went and told the Court all they had said. I was not able to send a report to India because there were too many German Americans watching me and I was not able to inform the authorities as to who has been arrested and who had given information etc. and was not even able to tell the Frisco Police everything because among them there were German agents. I know they will try and kill me some day. These German fellows are doing us a vast amount of damage."

From Sawan Singh, Lance Dafadar Instructor, 25th Cavalry, c/o., Mr Ram Singh, 411 C. (or E.) 4th Street, Los Angeles, California to the Commanding Officer, 25th Cavalry, c/o., India Office. (Urdu dated the 5th October 1917).

*****

"Oh Brethren, do not be hasty; we will show our bravery. We will make them reap the same harvest which they have made us reap. We have conquered many countries; we will pitch our camp in our own country. We will never sit silent but will spread disaffection. We have prepared ourselves to die; we will cause a rebellion to break out in India. Once and for all. We will never hesitate, as long as we are alive: we will exert ourselves to the utmost of our power. We will never entreaty to the *badmashes (Feringhis)*. We will make them straight (*Feringhis*) with sticks. We have lost our money and heart; we will never shrink from laying down our lives. On reaching our country we will spread agitation. We will drive out the white men holding on to their ears. We will teach them a lesson in return for their oppression by committing a general massacre. We will cut out the tongues of the *Feringhis* in order to teach them not to use the word "tum". The tyranny of the *Feringhis* shall be reckoned up in order to kill twice the number of *Feringhis*. As long as there is life in us India cannot die; we will show our chivalry to the world. The blood of our forefathers still exists in us; we will prove to the *Feringhis* how brave we are. The *Feringhis* should regard us as arranged in the battlefield; we will slay them like goats. All Hindus and Muhammadans will unite and destroy the *Feringhis*, root and branch. We are the children of the old Ghazis; we will take revenge on behalf of Turkey and Persia. The *Feringhis* have spread the germ of disunion in order to divide us; we will teach them a lesson in return for their action.

Rise, Oh Indians; we must do our duty. Our grievances are so many that they cannot be redressed. We will surely carry out our aims in the terms we have written."

Extracts (translated) from three books found on board and given to the Committee by Captain Yamamoto of the S.S. "Komagata Maru".

Translation of a Gurmukhi poem in the note-book of Lal Singh. Poem No.3, page 20.

*****

"Oh Indians, give heed: why do we not today possess the characteristics of our ancestors? Oh Lions, you have become weak. Why do you not reflect on this? Our forefathers became martyrs for the sake of religion. Why is it not their example that we follow now? Why does not the spirit of Guru Gobind Singh and Hari Singh Nalwa exist in these days? Did not S. Sham Singh of Atari kill lakhs in his old age? The names of such warriors will live forever. Why is there no one in the world, who knows of them? Those, who become martyrs, will never die.

Don't go so far back. Listen to the tale of the present day. Are there not thousands of wanderers like Mr. Tilak, Ajit, Bhagwan, Barkatullah, Ghosh, Ram Chandar, and

Hardyal? Of these, some were imprisoned, and others hanged. Oh brothers, why do you not look towards such heroes? There are persons like Madame Cama, the Devi, Krishna Varma, Pindi Das, Savarkar, Nand Gopal, Hazrat Sufi, Bindar, Mohan Ghosh and Liakat Husain, who have done such marvellous work. Although these persons are out of sight, why are not such gems given a place in your heart?

What fault have they committed, Oh Mother? Why do they not live in comfort? Lakhs of learned men have been transported. Oh, Simpletons, why do we not think about them? Our Gurdwara at Sisganj has been dismantled. Say, Oh Sikhs, are we not in bad condition? You are drawing lines on paper. Why do you not take up the sword and shield? Why are we making entreaties? Why do you not think as lions should? Each step we take is a backward step of trepidation; why is not ours the gait of men?

Why do you boast? Why are you not ashamed?

You swagger in the enjoyment of liquor and turbans, why do not your hearts hold thoughts of your country?

Look at China and Japan and see what comfort they enjoy. We are men of six-foot stature. Why? What a pity that we are not accorded even a scrap of respect.

Oh Hindus of Canada and America, why do you not die of shame?

You speak futile words. Why do you not speak plain words to your enemy? The sleeping Punjab should come to its senses. Why should not the Punjab be prodded into waking? If you step forward, will not our brothers follow you? Oh Hindus of Canada, why put the blame on the shoulder of your countrymen? Why do you not become its protectors? What can those who are slaves do? Why do you not rise, you who enjoy liberty?

Let us return to India, lion-hearts; is not our predicament pitiable?

Come let us preach to our countrymen, why should we not let them know how they are oppressed? Our work lies incomplete, for we lack wealth.

We should rob the white men. Why should we not become rich?

We must open funds to relieve India, our country. Why should not our condition be changed very shortly? We should publish the Gadhr in our country. Why should we not spread agitation? We should appoint sabhas and fix their duties. Why should we not reduce the powers, disgracing them? You should punish the Indian killers; why do you not put an end to the lives of the tyrants? Oh Martyrs, why sit silent?

Why do you not care for what passes in our minds? The mother weeps on seeing our disgrace. Why does not our blood boil? The Indians die of famine, why do their faces not grow red in wrath?

If you have any regard for your honour, why do you not leap forward like lions? What has become of the Akalian da bagh (a temple garden in Amritsar)? Are not our temples in a bad condition? The Khalsa College has lately been taken away from us, has not the wall at Delhi been pulled down?

You have shut your eyes like gandus (catamites). Why do not the heroes of the Guru come forward? Thus was the Punjab lost, why do you not understand their (the Englishmen's) deceitful ways? Those, who sing the songs of loyalty, are they not bastards?

Where has Sat Guru (true Guru) ordered you to become slaves? Why are you not ashamed?

Oh Martyrs, come and hold the flag. Why do you not enter your country at once? What thoughts do you think? Why do you not realise (the waste of) valuable time? Those who like to play with golal (golal is the red coloured water squirted on friends on the holiday; here the word means blood), why do not the sons of India come forward? We should go to India; none hears us from abroad.

The aggrieved repeats his story unendingly. Why do not the well-wishers of India act upon it?"

Translation of a Gurmukhi poem in the note-book of Lal Singh. Poem No.4, page 22.

*****

"This news will be read throughout India in general and in the Khalsa Panth in particular with great interest and joy, that through the grace of Guru Nanak and Guru Govind Singh Ji, the foundation of the Siri Guru Nanak Steamship Co., has been laid and the first steamer, Komagata Maru, which has been hired, has left for Vancouver (Canada) on the 29th March 1914.

It may be known to all, that in our country and especially in the Punjab there are many rich men, but none has dared take up foreign trade up to this time. It is the kindness of the Gurus that they have bestowed upon me courage to do this big work.

What led me to do this work is that when I came to Hongkong [sic] in January 1914 I could not bear the trouble of those, who were in the Gurdwarah waiting to go to Vancouver. They were waiting there for years and living at their own expense: how tyrannical and hard was this on our brothers!

This affected my mind with the result that I resolved to take them to Vancouver under any circumstances. I promised the passengers that if no company will issue tickets to them and they wrote to me, I would do the needful and fight out the case in the Supreme Courts of Vancouver to get the matter settled for ever. If the Canadian Government will prevent us from landing, I will ask many questions of our Government, and will not return until the matter is finally settled and will notify the full details of these proceedings to the people of India.

For this reason I have hired the ship for six months on the 24th March 1914 because when the ship is ours we will stop it where we like and will arrange for landing the passengers and will devise plans for trading. In the first instance, it is expected that there will be 300 passengers at Shanghai, but on the second voyage the ship will start from Calcutta.

The ship belongs to a Japanese Company. Its name is Komagata Maru and the arrangements were made through an Agent named Mr. A. Bune. If anyone wants to get more information, he can have it from the aforesaid gentleman.

The ship has been engaged for six months for $66,000. I will be responsible for all the expenses.

It is now fully believed that the steamers of the Sri Guru Nanak Steamship Company will go all over the world, and it is hoped that the Company will be registered at Vancouver. I have taken over the whole concern, because no one else has taken any shares. I hope that after the venture succeeds, many will take shares.

The recitation of the Granth:-

Before chartering the ship, the recitation of the Granth Sahib was concluded on the 22nd March 1914 at 3 A.M. The ship left Hongkong on the 29th March 1914 at 10 A.M. May the Guru Ji get the passengers of the steamer landed at a proper place with all ease and comfort.

DELAY

The delay from January to March was due to objections raised by Thaman Singh, Daljit Singh and Bir Singh to the effect that the ship ought to start from Calcutta. Therefore I came to Hongkong. There only a few passengers presented themselves and many obstacles had to be overcome which I shall narrate later on. Suffice it to say that by the grace of Guru Nanak the ship is ready.

1. 29th March 1914 starting from Hongkong at 10 A.M.
2. 6th April 1914 starting from Shanghai.
3. 10th April 1914 starting from Nagasaki.
4. 14th April starting from Yokohama.
5. 26 (29th) April starting from Victoria.
6. 30th April 1914 arrival at Vancouver.

On return from Vancouver, the passengers will land free of charge at Singapore, Kuala Lumpur, Penang, Calcutta and Malay States. In July, she ship will again sail from Calcutta to Vancouver.

Panth Da Dass
(Obedient servant of the Sikh nation).
Gurdit Singh,
Manager.
Sri Guru Nanak Steamship Co.,
Gurdwara, Singapore."

Translation of Gurmukhi notice issued by Gurdit Singh.

*****

"The law for the Indian immigration, which was passed by the Canadian Government on 9th May 1910, made many Indians to suffer many hardships. Now we have arranged to meet with the requirements of the Canadian laws that to book passengers directly from India and to show $75 which equal Rs. 225, there before landing.

We have just received a telegram from Ottawa saying that intending immigration should book directly from India and show $200 on landing, so we have arranged for the both.

To go direct we have chartered a steamer and have asked Mr. A. W. King to do this for us. The passengers shall be taken directly to Vancouver and landed there. Rupees 350 shall be charged as passage ticket and Rs. 50 shall be provided to passengers with regard to their religious scruples. Those who provided themselves with their own food shall not be charged for diet. The date of departure of the steamer shall be notified through Punjabi and other newspapers and headmen of the villages shall be informed about the day. The head-office of the Company shall be in Calcutta and there shall be branches all over the world. The departure date shall not be notified through papers this time but shall be wired to some of the Gurdwaras.

Further information from the undersigned: if any person wants to ascertain more about it he can send the letter to this address – Director, Siri Guru Nanak Steamer Company, Gurdwara, Howrah, Calcutta."

B.G.S.
Calcutta,

The 21st February 1914.

Translation of the foot-note in Gurmukhi at the bottom of the Advertisement.

"It should be noticed that the vessel will leave Calcutta on or about the 15th of March 1914 for the first time and the passengers concerned shall be given every assurance of their being allowed to land at America before they embark.

If anyone has any doubts, he should refer to the undersigned without any hesitation."

Notice dated 21st February 1914, published by Gurdit Singh, advertising that he has chartered a ship to take emigrants to Canada.

*****

Sikhs on board the *Komagata Maru*, Vancouver, BC. (Library and Archives Canada/Henry Herbert Stevens fonds/c075261)

*****

BRAVE IS HE WHO FIGHTS FOR HIS RELIGION! THOUGH BE CUT TO PIECES, HE WILL NOT LEAVE THE BATTLEFIELD!!

"Oh brave Indian people, you may have seen and heard that the Guru Nanak Company's steamer, Komagata Maru, whose arrival has been expected and awaited [sic] for a long time, reached Vancouver on the 23rd May 1914 with 376 passengers on board.

The Immigration authorities have not given any decision about her, and no Indian (residing in America) can see the passengers. The steamer is guarded on every side by the police on the sea, so much so that not even the passengers' Counsel is allowed an interview. The blood of the Indians is raging at the injustice. (Indian) brothers are very keen in collecting subscriptions from Vancouver suburbs, because the trick on which Immigration authorities are determined is that the steamer should return just as it is with the passengers on board. There is great excitement among the Indians resident in Canada, and we will never accept defeat at the hands of the Immigration authorities. We will never allow the 376 passengers to return to their country. We are ready to fight up to the walls of Vancouver, Ottawa and London. With this object in view, every friend is collecting subscriptions, because this is a question of vital importance.

The whole world is anxiously waiting to see how the fate of the Komagata Maru is decided; because the decision about her fate will make a mark in the history of the world.

The time has come when we must show our activity, union, courage and valour –this critical time should be considered the test of the above-mentioned virtues. So, sons of Mother India, consider this to be a real examination; it is not the time to talk, but to show work. At least 25,000 dollars are required for this purpose. So you should offer a handsome subscription after reading this.

Bhai Balwant Singh Ji, who went to India in order to remove the grievances of Indians resident in Canada, has now returned.

Below this follows a list of passengers and then another notice entitled:

"Voyage of the ship"

It is needless to describe the condition of Indians who, on their way to Canada, are being subjected to several hardships at different places like Calcutta and Hongkong.

Since last year about 200 brothers have been waiting at the Gurdwara, Hongkong, for some Steam Navigation Company to book their passage to Canada. But no company has been good enough to book these unfortunate Indians. It was by strange co-incidence that Sardar Gurdit Singh Ji happened to pay a visit to Hongkong on some private affairs and, on seeing the conditions of the Indians who were lying in the Gurdwara, he promised his brethren to take them to America somehow or other; and for this purpose the Sardar Sahib chartered the Komagata Maru. When he was making preparations for the ship he suffered several troubles at the hands of the Captain of the Police. But on finding that the Sardar Ji was not exceeding the limits of the law, the police had to withhold their hands. He was again put to trouble when he got a passenger certificate, and it took him three days to secure it; and for this a notice for damages of 20,000 dollars was served on the Hongkong Government; and the Colonial Secretary had to issue a certificate eventually. There was a wonderful sight when the ship sailed: regimental bands, soldiers and several regimental companies were present. Cries of Sat Sri Akaal and Ali Ali were raised when the ship set sail. Brothers, there was a time when the different communities in India were always quarrelling with each other on religious points, and they hated each other. Today the time has come when we see a Sikh place of worship on one side of the Komagata Maru and a Muhammadan place of worship on the other. After undergoing several hardships, this steamer has reached the coast of Vancouver.

The decision of the fate of this steamer will not be the decision of the fate of 376 passengers only but will be the decision of the fate of 33 crores of Indians.

All Indians have been anxiously waiting to see the ultimate result of this ship. Oh! Indian brothers, you must shake off sloth now and be prepared to come forward and fight for the fate of 33 crores of Indians. We shall take no rest unless we succeed in winning this trench.

Please send money to the following address:
Bhai Bhag Singh, Mr. Rahim,
1866, 2nd Avenue, W., Vancouver, B.C."

Translation of an appeal for money, printed in Gurmukhi, issued from Vancouver.

*****

Sikhs on board the Komagata Maru in English Bay, Vancouver, BC 1914. (Library and Archives Canada/Natural Resources Canada fonds/a034014)

*****

Friday, 17th July 1914

"It was a day, very injurious to the passengers, because the faithless and tyrannical Immigration Department issued orders for the deportation of all the passengers. We have travelled over the sea thousands of miles and have suffered four months imprisonment on the ship, but the tyrants have shown us no mercy. They have not considered our loss of lakhs of rupees and have shown no mercy to us. The executioners have not hesitated to drink our blood and have now passed the serious sentence of deportation. We do not care; man has to meet such troubles. It is not to be deplored, as it is God's will. Perhaps Waheguru (God) desires that we should be saved from lifting timber and being called labourers, but we are feeling much regret; perhaps, this may bear sweet fruit. Today we are giving up hopes of Vancouver from our minds, but sweet songs of the liberty of India are being sung. Have your minds now been affected by the taste of the oppression of the tyrants? It is a matter for gratitude that feelings for our country will be increased.

The order for the deportation of all has been passed, but the faithless doctor is being shown favour while landing. £17 has been taken from the disloyal traitor and he has been allowed to go. A good treatment for this hog.

We have written several letters for provisions, but no one pays attention to them. At last it was proposed to hold a meeting, and in the meeting a resolution was passed to rid ourselves of all these troubles. It was proposed to take the ship into harbour and to land by force. This is against the law, but we have been hungry for a long time and there is no law to help us. So let these laws be done away with.

At 1 A.M. a boat load of immigration officials comes near us and wants the Captain of the ship. Our sentries told them that this was not the time (to come) and that they should come again in the morning, but they replied that they wanted the Captain on urgent business. The sentries told them that there was no necessity (to see the Captain). At last Hopkinson said they had better give him a letter to him, and it was taken on board fastened to a *pagri*.

The letter was a peculiar sort. It was written that he had better start the ship that night, otherwise he would be fined. If the lifting of the anchor was not allowed, the police would do so by force. There was a hue and cry when the letter was read, and all the people gathered at the side of the ship. The people were so annoyed with the Immigration tyrants, that they would have killed them if they had been able to get hold of anything, but they could not do anything. As a receipt was asked for, the letter was signed by the Captain and then handed over to them. That *sala* (a term of abuse) opened the letter immediately and was confused to see the signature of Daljit Singh (as though struck by a bullet) and he told Daljit Singh to call the Captain, who did so. Then the Captain was asked by Reed whether he was the Captain or Daljit Singh, and why he has not replied to the letter. Whether he wanted to go or not, but the cowardly Captain said he wanted to go, but the Hindus would not allow him to go. He was told that if he was not being allowed to go, he could have help from the police and must lift anchor. The passengers at the same time said that they did not care in the least, "let the police come". The Captain was told to go on shore, and that coward became ready to go there. While going he was told that the sentries would not allow him to go during the night; it would be better for him to remain on shore. The Captain left, but the passengers were ready for the police.

I forgot to write that after the order of deportation was announced, the faithless Gardiner Johnson came on board at 7 P.M. in the evening and began to make a speech before the passengers that he was sorry, but they must now return in silence and the provisions would be sent to them when 70 miles away. On this the passengers told him that they were ready to go silently, but they should get provisions to take them to Calcutta and also should be allowed to see their relatives. He replied that they would get provisions to take them to Hongkong and that only when 70 miles away from Vancouver. The passengers enquired who would lift anchor. That faithless man replied it is your will, but the police will have to use force. The reply given was that is mattered little. The faithless man closed his ears and left with this short reply.

Before this Johnson sent all necessary papers, certificates of departure of the ship, health certificate, by a little boy, who wanted to hand them over to the Captain unnoticed, but Daljit Singh was informed by someone that a boy had thus entered the Captain's room. Daljit Singh went into the Captain's room. The Captain was dressing. Daljit Singh saw those papers on the table, took them and was on the point of reading them when the boy raised a cry. Daljit Singh thought that these were some secret papers. He came to me and informed me that these papers should be seen. When we went to the Captain's room Daljit Singh took the papers and saw that they were about the departure of the ship, and that the last port was Hongkong. We informed the Captain that the passengers would not allow him to lift anchor until they saw the passport for Calcutta. The Captain left the ship.

Saturday, 18th July 1914.

Today at 10 A.M. faithless Jano (Gardiner Johnson) came on board and began to say it was better to start the ship, otherwise the police would be sent to force them to go. We replied, "It does not matter; let the police come." We have got no provisions, no medicine; we prefer to die as martyrs while fighting with the police, then to die hungry on the way. By this our ignorant, non-patriotic Indians will know that patriotism is something and how badly these white men treat us and are thirsty of our lives. O Jano (Johnson), go away from before our eyes and send your police, so we may see this result. Badzat (ill-born) Johnson left murmuring something.

A letter was sent by the passengers' committee to Gardiner Johnson containing great and powerful proofs.

A telegram of appeal was sent to the Governor-General, Ottawa. We were placed under stricter surveillance than before, and we did not know whether Johnson would really bring the police and show his foolishness to the world. We were pondering this in our minds........"

Extracts from note-book No.1 (Diary taken from Gurdit Singh's box) giving an account of the S.S. "Komagata Maru" while at Vancouver.

*****

"Amar Singh:

I would like you to be in the same position as we have been here for three days without water, and see how you feel about it individually, and what must be the case of men collectively as in this case. You are getting your food three times a day and your water [;] we are getting nothing. If you were starving for three or four hours, you would soon take action to get something for yourself, but we have had nothing for three days or so.

You have come on this boat possibly three times from the time she has been here. We have addressed you letters and complaints with regards to several matters. We have made enquiries for you from your officers that have come on this boat; but they have always said: "Mr. Reid is attending to the matter", or "I do not know". You have never put in an appearance on this boat except on the three occasions, and now that you are here we would like to hold you until such time as your promise of the sending of provisions and water is fulfilled."

Meeting of the committee appointed by the passengers on board S.S. "Komagata Maru": who have taken the matter out of Gurdit Singh's hands:

Vancouver, B.C., 9th July 1914.

*****

Sikhs on board the *Komagata Maru*, Vancouver, BC. (Library and Archives Canada/Henry Herbert Stevens fonds/c075260)

*****

A BIG BATTLE AT SEA

"This chapter refers to a defeat inflicted on the British man-o-war and army by the unarmed Indian bahadurs. The Indians only used coal.

On the 27th July the Captain received an order from Mr. Johnson to weigh anchor. The ferenghis had arranged for the ship to sail when all the passengers were fast asleep, so that they might not prevent the Captain from sailing. But how were the hungry passengers to sleep? When the Captain was making arrangements to weigh anchor, the passengers objected to his sailing. The Captain showed a letter from Johnson. The result was that the Captain took the letter and one from the passengers and went at once to Mr. Johnson. Next day, the Captain returned with Mr. Johnson, who advised the passengers to return to their country peacefully, otherwise force would probably be used. The passengers replied that they would never go back without provisions, medicine and the written permission of the characters (the Sikh Committee). They further added that in the event of any of these terms being refused they were prepared to resist the soldiers. Mr. Johnson, however, began to threaten them. On this, the Sikhs said "Oh Badzat (low caste) owl, hold your peace. If you speak again you will be killed." The coward began to tremble and replied that provisions would be sent when the ship had steamed out a distance of 70 miles.

On the 18th July, a telegram was sent protesting against the decision of the Immigration Officers. A reply was received, "We are considering." In short, 400 soldiers surrounded the ship at 1.30 A.M. There was a man-o-war to assist the police, but the passengers had sticks and coal only. The latter eventually defeated the man-o-war and the police and put them to flight. The police wanted to climb on board; but the passengers cut the ropes. On this, the police began to pump water over us to drive us away and so be able to climb on board easily. The Sikh leaders, whose names it is not desirable to disclose, began to oppose the police and asked the other Sikhs to bring up coal on deck. When the Sikhs began to cut the ropes the enemy began to fire on us; but in the meantime a sufficient store of coal had been brought. About 30 Sikhs began to fight with coal, which were showered like rain, although the enemy fired two more shots. The enemy was repulsed and was unable to stand the shower of coal. The result was that some of the soldiers were drowned and others received injuries. One of the soldiers plucked up the courage to fire a revolver, but a Sikh succeeded in knocking the revolver into the sea. Great consternation spread among the soldiers. Even the deck of their ship was covered with blood. One of the passengers wanted to find out with his glasses whether Messrs. Reid and Hopkinson were on the ship or not. The Sikhs had intended to jump down on to the enemy's ship and kill them (Messrs. Reid and Hopkinson); but some Hindu had meanwhile cut the rope. This was a great mistake; otherwise all the soldiers would have been killed and their blood would have sufficed to slake the thirst and hunger of the Sikhs.

The following ultimatum was sent from Ottawa to the Hindus through the Immigration department:

"We have been directed by the Canadian Government to say that it will be most regrettable if blood-shed occurs. It is, therefore, directed that the order of the Government and the rules framed under the law should be complied with peacefully.

Your case has been fully argued in court; and the decision has gone against you. The Government has ordered that you be sent back. As your case is an unusual one, the Government has agreed to supply you with provisions, which will be sent on board when you show yourselves well-behaved and allow the Captain to sail. The Government regrets that you have committed the offence of disobeying the law, viz., first, in not complying with the orders of the Immigration Officers; second, in not allowing the Captain to sail; third, in opposing the military. If you refuse to comply with the rules and orders, the military authorities will be ordered to drive your ship by gun fire."

The ultimatum was not handed over to us. What has been set forth in the ultimatum is wrong. We were never allowed to see our lawyer; nor were we permitted to appear in court. We could not accept the order of the Government, as the Judge was both plaintiff and defendant.

A European made enquiries, signalling with a flag, whether anyone of the passengers would come ashore to settle the terms of settlement. We replied that the Hindus of Vancouver should be consulted. A meeting was held at about 2.15 P.M. at the Immigration Office, at which the following were present:

(1) Mr. Hopkinson (badzat); (2) Natha Singh; (3) Sohan Lal; (4) Kartar Singh; (5) Indar Singh; (6) Hari Singh; (7) Arjun Singh.

Later on, all these persons came on a boat to visit our ship; but we refused to see them until provisions were given to us. The provisions were then supplied. After we had eaten we spoke to them; and they advised us to return. The passengers replied, however, that they would give no answer until they had seen Bhai Bhag Singh, Balwant Singh, and Mr. Rahim. The above mentioned Hindus said that Balwant Singh and Bhag Singh had been implicated in an Arms Act case. They further added that they (Balwant Singh and Bhag Singh) had been collecting 35,000 dollars for the passengers, but that the Badzat Sarkar of Canada had fabricated a case under the Arms Act alleging that they were endeavouring to purchase arms for the Hindus. We insisted on seeing Mr. Rahim.

On the 12th July Mr. Rahim came. After a great discussion, the passengers agreed to return.

The Japanese Consul came to the ship and assured us that the ship would certainly go to Hongkong and that the dispute about the coal between Gurdit Singh and the owners of the ship would be settled in Hongkong. On these conditions, the Indians agreed to return.

Twenty-four thousand dollars' worth of provisions were supplied to us. To copy the example of the avaricious and deceitful feranghis, we said that we would not set sail until a 100 goats, fowls and eggs had been supplied. We began to have faith in our own strength. We got 24,000 dollars' worth of provisions by shoe-beating a few; more threatening would surely bring us goats, eggs and fowls. The, Oh Indian brother, be ready to become martyrs, and your wishes will be fulfilled.

The newspapers had begun to write that the Indians had again become desperate. The Immigration Officers sent the Hindus of Vancouver to see us and advise us to return, although they had not before been allowed such a concession. The reason was that, to achieve their aim. They (Immigration Officers) had begun to kiss the feet of the Hindus, whom they despised as curs. Eventually it was agreed that we were to go back.

At this period, a telegram was received from Bhai Bhag Singh. He said that he was the charterer and that the ship was not to sail without his permission. On this, the Sikhs began to become desperate (bigaram). But Mr. Rahim gave his permission; and the objection was withdrawn.

As we returned we made an appeal as passengers on the Komagata Maru to God. It was as follows:

"Oh Akalpurkh (God)! send some powerful enemy to bombard the men-of-war of these Canadians who have driven innocent people like us from their coast with the help of their men-of-war, so that the tyrants may be punished for their oppression."

A manuscript giving a history of the voyage of the S.S. "Komagata Maru", written in Gurmukhi, apparently in the handwriting of Daljit Singh (extracts).

*****

"My name is Amar Singh. My father's name is Khajan Singh. I am caste Sidhu Sikh, and by occupation a cultivator. My home is at mauza Sanpura, thana Khalra, district Lahore. I reside at home.

Q. – I am a Hakim, a deputy Magistrate. If you say anything I shall write it down. You have nothing to fear, nor have you got anything to do with the police and need fear no one. Say what you wish to. Whatever you say I shall take down. It will all be produced in Sarkar's court, and orders will then be passed on it according to law.

A. – Question me, and I shall say.

Q. – Tell me in detail what happened after you reached Canada and on your way back from there.

A. – When we reached Canada we were not allowed to land there. The English officer at Canada told us that he would let us know the order when received from Ottawa. We remained there for full two months. Then he gave orders "You go back. Take your ship away." To this Gurdit Singh said, "Give us supplies of food and water and we shall take back our ship." Then Mr. Reed said, "You take your ship away. Provisions will be supplied to you at Victoria." Gurdit Singh replied, "Give us the provisions first, then we shall depart." Then one night Mr. Reed brought up the military and they poured water through pipes on to the ship. Thereupon, coals were thrown at them from our ship. The military then withdrew. When they gave us provisions, we weighed our anchor and returned. On our journey back, Gurdit Singh and Daljit Singh used to say, "We starved for full six days and the Sarkar did not permit us to land nor gave us any food. They did not allow us to land at Canada, then why did they not tell us so at Yokohama? We would have returned from there. They also said that the English have killed our karobar and (gives us dhoka) deceives us. I do not remember in detail all that happened. I am an illiterate man. You will find all the papers in Gurdit Singh's box. Everything will be found out from them.

Q. – Who was Daljit Singh?

A. – He was Gurdit Singh's Secretary. Call him Secretary or Treasurer. He was everything. He knows English and has read in school. On the ship, we used to have discourses on the Granth Saheb as we do at home. There was a separate place for the Granth Saheb in the ship. In those discourses, there used to be no talk about the

Sarkar. Whatever Gurdit Singh had to speak against the Sarkar he did in his cabin. He used to only sleep in that cabin. All the talking he used to do in his office cabin.

When our ship came near Calcutta, then three or four European and six Punjabi officers boarded our ship and conducted a search all over the ship. They examined our luggage. Our ship remained there for two days. Then she was taken to Budge-Budge and we all landed there. When I was asked to get into the train I told them that I was afraid to get in: "take me to Howrah, I shall go to my home from there."

Q. – What was it you were afraid of?

A. – Everyone coming from China entrains at Howrah. I was about 20 steps behind. I do not know where was Gurdit Singh exactly then. I was at the head of our men with a dholki. I heard report of a gun behind and hearing it I ran away.

Q. – From where did the Sikhs get pistols: (revolvers)?

A. – I don't know. Men of Gurdit Singh's own village might know. I did not even know him before and saw him first at Shanghai.

(Sd.) Amar Singh
(In Hindi.)
(Signature of the accused.)"

The statement of Amar Singh, age 26 years, made before Mr. N. R. Mukharji, Magistrate of the 1st Class, Alipore, 24-Parganas, on the 22nd October 1914, in the Hindi language.

*****

"I joined the ship of Gurdit Singh at Yokohama, where I paid him £19. We were not allowed to land at Vancouver, so returned in the same steamer. Government gave us rations at Vancouver. We came to Kobe; the passengers went to see the Consul there, and asked him for assistance, as otherwise we could not get to India. He gave us water and paid for coal and gave 9,000 dollars for rations; the Consul said that this was for enabling the passengers to reach home, and not for the sake of Gurdit Singh. Gurdit Singh spent 200 dollars in purchasing fowls, lemonade, and vegetables and dal. We came to Singapore, and thence to the Hooghly. On the ship we were told by Sahebs that trains were ready to take us to our homes. The 9,000 dollars were never divided. Gurdit Singh took the cheque to the bank and got sovereigns. With him were Diljit Singh, Mir Muhammad, the Munshi, and Amar Singh, Nihang and Babu Pohlo Ram; they went to cash the cheque. Both before we landed and after we landed Gurdit Singh told us that the train for the Punjab went from Howrah, from the other side of the river, and that the Sahebs were deceiving us and would take us somewhere else. Four or five of our people went to the station to ask if the train would go to the Punjab and were told it would; they told us to come to the station. We all came as far as the level crossing with the Granth Sahib, singing shabad (hymns); there we stopped, and asked Gurdit Singh whether we should go to the railway or not. He said, 'Please yourselves, but they will not take you to your homes, but will shut you up in some fort.' We stayed there singing and talking for a long time, for an hour or an hour and a half. Gurdit Singh told us to ask the Seth Sahebs, the two Sindi Sahebs. They told us to go to the railway, and not to make mischief; if they are going to kill you, they will kill you, otherwise they will take you home. Gurdit Singh then told us to get into the train. Puran Singh and Thakur Singh and Bhajan Singh said that we must first take the Granth Saheb to the Gurdwara in Howrah, and after that we could get into the train at any station we liked. The Granth Saheb was lifted up and we crossed the railway and started along the road. The Sahebs warned us at the crossing not to go along the road, but to go to the railway. We went along the road, the police going with us: there were 13 or 14 police. We went about 3 miles along the road, when we met some 12 sahebs. They told us to stop. We stopped, and European soldiers came. An officer of the soldiers came and called Gurdit Singh and told him to go back to Budge-Budge. Gurdit Singh said that nobody does us justice. The officer said that justice would be done at Budge-Budge. We all then returned by the orders of the officers. Gurdit Singh told us to go back. We came back to the railway. On the way out a bicycle had been obtained on which sometimes Gurdit Singh and sometimes the Seth Saheb rode. We all came on to the platform. Police sahebs who had come with us then came and told us to go back to the ship from which we had come. We all went out by the railway crossing and stood in front of the shops. We all said that we had got thirsty. The sahebs told us to sit down, and we would be given water. We all sat down, and then the soldiers shot at us. I did not see any weapon with our people, nor did I see any of them firing. I ran away along the railway line. Rala Singh was with me. We went to sleep in a house and were caught there by the police.

When we came to the station for the first time the sahebs told us to go and fetch our luggage. We said coolies might bring it. Gurdit Singh told us that he had to fight a case and wanted the money given us at Kobe for the vakils and other expenses. Gurdit Singh told us on the ship that the Government did not want us to do trade, so that we might not become learned, and manage our own business."

Statement of Mela Singh, son of Achhar Singh of Khurdpur, district Jallandar, Punjab, stated (after being warned that he was speaking before a Magistrate and that the statement might be taken as evidence against him) - 1st October 1914.

*****

"Humanity throughout the world is now awake. Oh sleeping India, why don't you arise?

Your clothes are torn, and your body emaciated. Why is there no zeal in your body or strength in your heart?

The world calls us "black thieves." Where is our old prosperity and happiness?

Neither your colour nor your looks resemble that of old. Where did you lose your pomp and self-respect?

You have no education or goodness or wealth. Where even is your sense of politics and your self-respect?

Why are there no persons such as the great poet Kalidas, the philanthropic ruler Bhoj, or strong men like Arjuna?

Why are there no strong Hindus of India nor strong Muslims, the sons of crusaders.

After dividing them, the oppressor has finished them both. Why don't you turn into poison to kill him?

Repression is at its height and hell is loose. Why don't the Sikhs rise and attack?

The world calls us "coolie." Why doesn't our flag fly anywhere?

We are faced with innumerable miseries. Why aren't our hearts upset?

It seems that we are good for nothing. Why aren't we honoured anywhere?

From the beginning we have been yoked to thraldom. Why don't we even dream of freedom?

How shall we survive, are we slaves forever? Why aren't we involved in politics?

Wherever we go, we are treated like dogs. Why is no person kind to us?

The goal is far away, and our pace is slow. Why are we inert?

The blood has dried and only the skeleton remains. Why don't we burn it at the cremation ground?

In the conflagration our house is ablaze. Why don't we put out the fire?

Only a handful of oppressors have taken our fields. Why has no Indian cultivator risen and protected his land?

Our children cry for want of education. Why don't we open science colleges?

Have we ever been brave heroes? Are there no battlefields on which we can play?

We have many tricksters among us who are killing the nation. Why shouldn't these dishonest men die?

Are there no valiant heroes, sons of India like Tilak? Why doesn't our jewel, Sri Aurobindo, shine like a light of humanity?

Har Dyal has been kind to India. Why doesn't our friend Ajit Singh offer sacrifice?

The time will come, and our eyes will bear witness. Why doesn't God avenge those who spend their lives in misery?

Our weapons have been hidden. Why doesn't the kirpan (sword) shine like thunder?

Oh brave Singhs, the time is not for sleeping. Why don't you look at the world around you?

The oppressor is acting like a monkey. Why don't you take his life?

He has devoured Turkey, Iran and China. Why doesn't Japan awake and lead?

Oh Ye, the blood of our revered fathers. If you unite, Satan must die.

If you Singhs show courage, you can achieve success. Having lived a long life, why can't you sacrifice yourselves?"

Extract taken from the Punjabi Shamsher Khalsa ("Sword of the Khalsa") published in Stockton, California, July 1914.

*****

Ghadr-di-Gunj

Perversions	Suggestions
1. Our children are thirsting for knowledge. Colleges are certainly started, but not to impart knowledge.	1. Establish secret Raj societies; make friendship with the Mahrattas and the Bengalis.
2. Respectable persons are wandering about about and have no homes.	2. First deal with the traitors to the motherland; and then sit on the chests of your enemies.
3. Look how they have ruined the gardens like Shalimar by giving feasts therein.	3. Commit dacoities at some places.
4. They, faithless enemies, have violated the privacy of our sisters and daughters.	4. O Hindus, Sikhs, Muhammadans make haste! Be supporters of one another!
5. They have drained all the money from India, and taken it to England.	5. Drink the blood of the nation of the infidel Christians; quench your thirst and appease yourselves.
6. Bulgaria nominally picked up a quarrel with Turkey while really tyrannical England waged war secretly.	6. Empty bragging is of no use. The time has come to wage war!
7. They could not come here had they not been brought by the Nabha and Patiala States: they conquered the Punjab with the help of those who were not faithful to their country. Nabha and Patiala did acts which are not done even by a *chandal*, (i.e. the lowest dregs of society).	7. On perusal of the Ghadr I learnt that time has come to set up rebellion.
8. The Khalsa College which was started has now been taken possession of by white monkeys. Sundar Singh Majithia ruined it.	8. If cow, swine and *Jhatka* are causes of disputes between Indians, the whites are eaters of all three.
9. (Talking of mutiny) Several thousand children and women weltered in blood for the sake of their country.	9. Go and arouse the armies; why are you sleeping O wielders of the sword. O Musalmans, Pathans, sturdy Dogras and the brave war-like Sikhs!!! The power of the European is not great. All the Indians should make a united attack.
10. The tyrannical Europeans have plundered the country; and so on.	10. When will the Khalsas (Sikhs) unsheath their swords and slaughter the whites in large numbers.
	11. Prepare for mutiny quickly. Why have you given up the desire to regain the country?
	12. It is our duty to support "the Ghadr"; think of it as your child. Besides, it is our duty to set up mutiny.

	13. Hardyal, a promising youth of Bhart Varsh, has become popular, O Singhs!
	14. Stanza xiv is in praise of the *Ghadr.*
	15. We should suck the blood of all Europeans.
	16. Let us first practice with a knife thoroughly, lest our minds should become frightened on seeing a spear.
	17. We should commit dacoity on the Government, and awake the whole of the Punjab. We should fight guerrilla wars at some places, and adopt such measure as are feasible. O Brothers! Arise like the Bengalis!
	18. We should raise the beautiful three-coloured standard.
	19. If the English remain here for 25 years more, no trace of us will be left, O brothers! Make hasty preparation for rebellion!
	20. Be influenced by observances of *Chutt Chatt* (scruples of interdining) and caste divisions, they took a wrong step. Such things created factions.
	21. Stanza xxi praises the leaders of the Mutiny of 1857.
	22. Let us break jails, and release the men who served the nation and remained faithful in their love for the country.
	23. Go to your country and set up rebellion at once!
	24. It is time! Plunder the treasuries! The doors to martyrdom are open.
	25. Be determined to wage war!
	26. Come let us go to our country at once, and preach sermons to the armies to the effect that we must kill the whites and cut them to pieces. Be determined to hoist your flag![6]

*****

6 Isemonger, *An account of the Ghadr conspiracy*, pp. 23-25.

Epilogue

One who dies fighting in the hour of peril and recites the Word in the ambrosial hour is known as the true warrior.

From this village 176 men went to the Great War 1914–1919 of these 8 gave up their lives.

We were told that this was a war for freedom …

As Sikh servicemen started to return to the Punjab after the armistice, they may have expected to be welcomed home as conquering heroes. But the Punjab that some had left four years ago was a different place. The enormous contribution that Sikh soldiers had made on the battlefields of the Great War, through their blood and sweat was forgotten all too quickly by the British. The reward for their sacrifices was an even greater act of betrayal. Promises made to the Sikhs did not manifest themselves. This 'frailty of heroes' was effectively deceived by the very Government that they had served.

Sikhs soldiers had returned from the Great War to their homeland full of vigour and enthusiasm for the future. The British had offered many incentives to the soldiers as well as the promise to share power with the Indian people. The Sikhs felt that they had more than earned their rewards by the sheer scale of their contribution to the British war effort. However, the Punjab they returned to was effectively a 'garrison' state. Promises made about self-government by the Montagu-Chelmsford reforms of 1917 turned out to be half-baked untruths and were perhaps a recruitment tactic. Prominent Sikh educational and religious places were still being run by 'non-Sikhs'. Sikhs had little or no representation on local boards or committees. Grain prices were high across the Punjab and people were dying from a flu epidemic. Most infuriatingly hundreds of Sikh Gurdwaras were still under the control of the British.

However, Sikh soldiers were now armed with new knowledge about the feeling of freedom, garnered from the people of France and other places they had visited in Europe. An interview conducted in 1972 with a veteran Sikh sepoy, Ralk Singh of the 45th Sikh Infantry, highlights his indignation over the difference in attitudes of the French and British:

> We came to know that the British had no respect for the Indians. They regarded us as their servants. The British soldiers used to get four times more than our salary. Their sepoy did not salute our Subedar-Major or any N.C.O.[1]

1 Ellinwood, *India and World War I*, p. 224.

On their return to the Punjab, soldiers would also lament the state of their Gurdwaras under *de facto* British rule. Some attempts had been made during the Great War years by the Chief Khalsa Diwan for reform of Gurdwara control, an English leaflet, advocating such reform was written in 1915, however prominent Sikhs not hopeful of achieving any success lacked conviction and the proposal was dropped as impracticable.[2] Other Sikhs who took such grievances to the courts saw their cases stuck in the legal system for many years and only achieved limited success.

Thus, the soldiers had come to realise that as 'one colonial hand fed them, the other hid the keys to their community institutions in its grasp (literally, in the case of the Golden Temple).'[3] The newspaper, *The Panth Sewak*, 26 February 1919, writes about the Golden Temple:

> The shrine is no longer the charge of the Khalsa, the offerings are not for the Panth, the management is not by the Sikhs ... To an ordinary mind, it is something inexplicable why a Christian Government should treat the management of this shrine as a department of the Government. What on earth, one sometimes irresistibly asks oneself, has the Government to do with the premier Sikh shrine? If the churches are managed by the Christians, the mosques by the Muhammadans, why is the Sikh Harmandir under the thumb of a Government official and his nominee?... The Deputy Commissioner of Amritsar lords it over with as absolute power and even more sometimes, in the management of the Golden Temple as in the workings of the office of his S.V.O.; and a Government appointed Manager treats it as a concern to be run as his whim or pleasure dictates, uncontrolled by the voice of the Panth or opinion of any public body in the land...The real sentiment of the community asks for the shrine to be handed over to them and to be run by themselves which was created by their Gurus and to which they and they alone have the right of ownership. If the inhabitants of Palestine and the German colonies are considered fit for the principle of self-determination in the sphere of the government of their lands, are the Sikhs not even fit to look after their own shrine?... May we hope that the Government will lay aside its policy of ignoring the just feelings of the community and revise its view?

In 1918, a non-Sikh was appointed as the manager of the religiously significant Kartarpur Gurdwara and there were many stories circulating of misappropriation of funds in important Sikh shrines. Demobilised Sikh soldiers returning to their native villages only added further to the growing woes of the people and faced arbitrary cuts in their pensions. Their disappointment exacerbated at the non-fulfilment of various promises of rewards made to them for loyal services during the war.[4]

War time restrictions on the press were re-imposed. There was no medium for Sikh voices to be heard. The returning Sikh soldiers started to think that the British were denying them their rights. Veteran Lance Naik, Khela Singh of the Patiala State Force, interviewed in 1972 summarised his views:

2 Teja Singh, *The Gurdwara Reform Movement and the Sikh Awakening* (Lahore: The Mercantile Press, 1922), p. 94.

3 Richard G. Fox, *Lions of the Punjab: Culture in the Making* (London: University of California Press, 1985), p. 140.

4 Mohinder Singh, *The Akali Movement* (New Delhi: National Institute of Panjab Studies, 1997), p. 12.

> Previously, we remained satisfied with the existing circumstances. But when we saw various peoples and got their views, we started protesting against the inequalities and disparities which the British had created between white and black. We had come to know about the cunningness of the British.[5]

The very Sikh soldiers that the British had 'controlled' and 'maintained' in the orthodox traditions of the army were now to become the very 'agents of change' in the Punjab that the British had hoped to prevent in the first place. These "change agents" would give impetus to the notion that the British had been subjugating them in their own country.

By far the greatest betrayal was the passing of the infamous Rowlatt Act on 19 March 1919. The Act effectively allowed the Government to arrest anyone suspected of revolutionary acts and to be interned without trial. In reality it meant that they could arrest anyone under mere suspicion. Coming just over four months after the end of the Great War, the Rowlatt Act was the first turning point in the future of the Punjab.

Then, on 13 April 1919 an event would take place which would change the Punjab forever. The people of the Punjab were celebrating the festival of *Baisakhi* in Amritsar. At Jallianwala Bagh, a park in Amritsar, Sikhs and Punjabis were gathered listening to speakers in the park. Colonel Reginald Dyer commanding troops of the British Indian army decided to fire indiscriminately at the gathered people. The park had only one entrance which was blocked by the soldiers firing at them, so there was no way out for the unarmed people. Some jumped into wells to escape the bullets. Official sources put the death toll at 379 with 1,200 wounded; other estimates were much higher. A good proportion of the gathered crowd were Sikhs. The Amritsar Massacre, as it would become known, ignited the Punjab and 1919 was the beginning of the end of British rule in the eyes of many.

After the Amritsar massacre the Sikhs understood more as a collective entity that they were being deprived of their rights. *The Khalsa Advocate*, 9 September 1919, writes about the feelings of the Sikhs:

> Disappointment and failure are the lot of Sikhs. Nothing has availed them. Not even their unparalleled sacrifices for, and loyal devotion to, the King-Emperor and his Empire have brought in any substantial recognition excepting of course some lip appreciations. The services which the Sikhs have put in for the cause of the British Government ever since the annexation of the Punjab failed to find a parallel in the annals of any subject race. They have supplied one fifth of the entire Indian military strength besides a very large number of non-combatants during the recent world war. They have won quite a third of the war awards. Still their martial superiority has failed to secure them their due share of army commissions ... But for the gallant and bold front put in by the Sikhs, the battle of Ypres would have been lost and still those same Sikhs have failed to find admission to Sandhurst. Not to speak of Government favours, the Sikhs could not be trusted in the control of their domestic and religious affairs even. Their Holiest of Holy, the centres of their religion, must be controlled and managed by men not of their own choice. Even their biggest educational institution is not to be

5 Ellinwood, *India and World War I*, p. 224.

> trusted to their charge. The despair of the Sikhs does not end here. Contrary to all their religious behests and traditions and in utter disregard of their past is history and in the teeth of strong opposition and in the face of declared views the renegades and apostates become declared Sikhs and are thrust upon them as their guardians. A grosser sort of calumny on their communal existence cannot be conceived. Delicate cords have thus been touched. Strong sentiments have been roused, religious susceptibilities have been wounded; and still the paternal Government has not fought fit to save them from the most disgraceful showers of abuse heaped upon them by some insolent sections of various religious persuasions. In short, it seems that the more magnificent the record of their services the greater their incapability to manage their own house and disqualifications for public service. Substantiate to any extent the facts and figures about the invaluable services of the Sikhs; the fact remains that their most cherished hopes have met a most callous rebuff both at the hands of Government and the leaders of Indian public opinion. A more glaring instance of the ingrateful discharge of one's obligations towards a benevolent race, as the Sikhs, is hardly to be found ...

Their representative body, the Chief Khalsa Diwan (CKD) lost its remaining credibility and a new organisation, the Central Sikh League broke off from the CKD as they felt alienated by its inactivity. Other issues such as the treatment of Sikhs in Canada (and the colonies), the heart-rending stories of Sikhs hanged, jailed or transported for life, the miserable pay of a sepoy compared to the British soldier, general poverty and aerial bombings of Punjab villages by the British all contributed to growing Sikh disillusionment. Simultaneously, Sikhs were also becoming casualties in the Third Afghan war (1919) and the military intervention in the Russian civil war (1918-20).

The main difference now was that the disaffection of Sikhs was felt by all (soldiers and the rural and urban classes), especially the stories of laxity at major Sikh shrines such as Nankana Sahib (birthplace of Guru Nanak), started turning the people against the British. The Sikhs decided that the managers of 'their' Gurdwaras were the enemy within and as the British had appointed them as their guardians, they were enemies too. In the next few years (1920-25), the Sikhs decided to regain the control of their Gurdwaras; it would not be easy to take on the British. Countless thousands would be arrested, and many killed, but the 'Gurdwara reform movement', as it would become known had begun ...

Finally, relevant British history texts do not mention the story of the sons of Guru Gobind Singh (the Sikhs) on the battlefields of the Great War. Indian historians forgot them as soldiers who had fought for the imperial power. Thus, Sikh soldiers found themselves in a 'no man's land' of the Great War memory. These 'sons of the soil' went to fight and win a war which they may have thought was their own. They are joined at this time by the *Ghadarites*, those on the *Komagata Maru* and the Lahore "conspirators". For differing reasons they were Sikhs prepared to risk their lives for what they believed in. Perhaps, for an alternative set of five K's: their Kin, their King-Emperor, their Karma, their Kartaar (God) and for the Khalsa. Above all, they were willing make the supreme sacrifice; and for this, they were undeniably heroes and deserve to be remembered by future generations.

Appendix I

Sources of chapter subtitles

Preface

1. British Library: L/MIL/5/825-828, 'Reports of the censor of Indian mails in France: printed reports and abstracts, with related correspondence.'
2. Ibid.

Introduction:

1. Poem, *The Khalsa Advocate*, Saturday, 20 November 1915.
2. Lt Col Merewether and Sir Frederick Smith, *The Indian Corps in France* (London: John Murray, 1918), p. 483.
3. BL: L/MIL/5/825-828, 'Reports of the censor of Indian mails in France.'
4. Muhay, *A zeal for martyrdom*, p. 106.

Chapter 1

1. BL: L/MIL/5/825-828, 'Reports of the censor of Indian mails in France.'
2. Ibid.
3. Ibid.
4. Ellinwood, *India and Word War I*, p. 223.

Chapter 2

1. BL: L/MIL/5/825-828, 'Reports of the censor of Indian mails in France.'
2. Ibid.
3. Ibid.
4. Ibid.

Chapter 3

1. BL: L/MIL/5/825-828, 'Reports of the censor of Indian mails in France.'
2. Ibid.
3. Ibid.
4. Ibid.

Chapter 4

1. Anon, *47th Sikhs war record*, p. 115.
2. BL: L/MIL/5/825-828, 'Reports of the censor of Indian mails in France.'
3. British Library: L/PJ/6/1451, File 3378, 'Loyal Addresses to the British Crown from Sikhs of Malay States.'
4. Article, *The Khalsa Advocate*, Saturday, 26 June 1915.

Chapter 5

1. BL: L/MIL/5/825-828, 'Reports of the censor of Indian mails in France.'
2. Ibid.
3. Ibid.
4. Ibid.
5. Ibid.

Chapter 6

1. BL: L/MIL/5/825-828, 'Reports of the censor of Indian mails in France.'
2. Andrew Roberts, *Love, Tommy: Letters Home, from the Great War to the Present Day* (Oxford: Osprey, 2012), p. 55.
3. BL: L/MIL/5/825-828, 'Reports of the censor of Indian mails in France.'
4. Ibid.
5. University of Cambridge Library: GBR/0012/MS Add.6170, 'Letters from Indian Army Troops.'

Chapter 7

1. BL: L/MIL/5/825-828, 'Reports of the censor of Indian mails in France.'
2. Article, *The Khalsa Akhbar* (Lahore), 2 February 1917.
3. BL: L/MIL/5/825-828, 'Reports of the censor of Indian mails in France.'
4. Ibid.

Chapter 8

1. BL: L/MIL/5/825-828, 'Reports of the censor of Indian mails in France.'
2. Ibid.
3. Ibid.
4. Ibid.

Chapter 9

1. BL: L/MIL/5/825-828, 'Reports of the censor of Indian mails in France.'
2. Ibid.
3. Ibid.
4. Singh, *Jail Chitian*, p. 26.

Chapter 10

1. Singh, *The Ghadar heroes*, p. 23.
2. British Library: L/PJ/6/1338, File 5028, 'Papers on the Budge Budge riot and passengers on the Komagata Maru.'
3. Ibid.
4. Ibid.

Epilogue

1. Sikh Holy writings of Bhai Gurdas, *Vaar* 30, *Pauri* 14.
2. Plaques dotted across the villages of the Punjab.
3. Malik, *A little work, a little play*, p. 16.

Appendix II

Indian Army Ranks 1914-18[1]

Infantry	Cavalry	British Equivalent
Sepoy	Sowar	Private
Lance Naik	Acting Lance Daffadar	Lance Corporal
Naik	Lance Daffadar	Corporal
Havildar	Daffadar	Sergeant
Havildar Major	Kot Daffadar	Sergeant Major
Jemadar	Jemadar	Lieutenant
Subedar	Risaldar	Captain
Subedar Major	Risaldar Major	Major

Other

Ressaidar: A rank of Indian cavalry officer intermediate between Jemadar and Risaldar. In April 1921 the rank of Ressaidar was abolished, all existing Ressaidars being regraded as Risaldars.

1 https://indiafamily.bl.uk/ui/Dictionary.aspx

Appendix III

Quality of Sikh recruits by district[2]

District	Tehsils	Value
Amritsar	Amritsar	Very good.
	Tarn Taran	Do.
	Ajnala	Fair.
Lahore	Lahore	Very good.
	Kasur	Do.
	Chunian	Good.
	Sharakpur	Bad.
Ferozepore	Ferozepore	Very good.
	Moga	Do.
	Zira	Do.
	Muktsar	Fair.
	Fazilka	Bad.
Ludhiana	Ludhiana	Good.
	Jagraon	Very good.
	Samrala	Fair.
Patiala	Patiala	Good.
	Amargarh	Very good.
	Phul	Do.
	Sangrur	Good.
	Punjour	Fair.
	Anahadgarh	Do.

2 Falcon, *Handbook on Sikhs*, pp. 69-70.

	Karaingarh	Do.
Nabha	Nabha	Good.
Faridkot	Faridkot	Very good.
Jalandhar	Jalandhar	Fair.
	Nakodar	Good.
	Phillour	Fair.
	Nawa Shahr	Do.
Kapurthala	Kapurthala	Good.
Gurdaspur	Gurdaspur	Bad.
	Batala	Fair.
	Shakargarh	Very bad.
	Pathankote	Do.
Malerkotla	Malerkotla	Good.
Hushiarpur	Hushiarpur	Bad.
	Dasuya	Very bad.
	Gharshankar	Bad.
	Una	Very bad.
Gujranwala	Gujranwala	Good.
	Hafizabad	Do.
	Wazirabad	Fair.
Ambala	Ambala	Poor.
	Rupar	Bad.
	Kharar	Do.
	Naraingarh	Do.
	Pipli	Very bad.
	Jagadhri	Do.
Jind	Jind	Fair.
Kalsia	Kalsia	Bad.
Sialkot	Sialkot	Very bad.
	Raya	Fair.
	Pasrur	Do.
	Zafarwal	Very bad.
	Daska	Fair.
Hissar	Hissar	Very bad.
	Hansi	Do.

	Bhiwani	Do.
	Sirsa	Bad.
	Fatehabad	Do.
Gujrat	Gujrat	Very bad.
	Kharian	Do.
	Phalia	Do.
Karnal	Tehsils unnecessary	All very bad.
Montgomery	"	"
Shahpur	"	"
Jhelum	"	"
Rawalpindi	"	"
Rohtak	"	"
Gurgaon	"	"
Delhi	"	"

Appendix IV

First Lahore Conspiracy Trial: Schedule of Results[3]

No.	Name.	Convicted under section.		Sentence or acquittal.
2	Arjan Singh	121 A, 302-109, 121,	I.P.C.	Transportation for life.
*3	Attar Singh	121, 121 A	"	Ditto.
*5	Bogh Singh	121, 121 A	"	Ditto.
6	Bir Singh	121, 396, 302-109	"	Death.
7	Bishen Singh	121, 395-109	"	Transportation for life.
8	Budha Singh	121	"	Ditto.
9	Chanda Singh			Acquitted.
*10	Dalep Singh	121	"	Transportation for life.
12	Dhan Singh			Acquitted.
13	Dharm Singh			Do.
*14	Ganda Singh	121	"	Transportation for life.
15	Ganda Singh	121	"	Ditto.
16	Ganda Singh			Acquitted.
18	Gujar Singh	121	"	Transportation for life.
*19	Harbhajan Singh	121	"	Ditto.
21	Hari Singh			Acquitted.
22	Hari Singh	121	"	Transportation for life.
23	Harnam Singh	121	"	Ditto.
24	Harnam Singh	121	"	Ditto.
26	Harnam Singh	121, 121 A, 131	"	Ditto.
28	Hira Singh	121, 121 A, 131	"	Death.

3 British Library: L/PJ/6/1405, File 4095, *Lahore Conspiracy Case and the Lahore Supplementary Conspiracy Case.*

29	Ijaib Singh			Acquitted.
30	Inder Singh	121	"	Transportation for life.
32	Ishar Singh	121, 302-109, 121 A	"	Death.
*33	Jagat Singh	121	"	Transportation for life.
34	Jammu	202	"	Six months' rigorous imprisonment.
35	Jassa Singh	121 A, 124 A	"	Ditto.
*37	Inder Singh	121	"	Transportation for life.
38	Kahan Singh	124 A	"	Four year's rigorous imprisonment.
40	Karm Chand			Acquitted.
41	Karm Singh	121, 395	"	Transportation for life.
42	Kartar Singh	121	"	Ditto.
*45	Kesar Singh	121	"	Ditto.
46	Kirpa Singh	121, 131	"	Ditto.
48	Labh Singh	121, 121 A, 131	"	Ditto.
*49	Labh Singh	121	"	Ditto.
*50	Lal Singh	121	"	Ditto.
51	Maghar Singh			Acquitted.
52	Maharaj Singh	121	"	Transportation for life.
53	Mahendar Singh	121 A	"	Three years' rigorous imprisonment.
*54	Mahendar Singh	121, 121 A	"	Transportation for life.
55	Mangl Singh			Acquitted.
*56	Mangl Singh	121	"	Transportation for life.
*58	Mastan Singh	121	"	Ditto.
*59	Nahar Singh	121, 121 A	"	Ditto.
*61	Nathu Dhun	121	"	Ditto.
62	Pakhar Singh	121	"	Ditto.
63	Pala Singh	121 A	"	Three years' rigorous imprisonment.
*64	Pala Singh	121	"	Transportation for life.
65	Phera Singh	121 A	"	Two years' rigorous imprisonment.
66	Phumman Singh			Acquitted.
*68	Ram Singh	121	"	Transportation for life.
69	Randhir Singh	121 A, 121	"	Ditto.
70	Ranga Singh	121, 302-109	"	Death.
72	Rur Singh	121, 302	"	Do.
73	Sadhu Singh			Acquitted.

74	Sajjan Singh	121, 131	"	Transportation for life.
75	Sama Singh			Acquitted.
*77	Santa Singh	121	"	Transportation for life.
78	Sarwan Singh			Acquitted.
80	Sham Singh	121 A	"	Three years' rigorous imprisonment.
81	Sher Singh	121 A, 124 A	"	One year's rigorous imprisonment.
82	Sucha Singh	121, 131	"	Transportation for life.
*84	Sultan Shah	121	"	Ditto.
85	Sundar Singh	121	"	Ditto.
*88	Suga Singh	121	"	Ditto.
*89	Surjan Singh	121	"	Ditto.
*90	Teja Singh	121	"	Ditto.
91	Teja Singh			Acquitted.
*93	Thakur Singh	121	"	Transportation for life.
*94	Thakur Singh			Acquitted.
96	Udham Singh	121	"	Transportation for life.
98	Uttam Singh	121, 395, 302-109	"	Death.
*100	Wasakha Singh	121	"	Transportation for life.

Those marked * were recommended for mercy.
I.P.C. – Indian Penal Code.

Appendix V

Lahore Division and Meerut Division Orders of Battle 1914-15[4]

Lahore Division

Commander: Lt-General H.B.B. Watkis, C.B.
Ferozepore Brigade
Commander: Brigadier-General R.M. Egerton, C.B.
1st Battalion Connaught Rangers
129th Duke of Connaught's Own Baluchis
57th Wilde's Rifles (Frontier Force)
9th Bhopal Infantry
Jullundur Brigade
Commander: Major-General P.M. Carnegy, C.B.
1st Battalion Manchester Regiment
15th Ludhiana Sikhs
47th Sikhs
59th Scinde Rifles (Frontier Force).
Sirhind Brigade
Commander: Major-General J.M.S. Brunker
1st Battalion Highland Light Infantry
1st Battalion 1st King George's Own Gurkha Rifles
1st Battalion 4th Gurkha Rifles
125th Napier's Rifles
Divisional Troops
15th Lancers (Cureton's Multanis)
Headquarters Divisional Engineers
No. 20 Company Sappers and Miners
No. 21 Company Sappers and Miners
Signal Company

4 Merewether, *The Indian Corps in France*, pp. 10-12.

34th Sikh Pioneers
Artillery
Headquarters Divisional Artillery
5th Brigade R.F.A. and Ammunition Column
11th Brigade R.F.A. and Ammunition Column
18th Brigade R.F.A. and Ammunition Column
109th Heavy Battery

Meerut Division

Commander: Lt-General C.A. Anderson, C.B.
Dehra Dun Brigade
Commander: Brigadier-General C.E. Johnson
1st Battalion Seaforth Highlanders
1st Battalion 9th Gurkha Rifles
2nd Battalion 2nd King Edward's Own Gurkha Rifles
6th Jat Light Infantry
Garhwal Brigade
Commander: Major-General H. D'U. Keary, C.B., D.S.O.
2nd Battalion Leicestershire Regiment
2nd Battalion 3rd Queen Alexandra's Own Gurkha Rifles
1st Battalion 39th Garhwal Rifles
2nd Battalion 39th Garhwal Rifles
Bareilly Brigade
Commander: Major-General F. Macbean, C.V.O., C.B.
2nd Battalion Black Watch
41st Dogras
58th Vaughan's Rifles (Frontier Force)
2nd Battalion 8th Gurkha Rifles
Divisional Troops
4th Cavalry
No. 3 Company Sappers and Miners
No. 4 Company Sappers and Miners
Signal Company
107th Pioneers
Headquarters Divisional Engineers
Artillery
Head Quarters Divisional Artillery
4th Brigade R.F.A. and Ammunition Column
9th Brigade R.F.A. and Ammunition Column
13th Brigade R.F.A. and Ammunition Column
110th Heavy Battery

Appendix VI

Holy Words of the Guru

Guru Nanak

There is One God
Truth is his name, He is the creator
He is without fear, He is without hate
He is timeless and without form
He is beyond birth and death. The enlightened one
He can be known as the Guru's Grace
Meditate on the name
He was true before the creation
He was true when ages commenced
He is true now
He will always be true

Guru Nanak, Page 1, Guru Granth Sahib.

Guru Gobind Singh

I will
make manifest my kingdom,
merge the four castes into one,
and make all contemplate the mantra
'Waheguru' ('Wondrous Enlightenment').

On beholding my warriors mounted on steeds and
flying hawks, the Turks will take flight.

I will
have a single warrior fight 125,000 and
grant salvation to the Singh who wages war.
Lances will sway and elephants will be adorned.
At every door the battle drum will resound.

When 125,000 matchlock fuses smoulder,
the Khalsa will conquer all the lands under the sun.

Guru Gobind Singh's prophecy of sovereignty for his loyal followers in the face of tyrannical Mughal rule, as told to his devotee Bhai Nand Lal (source: Tankhah Nama).

Bibliography

Archival

India Office Records (IOR), British Library, London

L/MIL/5/825-828, 'Reports of the censor of Indian mails in France: printed reports and abstracts, with related correspondence.'

L/MIL/7/17347, (Collection 425/188), 'Censorship of correspondence to and from Indian Expeditionary Force in France.'

L/MIL/7/18480 (Collection 425/1308), 'German propaganda work among British and Indian prisoners of war: extracts from the Lausanne Gazette.'

L/MIL/7/18753 (Collection 425/1509), 'Breaches of law and customs of war by German authorities, with special reference to the treatment of Indian combatants of war in East Africa.'

L/MIL/7/18904, (Collection 425/1656), 'Alleged ill treatment by the Turks of certain Sikh prisoners of war.'

L/MIL/7/18937, (Collection 425/1689), 'Miscellaneous papers regarding the treatment of Indian prisoners of war by the Turks.'

L/MIL/17/5/2152, 'Recruiting in India, before and during the war of 1914-18. Delhi: Army HQ India, Oct 1919.'

L/MIL/17/5/2313, 'A short history in English, Gurmukhi & Urdu of the Royal Pavilion Brighton and a description of it as a hospital for Indian soldiers, 1915. Brighton Corporation.'

L/MIL/17/19/48, 'Report in connection with mutiny of 5th Light Infantry at Singapore 1915. Part 1 - Proceedings of court of enquiry. Part 2 - Report by H.E. the Governor of the Straits Settlements and the G.O.C. at Singapore. Simla: Govt of India, 1915.'

L/PJ/6/1325, File 3601, 'Canadian immigration; the Komagata Maru incident.'

L/PJ/6/1326, File 3903, 'Canada; scheme for raising a Sikh regiment.'

L/PJ/6/1338, File 5028, 'Papers on the Budge Budge riot and passengers on the Komagata Maru.'

L/PJ/6/1354, File 759, 'Indians in East Africa: translation of letter written 6th Nov 1914, by Uttam Singh, Uganda Railway and addressed to Hari Singh, Public Works Department, Kashmir State.'

L/PJ/6/1405, File 4095, 'Lahore Conspiracy Case and the Lahore Supplementary Conspiracy Case.'

L/PJ/6/1451, File 3378, 'Loyal Addresses to the British Crown from Sikhs of Malay States.'

L/PJ/6/1457, File 3818, 'Indian colonisation and German East Africa; proposal to establish a Sikh reservation on territory conquered from the Germans.'

L/PJ/6/1488, File 2279, 'Supplementary Lahore Conspiracy Cases.'
L/PS/11/116, P 201/1917, 'Mesopotamia: the proposal to erect a gurudwara for Sikh troops at Basra.'
L/PS/11/136, P 2375/1918, 'Criminal Intelligence Office: report on Indian Sedition in the Far East in 1917.'
L/R/5/195-201, 'Punjab Newspaper Reports', 1914-1919.
Mss Eur F143/75, 'Letters about the twice weekly Hindi and Urdu paper Akbar-I-Jung, with copies of the letters written by Indian soldiers to the paper.'
Mss Eur F143/96, 'Volume of newspaper-cuttings about the Brighton Indian hospitals.'
Mss Eur F161/152, 'Conspiracy: Report of the Committee on Revolutionary Conspiracies in India (1918).'

© The British Library Board.

Centre of South Asian Studies, Cambridge
Khalsa Advocate archive 1914-1919.

University of Cambridge Library, Cambridge
Letters from Indian Army Troops, Ref: GBR/0012/MS Add.6170.
The Syndics of Cambridge University Library.

National Archives of Australia, Canberra
B2455, SINGH SARN, AIF personnel files.

Published Works

Anderson, Lieut-Colonel R.H., *Regimental History of the 45th Rattray's Sikhs, during the Great War and after 1914-1921* (East Sussex: Naval & Military Press reprint of 1925 edition).
Andrews, William Linton, *Haunting Years, The Commentaries of a War Territorial* (London: Hutchinson & Co, undated).
Anon, *47th Sikhs War Record The Great War, 1914-1918* (Chippenham: Picton Publishing, 1992).
Anon, *Teja Singh Khalsa joins the army* (Simla: Govt P., 1918).
Barker, A.J., *The First Iraq War 1914-1918: Britain's Mesopotamian Campaign* (New York: Enigma, 2009).
Barrier, Norman, *The Sikhs and their literature: A guide to tracts, books and periodicals, 1849-1919* (New Delhi: Manohar Bk. Service, 1970).
Barrier, Gerald.N and Dusenbery, Verne.A (eds.), *The Sikh Diaspora: Migration and the experience beyond Punjab* (Delhi: Chanakya Publications, 1989).
Basu, Shrabani, *For King and another Country: Indian Soldiers on the Western Front 1914-18* (New Delhi: Bloomsbury, 2015).
Bingley, A.H., *Handbooks for the Indian Army: Sikhs* (Simla: Government of India, 1899).
Candler, Edmund, *The Sepoy* (New Delhi: Lancer, 2008).
Corrigan, Gordon, *Sepoys in the Trenches: The Indian Corps on the Western Front 1914-15* (Gloucestershire: Spellmount, 2006).

Dane, Edward and Jones, Jefferson, *'Side-Show' Theatres of the Great War* (East Riding of Yorkshire: Leonaur, 2013).
Das, Santanu, *Race, Empire and First World War Writing* (New York: Cambridge University Press, 2011).
Datta, V.N., *New light on the Punjab disturbances in 1919: Volumes VI and VII of Disorders Inquiry Committee evidence. Vol 1* (Simla: Indian Institute of Advanced Study, 1975).
David, Saul, *Victoria's Wars* (London: Penguin, 2007).
Dhesi, Narinder Singh, *Sikh Soldier, Volume Three, Policing the Empire* (East Sussex: Naval & Military Press, undated).
Doyle, Peter and Schafer, Robin, *Fritz and Tommy: Across the Barbed Wire* (Gloucestershire: History Press, 2015).
Ellinwood, De Witt C. and Pradhan S.D. (ed.), *India and World War I* (New Delhi: Manohar, 1978).
Evans, Martin Marix, *Over the Top, Great Battles of the First World War* (London: Arcturus, 2002).
Falcon, Robert Worgan, *Handbook on Sikhs for the use of Regimental Officers* (Allahabad: Pioneer Press, 1896).
Farooqui, Mahmood, *Besieged, 1857 Voices from Delhi* (Haryana: Penguin, 2010).
Fenech, Louis E., *Martyrdom in the Sikh Tradition: Playing the 'Game of Love'* (New Delhi: Oxford Press, 2000).
Fox, Richard G., *Lions of the Punjab, Culture in the Making* (London: University of California Press, 1985).
Government of India, *India's Contribution to the Great War* (Calcutta: Superintendent of Government Printing, 1923).
Government of India Army Department, *Manual of Indian Military Law, 1911* (Calcutta: Superintendent Government Printing, 1922).
Isemonger, F.C. and Slattery, J., *An account of the Ghadr conspiracy: 1913-1915* (Lahore: Superintendent, Govt. Print., 1919).
Kahlon, Swarn Singh, *Sikhs in Latin America: Travels among the Sikh diaspora* (New Delhi: Manohar Publishers & Distributors, 2012).
Kaul, Chandrika, *Reporting the Raj: The British Press and India, C. 1880-1922* (Manchester: Manchester University Press, 2003).
Lee, J. Fitzgerald, *The "D" Force (Mesopotamia) in the Great War* (East Sussex: Naval & Military Press, undated).
Leigh, M.S., *The Punjab and the War* (Lahore: Superintendent of Government Printing, 1922).
Lock, Henry Osmond, *With the British Army in the Holy Land* (East Riding of Yorkshire: Leonaur, 2012).
Macauliffe, Max Arthur, *The Sikh Religion: Its Gurus, Sacred Writings and Authors* (New Delhi: S. Chand & Company, 1985).
Macauliffe, Max, *A lecture on the Sikh religion and its advantages to the state* (Simla: Government Central Printing Office: United Service Institution of India, 1903).
Malik, Hardit Singh, *A little work, a little play: The autobiography of H.S. Malik* (New Delhi: Bookwise India, 2009).
Mazumder, Rajit, *The Indian Army and the Making of the Punjab* (New Delhi: Permanent Black, 2011).

Merewether, Lt Col and Smith, Sir Frederick, *The Indian Corps in France* (London: John Murray, 1918).
Mittal, S.C., *Freedom movement in Punjab, 1905-29* (Delhi: Concept Pub. Co., 1977).
Muhay, Gurcharan Singh, *A zeal for martyrdom: Kartar Singh Sarabha* (Ludhiana: Lahore Book Shop, 2005).
O'Dwyer, Michael, *War Speeches* (Lahore: Superintendent Government Printing, 1918).
O'Dwyer, Michael, *India as I knew it 1885-1925* (London: Constable & Co., 1925).
Ogle, Colonel N. and Johnston, Lieut. Colonel H.W., *History of the 1st Battalion 2nd Punjab Regiment: Late 67th Punjabis and originally the Madras Infantry, 1761-1928* (East Sussex: Naval & Military Press 2014 reprint of 1928 edition).
Olusoga, David, *The World's War: Forgotten Soldiers of Empire* (London: Head of Zeus, 2014).
Omissi, David, *Indian Voices of the Great War, Soldier' Letters, 1914-18* (London: Palgrave Macmillan, 1999).
Petrie, David, *Developments in Sikh Politics, 1900-1911: A Report* (Amritsar: Chief Khalsa Diwan, 1972).
Roberts, Andrew, *Love, Tommy: Letters Home, from the Great War to the Present Day* (Oxford: Osprey, 2012).
Sidhu, Amarpal S., *The First Anglo-Sikh War* (Gloucestershire: Amberley, 2010).
Singh, Bhupindra, *War speeches of H.H. Maharajah of Patiala* (Madras: Weekly Newspapers Press, 1920).
Singh, Gajendra, *The Testimonies of Indian Soldiers and the Two World Wars* (London: Bloomsbury, 2014).
Singh, Harnam and Singh, Teja, *Tales from the Sikh History of Rawalpindi, Attock & Peshawar Districts* (Rawalpindi: Khalsa Historical and Literary Society, 1918).
Singh, Khushwant, *A History of the Sikhs, Volume II: 1839-2004* (New Delhi: Oxford, 2004).
Singh, Mohinder, *History and culture of Panjab* (New Delhi: Atlantic Publishers and Distributors, 1988).
Singh, Mohinder, *The Akali Movement* (New Delhi: National Institute of Panjab Studies, 1997).
Singh, Pashaura and Barrier, Gerald (eds.), *Sikhism and History* (New Delhi: Oxford, 2004).
Singh, Patwant, *The Sikhs* (London: John Murray, 1999).
Singh, Randhir, *The Ghadar Heroes: Forgotten story of the Punjab revolutionaries of 1914-15* (Bombay: People's Pub. House, 1945).
Singh, Randhir, *Jail Chitian, Autobiography of Bhai Sahib Randhir Singh* (London: Bhai Sahib Randhir Singh Trust UK, 2012).
Singh, Savitri Devi Rup, *Sikh Education II: A paper read ... at the tenth session of the Sikh Educational Conference, held at Lahore, on 7th April 1917* (Lahore: Mercantile Electric Press, 1917).
Singh, Teja, *Guru Nanak and his Mission. Part 1* (Mahilpore: Sikh Tract Society, 1918).
Singh, Teja, *The Gurdwara Reform Movement and the Sikh Awakening* (Lahore: Mercantile Press, 1922).
Singh, Teja, *The Khalsa – A Universal Brotherhood* (Tarn Taran: Sikh Tract Society, 1918).
Singh, Teja, *The Sword & Religion* (Lahore: Sikh Tract Society, 1918).
Spackman, W.C. Colonel, *Captured at Kut: Prisoner of the Turks* (Yorkshire: Pen & Sword, 2008).
Stanley, Peter, *Die in Battle, Do not Despair, The Indians on Gallipoli, 1915* (Solihull: Helion & Company, 2015).
Stevens, Philip, *The Great War Explained* (Yorkshire: Pen & Sword, 2012).

Talbot, F.E.G., *The 14th King George's Own Sikhs 1846-1933* (London: RUSI, 1937).
Talib, Gurcharan Singh and Singh, Attar (eds.), *Bhai Vir Singh: Life, times & works* (Chandigarh: Publication Bureau, Panjab University, 1973).
Tan, Tai Yong, *The Garrison State: The military, government and society in colonial Punjab, 1849-1947* (London: Sage, 2005).
Tandon, Prakash, *Punjabi Century 1857-1947* (Oakland, California: University of California Press, 1968).
Tharoor, Shashi, *Inglorious Empire, What the British Did to India* (London: Hurst & Co, 2017).
Willcocks, James, *With the Indians in France* (London: Constable and Company Ltd, 1920).
Willmott, H.P., *World War I* (London: DK Publishing, 2003).
Ziemann, Benjamin and Ulrich, Bernd (eds.), *German Soldiers in the Great War: Letters and Eyewitness Accounts* (Barnsley: Pen & Sword, 2010).

Electronic Sources

The Collected Works of Mahatma Gandhi (Electronic Book), New Delhi, Publications Division Government of India, 1999, 98 volumes <http://www.gandhiashramsevagram.org/gandhi-literature/collected-works-of-mahatma-gandhi-volume-1-to-98.php>
https://indiafamily.bl.uk/ui/Dictionary.aspx

Index

INDEX OF PEOPLE

INDEX OF PLACES

INDEX OF FORMATIONS & UNITS

INDEX OF GENERAL & MISCELLANEOUS TERMS